MW01620333

The Ghent Altarpiece

Research and Conservation of the Interior:

the Lower Register

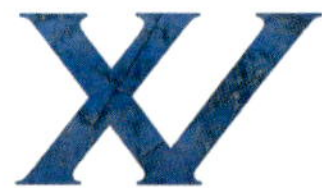

Contributions to the Study of the Flemish Primitives

16

The KIK-IRPA produces three series of scientific publications on 15th- and early 16th-century paintings: the Corpus, the Repertory and the Contributions.

D/2021/0613/1
ISBN 978-2-930054-41-4

Translations: Ted Alkins (from French)
Editing: Paul van Calster, with the collaboration of Elisabeth Van Eyck and Catherine Bourguignon
Image processing: Bernard Petit
Layout: Véronique Lux
Cover illustration: Jan van Eyck, *Adoration of the Lamb*, detail of the *Ghent Altarpiece* (Ghent, St Bavo's Cathedral)

Published by the Royal Institute for Cultural Heritage (KIK-IRPA), Brussels **with the support of** the Périer-D'Ieteren Foundation.

Research and Conservation supported by the Flemish Government; Saint Bavo's Cathedral, Ghent; Ghent University; University of Antwerp; MSK (Museum of Fine Arts), Ghent; Baillet Latour Fund; Gieskes-Strijbis Fund; Getty Foundation; Belgian Science Policy (BELSPO); Research Foundation – Flanders (FWO); University of Chemistry and Technology, Prague.

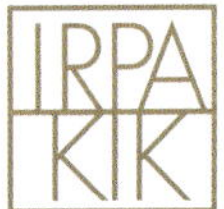

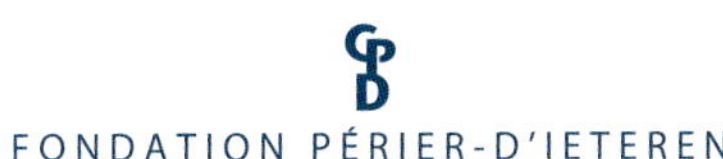

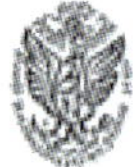
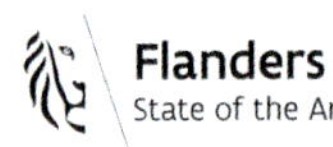

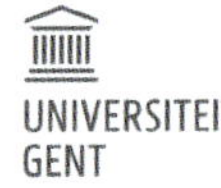

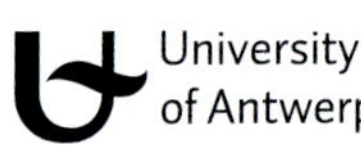

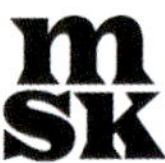

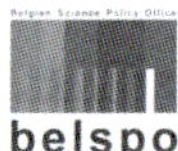

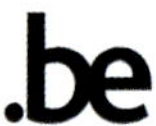

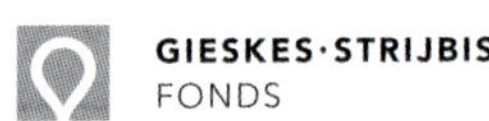

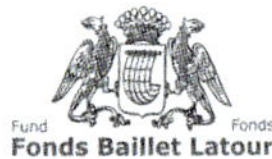

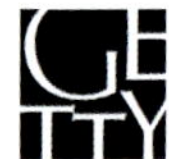
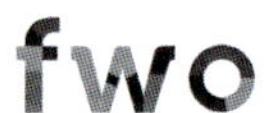

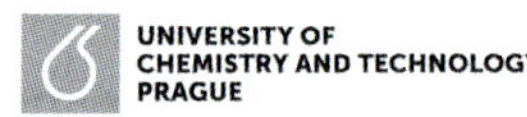

The Ghent Altarpiece

Research and Conservation of the Interior: the Lower Register

Main Authors
Griet Steyaert, Marie Postec, Jana Sanyova, Hélène Dubois

with observations, research and documents by

Painting Conservators-Restorers
Kathleen Froyen, Nathalie Laquière, Laure Mortiaux, Françoise Rosier,
Bart Devolder, Cécile de Boulard

Chemical Research Scientists
Geert Van der Snickt, Francisco Mederos-Henry, Cécile Glaude, Frederik Vanmeert,
Steven De Meyer, Stijn Legrand, Alexia Coudray, Štěpánka Kučková, Koen Janssens

Specialists in Scientific Imagery and Photography
Christina Currie, Sophie De Potter, Katrien Van Acker, Catherine Fondaire,
Stéphane Bazzo, Hervé Pigeolet

Making extensive use of the Closer to Van Eyck Website

Royal Institute for Cultural Heritage
Brussels
2021

Contents

Foreword

When the conservation project of the Van Eyck brothers' *Adoration of the Mystic Lamb* – the *Ghent Altarpiece* – started in 2012, expectations ran high. They were certainly met, and even exceeded, thanks to the extraordinary results of the treatment and of the associated scientific research. In the course of the first phase, the project was significantly modified due to the unexpected discovery – during varnish removal on the exterior of the polyptych – of overpaints covering the major part of the surface. Thanks to the flexibility and the confidence of the Church Council of St Bavo's Cathedral and generous funding by the Flemish Government and the Baillet Latour Fund, the same rigorous approach could be continued during the second phase of the project. Work was carried out in public in the purpose-built glazed workshop at the Ghent Museum of Fine Arts (MSK), which also generously supported the project and the team on a daily basis.

As in any other conservation project undertaken by the Royal Institute for Cultural Heritage (KIK-IRPA), an interdisciplinary approach was applied, involving highly experienced conservator-restorers, scientists and art historians, always keeping up with the latest research in their own field. Results of the conservation and research carried out during the second phase of the treatment (2016–19) are published here. They concern the lower register of the altarpiece interior: the eponymous central panel of the *Adoration of the Lamb*, the *Knights of Christ*, the *Hermits* and the *Pilgrims*.

Paul Coremans, the founder of our institute and instigator of the conservation of the *Ghent Altarpiece* in 1950–51, was a visionary. His dedication to interdisciplinary research and fascination for the painting technique of the Flemish Primitives led to pioneering results. Seven decades later, Coremans's legacy certainly lives on in our interdisciplinary research and collaboration with Belgian universities and foreign institutions while new analytical and imaging techniques are being developed, and samples are even analysed in synchrotron facilities. This intense collaborative effort lifts the veil on a persistent enigma in the history of Western art: the Van Eyck brothers' respective shares in the conception and execution of the *Ghent Altarpiece*, and their fascinating technical 'secrets'.

This book was written in the transitory period between the second and third phases of the conservation and restoration project. It is based on first-hand information gathered by the conservators and scientists who have been in direct contact with the paintings for several years. They have acquired a unique knowledge of the Van Eycks' painting technique and their subtle variations of paint handling. Combined with the laboratory-based scientific analyses and the art-historical facts, their findings will transform scholarly – and popular – perceptions of the achievements of Hubert and Jan van Eyck.

I would finally like to extend my sincere gratitude for the sustained collaboration with research partners and institutions, in particular with the universities of Antwerp and Ghent. We are also extremely grateful to the advising bodies who are too numerous to be listed here,[1] to the Gieskes-Strijbis Fund, which sponsored research, and to the Périer-D'Ieteren Foundation for its support towards the present publication.

Hilde De Clercq
Acting Director-General, KIK-IRPA, Brussels

Notes

1 A list of project participants is published on the website 'Closer to Van Eyck': http://closertovaneyck.kikirpa.be/ghentaltarpiece/#home/sub=credits&goto=credits2012 (2012–17); http://closertovaneyck.kikirpa.be/ghentaltarpiece/#home/sub=credits (2018–20); see also Project Participants in this volume.

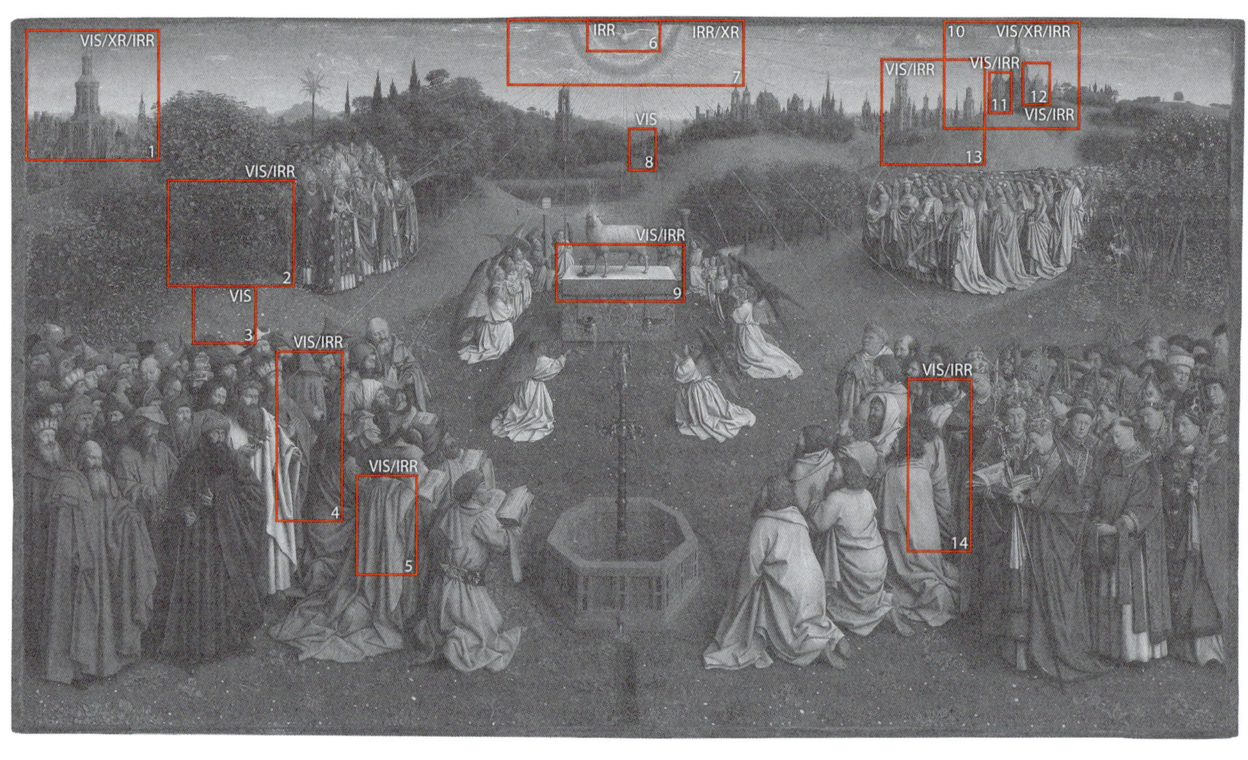
VIS/XR/IRR
1
IRR
6
IRR/XR
7
10
VIS/XR/IRR
VIS/IRR
VIS/IRR
11
12
VIS/IRR
13
VIS
8
VIS/IRR
2
VIS/IRR
9
VIS
3
VIS/IRR
VIS/IRR
4
VIS/IRR
5
14

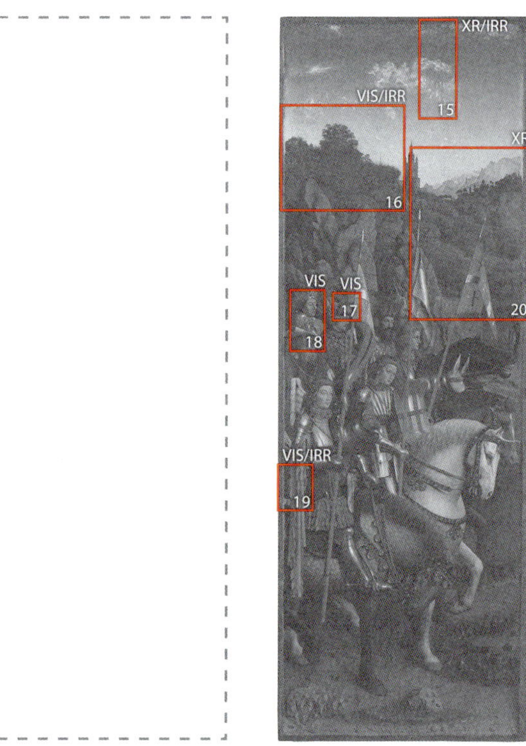
XR/IRR
VIS/IRR
15
XR
16
VIS
VIS
17
18
20
VIS/IRR
19

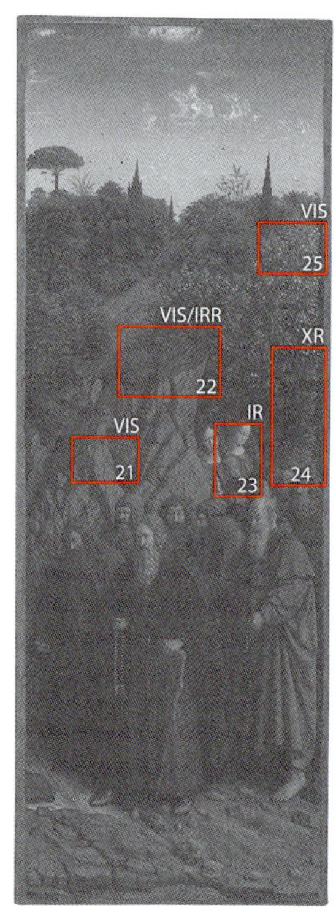
VIS
25
VIS/IRR
XR
22
VIS
IR
21
23
24

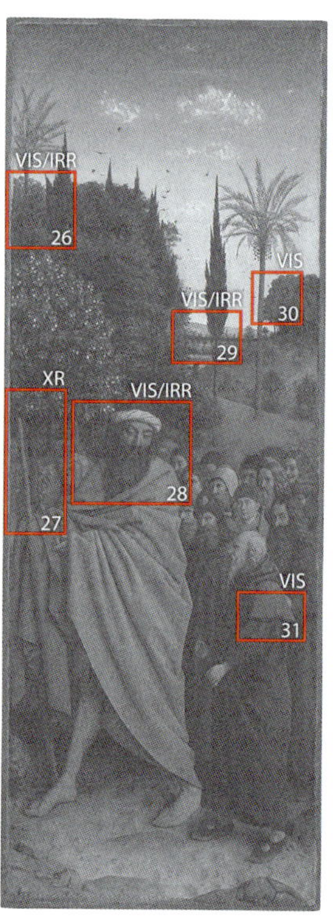
VIS/IRR
26
VIS
VIS/IRR
30
29
XR
VIS/IRR
28
27
VIS
31

Note to the Reader

Abbreviation 'cve'

The abbreviation 'cve' stands for 'Closer to Van Eyck' (http://closertovaneyck.kikirpa.be/). Although the present publication is richly illustrated, we have also provided references to certain details that can be viewed online. These references are indicated in the text in the form 'cve-1', 'cve-2', etc. The diagram on the facing page shows the location of the relevant details – vis, ir or irr.

'Eyckian' and 'non-Eyckian'

The term 'pre-Eyckian' is well established in art-historical discourse.[1] '"Eyckian" is often used to describe a later style derived from (Jan) van Eyck's work, but also in connection with Jan van Eyck or the Van Eyck brothers.'[2] In this volume, we use the terms 'Eyckian' for everything that could have been executed by Hubert or by Jan, and 'non-Eyckian' for everything that was not executed by either of the two brothers. However, this does not exclude the intervention of a contemporary painter.

Cross-section numbering

The cross-sections in chapters 2 and 3 are identified by compound numbers (*x*/*y*) in parentheses corresponding to the sample record in KIK-IRPA's laboratory archive. The number before the slash (*x*) refers to the sampled panel in the *Ghent Altarpiece*: 9 *Knights of Christ*, 10 *Adoration of the Lamb*, 11 *Hermits*, 12 *Pilgrims*, 13 *Archangel*, 14 *City View*, 15 *Interior with Lavabo*, 16 *Virgin Annunciate*, 17 *Joos Vijd*, 18 *John the Baptist* (grisaille), 19 *John the Evangelist* (grisaille), 20 *Elisabeth Borluut*; the second number (*y*) refers to the sequential order of the sample.

Notes

1 Deneffe et al. 2009, pp. 16–17.

2 Smeyers 1996; Verougstraete, Van Schoute 2000; Stroo, Martens 2020, p. 353.

To the memory of J.R.J. Van Asperen de Boer

Introduction

Restoration campaigns offer a privileged opportunity to study works of art. The Van Eyck brothers' *Ghent Altarpiece* was one of the first works for which restoration was followed by a scholarly publication: *L'Agneau mystique au laboratoire*, edited by Paul Coremans, appeared in 1953, following the treatment performed in 1950–51 at the Laboratoire central des musées de Belgique, KIK-IRPA's precursor.[1] That publication and *A Scientific Re-examination of the Ghent Altarpiece*, written by J.R.J. Van Asperen de Boer in 1979, are still landmark references[2] among the technical and material studies devoted to the polyptych. While the authors of both publications provided a great deal of highly pertinent information and observations, their interpretation has often remained incomplete for two main reasons. Firstly, they did not have access to the research tools we can call on today, while secondly and most importantly, they lacked one key piece of information that hindered their conclusions: the fact that the panels were largely covered by very early overpaints,[3] mostly dating back to the sixteenth century.[4]

The current conservation and restoration project began in 2012, preceded by a preliminary study in 2010.[5] Given the size of the *Ghent Altarpiece*, the intention from the outset was to execute the project in three successive phases: a first phase devoted to the study and treatment of the paintings of the altarpiece exterior; a second focusing on those of the lower register of the altarpiece interior; and, lastly, a third phase to treat the paintings of the upper register of the altarpiece interior. The first phase was carried out between 2012 and 2016 and the second between 2016 and 2019, both in public at the Museum voor Schone Kunsten (MSK) in Ghent.[6] The third phase, which will bring this ambitious programme to a close, has yet to commence.

Significant resources were deployed from the outset to fund the restoration process but also the research and sharing of information that occurred in parallel, beginning with the placement of important documentation online through the 'Closer to Van Eyck' website. Information of major importance was already presented at the symposium organized in 2012 by KIK-IRPA and its Centre for the Study of the Flemish Primitives.[7] Indeed, dendrochronology had established that the *Ghent Altarpiece* had been conceived from the outset as a polyptych comprising twelve panels[8] and that the lower register had not been executed separately and then integrated by Jan at a later date in a larger ensemble, as certain authors had suggested.[9] The first phase of treatment also revealed that the panels had been substantially overpainted. The restoration treatment of the huge ensemble undertaken in 2012 has involved the removal of these overpaints, revealing the Van Eycks' painting, which had been hidden for several centuries. All these data opened up fresh new perspectives in the study of this world-famous polyptych.

A scholarly publication, *The Ghent Altarpiece – Research and Conservation of the Exterior*,[10] followed the first phase of conservation and restoration. It describes the progressive treatment that led to the removal of overpaints, as well as the technical and scientific study of the paintings and their frames. The latter came as a genuine revelation during this round of treatment. Restoration of the frames also allowed investigation and confirmation of the originality of the quatrain[11] painted on the frames of the closed altarpiece, which mentions the participation of the two Van Eyck brothers. Ever since the quatrain was discovered in 1823, one of the key questions intriguing the experts has been the respective participation of the two brothers. The quatrain states that Hubert began the work, that his brother Jan completed it and that it was presented in 1432. We know, moreover, that Hubert died in 1426.[12] Having previously been contested,[13] Hubert's existence and the authenticity of the quatrain are both now generally accepted. Taken in combination with the dendrochronological results, this information suggests that prior to his death Hubert had played an important part in the genesis of the altarpiece and possibly in its initial execution.

The second restoration phase, conducted between 2016 and 2019, concerned the lower register of the open altarpiece. It allowed both the research and the removal of overpaints to be continued. As Coremans and Van Asperen de Boer had already noted, it quickly became apparent that the paintings in this zone of the altarpiece showed evidence of successive stages of development as well as reworking, indicating that numerous changes were made before the paintings were finalized: far more numerous indeed than had been expected. In-depth technical and scientific research continued during this second phase, supported by the International Advisory Commission,[14] which has supervised the treatment since the beginning of the project. Its views and encouragement have been invaluable:

> *The team's new discoveries of a complex history of very early revisions to the altarpiece have raised intriguing questions: in addition to the work of Jan van Eyck, do we now see evidence for the work of Hubert van Eyck or the Eyckian workshop? Hints that the production of the altarpiece may have extended over some time – that some passages may have been extensively revised during the creative process, others may have been painted over early damages, and that there may be evidence for more than one artist – will spur new scholarship for years to come…*[15]

It made sense, therefore, to continue the publishing effort begun in 1953 and resumed in 2020 following the treatment and research carried out on the paintings and frames of the altarpiece exterior. The approach presented here deliberately differs, however, from the book published in 2020, a substantial proportion of which was devoted to the overpaints and their removal.

This volume places the emphasis on the pictorial layers of the newly restored paintings, given the importance of the discoveries. The work of removing the overpaints and its specific challenges, which are described in the first chapter of this book, gave us the opportunity to view the work in a state much closer to the original. Thanks to the removal of thick yellow varnishes and of the sixteenth-century overpaints, we can now make out more clearly the details of execution and the superimposition of paint layers and better appreciate the differences in quality. The study of these layers and the different stages of execution that have been observed is detailed in the second chapter, which is devoted to the technical execution of the paintings. The laboratory's contribution (chapter 3) focuses on the analysis of the paint layers, together with the results of the study of the materials used in the paintings of the altarpiece exterior.[16] Certain results regarding the upper register are also touched on, based on the samples retained from the 1950–51 restoration campaign. The book concludes with a stylistic study (chapter 4), which proposes attributions based on the new technical and scientific data revealed here. Research into the supports, frames and inscriptions is not included at this point: the results will be presented in the publication that will round off this immense project following completion of the third phase. Detailed conclusions in this regard will only be possible after the restoration of the upper register.

All the new data gathered during and after treatment has been made possible by a great deal of teamwork. The time and the number of experts assigned to the project have been important factors in allowing treatment and in-depth study on such a large scale – resources we enjoyed but that were not available to Albert Philippot during the previous restoration campaign in 1950–51.[17] The many hours that the conservators (some of whom are also art historians) spent treating the panels allowed them to observe the work in the closest possible detail, cleared of substantial overpaints, and to make discoveries – some anticipated in earlier studies, others hitherto unsuspected. This study has benefited from the comments and observations of all the conservators who took part in the treatment of the four paintings: Griet Steyaert for the *Knights of Christ*; Nathalie Laquière, Laure Mortiaux, Marie Postec, Hélène Dubois and Cécile de Boulard for the *Adoration of the Lamb*; Bart Devolder and Kathleen Froyen for the *Hermits*; and Françoise Rosier for the *Pilgrims*. The *Just Judges* panel, which was stolen in 1934 and never recovered, obviously did not form part of the study, although we do still have the original frame.[18] Isabel Bedos and Marta Darowska studied the frames and Jean-Albert Glatigny the supports.

The observations recorded by each conservator are very important, but they would have been incomplete and insufficient without the intensive collaboration of numerous specialists. Scientific imaging is an inexhaustible source of information that needs to be compared with direct observation of the works. The contribution of each participant has therefore been crucial: that of the photographers who made an ongoing visual record of the work as a whole and its details in normal, raking, ultraviolet and infrared light, as well as the specialists who produced X-radiographs and infrared reflectograms before, during and after treatment. Dialogue with the laboratory may provide support for hypotheses or raise new questions. KIK-IRPA scientists paid heed to the conservators' requests while in turn suggesting analyses with the potential to deliver fresh information. The same went for their colleagues at Belgian universities – primarily Antwerp University, but those in Ghent and Louvain-la Neuve, too – and at institutions abroad, such as the National Gallery, London, the Doerner Institute, Munich, and the Kunsthistorisches Museum, Vienna, all of which complemented the analyses carried out at KIK-IRPA. The discoveries were further facilitated by new and much more effective analytical methods, including Macro X-ray Fluorescence scans (MA-XRF) and Macro X-ray Powder Diffraction (MA-XRPD).[19] We were likewise able to call on much better microscopes than those used in the twentieth century, not to mention far more advanced analysis of stratigraphic sections. The resolution of the infrared reflectograms is considerably higher now and the images can be digitally assembled to create ensembles that are easier to interpret. Macrophotographs are much higher resolution too – in both daylight and infrared – while X-radiographs are digitally assembled and the interference of the cradles is reduced nowadays. At the end of the day, everyone involved relied on the expertise of their peers – conservators-restorers, scientists and art historians – to place their individual analyses in a broader context. The expert commission, which has been overseeing this large-scale restoration campaign since 2012, provided valuable advice, as did our other partners in Belgium and abroad.

Not only have we benefited from an abundance of scientific imagery, the vast majority of the documents obtained can be readily consulted and compared online at the 'Closer to Van Eyck' website.[20] What is more, thanks to the Van Eyck Research in OpeN Access (VERONA) project,[21] this documentation can also be compared on the same site with all the works signed and dated by Jan van Eyck as well as those generally attributed to him, all documented by the same team of specialists and according to an identical protocol. Direct contact with the paintings themselves, however, remains an essential approach in terms of understanding the creative process of a work made several centuries ago, and even more so for the *Ghent Altarpiece*, which had a complex history even before its completion in 1432.[22]

As was the case with the exterior, treating the paintings from the lower register of the open altarpiece took a good deal of time: the time spent of examining the panels prior to each significant decision, the time taken for formulating and answering questions, and, of course, the time needed for each phase of the restoration process proper. No matter how long these treatment phases might seem – four years for the reverse sides of the shutters, three years for the lower register of the altarpiece interior – they turned out to be far from a luxury. On the contrary, in fact, the timing was actually quite tight. The time needed to raise and answer questions is rarely mentioned in the literature on restoration treatments, yet it is extremely important. The conservators inevitably accumulate a mass of documentation that then needs to be collated in order to create a coherent account. Each person records visual data, keeps notes on and photographs the things that they observe, admire or do not understand right away. Ideally, two or three additional days ought to be assigned for each day of restoration work, to allow the recorded data to be classified, analysed and linked to colleagues' observations and for carefully reasoned hypotheses to be developed. Regrettably, few projects allow such scope, so it has been a privilege to have been granted it by the KIK-IRPA to prepare this publication. Several members of the KIK-IRPA team, in collaboration with the scientists from Antwerp University,[23] involved with this second phase of the study and treatment of the *Ghent Altarpiece*, took advantage of this opportunity to collate all the observations made by the team, the photographs, the scientific imaging and the laboratory analyses, in order to study the question in more depth and propose new hypotheses.

The chemical analysis of the materials likewise entailed a degree of interpretation of the results based on a better understanding of pigment–binder interactions. This, too, required time and objective consideration. The laboratory results presented in chapter 3 highlight the degree to which fresh research and new analysis methods can cast doubt on data acquired in the past. They also show how vital it is in a study of this kind to contextualize our ever-increasing knowledge of the nature of the materials used in a pictorial layer. The relatively recent study of the additives used to modify the properties of the paint layer holds out the prospect of fascinating revelations concerning the formulation of the materials by these peerless artists.

The many hours needed to treat the paintings gave the conservators the opportunity to observe every millimetre of the painted surfaces. This work – done to a large degree via stereomicroscopes that allow the successive layers and their specific material characteristics to be distinguished – offers a unique understanding of the studied paintings. The present volume proposes a *status quaestionis* while also setting out fresh benchmarks, notably a clearer hypothesis as to how far advanced the paintings were on Hubert's death and what changes were made by Jan. The latter were formal in character, but iconographical too, most notably in the addition of the fountain in the *Adoration of the Lamb* panel and changes involving the dove of the Holy Spirit. Art historians will be certain to explore these new data. As such, the final-phase conservation and restoration treatment of the upper register of the open altarpiece will provide further, unprecedented information that will complete our knowledge of this prestigious ensemble and most likely answer some of the questions raised here.

Notes

1 Coremans 1953. The project very much planted the seed for the characteristic interdisciplinary work of KIK-IRPA. Claes et al. 2019.

2 Coremans 1953; Van Asperen de Boer 1979. Without attempting to be exhaustive, we will refer to other publications on the pictorial technique of the *Ghent Altarpiece* in the notes to the chapters that follow.

3 The term *surpeint* (overpaint) is nevertheless used widely in *L'Agneau mystique au laboratoire*, without always being clearly defined. Coremans 1953, see e.g. p. 19.

4 Dubois 2018a; Dubois 2020a; Sanyova et al. 2020.

5 Van Grevenstein et al. 2011. Regarding the progress of the project up to 2016, see Martens et al. 2020a.

6 We are grateful to the staff of the MSK and its succeeding directors, for their constant support.

7 Currie et al. 2017.

8 Fraiture 2017.

9 Panofsky 1953, pp. 207–22. Panofsky refers to earlier authors in note 208/3.

10 Fransen, Stroo 2020.

11 Jones, Augustyniak, Dubois 2020.

12 The date of Hubert's death is known from his epitaph. Duverger 1945, pp. 15–28; Martens 2019, pp. 125–26; Paviot 2020, p. 60.

13 The various hypotheses in this regard are summarized in Kemperdick 2014, pp. 19–29; Martens 2019. The physical authenticity of the quatrain was established by the interdisciplinary research carried out during the first phase of the conservation project: Jones, Augustyniak, Dubois 2020.

14 Maryan Ainsworth (The Metropolitan Museum, New York), Till-Holger Borchert (Musea Brugge), Véronique Bücken (Royal Museums of Fine Arts of Belgium, Brussels), Lorne Campbell (formerly The National Gallery, London), Leslie Carlyle (Universitade Nova de Lisboa), Bart Devolder (Princeton University Art Museum), Jill Dunkerton (The National Gallery, London), Susan Farnell (independent conservator-restorer), Michael Gallagher (The Metropolitan Museum of Art, New York), Melanie Gifford (National Gallery of Art, Washington), Nicole Goetghebeur (formerly KIK-IRPA), Anne van Grevenstein-Kruse (Universiteit van Amsterdam), Régine Guislain-Witteman (independent conservator-restorer), Babette Hartwieg (Gemäldegalerie, Berlin), Lizet Klaassen (Royal Museum of Fine Arts, Antwerp), Maximiliaan Martens (UGent), Uta Neidhardt (SKD, Dresden), Elke Oberthaler (Kunsthistorisches Museum, Vienna), Catheline Périer-D'Ieteren (formerly Université Libre de Bruxelles), Marika Spring (The National Gallery, London), Ron Spronk (Queen's University Ontario/ Radbout Universiteit, Nijmegen), Jørgen Wadum (National Museum of Denmark, Copenhagen/Universiteit van Amsterdam).

15 Melanie Gifford, Michael Gallagher, Marika Spring, Lorne Campbell, Elke Oberthaler, Susan Farnell, *Report of the International Commission meeting for the conservation of the Ghent Altarpiece*, Ghent, Museum of Fine Arts, 7 June 2019 (KIK-IRPA archives).

16 Laboratory input for the book that was published after the treatment of the altarpiece exterior comprised analysis of the overpaints rather than the original pictorial layers.

17 That conservation treatment only lasted thirteen months. Paul Coremans mentioned the lack of time in the introduction to the publication: Coremans 2013, p. 10.

18 We have photographs of the missing work, as well as a copy of three XRs taken by Alan Burroughs in 1927. Burroughs 1938, pp. 180–93; Fondaire, Vanwijnsberghe 2008, pp. 283–84.

19 These analyses were carried out by the AXES Research Group at Antwerp University.

20 http://closertovaneyck.kikirpa.be/.

21 http://closertovaneyck.kikirpa.be/verona.

22 De Schryver, Marijnissen 1953; Dubois 2018a.

23 See especially chapter 3.

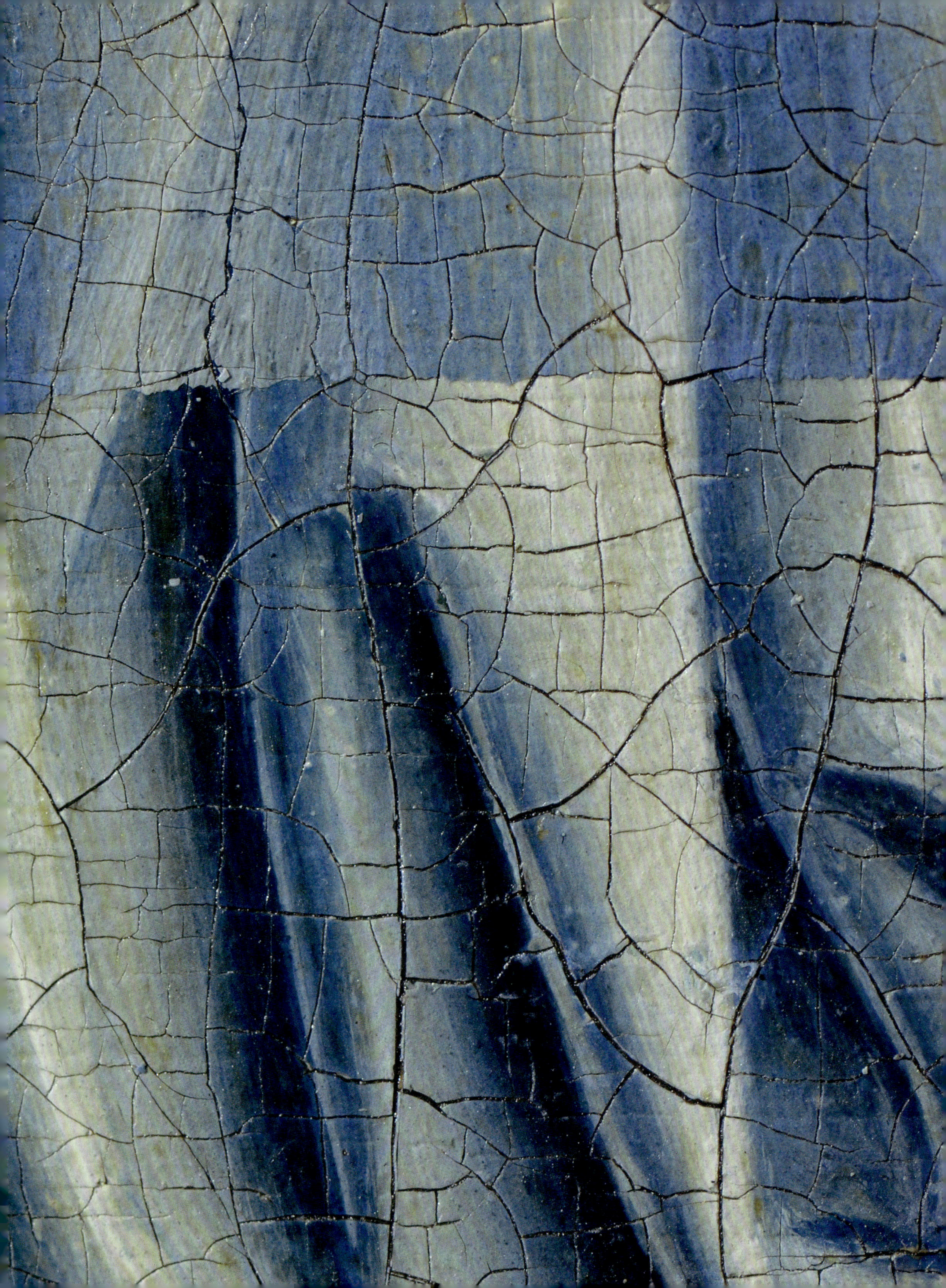

1

The Conservation-Restoration of the Interior Lower Register of the *Ghent Altarpiece*

Hélène Dubois, Kathleen Froyen, Griet Steyaert, Marie Postec,
Laure Mortiaux, Nathalie Laquière, Françoise Rosier,
Bart Devolder, Cécile de Boulard

Introduction

This chapter describes the methodology and results of the conservation and restoration of the paint surface of the *Knights of Christ*, the *Adoration of the Lamb*, the *Hermits* and the *Pilgrims* (figs. 1.1 and 1.2).[1]

The experience acquired during the restoration of the *Ghent Altarpiece*'s exterior led us to expect several layers of degraded varnish and restorations in the phase discussed here. These layers obscured the colour values, the subtle play of light and textures, and the spatial illusion of the original, Eyckian paint surface. Also, substantial lifting of small paint flakes could not be treated without removing these non original layers.

The restorers were naturally aware of the treatment by Albert Philippot in 1950–51, and of other restorations carried out in the nineteenth century, but their extent and location were not mapped precisely. Nor were they surprised to discover old overpaintings similar to those encountered on the closed polyptych, such as mid-sixteenth-century overpainting and, possibly, even older interventions that were completely hidden.[2] As described (albeit not very clearly) in Paul Coremans's *L'Agneau mystique au laboratoire*, Philippot removed some of the nineteenth-century restorations as well as some of those carried out in the sixteenth century (figs. 1.3 and 1.4).

Coremans and his team concluded that zones of the *Adoration of the Lamb* had been overpainted in the sixteenth century.[3] Their deduction was based on the pigment analysis of paint samples, on the examination of the paintings during their restoration, and on the fact that the overpainted areas were closely followed by Michiel Coxcie (1499–1592) in his copy of the *Ghent Altarpiece* of 1557–58.[4] Although a re-examination of the cross-sections taken during the 1950–51 campaign seemed to refute Coremans's assumptions,[5] his initial interpretation was eventually confirmed during the present restoration project.[6] Coremans also suggested that Jan van Scorel of Utrecht (1495–1562) and Lancelot Blondeel of Bruges (1498–1561) were the authors of these old overpaint.[7]

(facing page) *Adoration of the Lamb*: detail of the drapery of one of the virgins during overpaint removal (see also fig. 1.16).

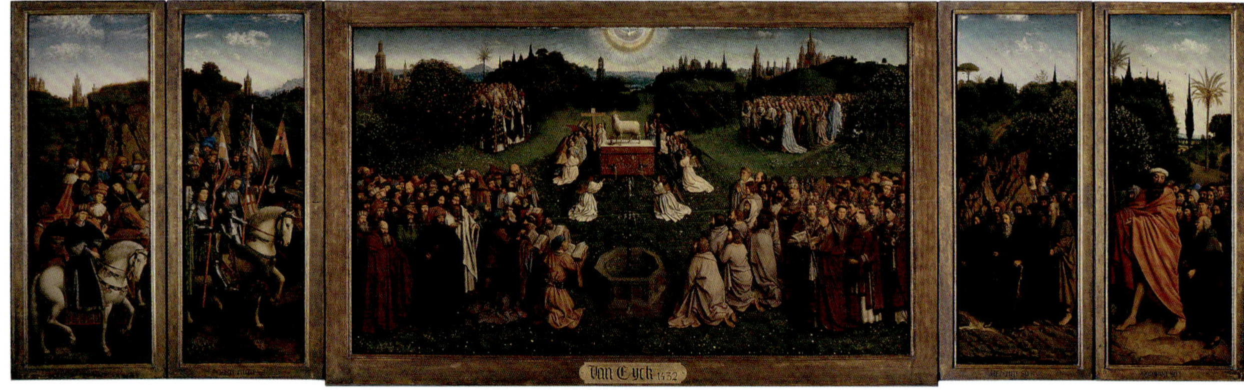

1.1

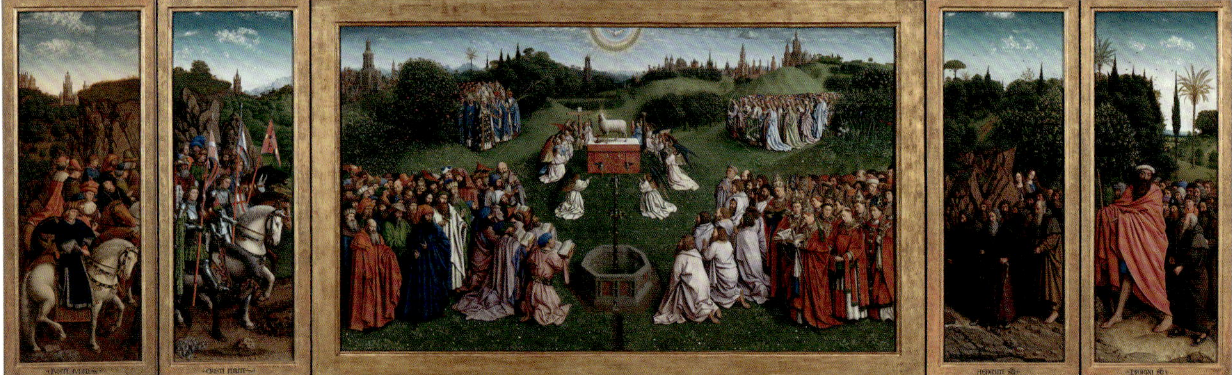

1.2

Fig. 1.1. Hubert and Jan van Eyck: lower interior register of the *Ghent Altarpiece*, before restoration, Ghent, St Bavo's Cathedral.

Fig. 1.2. Hubert and Jan van Eyck: lower interior register of the *Ghent Altarpiece*, after restoration, Ghent, St Bavo's Cathedral.

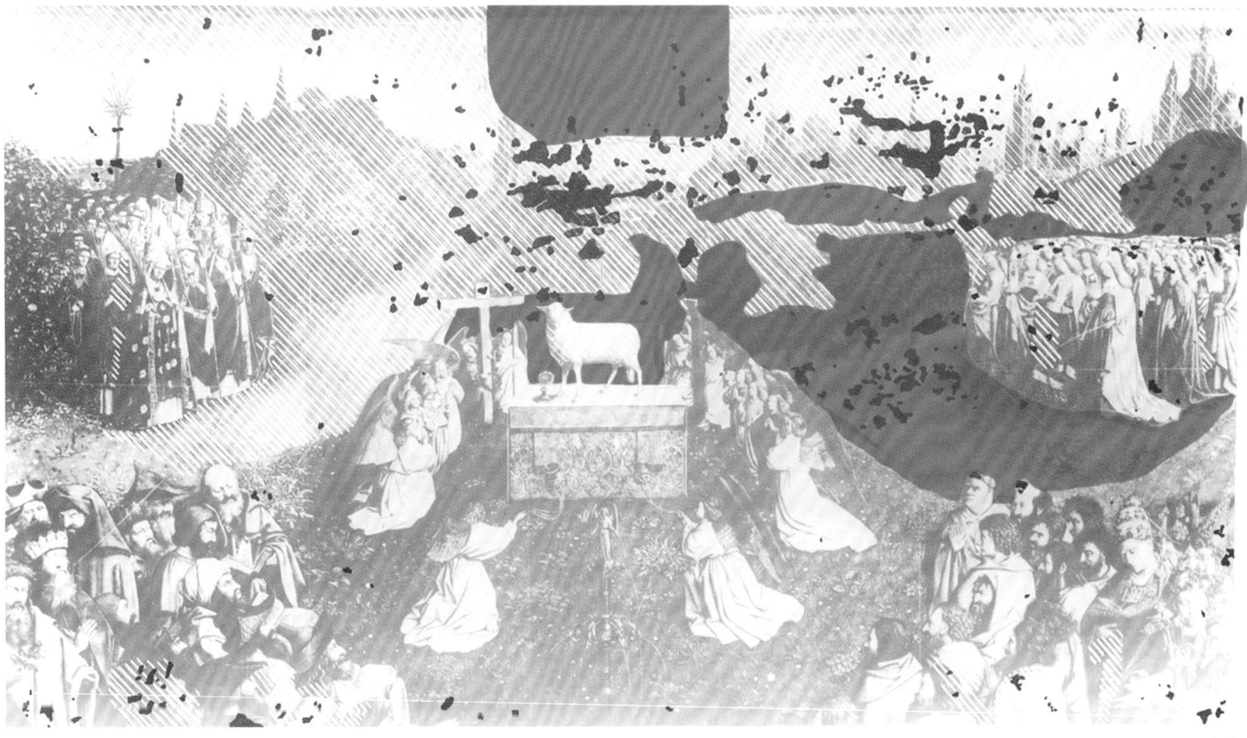

1.3

Fig. 1.3. *Adoration of the Lamb*, diagram of losses (dark grey) and overpaints from different periods (white hatching), published in Coremans 1953, Pl. XXXI. The areas where Albert Philippot removed overpaints are shown in green.

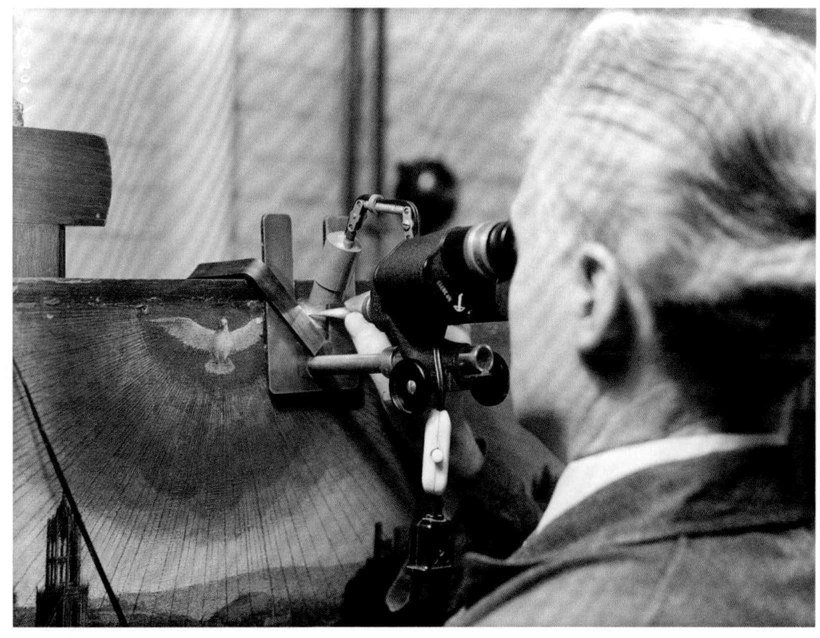

1.4

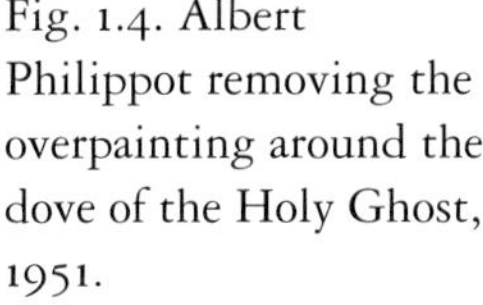

Fig. 1.4. Albert Philippot removing the overpainting around the dove of the Holy Ghost, 1951.

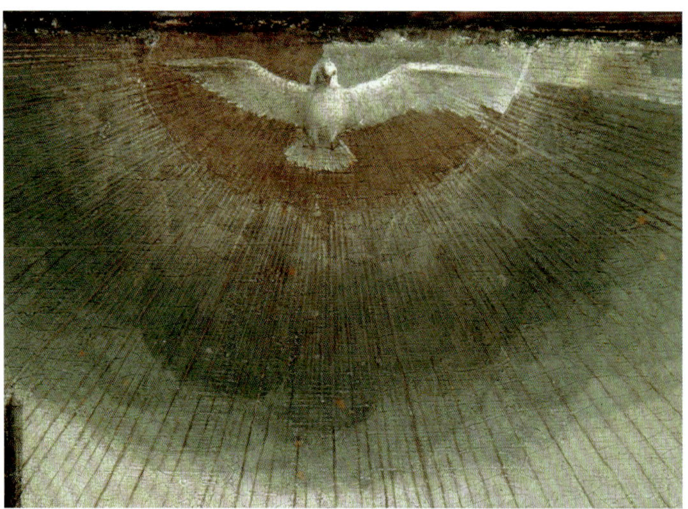

1.5a

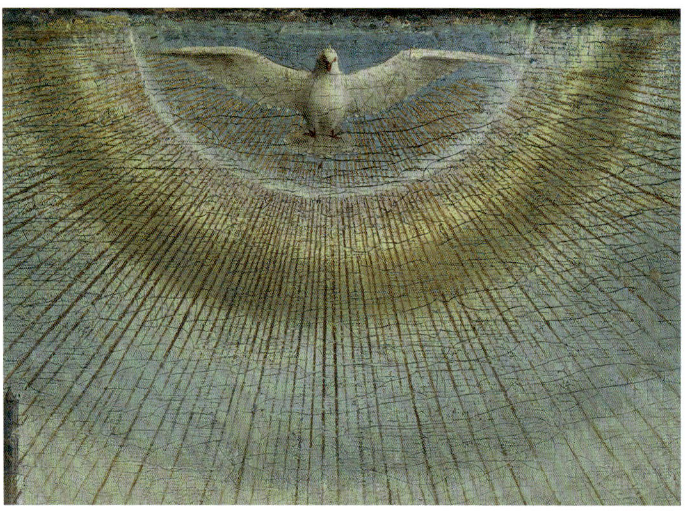

1.5b

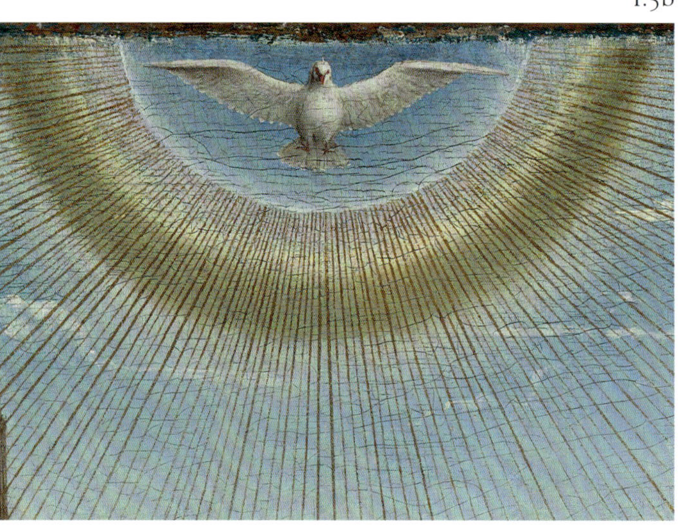

1.5c

Fig. 1.5a–c. *Adoration of the Lamb* (details). The zone of the dove during overpaint removal in 1951. Non original gilding has been removed on the right side, above the head and around the wing of the dove, and in the clouds (a); after varnish removal and before the removal of the overpainting in 2017 (b); after overpaint removal and restoration (c).

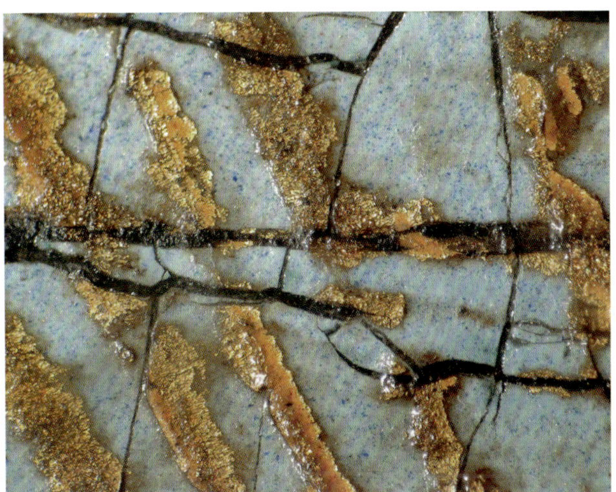
1.6

Fig. 1.6. *Adoration of the Lamb*, microphotograph of the mordant-gilded rays directly below the dove, before removal of the overpaint (in 2017). The rays overlap wide cracks in the blue semicircle, indicating that they were applied after this layer had aged and deteriorated.

A complete evaluation of both the complex paint build-up of the whole register and the condition of the original became possible only after the thinning of the thick darkened varnishes masking the differences in colour and texture between the original and later additions. The examination revealed that the central panel had suffered more early damage than the shutters and that it had been more extensively overpainted in the mid-sixteenth century. Furthermore, specific areas were restored in Paris in 1798[8] and twice in Ghent, in 1828 and in 1859.[9] The condition of the paint layer of the side panels, which were kept in Berlin between 1821 and 1920, was better, despite the intrusive structural treatment of 1894, when the panels, painted on both sides, were sawn through their thickness to obtain separate paintings.[10]

During the 1950–51 campaign, overpaints and varnish were removed to varying degrees according to their aesthetic impact on the whole.[11] For example, in the zone around the dove of the Holy Spirit, Philippot removed a golden glory and billowing clouds to reveal the underlying colourful halo and bright blue semicircle ringed with white (figs. 1.4, 1.5a and 1.5b), but he retained the obviously non-original mordant-gilded rays immediately around the dove (fig. 1.6).[12] He also left untouched the overall mid-sixteenth-century overpaint of the sky, consisting of a thick blue, azurite-containing layer, with mordant-gilded rays applied on top of it (figs. 1.7a–b and 1.23b),[13] and most of the nineteenth-century retouchings in that area. Philippot uncovered the original ears of the lamb when removing some sixteenth- and nineteenth-century overpaints in the surrounding meadow.[14] As a result the Mystic Lamb has ever since sported four ears: the original pair, revealed by Philippot, and those added higher up on the head in the sixteenth century, which were not removed in 1950–51 (fig. 1.8a). Coremans's team made many groundbreaking discoveries, but in some cases confused different overpainting stages.

Treatment procedures

Varnishes composed of synthetic resins applied since the 1950s were first removed. These were followed by uneven layers and residues of older, darkened natural resin and oil varnishes (figs. 1.7a and 1.9a–b), as well as local, thick and discoloured retouchings associated with these varnishing campaigns. This approach, already adopted during the first phase of the restoration, allowed a progressive insight into past interventions. There were only a few nineteenth-century retouchings on the shutters, but on the *Adoration of the Lamb* panel many restored areas thickly painted with pigments that did not come into use until the nineteenth century, such as cobalt blue, or chrome oxide green, spilled onto the original paint. Particularly crude and darkened were retouchings in the foreground figures (fig. 1.10). Their

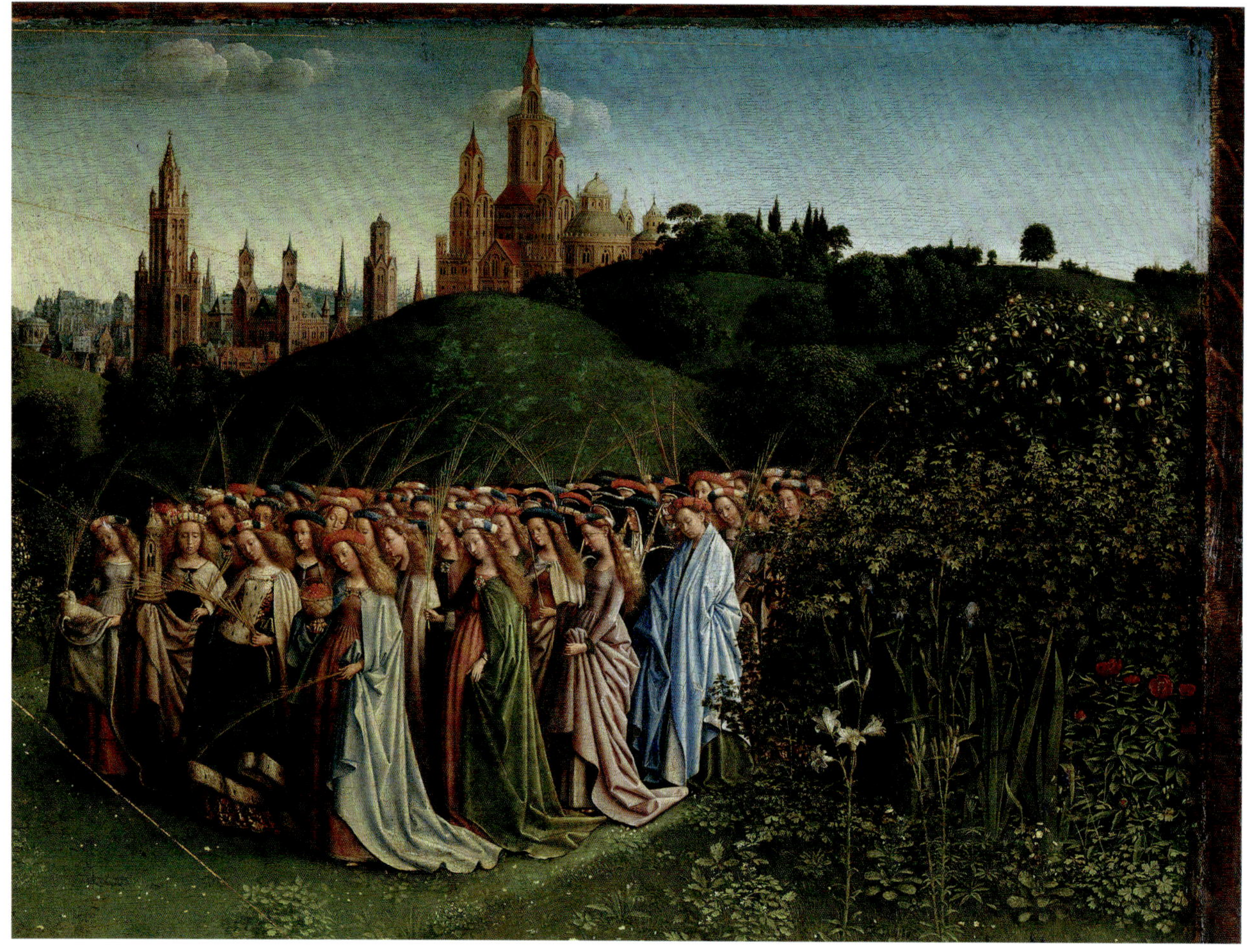

1.7a

Fig. 1.7a–b. *Adoration of the Lamb*, group of the virgins during removal of discoloured varnishes (a); during removal of the dark sixteenth-century overpaint, revealing the underlying brighter sky and hills. The palm branches above the women were part of the overpainting (b).

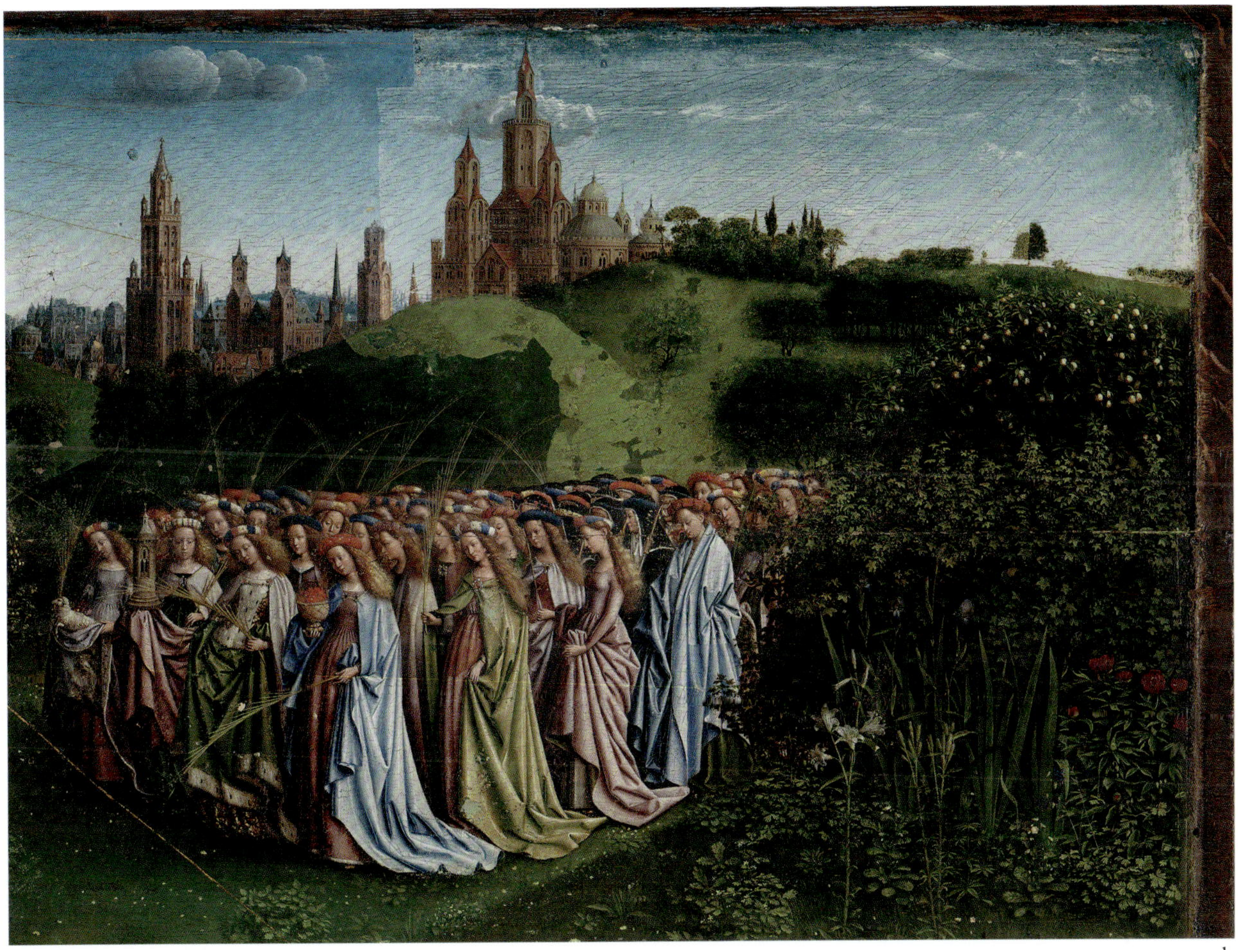

1.7b

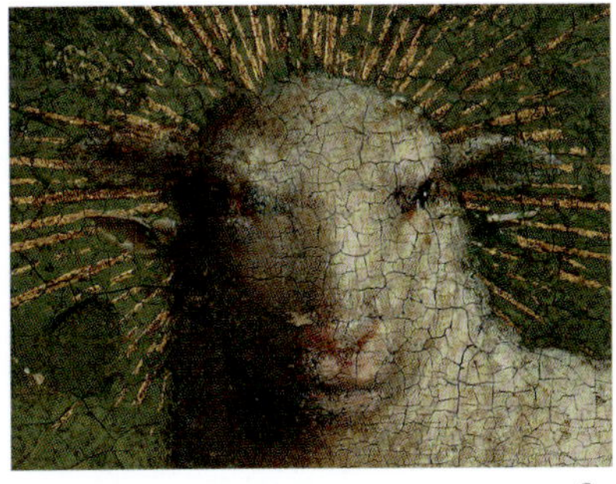

1.8a

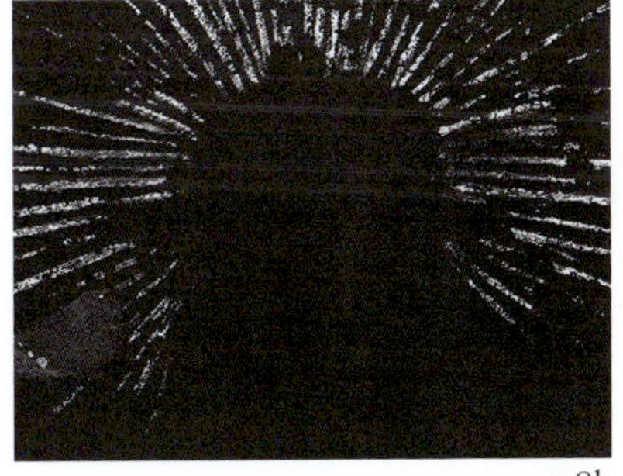

1.8b

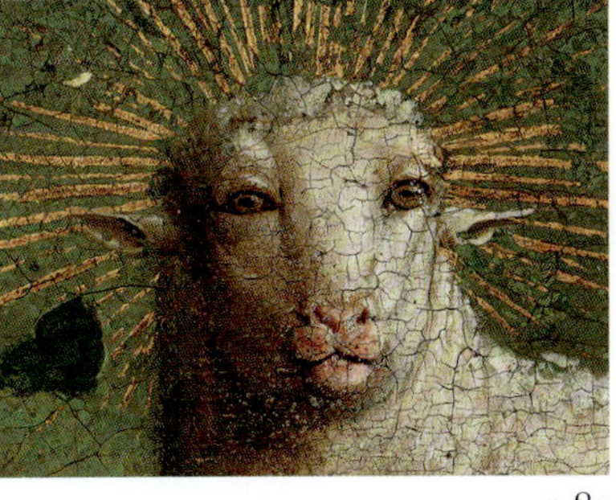

1.8c

Fig. 1.8a–c. *Adoration of the Lamb*, detail of the lamb, after varnish removal (a); MA-XRF Au-L map (gold), showing the mordant-gilded rays placed around the original ears and covered by the ears added in the sixteenth century (b); the lamb, after overpaint removal (c).

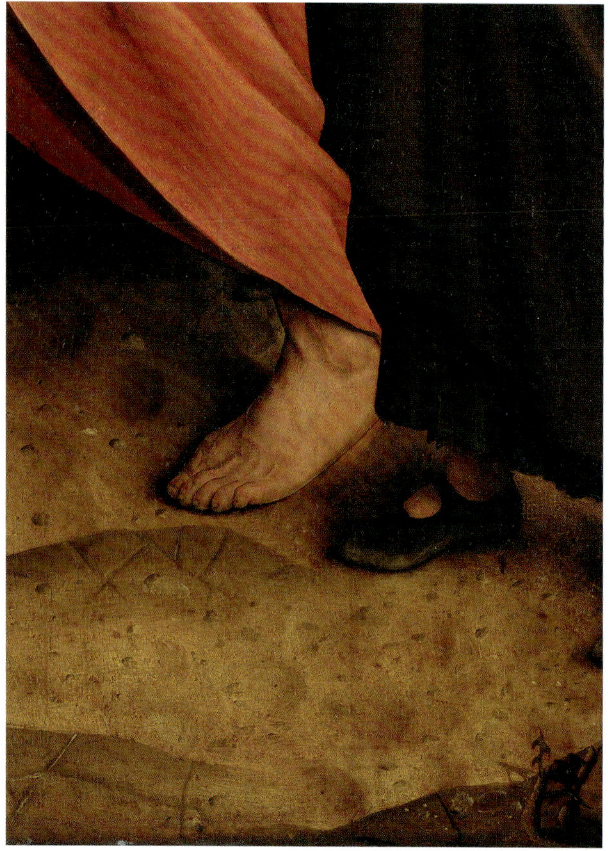

1.9a

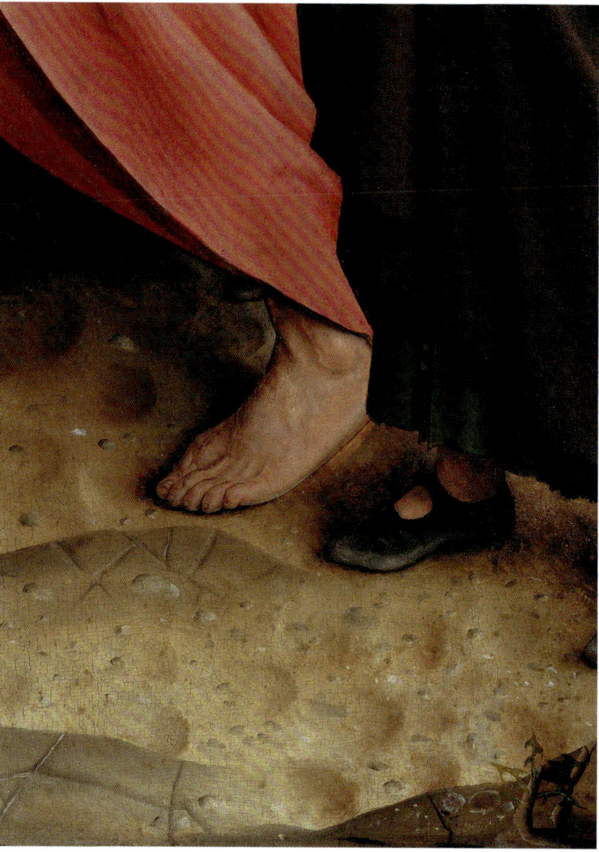

1.9b

Fig. 1.9a–b. Detail of the *Pilgrims*, before (a) and after (b) cleaning, showing the improvement in the rendering of depth and of the textures of rocks, sand, leather, fabrics and skin tones.

location and composition were documented before removal (fig. 1.11). Only at that point did it become possible to map overpaintings belonging to still older campaigns.

Several months of interdisciplinary examination were needed to allow us to conclude that over half of the surface of the *Adoration of the Lamb* and some smaller zones of the wings were covered with mid-sixteenth-century overpaints (fig. 1.12). The condition of the original paint was generally good, with only few losses and some abrasions (fig. 1.13). Several small test windows showed that the overpaint could be removed securely. In view of this evidence and due to the results of the restoration of the exterior, the International Commission of experts advising on the project recommended that this sixteenth-century overpaint should be removed in order to recover the Van Eycks' extraordinary painted surface, as long as it could be done safely.

For the paintings of the interior, with their exceedingly detailed scenes, the distinction between original 'Eyckian' phases and early additions by other hands was more difficult to resolve than for the paintings of the exterior. Various zones of the *Adoration of the Lamb*, long thought to be non-Eyckian additions, had to be thoroughly reassessed. A case in point was the dove of the Holy Ghost as to whose

Fig. 1.10. *Adoration of the Lamb* (detail), large, darkened retouchings in a kneeling prophet.

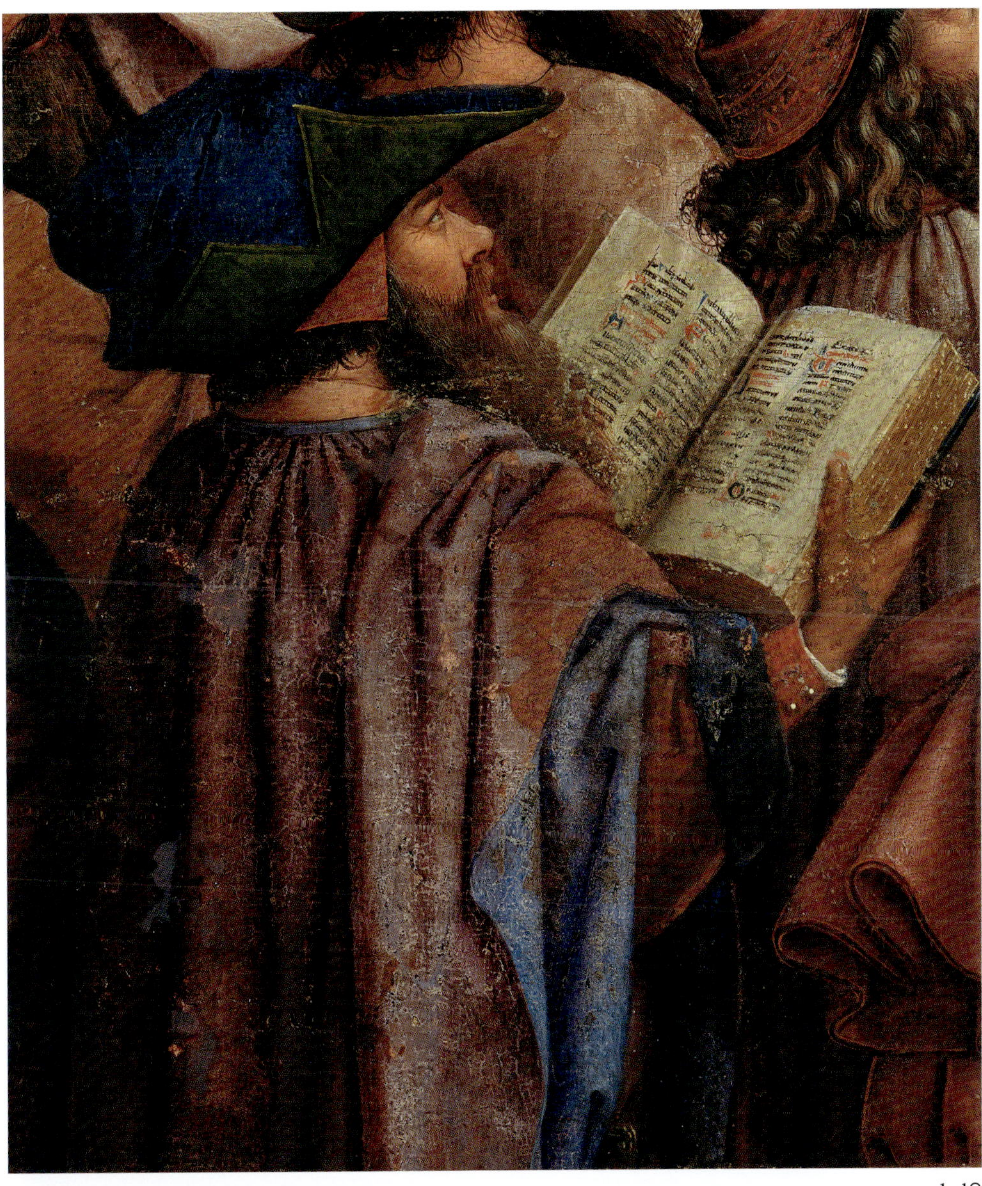

1. 10

Fig. 1.11. *Adoration of the Lamb*, diagram of the zone of the altar documenting nineteenth- and twentieth-century retouchings (in black) before their removal.

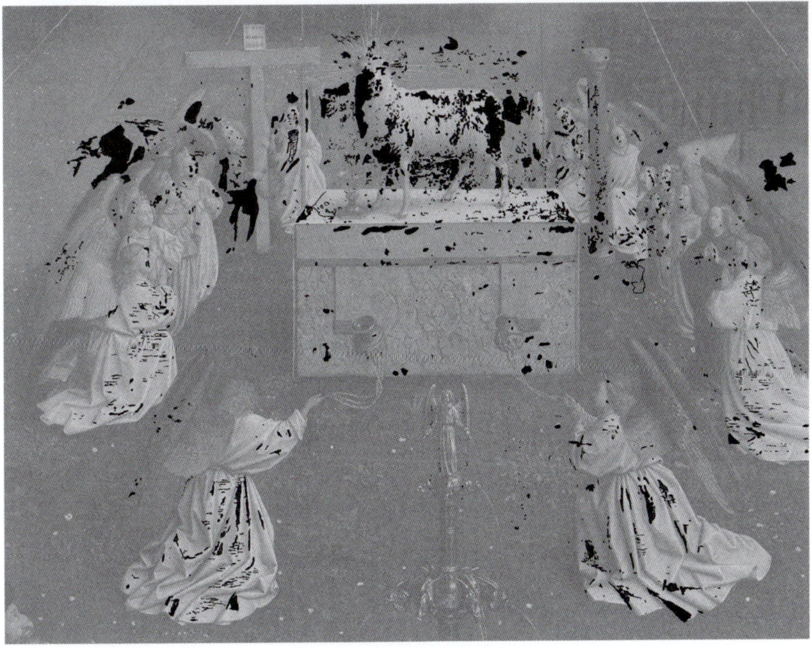

1. 11

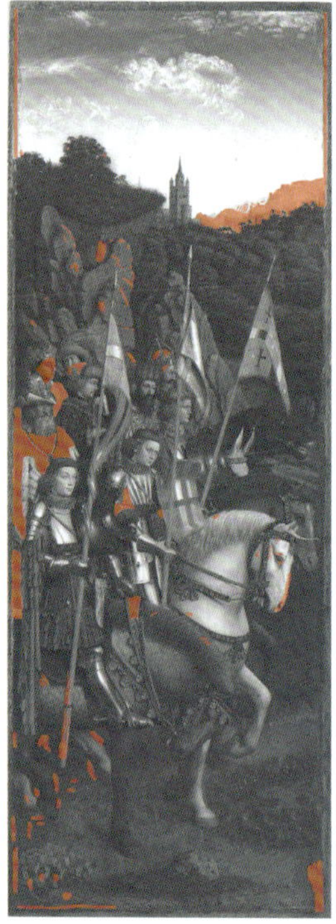

1.12a

1.12b

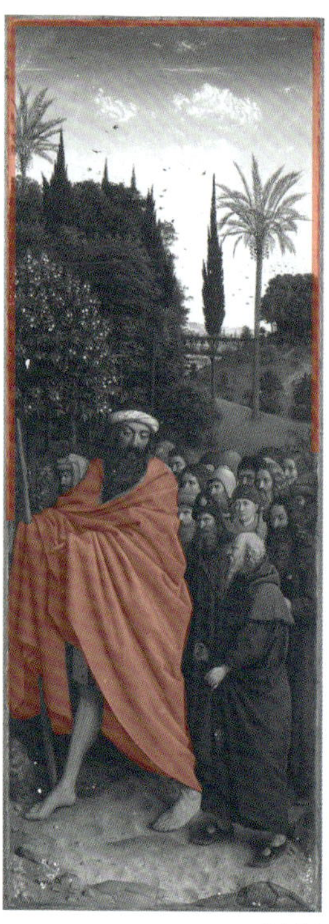

1.12c

Fig. 1.12a–d. Diagram of the extent of sixteenth-century overpainting (in red).

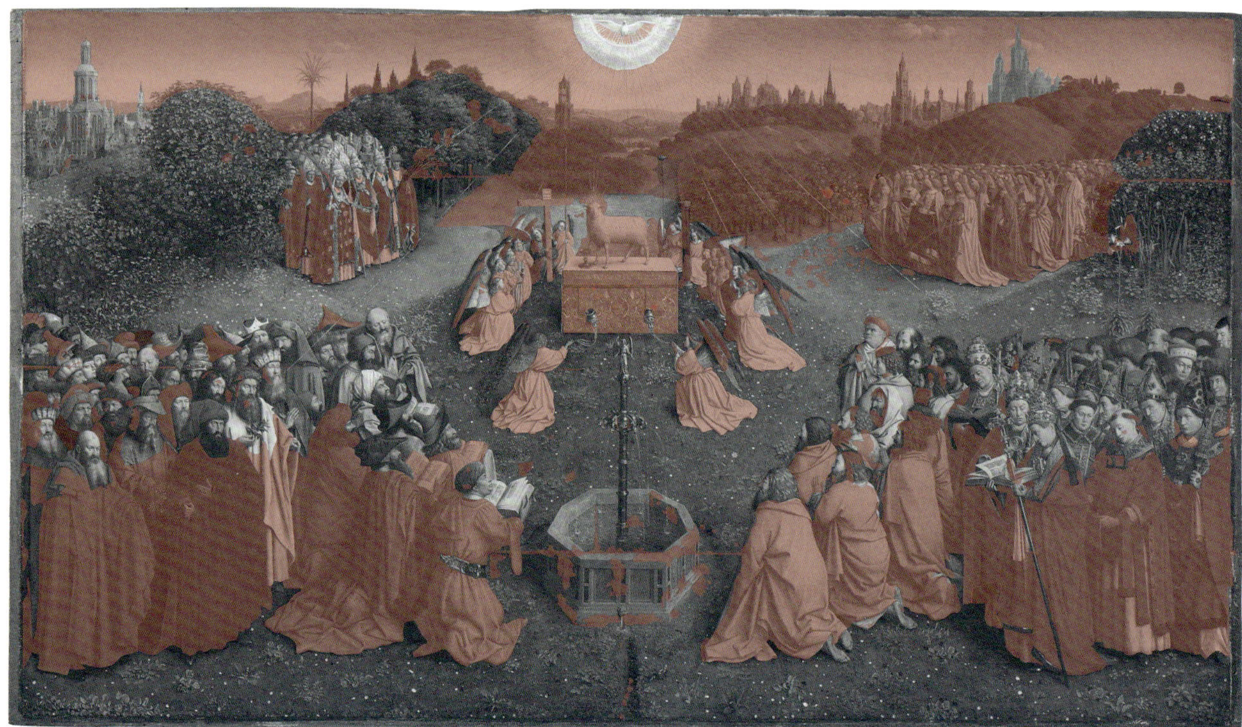

1.12d

Fig. 1.13a–d.
Diagram of the actual paint losses that were hidden by sixteenth-century overpaints (in red).

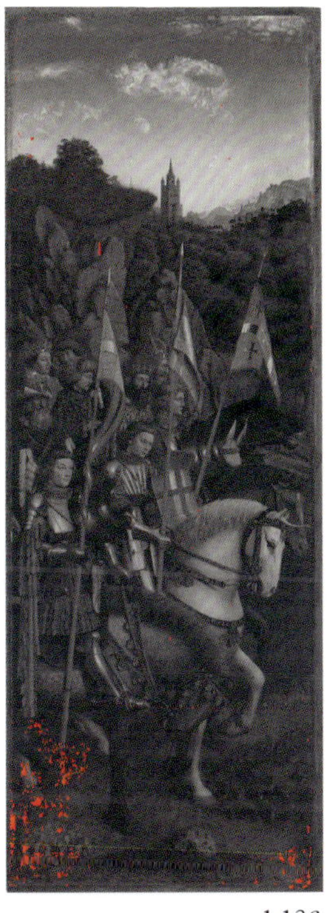

1.13a

1.13b

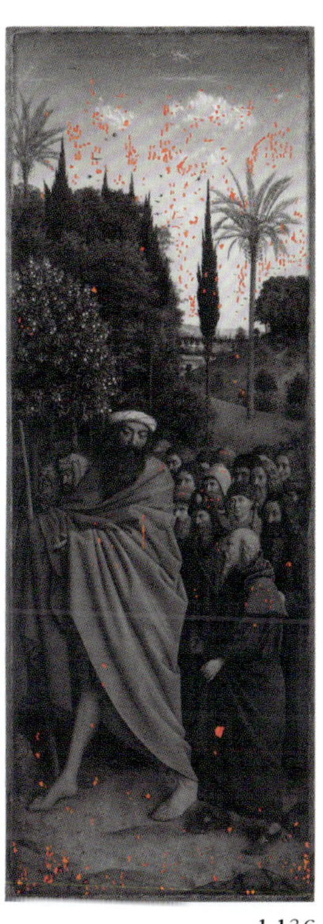

1.13c

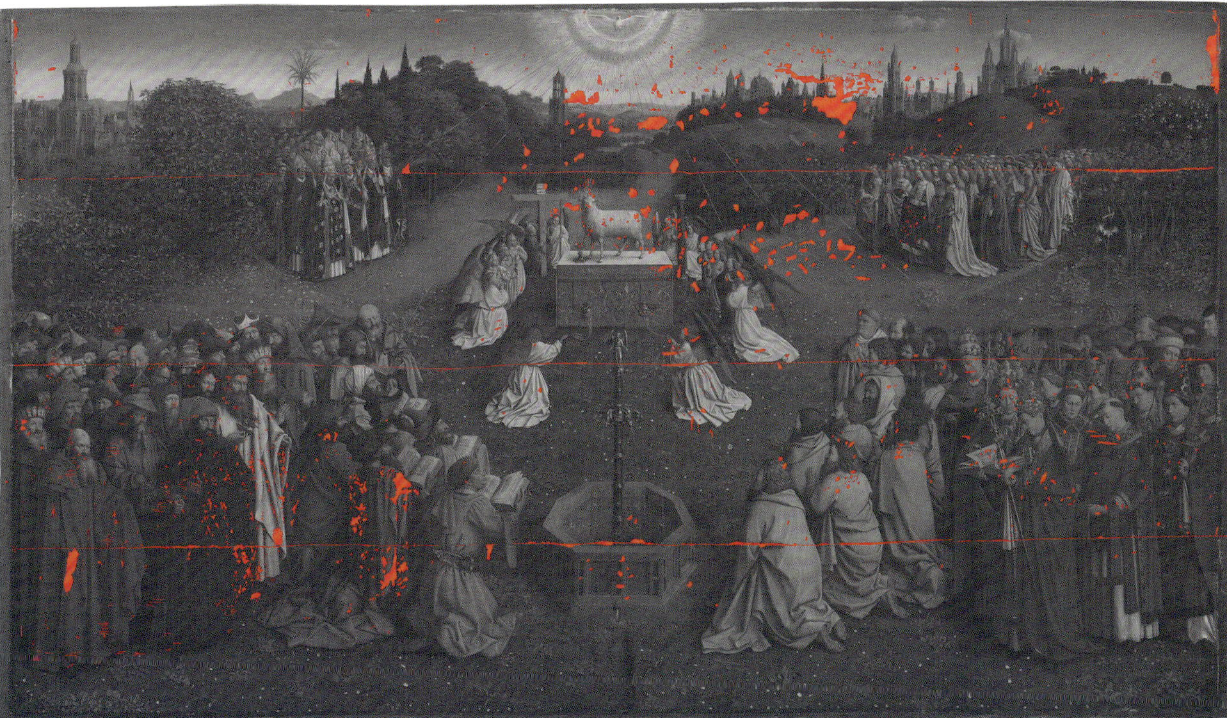

1.13d

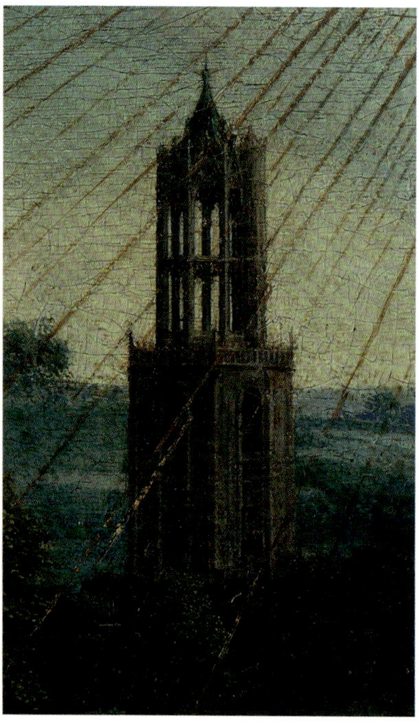
1.14a

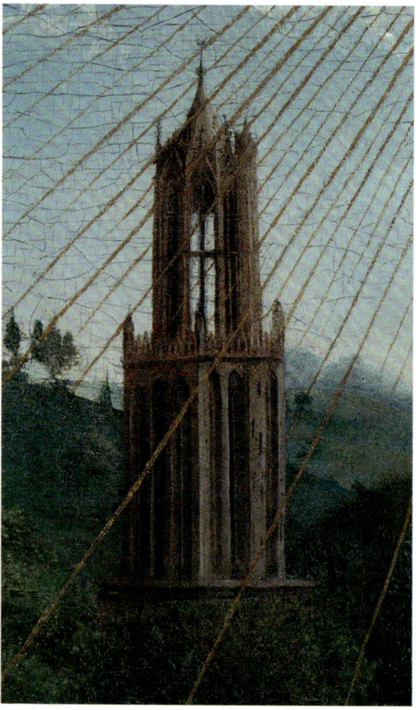
1.14b

Fig. 1.14a–b. *Adoration of the Lamb*, the tower of Utrecht cathedral, before (a) and after (b) overpaint removal, during restoration.

originality several scholars had expressed doubts.[15] Furthermore, Coremans had suggested that the tower of Utrecht cathedral in the background might have been added by Jan van Scorel around 1550 (fig. 1.14a).[16]

Contrary to the assertion made in *L'Agneau mystique au Laboratoire*,[17] the sky of the *Adoration of the Lamb* and parts of the landscape and the meadow had been damaged only superficially by the fire in Ghent cathedral in 1822. The large losses along the horizon detected by X-radiography (fig. 1.15) were in fact much older, since they were hidden by the thick mid-sixteenth-century overpaint. The same intervention also covered the hills and most of the trees of the wooded area. The billowing clouds around the dove, added on that same occasion and further heavily retouched in the nineteenth century, were removed by Philippot. The skies of the wing panels, on the other hand, were overpainted very thinly except along the edges, where the same overpaint – but more thickly applied – covered the unpainted edges that had

Fig. 1.15. XR of the sky of the *Adoration of the Lamb*, before treatment, showing losses filled with lead-white-based putty.

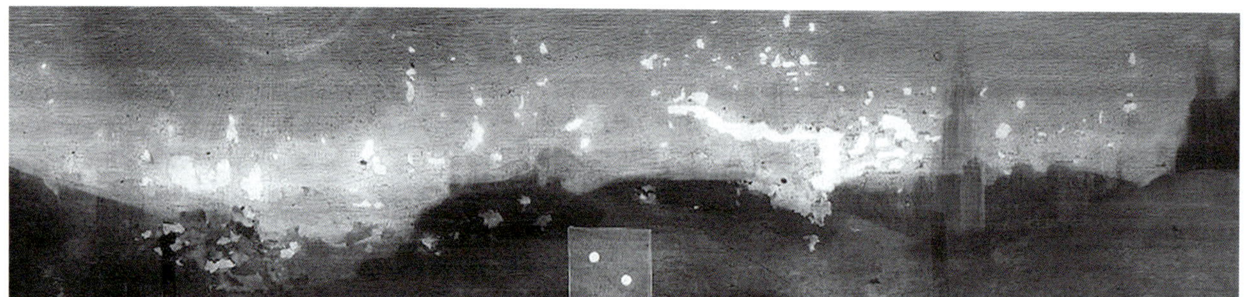
1.15

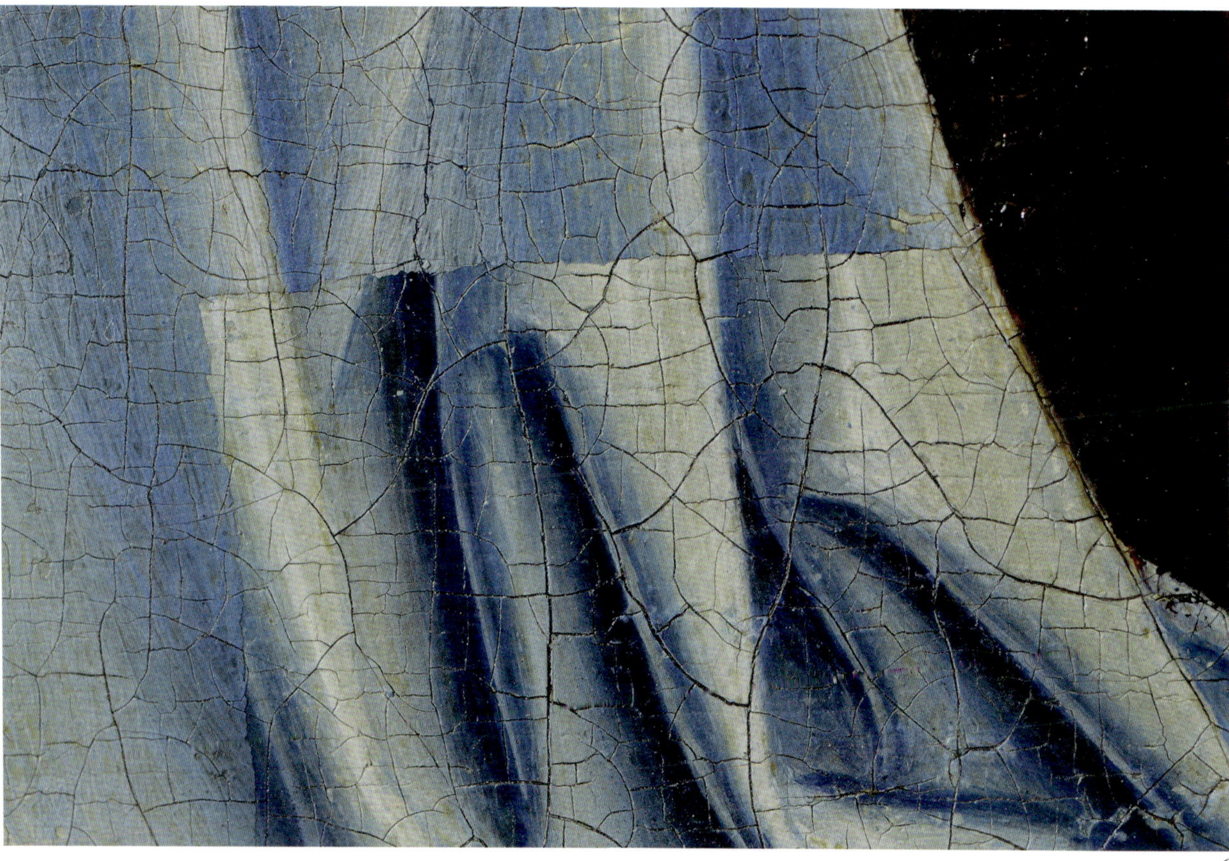

1. 16

Fig. 1.16. *Adoration of the Lamb*, detail of the drapery of one of the virgins during overpaint removal. The complex structure of the folds using several tones and the enamel-like surface of the original (below) contrast with the grittier paint and the simplified rendition in the mid-sixteenth-century overpaints (above).

Fig. 1.17. *Portrait of Joos Vijd* on the exterior of the polyptych, detail. Cleaning window made in 2013 in the overpainted drapery, showing the original dark shadows and the bright highlight along the fold.

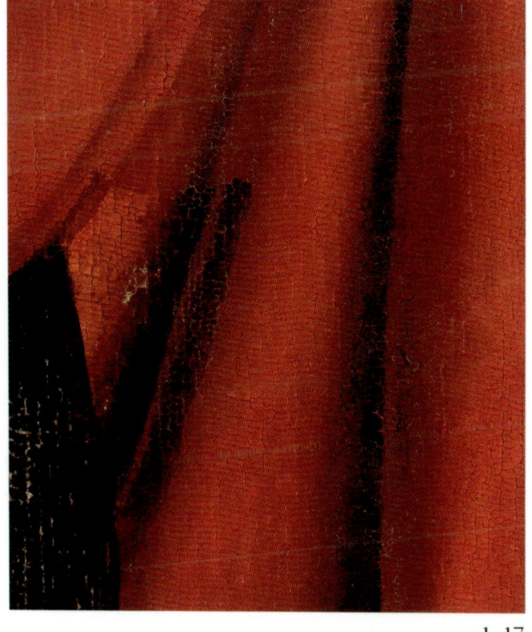

1. 17

become visible through the shrinkage of the panels in their frames. A few palms and leaves had been added to the vegetation.

The technique in the old overpaints of the clothes in the *Adoration of the Lamb* and in parts of the shutters closely resembled that of the donors on the exterior of the altarpiece. There can be no doubt that all these areas were overpainted during the same treatment: the sharp folds were softened and the high contrast of bright tones and deep shadows of the original subdued (figs. 1.16 and 1.17). Some draperies were also covered with thinner, glazing overpaint (fig. 1.18).[18] The contours were carefully followed, but the shapes were simplified. Small features such as palm branches were mostly repeated (fig. 1.19). In the group of the virgins, where the opening of a joint in the wooden support had caused localized damage, flesh tones were hidden under a chalky mask of overpaint (fig. 1.20a–b). Dainty trees in the hills of the *Adoration of the Lamb* were transformed into stubbier standardized versions, and leaves added to soften the transition to the overpainted sky. The rolling hills, originally bathed in sunlight, were covered with flat, dark and coarse layers (fig. 1.7b). In the central valley, a damaged landscape area was completely covered with bluish hills. Three buildings were uncovered here, one of them a reddish tower strongly recalling Our Lady's Church in Bruges,[19] and next to it, two structures apparently based on St Bavo's Abbey in Ghent, which was demolished in 1540 (fig. 1.21a–d).[20] Further to the right, a cityscape was changed into a suggestion of antique buildings and a fragmentary tower was hidden (fig. 1.22a–b). Most of the buildings along the horizon were covered, except the cityscape on the left and the large edifice on the right. Windows, archways, roofs and balustrades were altered, and the variegated and original bright colours were covered with a dull camaieu of greys, blues and violets. This was also the case of the tower of Utrecht cathedral, originally displaying delicate architectonic details, closely recalling the actual building (fig. 1.14b). The tower was not added as a new feature in the sixteenth century, but it owed its awkward appearance to overpaint from that period. The weakly painted dove of the Holy Ghost, however, was not covered in mid-sixteenth-century overpaint.[21] Whether this element should be considered part of the original Eyckian conception is discussed elsewhere in this volume.

Many marvellous details and nuances of the original re-emerged as work went on. The original features of the lamb's head, however, were largely anticipated by preliminary interdisciplinary research.[22] The recovery of the face of the lamb, with its large, frontally placed eyes revealed the original iconographic intent of the composition's central element (fig. 1.7a and c). The reasons why the lamb's head

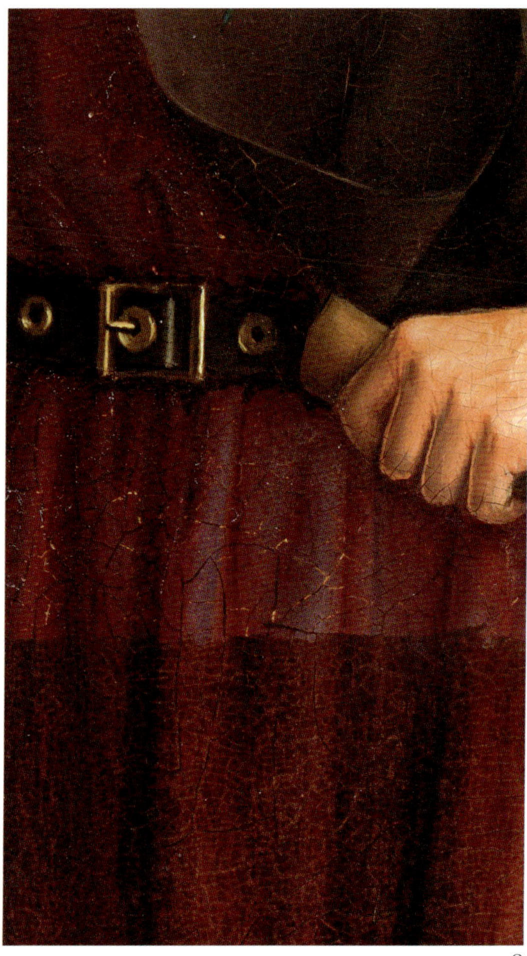

1.18

Fig. 1.18. *Hermits*, detail of St Anthony's cloak during the removal of overpaint.

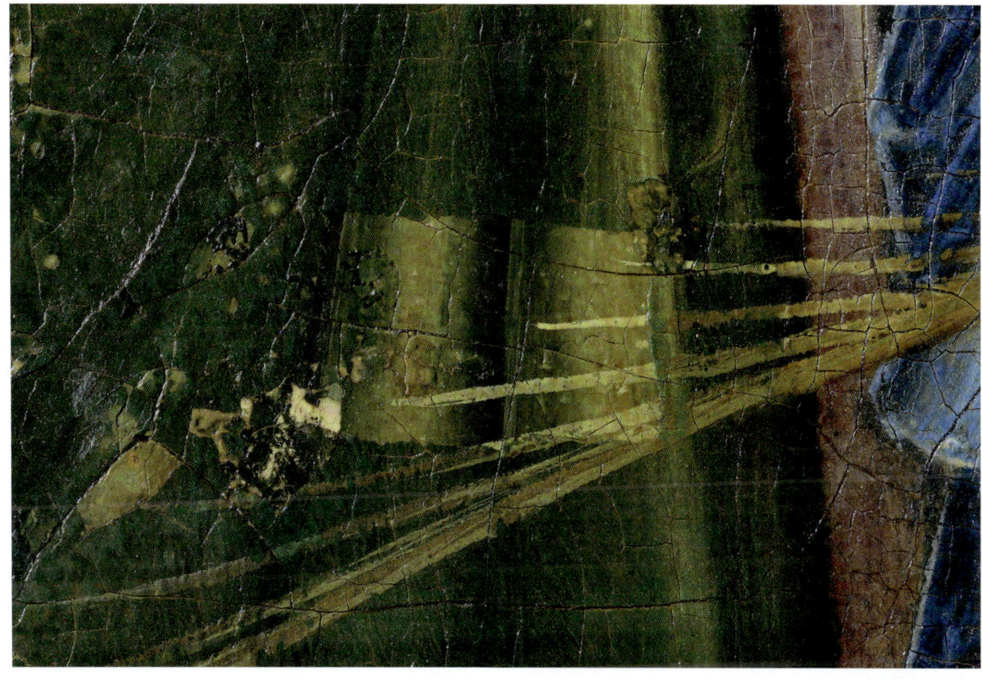

1. 19

Fig. 1.19. *Adoration of the Lamb*, detail of a cleaning window in the green dress of one of the virgins: the original palm branch was reproduced in the overpaint.

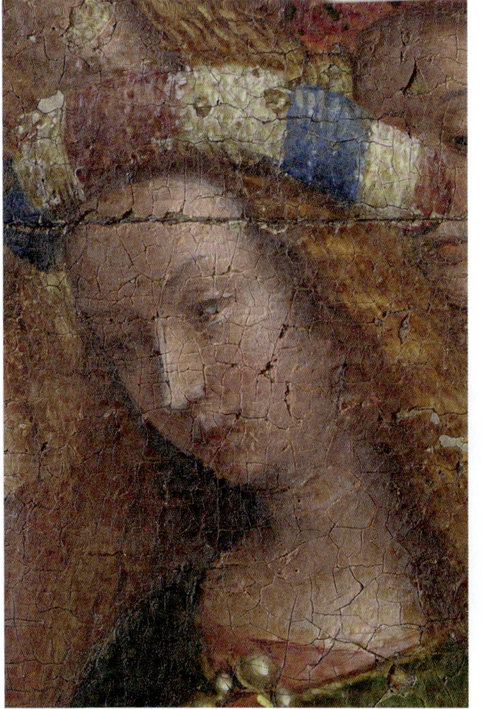

1.20a

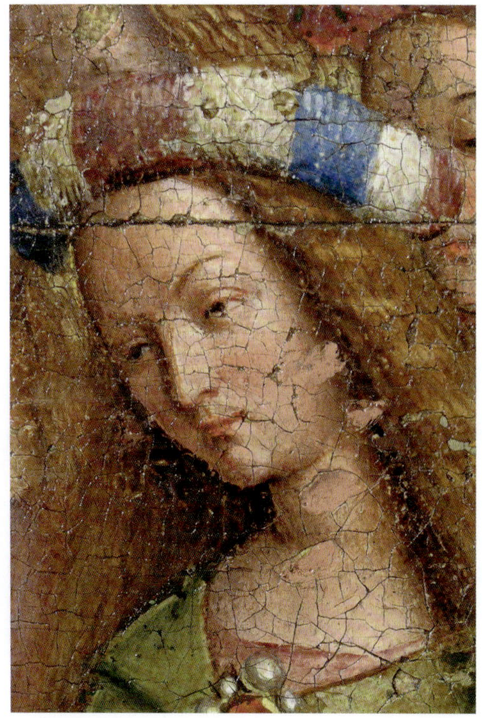

1.20b

Fig. 1.20a–b. *Adoration of the Lamb*, detail. Face of one of the virgins before (a) and after (b) the removal of overpaint.

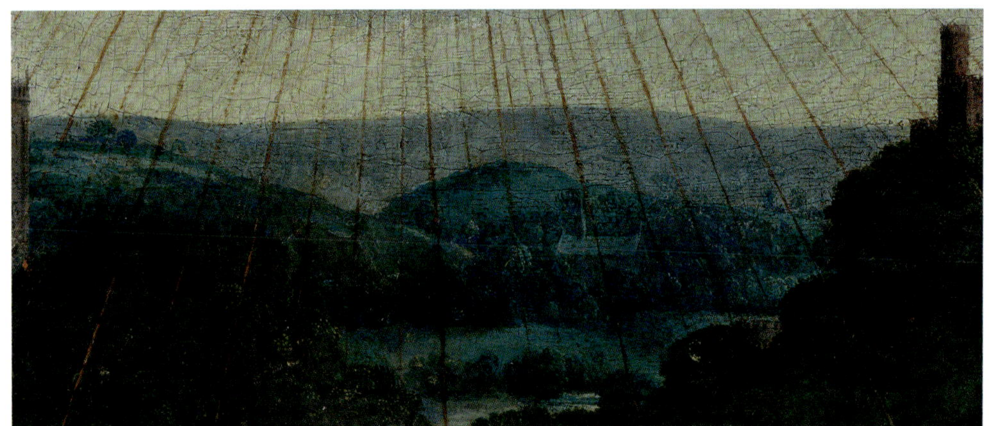

1.21a

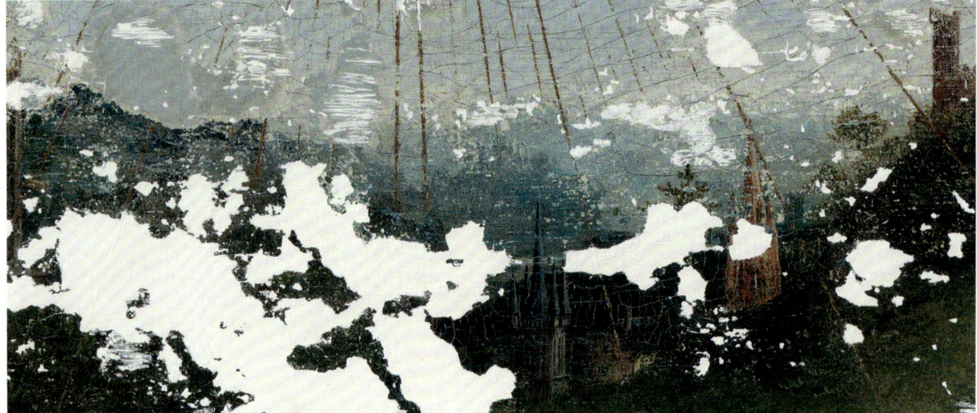

1.21b

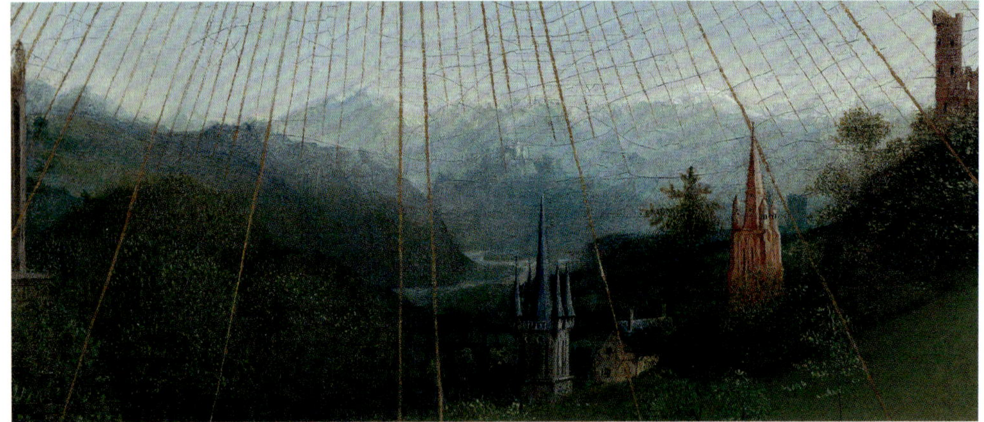

1.21c

Fig. 1.21a–d. *Adoration of the Lamb*, detail. Central landscape before overpaint removal (a); after cleaning and filling of the paint losses in the original (b); and after restoration (c). Detail of St Bavo's Abbey in the anonymous *View of Ghent of* 1534, canvas, Ghent, STAM, inv. 474 (d).

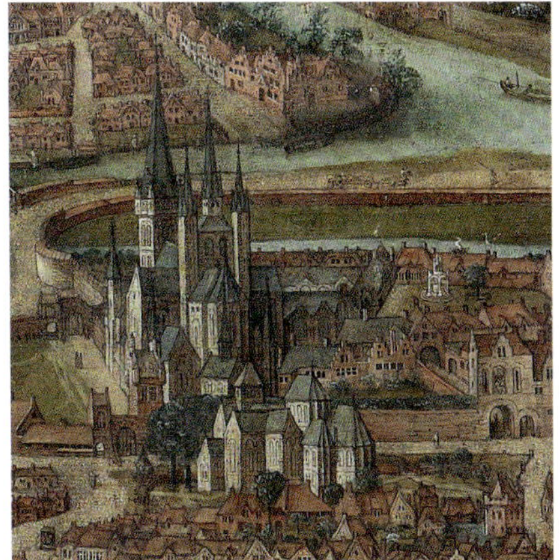

1.21d

was overpainted with a less evocative version, with eyes placed more laterally and ears higher up, are still under investigation.[23] The same goes for a few other iconographic modifications in the *Adoration of the Lamb*, including the row of twenty palm branches added above the group of virgins (fig. 1.7a–b), and the house painted in the left upper landscape, below the palm tree. These elements were also removed in order to restore the coherence and the luminosity of the original landscape.

Overpaint removal and consolidation of the paint layers

With the aid of stereo microscopes, surgical scalpels were used to remove the overpaint on top of intermediary layers of varnish of various thickness (fig. 1.23a–b). In some areas, solvent compresses or gels were applied to soften the overpaint, before removal.[24] The relative cohesion and solidity of the underlying layers was methodically taken into account, and the original paint was consolidated where necessary. Constant reference was made to technical documentation acquired through macro-X-ray fluorescence (MA-XRF), X-radiography (XR), infrared macrophotography (IR) and infrared reflectography (IRR) (fig. 1.8b).[25] Observations were discussed within the team and with visiting colleagues and experts. All this has contributed to the successful unveiling of the Van Eyck brothers' original paint

Fig. 1.22a–b. *Adoration of the Lamb*, detail. Cityscape on the right side of the horizon, before (a) and after (b) the removal of sixteenth-century overpaint.

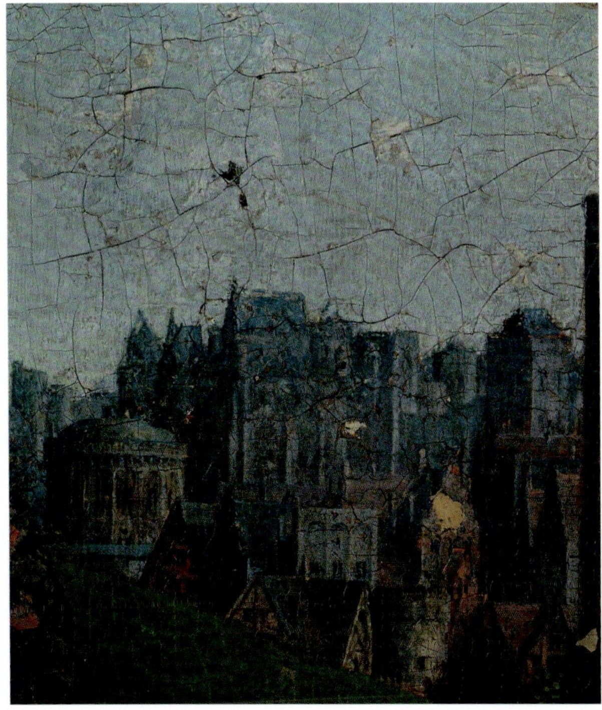

1.22a

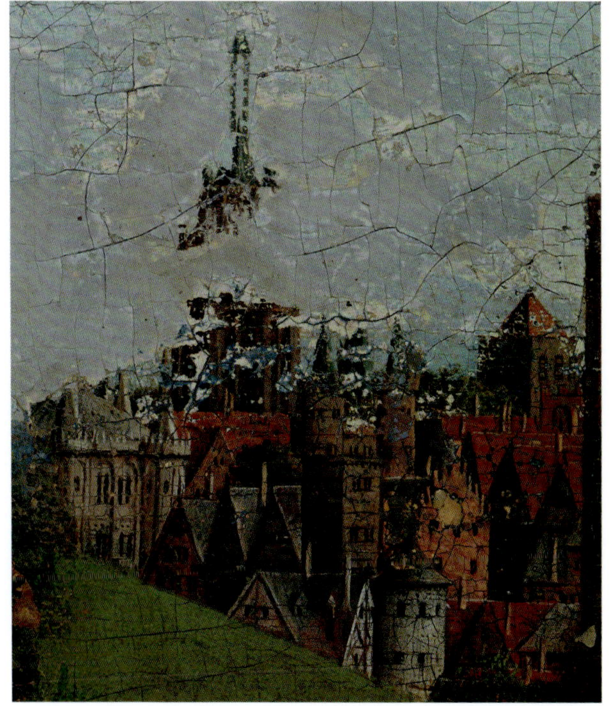

1.22b

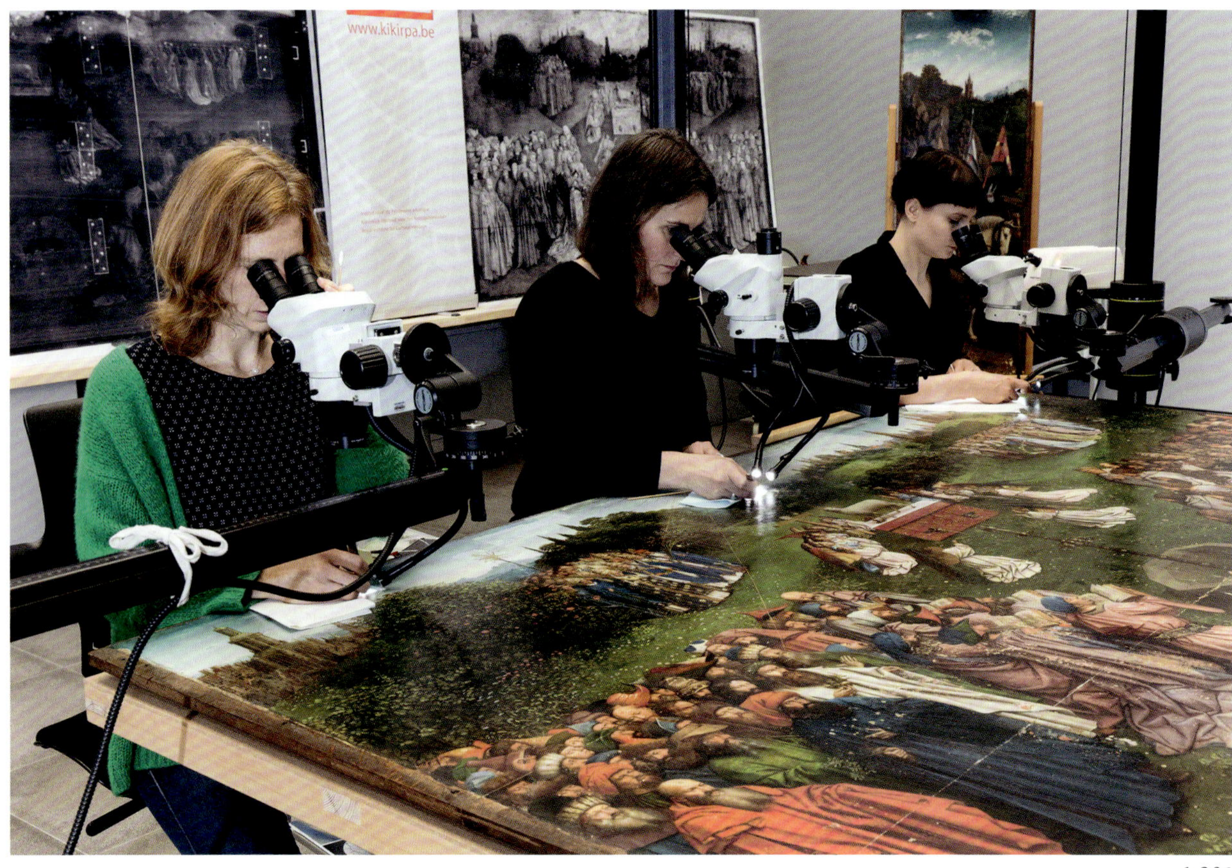

1.23a

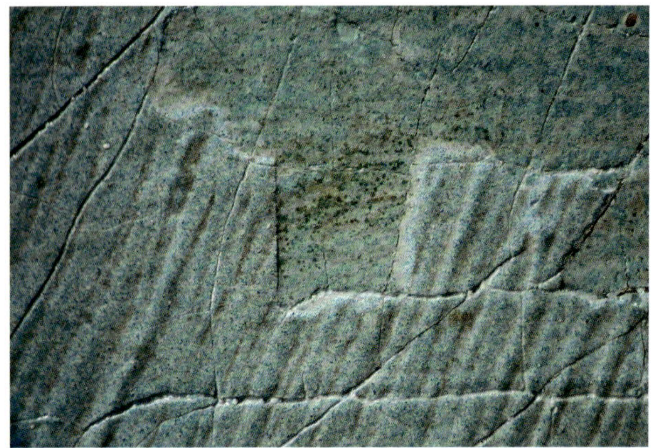

1.23b

Fig. 1.23a–b. During the removal of overpaint, the heavy panel of the *Adoration* was laid on a custom-made tilt table in order to allow several restorers to work together (a); *Adoration of the Lamb*, microphotograph of the sky taken during overpaint removal: the streaky and gritty texture of the overpaint contrasts with the smoother original. The dark stains on the original surface are remains of an intermediary varnish (b).

Fig. 1.24. *Knights of Christ*, detail. One of the knights after cleaning and restoration.

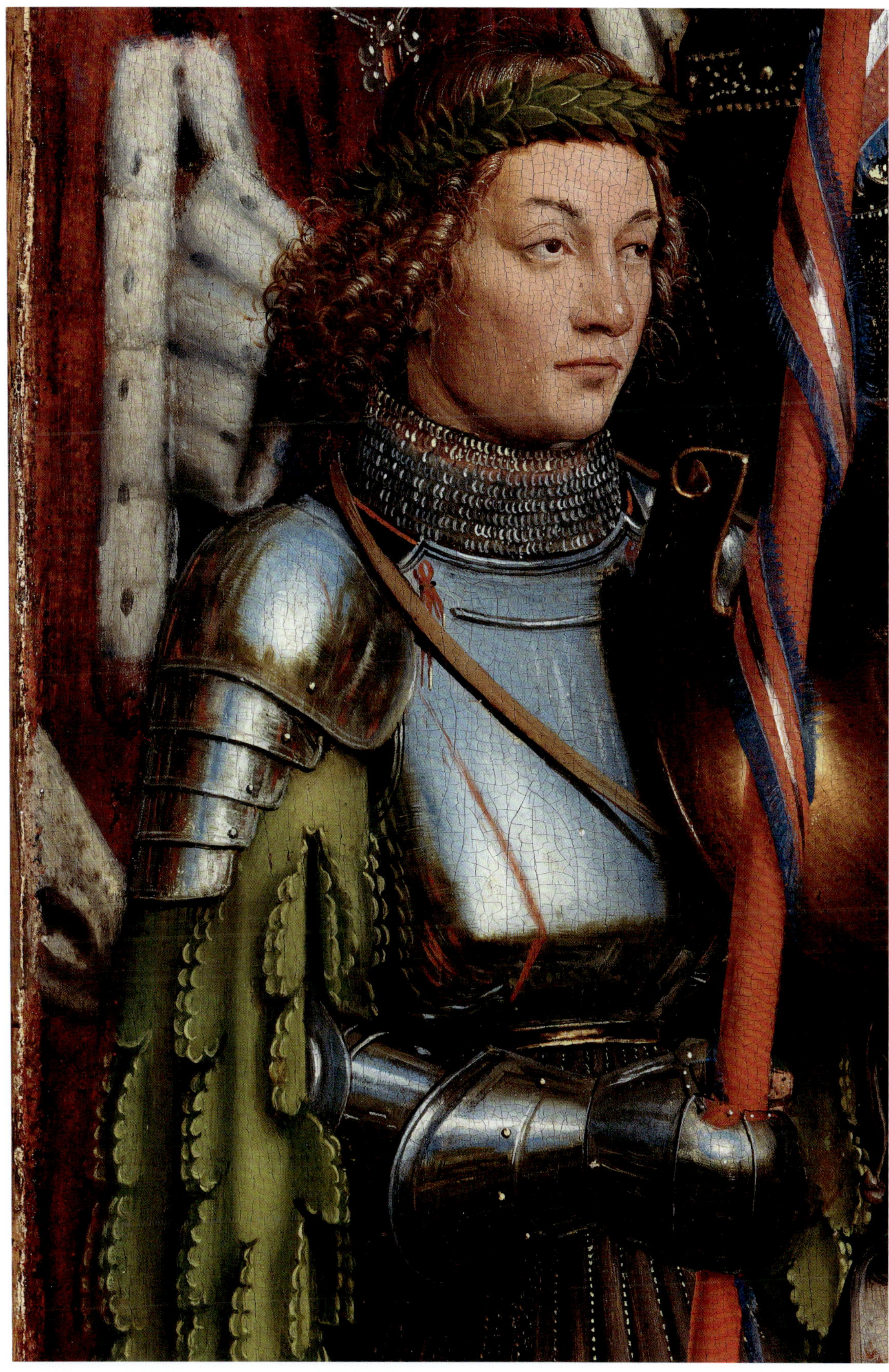

1.24

surface. The overpaint, varying in texture, hardness and thickness, was removed where it could be confidently identified and only where this could be done safely.

The finalization of the cleaning process included the removal of remnants of putty spread over the original surface, as well as thick, browned and uneven old varnish layers that had accumulated in the darker areas, particularly on the wings. This last step has further revealed the luminosity of the painted surface, the depth of the landscapes and the almost tactile appearance of painted metals, stones, plants and fabrics (fig. 1.24).[26]

The restoration treatment resulted in a major retrieval of areas of original paint, since the amount of actual paint loss preceding the mid-sixteenth-century restoration (about 5% in the *Adoration of the Lamb*, and even less on the wings) was only a fraction of the overpainted surface. Paint losses were caused by the cumulative effect of the natural degradation of materials, human intervention (such as opening and closing of the altarpiece and manipulations relating to the liturgy), accidental impacts and inept cleaning and restorations. Paint layer analysis suggests that, just as with the paintings of the exterior, the mid-sixteenth-century restorers started with a superficial cleaning. They did not remove all older varnishes or earlier restorations before they set about overpainting.

During the overpaint removal we have become aware of even older, carefully painted additions applied directly to the Van Eycks' paint surface. These additions were not removed because, at the time, they could not be confidently identified. Further research was needed and the first results thereof are described in this volume. It is not known whether the author(s) of these additions also worked on the exterior of the shutters: diverse types of restoration were found there under the mid-sixteenth-century overpainting and were removed when this could be done safely.[27]

Reintegration of losses and abrasions; varnishing

As with the restoration of the exterior, an illusionistic inpainting approach was adopted in order to avoid attracting attention to the damages and restore the legibility and visual unity of the paintings.[28] To prepare this, a thin layer of varnish was applied with a soft cloth. Some of the old fillings were preserved and the new ones filling the losses were applied meticulously to ensure the illusion of a continuous texture.

Small losses interrupting the perception of the subtle colour gradations and disturbing the visibility of specific details were meticulously inpainted to begin with. This increased the legibility of the spatial relationship between the various figures and restored the admirable sense of depth and the continuity of the scene from one panel to the next.[29]

The reintegration of some of the buildings and landscape elements required a strategic preparation. Abrasions and small losses were digitally retouched on high-resolution photographs in order to simulate the reconstructed appearance of the buildings (fig. 1.25a–c). These simulations were then discussed with specialists of medieval architecture in the Low Countries and with the experts of the International Commission before being used as guides for the reconstructions.[30]

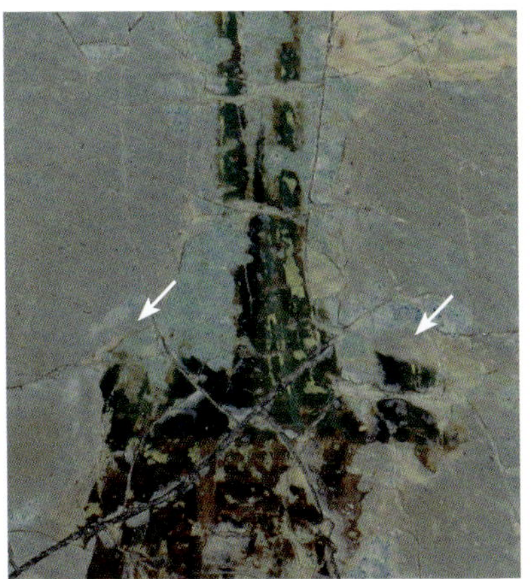

1.25a

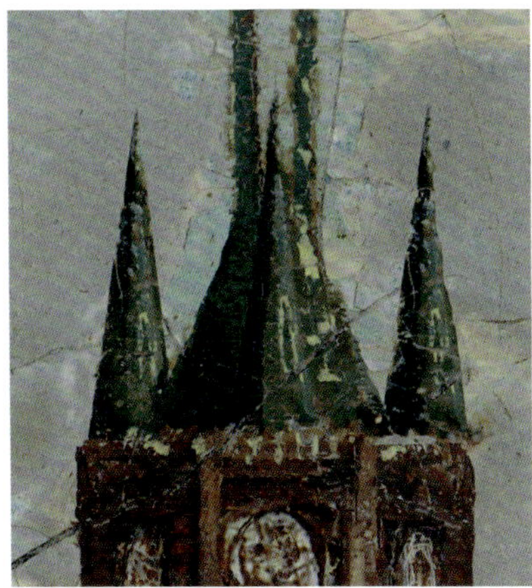

1.25b

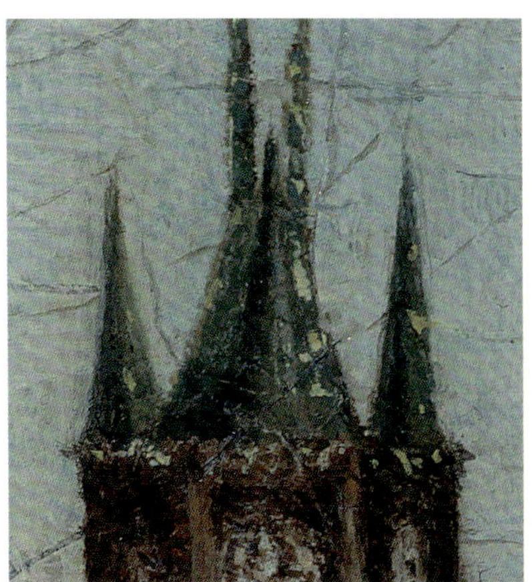

1.25c

Fig. 1.25a–c. *Adoration of the Lamb*, detail (ca. 1 cm wide). Reconstruction process of the roofs of a tower: condition after cleaning, before retouching, with only a few traces of the two lateral spires visible (a); digital reconstruction on the basis of the remaining spire (b); reconstruction on the painting (c).

In more heavily damaged zones, such as the landscape to the right of the tower of Utrecht cathedral, some of the transitions between remaining elements of snow-peaked mountains, hills, valleys and a river (fig. 1.21b–c) were reconstructed on the basis of preserved fragments and by referring to similar landscapes attributed to Van Eyck and his studio, such as the *Crucifixion* in the Metropolitan Museum of Art, New York (fig. 1.26).

A thin layer of varnish was brushed onto the paintings before the last retouching stage and a spray varnish was finally applied to saturate the colours and protect the

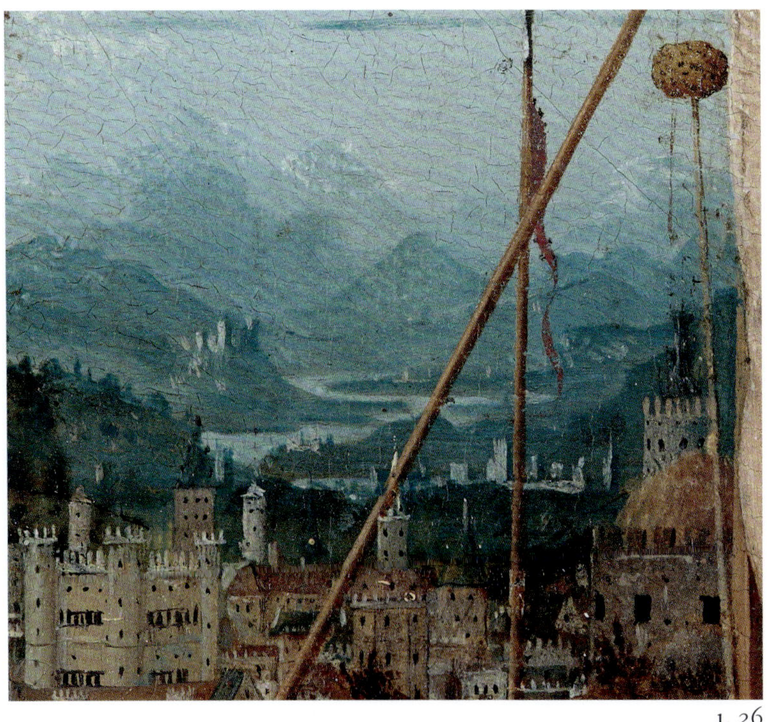

1. 26

Fig. 1.26. Attributed to Jan van Eyck (and workshop assistant), *The Crucifixion* (detail), New York, The Metropolitan Museum of Art, acc. 33.92ab.

surface after retouching. This coating, giving a soft, even sheen to all the paintings without masking their delicate textures, concluded the treatment.

As with the first phase of the restoration, the removal of the sixteenth-century overpaint from the lower register of the interior allowed the astounding recovery of the Van Eyck brothers' original paint surface and contributed to securing its conservation for future generations. The treatment of the upper interior panels – the third phase of the restoration – will no doubt lead to further revelations on this unique masterpiece.

Notes

1 Pending future research on the supports, treated by Jean-Albert Glatigny, and the frames, treated by Marta Darowska and Isabel Bedos, see 'Closer to Van Eyck' (http://closertovaneyck.kikirpa.be); Froyen, Dubois 2020, pp. 28–37 and 216–39. Materials and methods used for this second phase of the restoration are identical to those of the first phase: Augustyniak et al. 2017 and Depuydt-Elbaum et al. 2020. The twentieth-century copy of the stolen *Just Judges* was not restored. It was conserved in 2010 (Van Grevenstein et al. 2011, pp. 189–99), and its frame, which was not stolen, was restored during the present campaign.

2 On the discovery of old overpaint on the exterior, see Postec et al. 2016; Depuydt-Elbaum et al. 2020, pp. 124–35; Martens 2015; Van Grevenstein 2015.

3 Coremans, Loose, Thissen 1953, pp. 98–99 and 101–17. Old overpaints were also reported on the *Deisis* and on the Angels in the upper register.

4 On Coxcie's copying approach, see Dubois 2017.

5 Brinkman et al. 1988/89, pp. 35–37; Van Asperen de Boer (1979, pp. 155–63 and 172–78) was not convinced that the evidence presented by Coremans proved that large sections of the interior upper register were overpainted.

6 Depuydt-Elbaum et al. 2020, pp. 147–151. On the analytical detection of overpaint on the exterior, see Van der Snickt et al. 2017; Sanyova et al. 2020. Coremans and his team had not noticed that the exterior of the shutters was also overpainted.

7 See note 3, above. Dubois (2018a, pp. 756–60, and 2020a, pp. 23–29) argued that the campaign may have been motivated by the context of early Counter-Reformation initiatives in the orbit of the Habsburg court.

8 Dubois 2018b.

9 De Schryver, Marijnissen 1953, n. 54, pp. 50–52 and n. 65, pp. 55–56.

10 Stehr, Dubois 2014.

11 This approach was supported by the International Commission advising on the treatment at the time.

12 These rays were removed during the present restoration.

13 See also fig. 1.3.

14 Coremans (1953, pp. 114–15) thought that the lamb was overpainted after being damaged in the fire that occurred in 1822.

15 Panofsky 1953, pp. 218–19; Coremans 1953, p. 108; Van Asperen de Boer 1979, pp. 195–96 and 200–201.

16 Coremans 1953, pp. 109 and 112. Van Scorel was canon of St Mary's in Utrecht: Faries 1997, p. 107.

17 Philippot, Sneyers 1953, p. 83; Coremans, Loose, Thissen 1953, pp. 107, 115 and pls. XXX, XXXI and XL.

18 Cross-section showing the overpaint on top of thick varnish; see fig. 3.15b, cross-section 11/12 and fig. 2.11d, cross-section 10/73.

19 In spite of a large loss in the tower, its colour and proportions and the shape of its buttresses provided clues towards its identification.

20 UGent professors Marc Boone, Anne-Laure van Bruaene, Jan Dumolyn and Maximiliaan Martens, urban archaeologist Marie-Christine Laleman and architectural historian Luc Devliegher advised on the identification of the buildings.

21 Philippot may have removed old overpaint from the dove when he thinned down nineteenth-century restorations (Coremans 1953, p. 108).

22 Van der Snickt et al. 2020.

23 Danny Praet (UGent) and Barbara Baert (KULeuven).

24 Froyen, Dubois 2020, pp. 74–77.

25 Van der Snickt et al. 2020. See also several examples of this documentation in this volume.

26 These results are best observed on the website 'Closer to Van Eyck': http://closertovaneyck.kikirpa.be.

27 Depuydt-Elbaum et al. 2020, pp. 138–39. Older overpaint and zones of questionable authorship on the exterior are mapped in Augustyniak et al. 2017, pp. 225–26.

28 All materials used for filling and retouching are stable and reversible without causing any damage to the original; Depuydt-Elbaum et al. 2020, pp. 152–56.

29 See note 26.

30 See note 20.

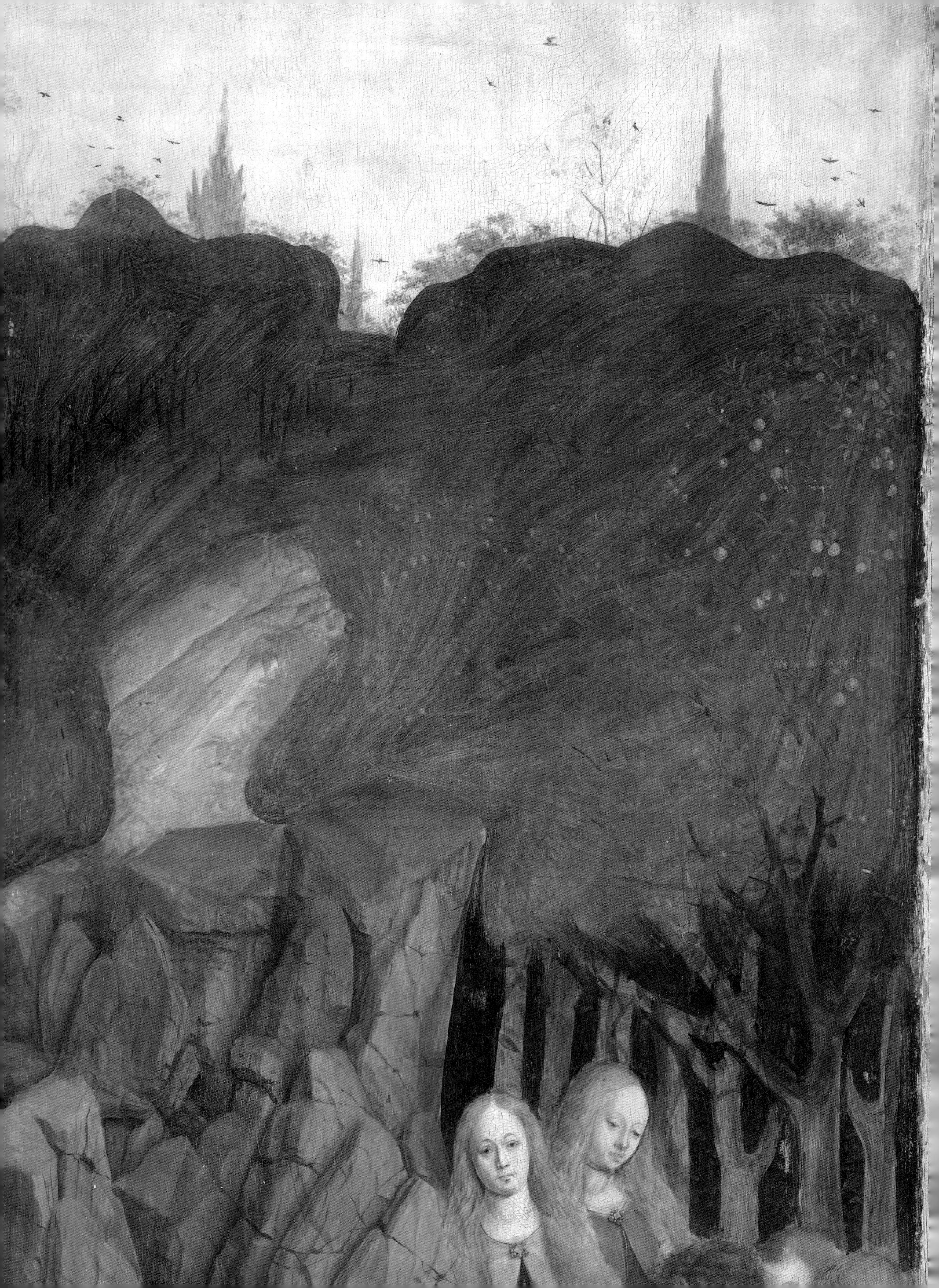

2

The Van Eycks' Creative Process and the Different Stages in the Execution of the Interior Lower Register of the *Ghent Altarpiece*

Marie Postec, Griet Steyaert

With contributions by our colleagues,
the researchers and specialists mentioned on the title page

Introduction

Interdisciplinary research is essential to understanding the genesis of the *Ghent Altarpiece*. According to the quatrain, Hubert began the work, his brother Jan completed it, and it was presented in 1432.[1] We know, meanwhile, that Hubert died in 1426.[2] The altarpiece originally comprised twelve panels, which – if we take account of those painted on both sides and the lost *Just Judges* – in its present condition add up to nineteen paintings.[3] In this contribution, we are studying only the four original paintings from the lower register of the altarpiece interior. Various authors have suggested that Hubert planned a smaller altarpiece and that Jan later expanded the project by creating a twelve-panel polyptych.[4] Thanks to recent dendrochronological research, however, we now know that this large altarpiece was conceived as a unified ensemble from the outset.[5] Jan and Hubert are likely to have come from the same tradition and to have received similar training. From an exclusively technical and scientific point of view, therefore, there will have been little difference in their respective work. Conversely, technical and scientific analysis allied with a thorough understanding of the stratigraphy of the paint layers is essential to understanding and correctly identifying such stylistic differences as do exist. As we will see, the stratigraphy of the paint layers – even after removal of the sixteenth-century overpaints – does indeed display an unusual number of layers, as well as multiple changes and reworkings, which allow different stages to be distinguished in the altarpiece's development.

The technical study of wich the results are presented here[6] has been much more complex than that of the panels of the altarpiece exterior,[7] as the compositions are considerably more detailed. Paul Coremans and J.R.J. van Asperen de Boer[8] – the authors of the two principal technical and material studies devoted to these paintings – faced a similar challenge. We therefore decided that it would make sense

(facing page) *Hermits*: plain black areas showing vigorous brushwork and trunks that were partly concealed by foliage can be seen in the IRR (see also figs. 2.50 and 2.47).

for our study to follow the approach suggested by these authors, with analysis of the paint layers by zones or by areas of representation (e.g. vegetation, architecture, figures). To avoid swamping the reader with details, we will begin by outlining the new hypotheses that are presented here. It should be noted that these are based not only on the technical and scientific studies and laboratory analyses, but also on the stylistic study discussed in chapter 4. The hypotheses we present may be introduced with reference to the central panel.

First stage

During the first stage of execution, a preliminary version of the composition was created, which contains a number of differences compared to what we see today. This first composition was already largely painted. The foreground of the *Adoration of the Lamb* did not include a fountain but probably a simple natural spring in the middle of a meadow, surrounded by the groups of people, as well as the altar with the lamb and the angels higher up. The central part of the horizon comprised a hilly landscape without buildings, while the painted cities on either side were not the same as their current counterparts. Rays of light were incised in the sky, but these were much less numerous and converged on a higher vanishing point, while in the end, these rays were neither gilded nor painted. This initial project appears subsequently to have been abandoned. The vegetation of the central panel was also less varied at first.

As we will see in chapter 4, some of the figures – especially those closest to the spring (now the fountain) – display different stylistic characteristics to those of many other figures in the *Adoration*, which we recognize as Jan's work. We seek to demonstrate, using stylistic arguments, that the central part of this initial stage (spring, first meadow and figures close to the spring) may be attributed to Hubert. If the foreground figures had already been painted at the time of this first stage, it is fair to assume that the rest of the composition was already well under way. However, in spite of the fact that fifteenth-century Flemish artists tended to follow the logic of painting the most distant elements of the composition first before tackling the foreground,[9] we cannot rule out the possibility that some areas were well advanced, while others remained at a preliminary stage.

Second stage

In the course of a second stage, a fountain was painted over what we believe to have been a spring and a second meadow was painted over the first. We argue in our stylistic analysis that the fountain and this second meadow can be attributed to Jan. As he executed the meadow, he carefully worked around some of the foreground figures who had already been painted by another artist during the first stage. We may assume that the painter before Jan was his brother Hubert who, as the quatrain states, began the work. Jan then painted the figures furthest from the fountain and retouched a number of the heads that his brother had commenced. We think that he also painted the lamb, even though this, too, might have been started by his brother. He likewise developed the flora by painting a wide variety of plants and applied at least one new layer of azurite to the sky. Jan reworked the urban landscapes on the horizon, adding a few buildings, including the tower of Utrecht cathedral, the former Abbey of St Bavo's and a tower reminiscent of Our Lady's Church in Bruges. To achieve this, he concealed the initial composition, while also retaining certain first-stage elements, which were incorporated into the final version. This makes it more complicated to distinguish clearly between the elements belonging to each of the first two stages of development. It might also have been Jan, lastly, who painted a first dove surrounded by a coloured halo, thus abandoning his brother's project with the rays.

Third stage

It appears that Jan was not the only person – or the last – to have reworked the lower register of the altarpiece interior. Numerous retouches, invariably on the surface and scattered more or less across the paintings studied here, were applied to zones we believe to have been painted and completed by Jan, but instead of enhancing them, they made them heavier.

The final paint layer in the sky of the central panel also raises questions: whereas the skies in the shutters were painted with a mixture of lead white and azurite, the top layer in the central panel comprises lead white and ultramarine. This ultramarine-based layer and most of the blue hills currently visible in the distance in the central panel were created during the same intervention, and clearly after completion of the second-stage buildings, which the ultramarine-based layer overlaps slightly. The presence of this latter stratum in the central panel modifies the overall tonality of the sky relative to that of the shutters. All this inclines us to question the originality of the ultramarine sky, although it undoubtedly belongs to the zone with the halo that is now visible around the dove. The halo was painted in two layers, however, so it is not impossible that Jan painted a first halo, with or without the dove. The dove we see today can hardly be attributed to him, but it, too, was painted in at least two layers.

While we cannot exclude the possibility that this was the work of one or more assistants, the interventions in question seem to post-date the Van Eycks. Even though we think that these interventions did not form part of the altarpiece's creative process, they are bound to come up frequently. Considering – and also localizing – them is important if we are to appreciate the Van Eycks' technique and attempt to distinguish between the contributions of the two brothers.

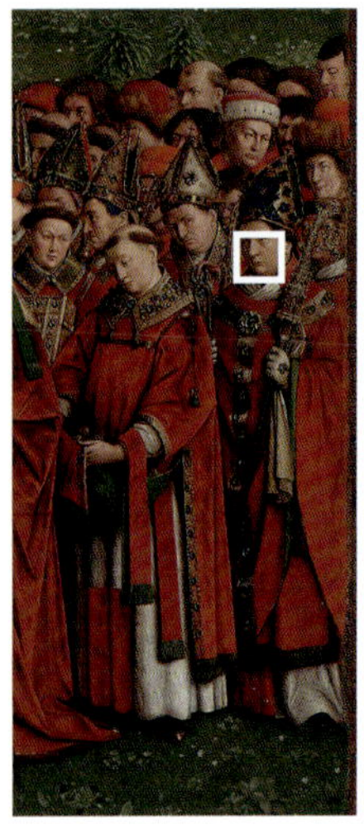
2.1a

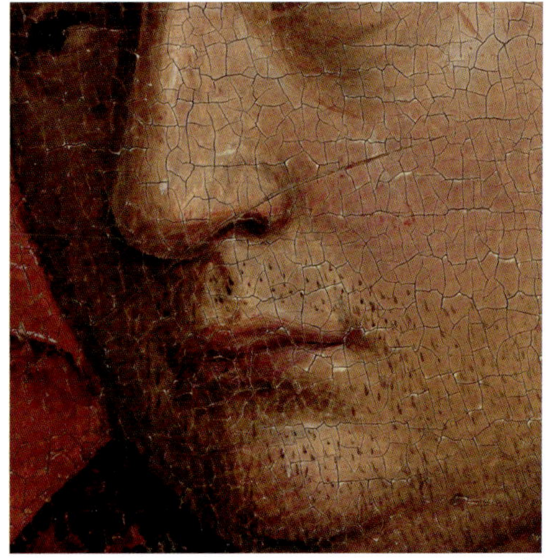
2.1b

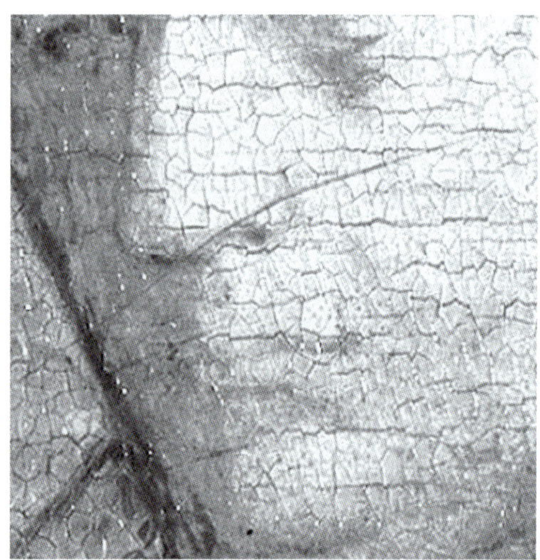
2.1c

Fig. 2.1a–c. *Adoration of the Lamb*, detail (a): bristle from a brush trapped in the ground layer – VIS (b); IRR (c).

We focus in this chapter on reporting the technical and stratigraphic characteristics in the development of these paintings. Where we deem it necessary, however, we will also refer to elements based on stylistic analysis.[10] If, as we suggest, Hubert was already well advanced in the painting stage, all of the preparatory layers must date from his time. We thus need to be extremely cautious when making comparisons with works securely ascribed to Jan, at least as far as the first strata are concerned.

Technical and stratigraphic characteristics of the paintings

The panels in the lower register of the altarpiece interior are made of Baltic oak – four planks laid horizontally for the central panel and three vertical planks for each wing.[11]

Preparatory layers

Ground

Both the composition and application of the ground do not seem to differ from those found on the altarpiece exterior. The ground layer – a mixture of chalk and animal glue – was applied in several layers[12] to the already framed panels and hence also to the mouldings of the frames. The presence of unpainted borders and barbs on each panel attests to this.

As in the case of the paintings of the altarpiece exterior, brushes and a spatula were used to apply the ground.[13] Few bristles from the brushes were found in this instance, however (fig. 2.1),[14] unlike the paintings of the closed polyptych, in which they were particularly numerous and mostly trapped in the ground layer.[15] Such bristles as were found were essentially located in the pictorial layer. Bristles trapped in the ground layer might be less obvious in the paintings studied here,

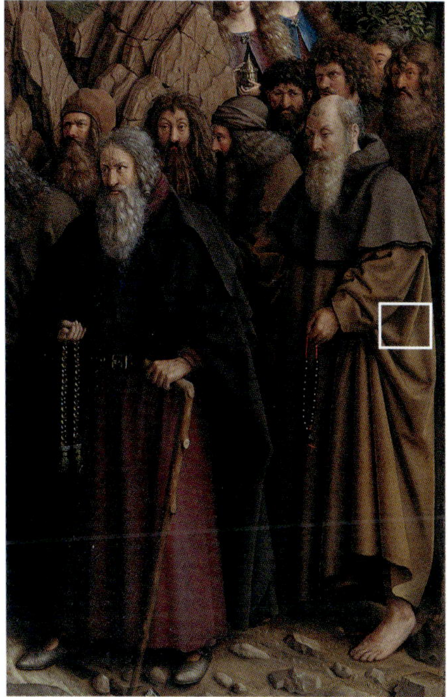

2.2a

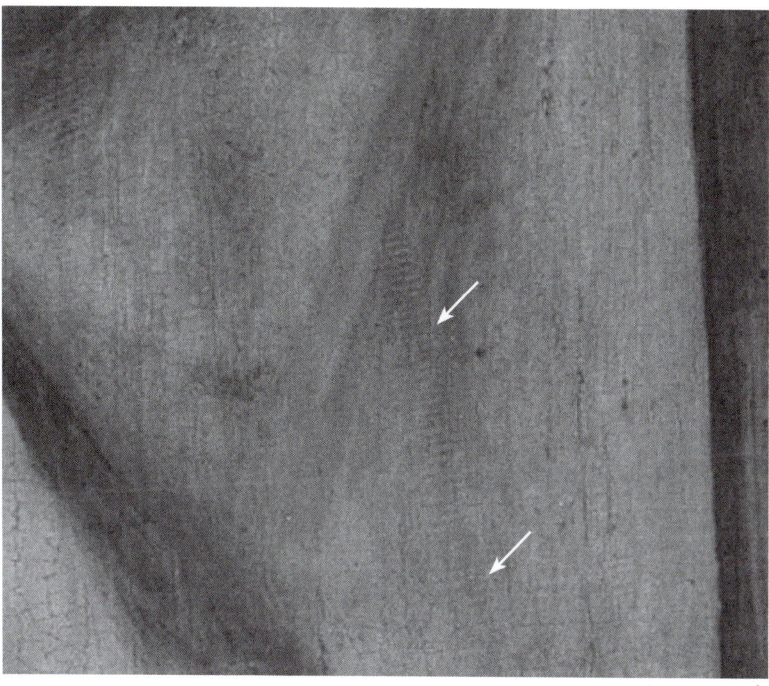

2.2b

Fig. 2.2a–b. *Hermits*, detail (a); striations indicating the use of a spatula in applying the ground, IRR detail (b).

given the larger number of paint layers.[16] A few striations demonstrating the use of a spatula have been identified, in the *Hermits*, for instance, along the right edge in the drapery of the tall, bald figure (fig. 2.2).

A strip of canvas was glued to a section of a joint in the central panel.[17] It was noted while restoring a loss (fig. 2.3) and can be seen in the infrared reflectogram and X-radiograph.[18] The strip, measuring approximately 28 by 4 cm, was glued in place before the ground was applied. Rather than being centred over the joint, it runs roughly 1 cm above it but approximately 3 cm below it. Although reinforcement of this kind has been found in a few pre-Eyckian works,[19] it becomes rarer in the course of the fifteenth century. In the *Virgin of Canon Van der Paele*, however, plant fibres were glued to the obverse side over the joints of both the panel and the frame.[20] The question in the *Adoration* is whether the canvas strip was intended to reinforce a weak point in the panel or to conceal some alteration in the wood.[21] Or might it have been a means of evening out a local difference in level between two planks?[22]

Underdrawing

The infrared photograph and reflectogram allow us to make out lines indicating the contours of the forms and the hatching of the modelling belonging to the underdrawing, but as we will see, in many places it is not the drawing that is legible in these documents but the first, already painted stage, which is now concealed.

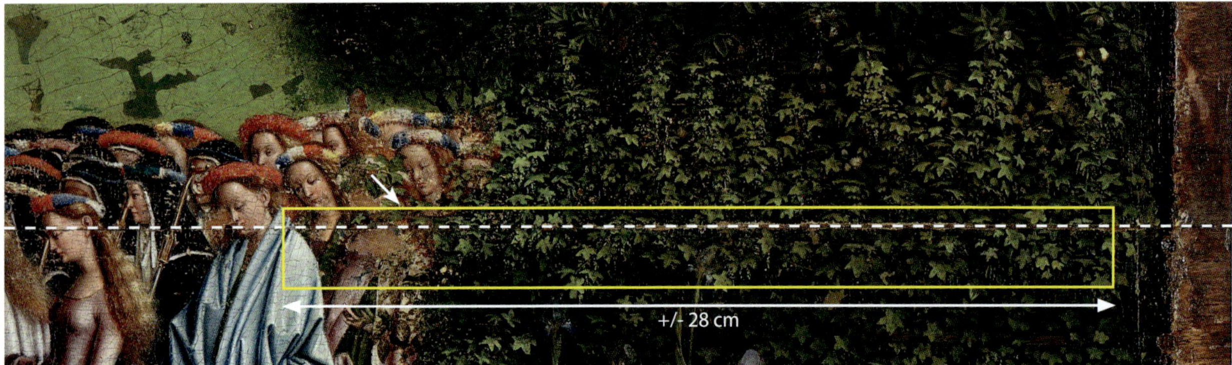

2.3a

Fig. 2.3a–b. *Adoration of the Lamb*, detail, diagram: strip of canvas (indicated by yellow frame) glued to a section of a joint (dotted line), under the ground layer (a) (see also same detail in IRR and XR on 'Closer to Van Eyck' website); canvas visible during restoration in a lacuna (b).

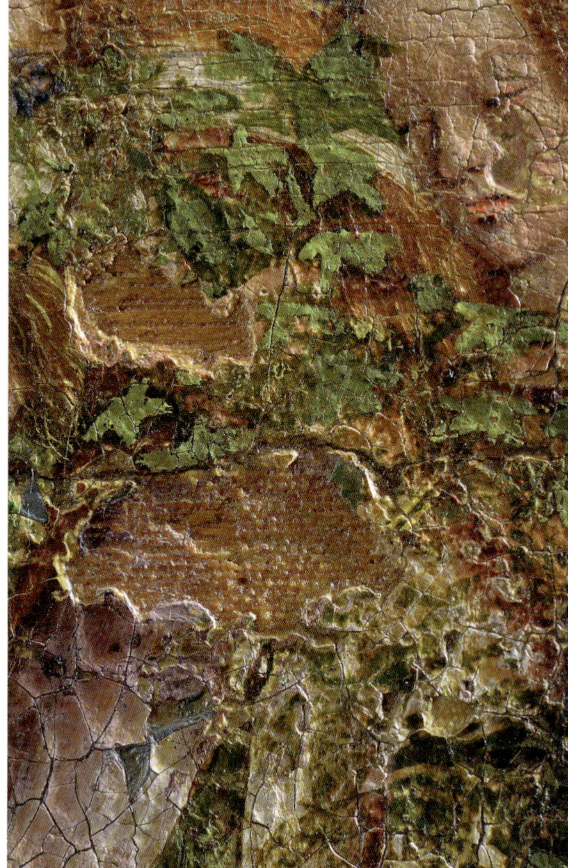

2.3b

More specifically, the drawing is visible in certain areas of the central panel with the *Adoration of the Lamb* and of the shutters, in some of the figures, animals and passages of rocks.[23] The painter carefully laid down the contour lines of the elements of the composition and already provided an indication of volume. The shadows of the folds in the drapery of the apostles, prophets, philosophers and angels around the altar are rendered with nervous strokes (fig. 2.4), short lines drawn with a certain verve, often curved, and intersecting the long lines demarcating the folds.[24]

In the infrared reflectogram, the areas of vegetation, by contrast, reveal fewer drawn lines than the draperies. As we will see, however, these zones are largely covered with a first, black paint layer, which serves as a background for the trees and bushes, and probably reduces the visibility of any drawing.

The infrared documents show lines and details in the buildings, such as windows, which do not correspond with the final painting. In most cases, however, these are not part of the preparatory drawing, but rather of the first or second painting stage, as is the case for the numerous windows painted in black on an underlying paint layer (fig. 2.40). The underdrawing can be seen more easily in the architecture with little or no second-stage modification (CVE-12).

Some changes appear between the preparatory drawing stage and that of the painting, whether in the rocks or in the position of human and animal figures and of certain details. Many of these were already described by Van Asperen de Boer.[25]

Nature of the drawing: dry and liquid medium

The study of the paintings on the exterior of the altarpiece identified different stages in the development of the drawing as well as different media – in this case a dry medium for the first laying out of the main elements of the composition, followed by a liquid medium for the more elaborate modelling of the forms, using lines and hatching of varying thickness, but also washes.

We also think that a first drawing stage using a dry medium can be seen in the lower register of the altarpiece interior which, as in the panels of the exterior, is rarely discernible and then only in locations where it was not followed by the liquid drawing. In the central panel, this is the case with a few of the foreground figures. The folds in the drapery of the prophet in the blue cloak differ from those actually painted and, above all, a rectangular shape – possibly a book that was not painted in the final composition – traverses the figure (fig. 2.5). A fairly similar form is found in one of the prophets kneeling in the foreground and seen from behind (CVE–5). These few lines visible in the infrared reflectogram seemingly display the characteristics of a dry medium, namely a discontinuous or even grainy line. They define summary shapes, without hatching for volume. Lines like this made using a dry medium do not show in the infrared reflectograms of the wing panels of the lower register of the exterior, although this does not mean they do not exist.[26]

As in the panels of the altarpiece exterior,[27] most of the underdrawing visible here in the infrared reflectogram seems to have been done in a brush loaded with an ink or a fluid paint. A few droplets at the end of lines in the underdrawing (fig. 2.6)

Fig. 2.4a–b. *Adoration of the Lamb*, detail (a); underdrawing with nervous strokes, short lines drawn with a certain verve, often curved, crossing the long lines demarcating the folds (IRR detail) (b).

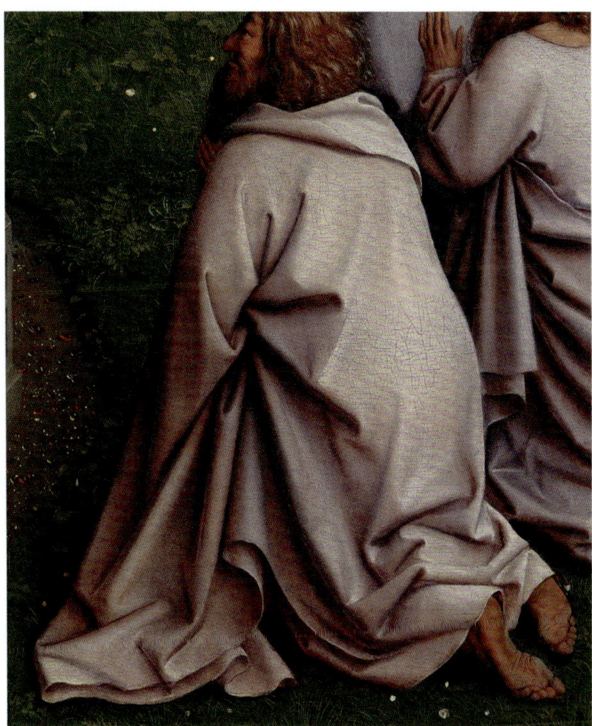

2.4a

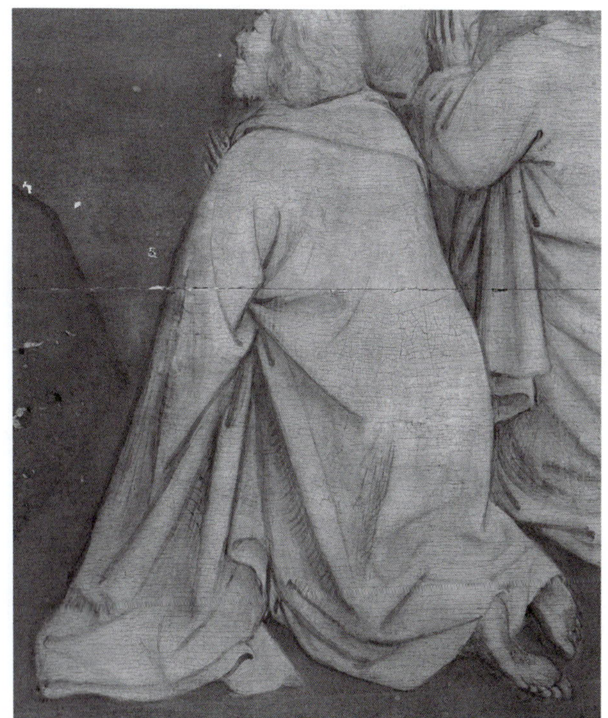

2.4b

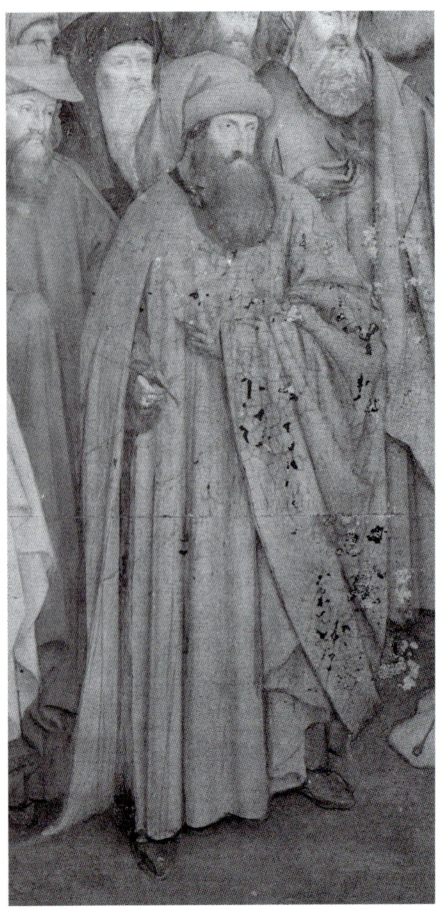
2.5a

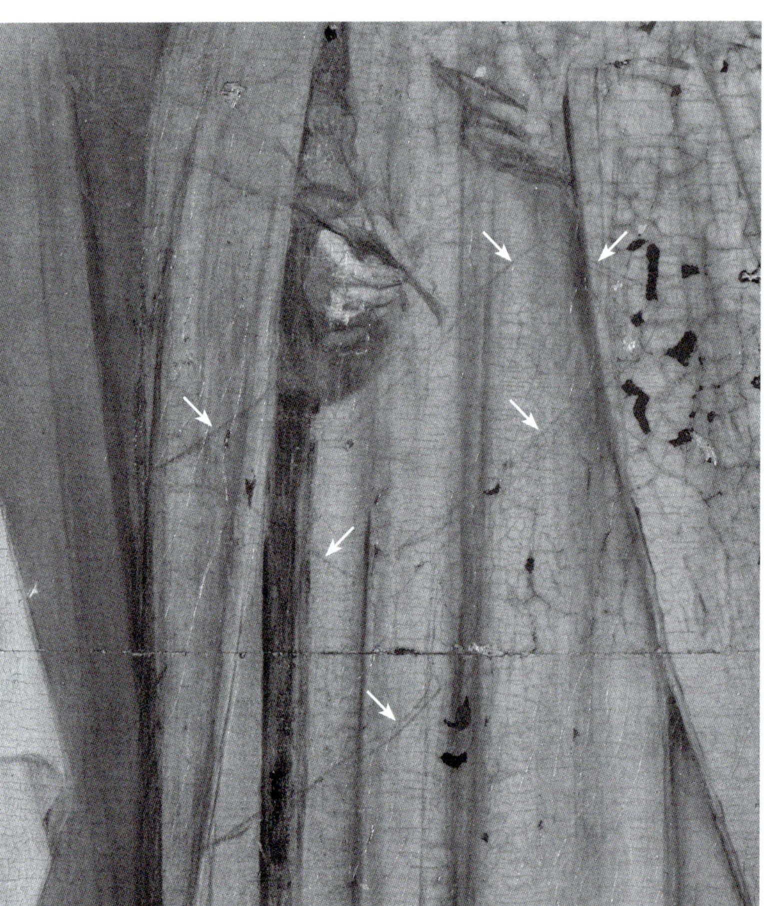
2.5b

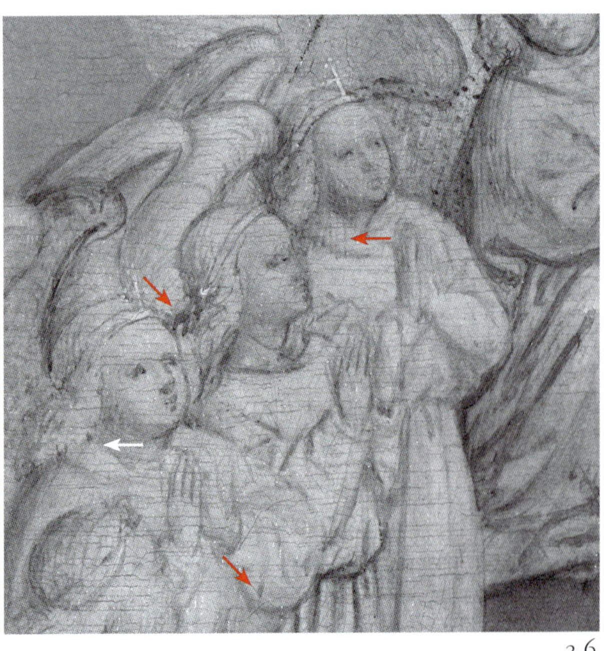
2.6

Fig. 2.5a–b. *Adoration of the Lamb* (IRR details): drawing in dry medium; elements corrected or omitted during the painting process.

Fig. 2.6 *Adoration of the Lamb* (IRR detail): traces of droplets at the end of lines point to the use of a liquid medium (red arrows) in the underdrawing; broad brushstrokes seem to indicate the use of washes (white arrow).

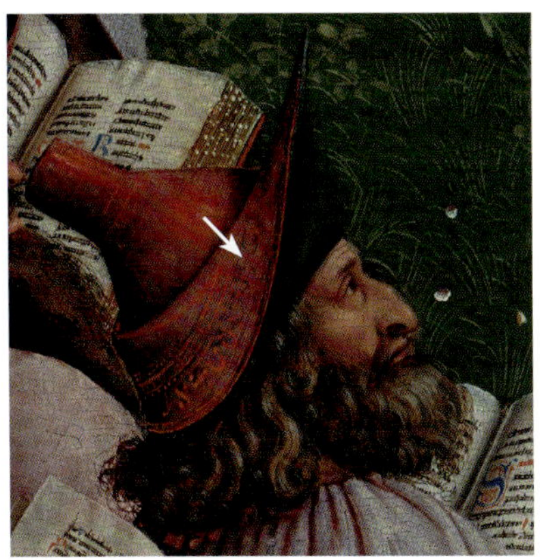
2.7a

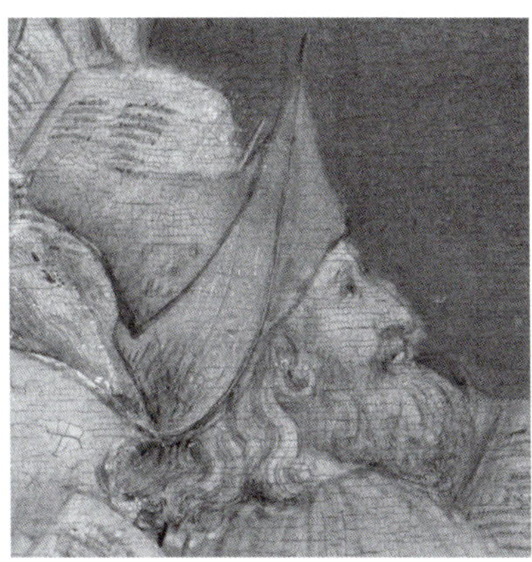
2.7b

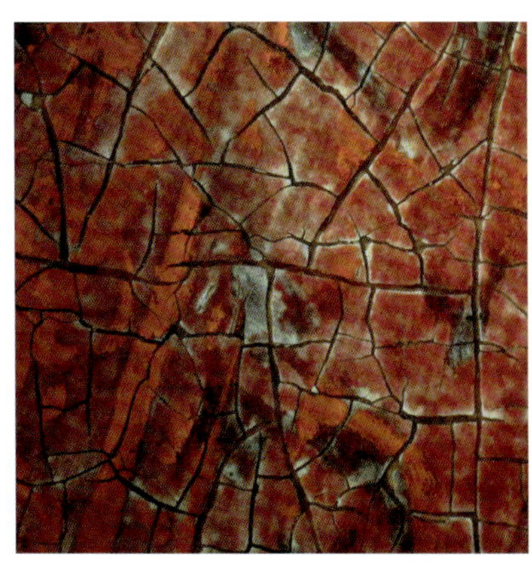
2.7c

Fig. 2.7a–c. *Adoration of the Lamb*, detail (a); drawing and/ or wash, visible in IRR (b); and in small losses in the paint layer (microphotograph) (c).

clearly show that we are dealing with a liquid medium. Some features of this drawing could be observed under a microscope in losses or uncovered areas (figs. 2.7 and 2.8). Other, more widely covered areas visible in the infrared reflectogram appear to have been done using a liquid medium in broadly applied brushstrokes. They probably resemble the washes (fig. 2.9) observed in the paintings of the altarpiece exterior, to which we will return in due course.

Drawing gone over with scored lines

The only underdrawn lines that are clearly visible in the sky of the central panel are those positioning the rays, which were drawn using a liquid medium but also by means of scored lines.[28] The latter are visible in the X-radiographs as fine, sharp white lines (CVE-7 and fig. 2.74a), because the radio-opaque pictorial

Fig. 2.8a–c. *Adoration of the Lamb* (IRR detail) (a); liquid drawing visible in a lacuna (microphotograph) (b); VIS (c).

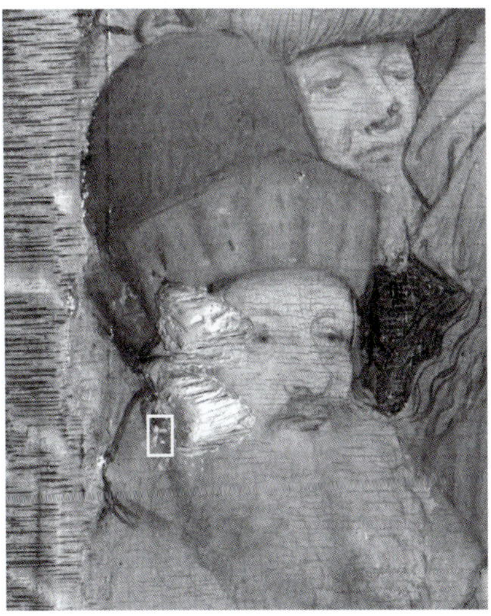
2.8a

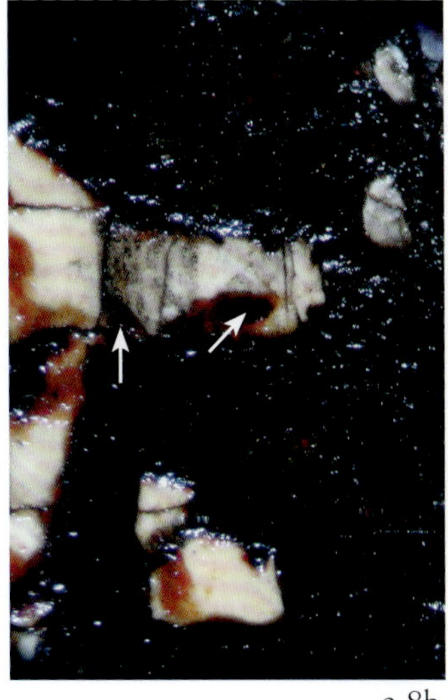
2.8b

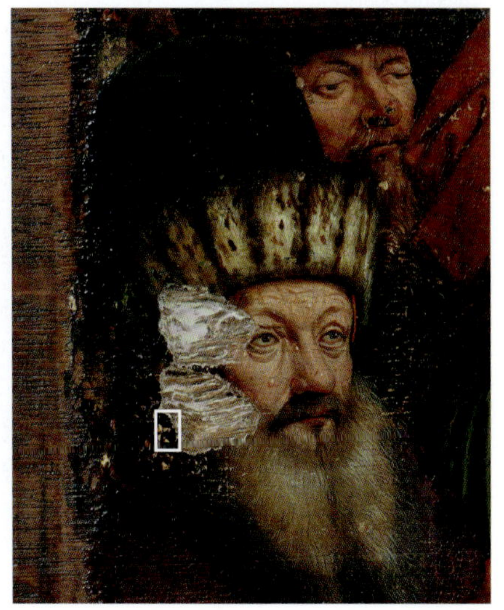
2.8c

material (containing lead white) filled the hollows left by these incisions. There are approximately 28 of these rays,[29] which do not correspond with the 129 gilded rays we see now. The latter also converge towards a point located near the barb of the paint layer, approximately 1 cm below the convergence point of the drawn and scored rays, which is located outside the limits of the panel. A small nail hole was located near the barb (fig. 2.10), as if a cord had been attached there to serve as a guide for drawing the future gilded rays. There is a certain concordance, therefore, between the drawn and the scored rays, but a substantial difference compared with the gilded rays. The latter point will be discussed further below.

The lines were probably scored using a stylus and a ruler to ensure they would be straight and remain visible, given that they would not be executed until after completion of all the pictorial layers, which would have obscured the black drawing.[30]

It should be noted that neither the scored nor the drawn rays were discontinued to leave space for the dove, for which no preparatory drawing is visible in the infrared reflectogram; this has prompted some authors to conclude that it was not initially planned.[31]

Other scored lines can be detected in large numbers at the fountain, but they were made at a later stage: they were not incised in the ground[32] but in the green pictorial layer on which the fountain is painted (figs. 2.27 and 2.28). We will return to this later. Van Asperen de Boer already noted in 1979 that no preparatory drawing could be detected below the fountain,[33] and this is confirmed by the new infrared reflectogram.

Fig. 2.9a–b. *Adoration of the Lamb*, detail (a); washes applied in broad brushstrokes (red arrow, IRR detail) (b).

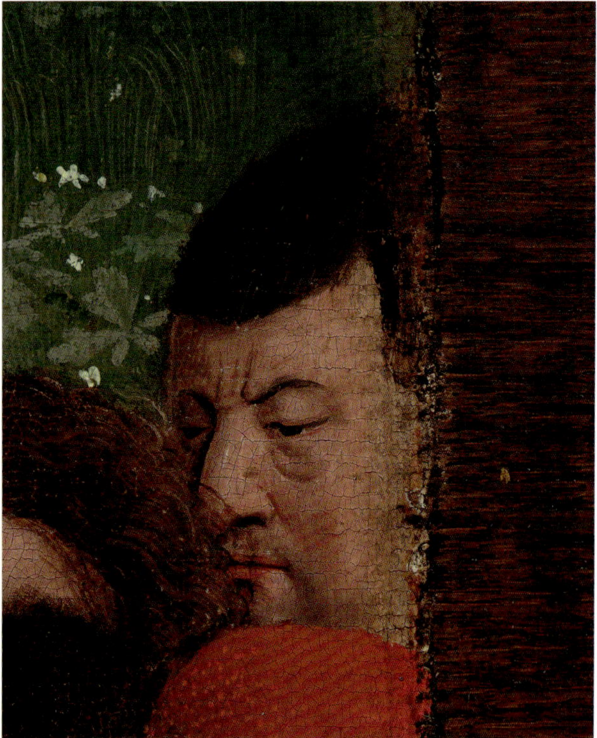

2.9a

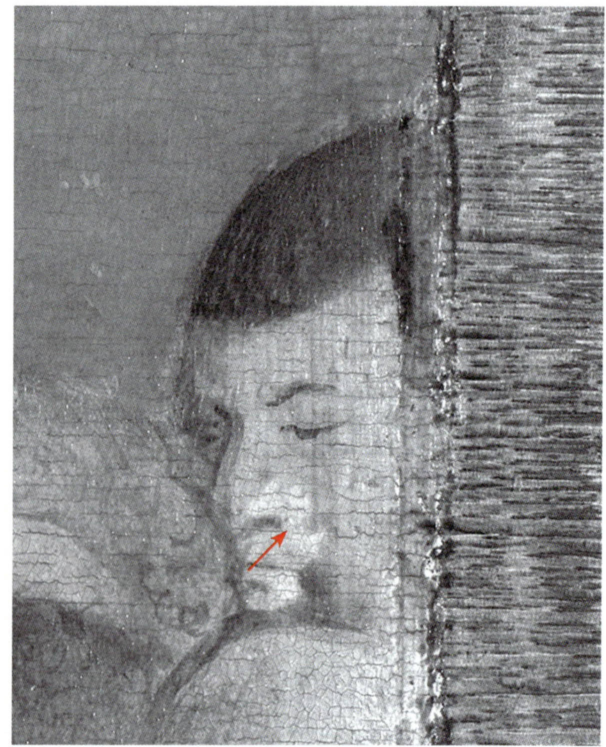

2.9b

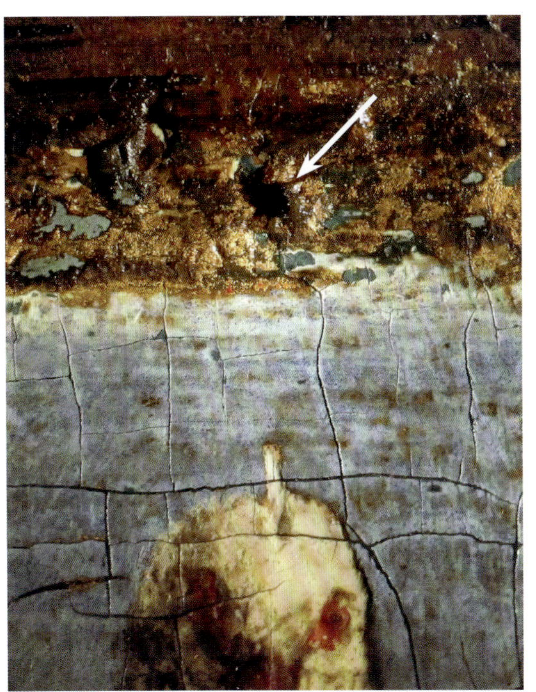
2.10

Fig. 2.10 *Adoration of the Lamb* (microphotograph): nail hole at the convergence point of the gilded rays.

Wash, isolating layer and priming

Regarding the hypotheses advanced in the technical study of the paintings of the altarpiece exterior,[34] we note a similar elaboration with more or less graphic and pictorial phases that were already combined and juxtaposed in the preparatory layers.

A wash[35] belongs to the stage in which the composition was laid out on the ground and before the application of any kind of isolating layer which would be more fatty. It comprises the same elements as the liquid drawing – a mixture of a single colour and a water-soluble binder, in this case a carbon-based black pigment in a binder most likely containing protein.[36] Different tones were obtained by varying the mixture's dilution. Disregarding the zones already painted, we believe this is what we see in Van Eyck's *St Barbara*.[37]

The purpose of the linear drawing and wash was to position the elements of the composition and allow the scenes to be visualized in terms of tonal values. The aim was to evaluate the gradations of the shadow and light areas independently of their hues, in order to lay out the forms and volumes. Washes have proved to be very hard to discern in the infrared documents. Particles of carbon – the black pigment used for the liquid linear drawing and the washes – are nevertheless nearly always present in the cross-sections, even in the zones without visible drawn lines in the infrared reflectogram (fig. 2.11). A few cross-sections from drawn lines visible in the infrared reflectogram (the folds of one of the prophets to the left of the fountain, fig. 2.12, and a ray around the dove) show a much greater concentration of black carbon particles than the cross-sections from either the zones without drawn lines or light areas. These observations suggest that the light areas are hardly, but nonetheless effectively covered by the washes. The infrared images also reveal the use in some cases of wide brushstrokes, which suggest the presence of washes, as we find along the right edge of the central panel (fig. 2.9).

This stratum of drawing and wash is covered by one or two thin translucent or semi-translucent layers, which appear in several cross-sections (figs. 2.11 and 2.12). The layers in question are rich in binder – they fluoresce under ultraviolet light – but the nature of the particles they contain is different: filler in the lower layer and pigments in the upper layer.[38] The first very likely corresponds with an isolating layer (layer 3 in figs. 2.11 and 2.12). Examination of the cross-sections shows that this layer is not entirely proteinaceous, for it does not seem to have been absorbed to any significant degree by the chalk and animal glue-based ground. Its oily nature has also been confirmed by laboratory analysis.[39] A certain plasticity can even be inferred for this layer, thanks to the examination of a sample taken from a ray incised near the dove (fig. 2.13).[40] The stylus used to score the drawing not only marked the ground layer (the scoring was subsequently filled with the pictorial layer of the sky), but it also cut across the translucent layer which, despite

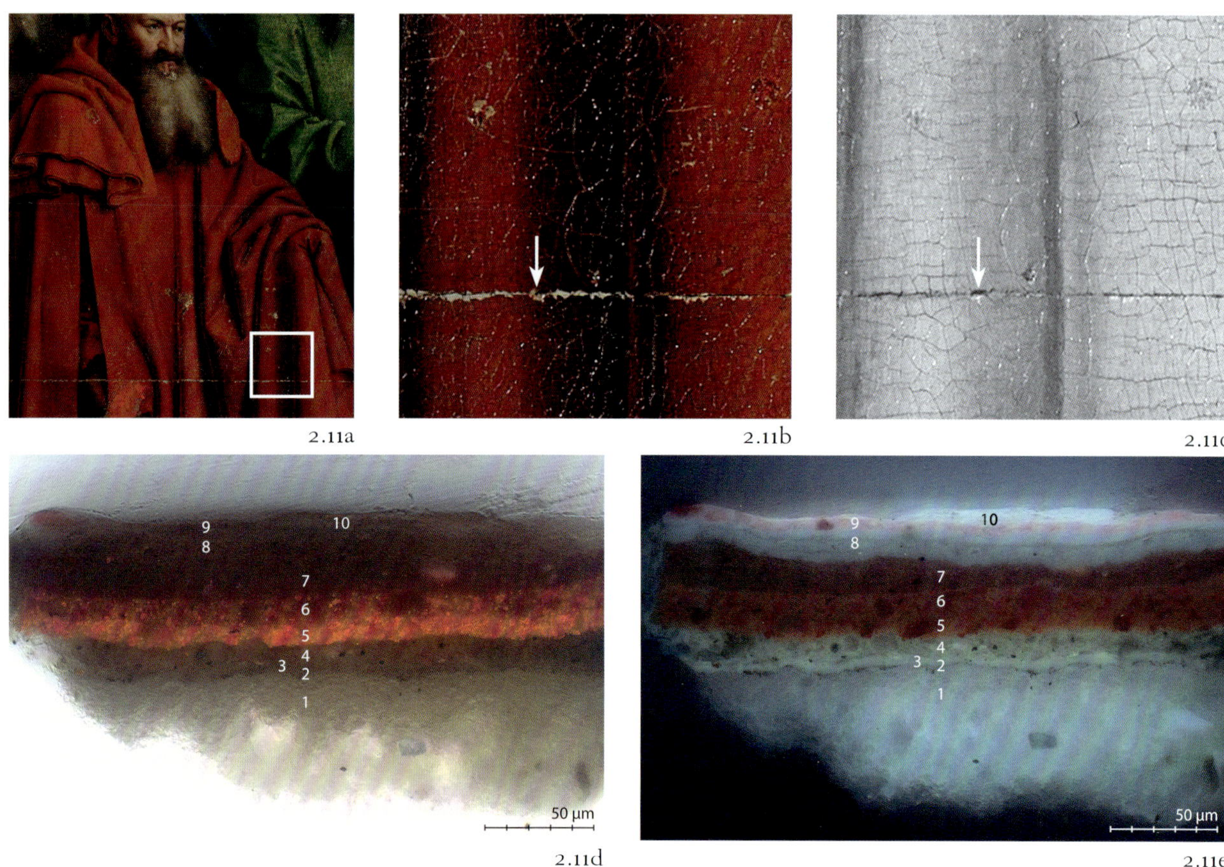

Fig. 2.11a–e. *Adoration of the Lamb*: location of sampling (a–b); IRR made during restoration, detail (c); cross-section 10/73 VIS (d) and UV light (e) taken in an area without discernible underdrawing and showing the following build-up: ground (1); fine layer with black particles (2); translucent layer (3); translucent layer with black particles (4); paint layers (5, 6, 7); overpaints and varnishes now removed (8, 9, 10).

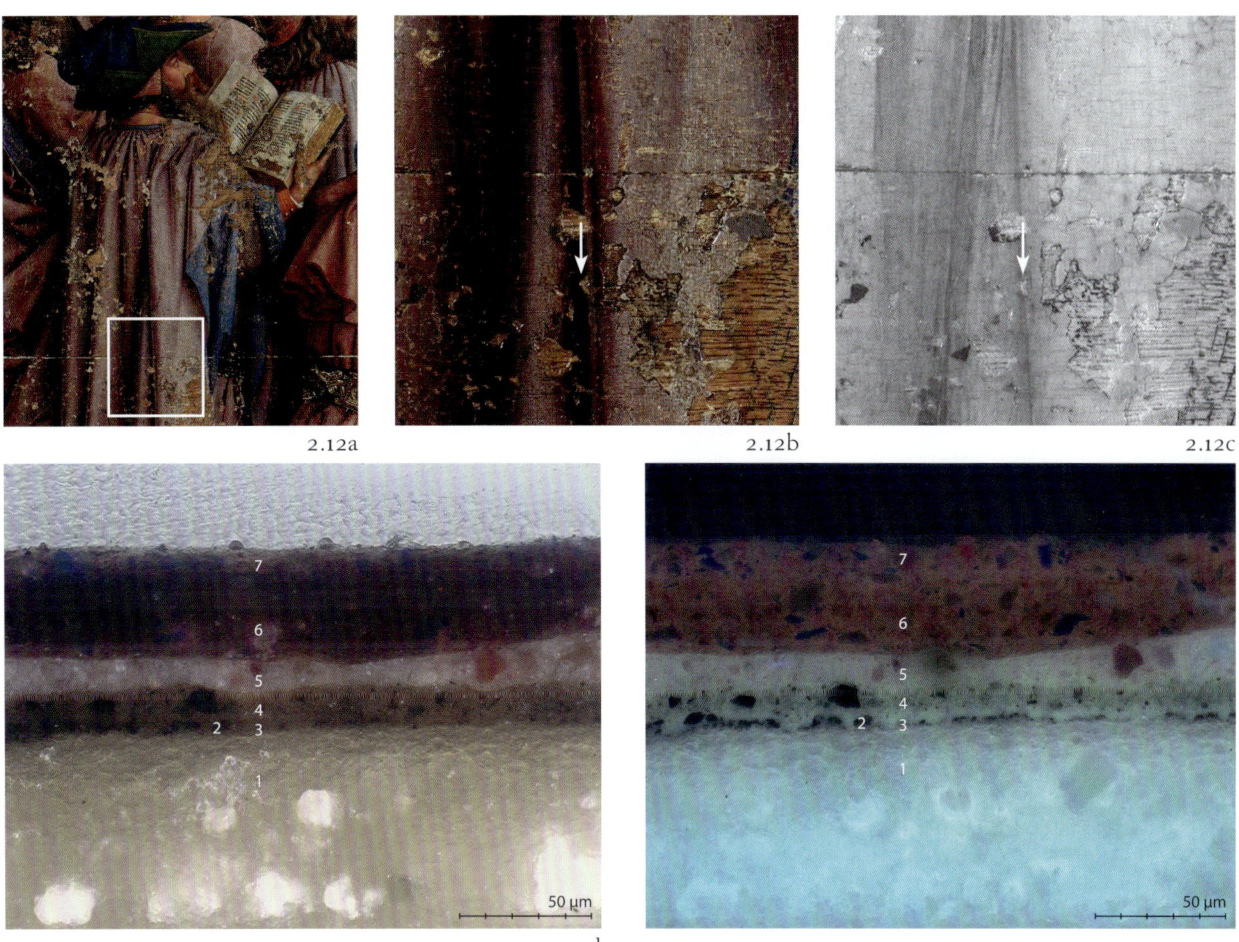

Fig. 2.12a–e. *Adoration of the Lamb*: location of sampling (a–b); IRR made during restoration, detail (c); cross-section 10/75 under VIS (d) and UV light (e), taken where a drawn line is visible in IRR and showing the following build-up: ground (1); fine layer with black particles (2); translucent layer (3); translucent layer with black particles (4); paint layers (5, 6, 7).

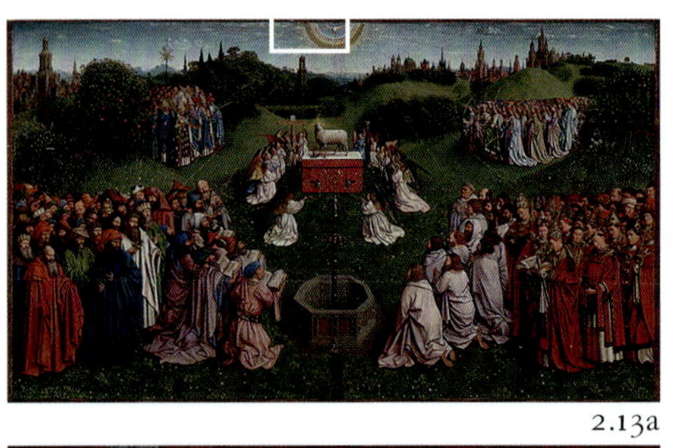

2.13a

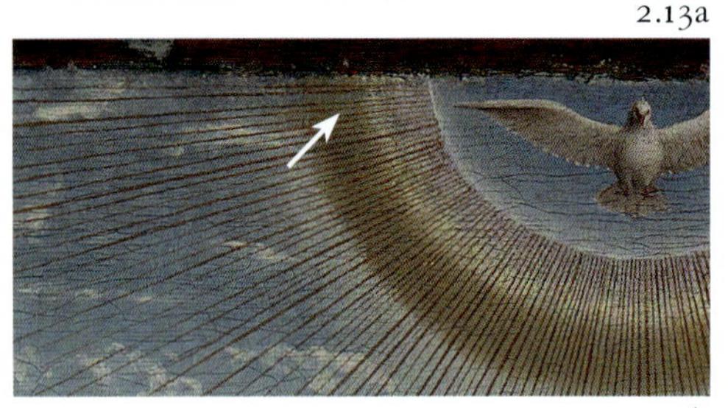

2.13b

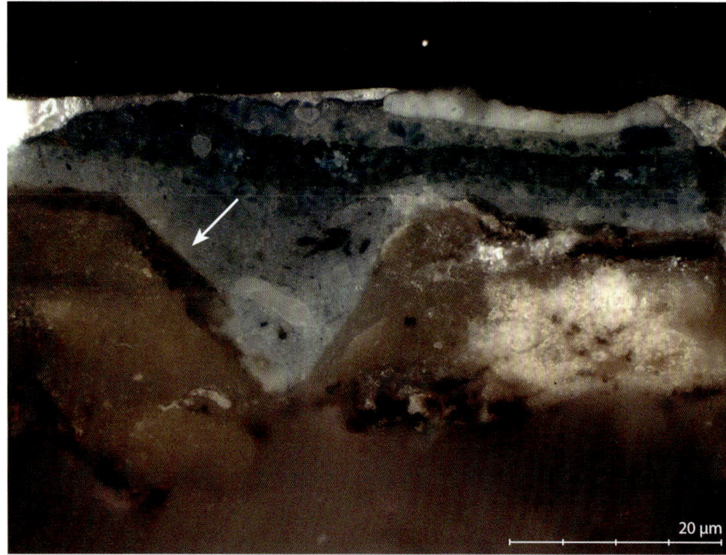

2.13c

Fig. 2.13a–c. *Adoration of the Lamb*: location of sampling (a–b); cross-section 10/69 VIS, incision made in the ground layer to mark the position of the rays surrounding the dove. The stylus used to score the drawing also cut across the translucent isolation layer (white arrow) (c).

having been broken, bent to follow the indentation of the incision. The second layer (layer 4 in figs. 2.11 and 2.12), itself translucent but more pigmented, is essentially composed of lead white, calcium carbonate, carbon black and a few red or ochre particles, giving it a warm tonality. This is most likely the priming, also called *imprimatura*, previously detected below the paintings of the altarpiece exterior and which corresponds with the pigmented intermediate layer that is very often present in medieval pictures painted in oil.[41]

Paint layers

Meadow and fountain

As Van Asperen de Boer already noted, not only has no preparatory drawing been detected beneath the fountain in the infrared reflectogram, the fountain was also painted over a layer of green paint[42] – basin and shaft alike. The recent research and analysis show that there was an initial project involving a different meadow with what we believe to be a spring at the centre. The stone fountain was added later and also appears to have been designed in two stages.

First stage MA-XRF analysis (fig. 2.14a-b) detected copper beneath the current fountain, suggesting a painted meadow.[43] This could also be made out during the restoration process in losses or abrasions in the stone basin (fig. 2.17). Microscopic observation and cross-section analysis identified a stratigraphy comprising several green layers including glazes.[44] Layering of this kind is traditional in Flemish painting,[45] with relatively light and opaque base layers consisting of verdigris and more opaque pigments such as lead white and/or lead-tin yellow, and a glaze consisting essentially of verdigris. The MA-XRF copper map also reveals a central area with almost no copper (black in the MA-XRF copper map) in the shape of an oval, the lower part of which shows a bulge towards the bottom of the panel (fig. 2.14a). This is a reserve, an area that was left blank in the meadow[46] (fig. 2.14b) and then painted black. The black, ovaloid form can be made out in the infrared reflectogram (fig. 2.14c–d). The black layer is also visible through abrasions in the pictorial layer of the stone basin, which was painted over it (fig. 2.18). The edges of the black oval shape overlap the edges of the green layer (visible in raking light) of the surrounding meadow (figs. 2.18 and 2.14e–f).

So what might this shape with its bulge at the bottom have represented? A manuscript illumination with *God Placing Adam in the Garden of Eden* by the Master of Berry's Clères Femmes, dating from around 1405 (fig. 2.15), appears to provide an answer.[47] It features two dark springs, square in shape here, with a similar bulge along their lower edges, from which the stream of water flows. These dark shapes were clearly painted over the surrounding grass. The dark tone evokes the depth of the springs, while the superimposition of the dark tone on the light green of the meadow – at the far end of the springs – suggests their edges and the transparency of the water. Comparison with this miniature suggests that the black oval in the *Adoration* served as the ground tone for the rendering of the water of the spring that was planned at that point. Although black, the paint – applied in large brushstrokes (visible in the IRR) – probably displayed a variety of shades according to the action of the brush that moved around more or less paint and so created variations in translucency. The same technique may be found in the *Meeting of the Magi* in the *Très Riches Heures du duc de Berry* (fig. 2.16),[48] where, once again, a dark layer overlaps onto the light tone of the surrounding rocky plateau to suggest the borders of the pools and water overflowing.

A sample taken from the reflection of the shaft of the fountain in the *Adoration* (fig. 2.19) allows this black layer – itself covered with light-green paint[49] before the brown paint of the shaft was added – to be observed. The light-green layer most likely represents water or some ripples. The spring thus appears to have been painted to an advanced degree. The surrounding meadow, consisting of several layers including a glaze, similarly suggests that the composition at the centre of the *Adoration* panel was well advanced. The documents at our disposal[50] do not allow us to verify whether a flow of water, originating at the spring, was painted. However, the initially painted shape with the bulge at the bottom and its comparison with the springs in the *Bible historiale* suggest that a ribbon of water of this kind was intended.

Within the overall composition of the polyptych, this presumed spring is located at the centre of the meadow zone, surrounded by all the groups of figures and beneath the altar. It is integrated in a perspective that gives full meaning to the initially planned shape with the bulge.[51]

Second stage It was decided at some point to turn this natural spring into an octagonal stone basin.[52] As noted, the fountain was painted over a meadow. In reality, the entire field in the central panel was repainted at this stage in two layers – first with a mixture giving a less translucent appearance than the final glaze of the first meadow, namely verdigris, lead white and lead-tin yellow, then with a

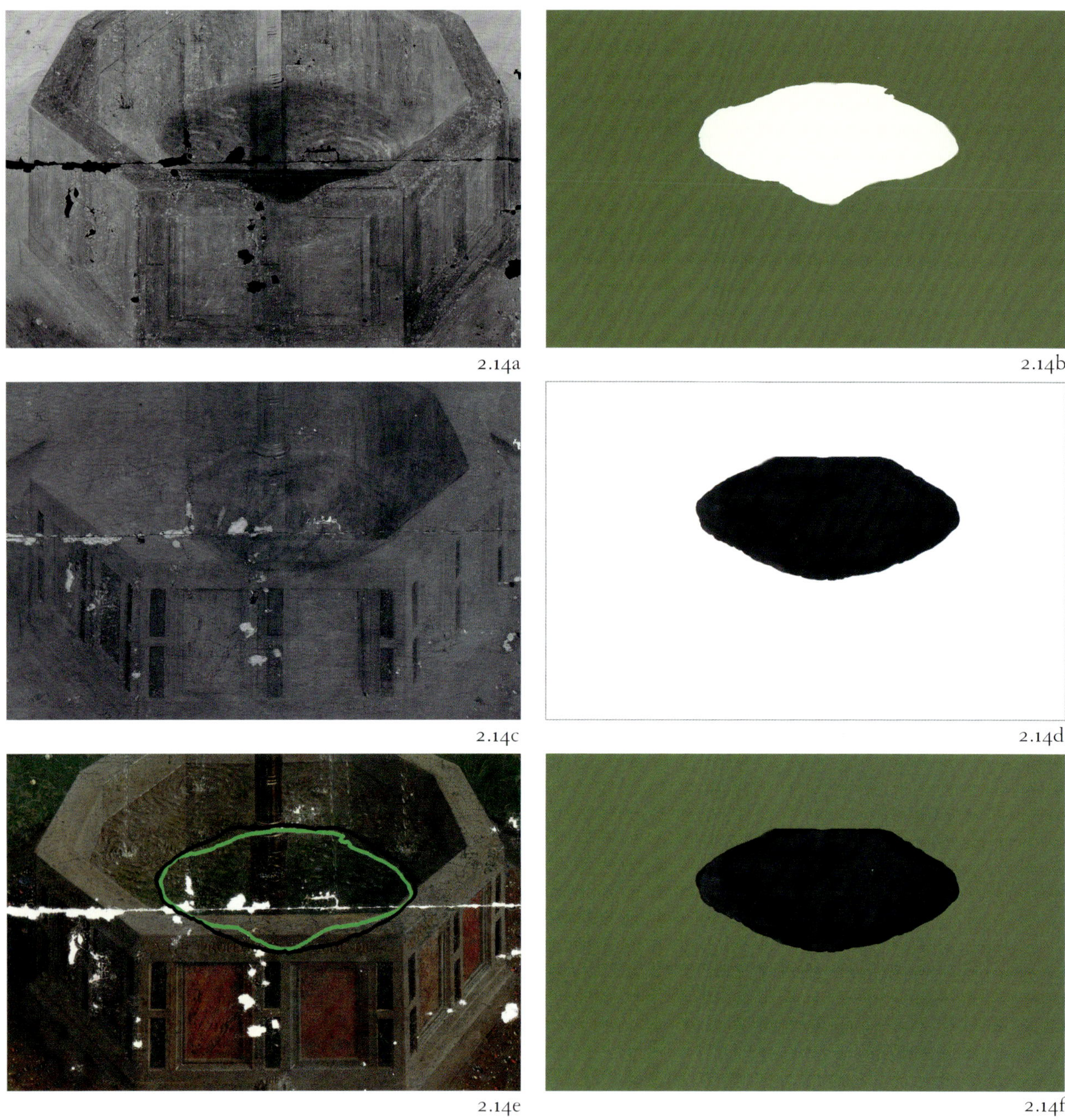

Fig. 2.14a–f. *Adoration of the Lamb*, the fountain with filled losses during restoration. Different steps in the realization of the hypothetical spring of the first stage. MA-XRF Cu-K map (a); diagram showing green layer of the first painted meadow, with oval shape left in reserve, visible in MA-XRF Cu-K map (b); IRR (c); diagram of the black, ovaloid form that can be made out in the IRR (d); diagram VIS with the overlapping outlines of the reserve (green) and the black, ovaloid form (black) (e); diagram layering the black, ovaloid form on top of the green and the reserve (f).

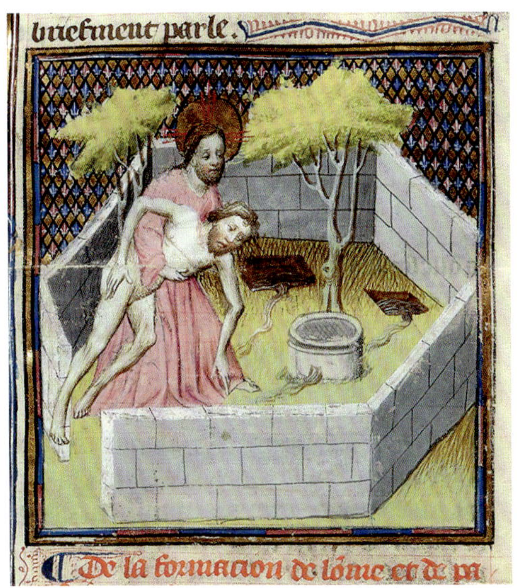

2.15a

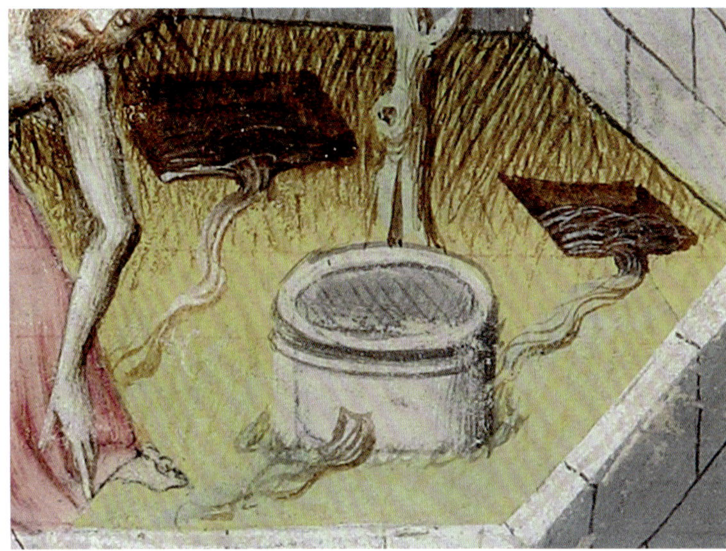

2.15b

Fig. 2.15a–b. Three springs in *God Placing Adam in the Garden of Eden*, miniature in Guyart des Moulins, *Bible historiale*, c. 1405, Paris, Bibliothèque de l'Arsenal MS 5057, fol. 8r.

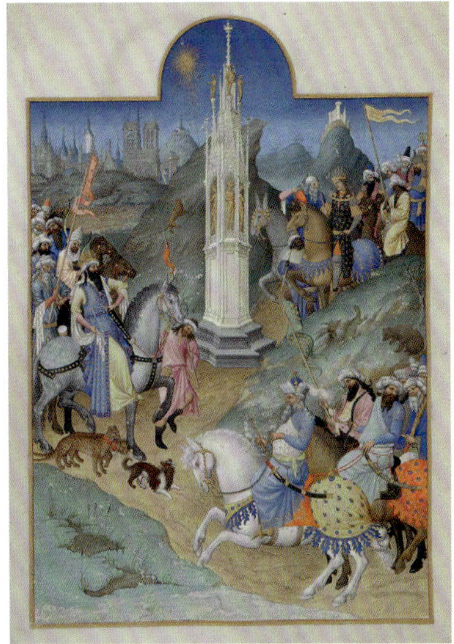

2.16a

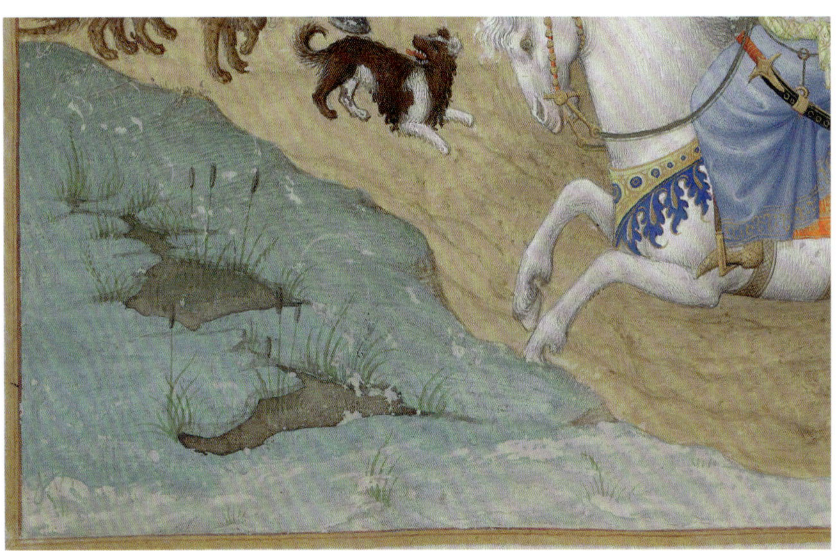

2.16b

Fig. 2.16 a–b. Two pools with reed tufts in the *Meeting of the Magi*, miniature in the Limbourg Brothers, *Les Très Riches Heures du duc de Berry*, Chantilly, Musée Condé, MS 65, fol. 51.

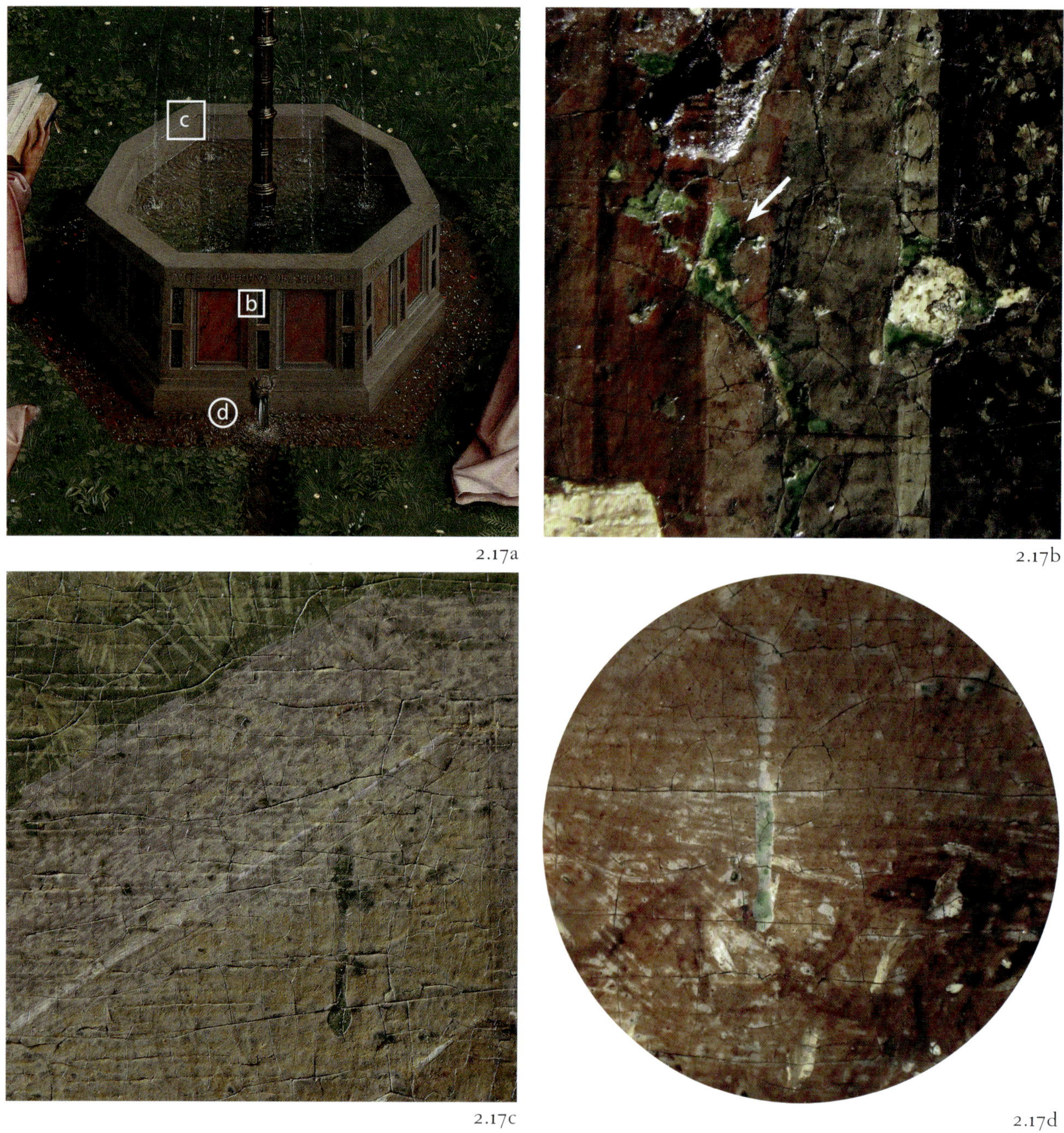

2.17a

2.17b

2.17c

2.17d

Fig. 2.17a–d. *Adoration of the Lamb*, detail (microphotographs, during restoration) (a): The fountain is painted on top of a 'complete stratigraphy' comprising several green layers, including glazes, visible in losses or abrasions in the basin (b) (white arrow); it also shows in trails of a corrosive substance that dissolved the paint of the basin and unveiled the green layer beneath (c–d).

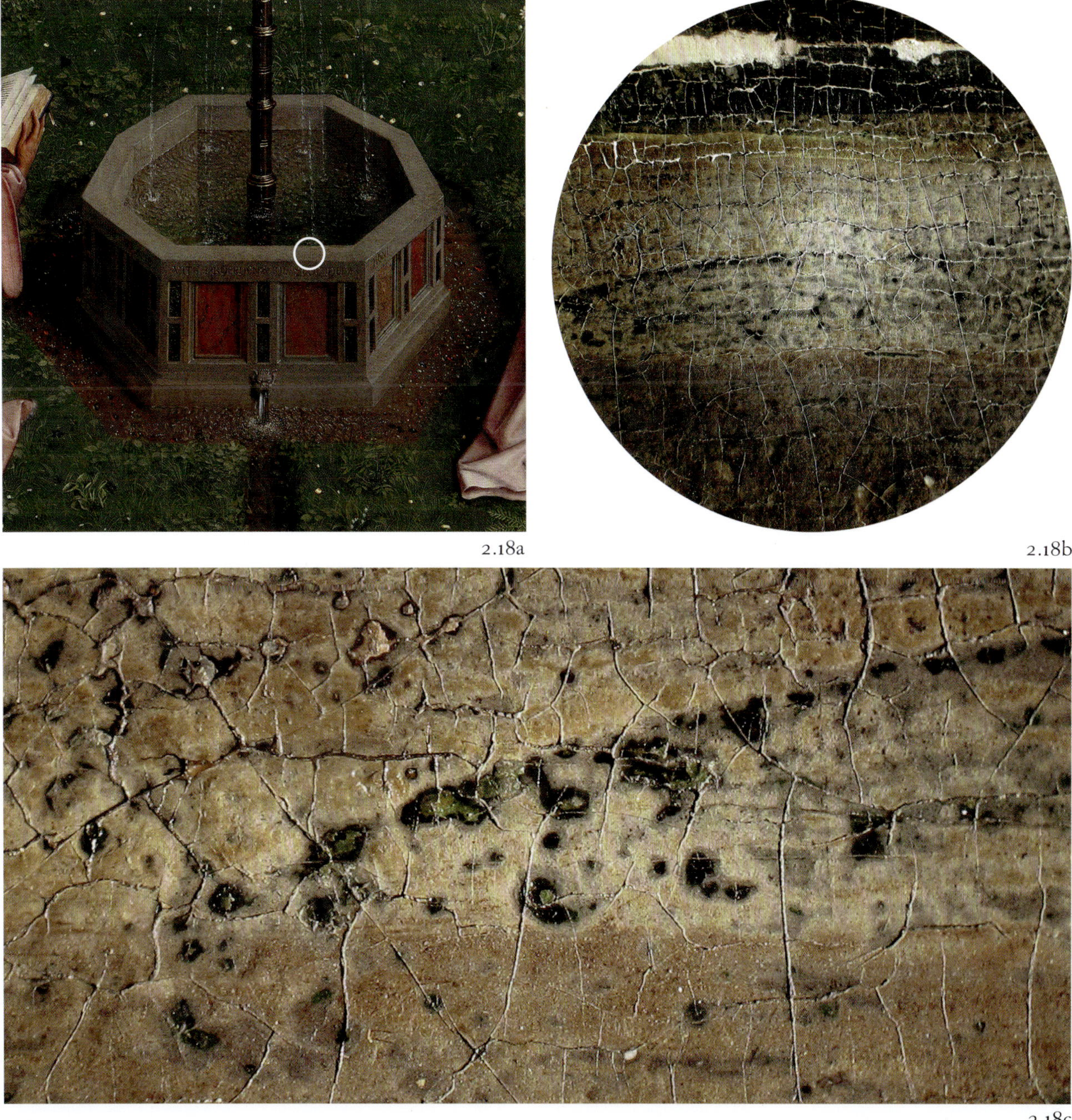

2.18a

2.18b

2.18c

Fig. 2.18a–c. *Adoration of the Lamb*, detail (microphotographs, during restoration) (a): superposition of the pictorial layers visible through abrasions in the basin – green (first meadow), black (spring), grey and brown layers.

translucent layer based on verdigris. This stratigraphy can clearly be seen in the paint samples taken from these locations. During the restoration treatment, the glaze of the first meadow was also detected in several losses (fig. 2.20).

The painter of this second stage did, however, use the glaze of the first meadow here and there to enliven the tufts of grass and the flowers he painted, although this did not prevent him from adding localized glazes himself, to indicate a small leaf here, a stem there (fig. 2.21). For their part, the flowers are painted by means of swiftly applied touches which, when viewed under the microscope, might give the impression that they are merely coloured patches resulting from the painter's playful handling of paint, but which actually represent perfectly identifiable varieties.[53] This is the case, for instance, for the rose campion (fig. 2.22) at the foot of the pomegranate tree to the left of the confessors. This was done by applying a preliminary red layer to which, once dry, the shades of the flower were added with touches of pure white and with red glazes, which were applied wet-in-wet, causing them to blend. Working wet-in-wet – blending the colours directly on the panel rather than the palette – allows layers that are not dry yet to be combined without totally mixing them. The touch has to be swift and precise, but it arises from a clear idea of the desired result and a perfect mastery of the gesture, because no reworking is possible without risking the loss of the intended effect, namely the creation of visual impressions rather than accurate lines and shapes. The painter's virtuosity is apparent in the splitting of blades of grass using the back of the brush in the fresh paint (CVE-3) or dabbing the glaze with the fingertips, leaving visible prints (fig. 2.23).

This second meadow skirts around several groups of figures, namely those with the large ones in the foreground, but also the more distant groups with the confessors and virgin martyrs, as well as the altar, the angels and the lamb, which were probably already finished, or at least well advanced. We will return to the latter in due course. This skirting of the forms is clearly noticeable in places by a ridge in the paint surface, marking the limits of the second meadow. This is the case around the figures of the prophets and the apostles on either side of the fountain (fig. 2.24). In some places, however – below the virgin martyrs, for instance – the transition between the two stages appears gentler. The first meadow is still partly

Fig. 2.19a–c. *Adoration of the Lamb*: location of sampling (a–b); cross-section 10/83 (c): preparatory layers (1, 2, 3); the black layer (4); a green layer (5); two brown layers corresponding to the reflection of the shaft in the water of the basin (6 and 7); non-original varnishes and retouches now removed (8, 9, 10).

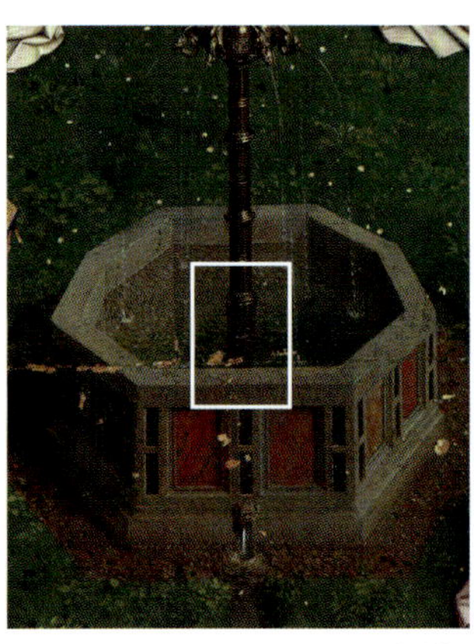

2.19a

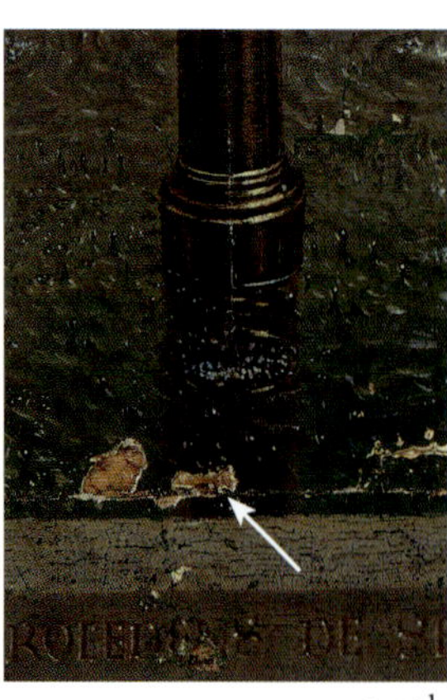

2.19b

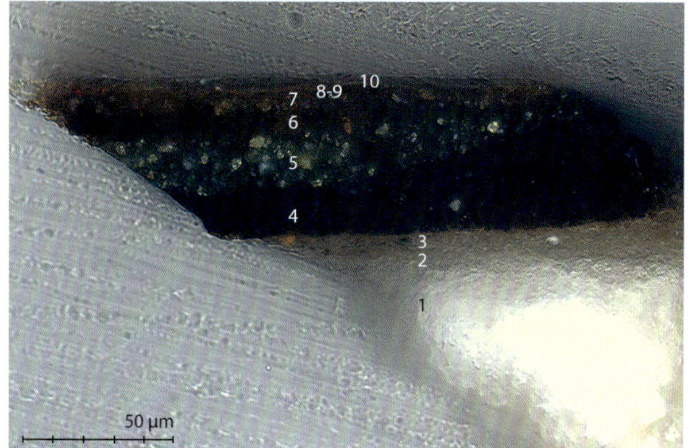

2.19c

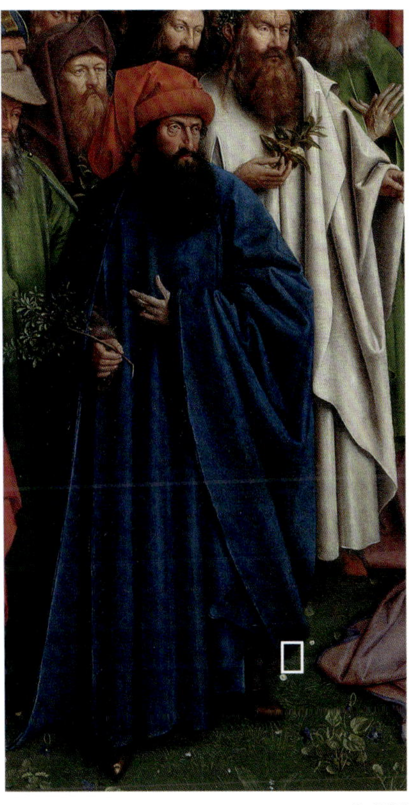

2.20a

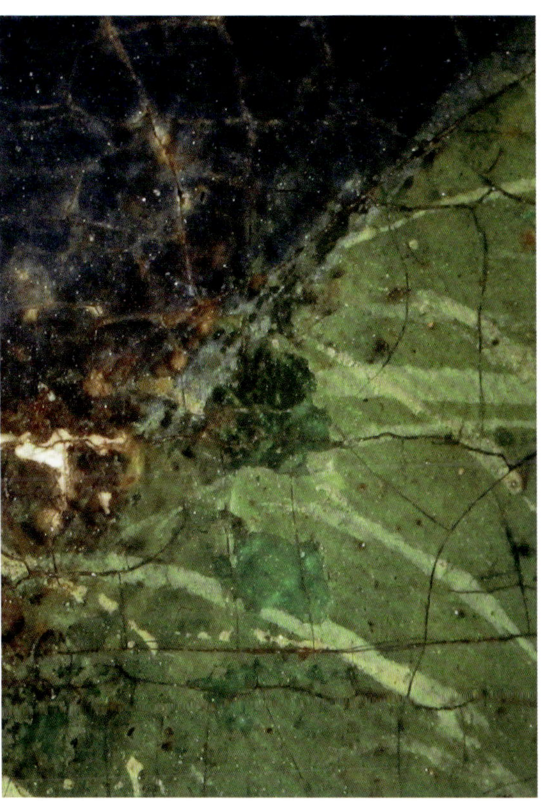

2.20b

Fig. 2.20a–b. *Adoration of the Lamb*, detail: green glaze of the first meadow visible in the losses of the second stage.

visible at the interface between figure and meadow (fig. 2.25), suggesting that the second-stage meadow stops just below the virgin martyrs group which, if not fully painted, will have been well advanced at least.

It is in the green layers of the second, freshly painted meadow that the contours of the octagonal fountain were traced by scoring (figs. 2.26 and 2.27).[54] The fountain was not drawn on the ground layer, as this had already been covered by the pictorial layers of the first stage. The scoring in question is multiple, indicating a search for the form of the basin, in the same way that a drawing would be subject to adjustments. It even appears that guide marks were drawn, possibly using a compass (fig. 2.28).[55]

The stone basin of the fountain was painted in two principal layers: a preliminary grey layer (apparently flat and uniform), followed by a second, more modulated grey-ochre layer along the more or less illuminated faces of the basin (fig. 2.29).[56] Veins or irregularities in the stone were suggested by translucent brown strokes.

The metal column was lower at this stage than in the final version. The final design of the fountain consists of a central metal column decorated with protruding rings spaced along the height of the shaft, then two series of dragon-like gargoyles spitting water. The final series of gargoyles ranged around a metal sphere is surmounted by the figure of an angel. It appears that the column was not initially intended to rise beyond the second ring, since the section below it was painted

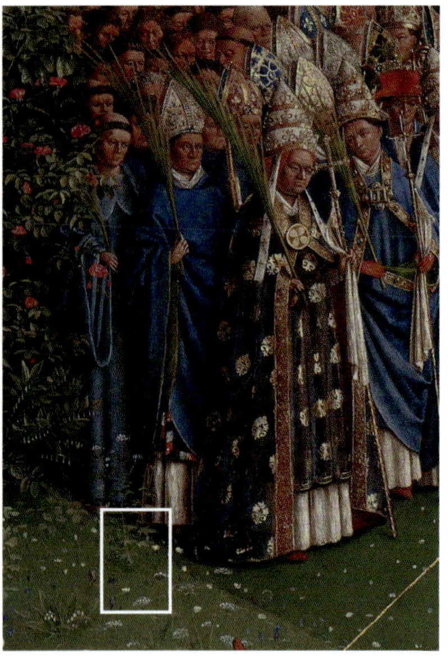
2.21a

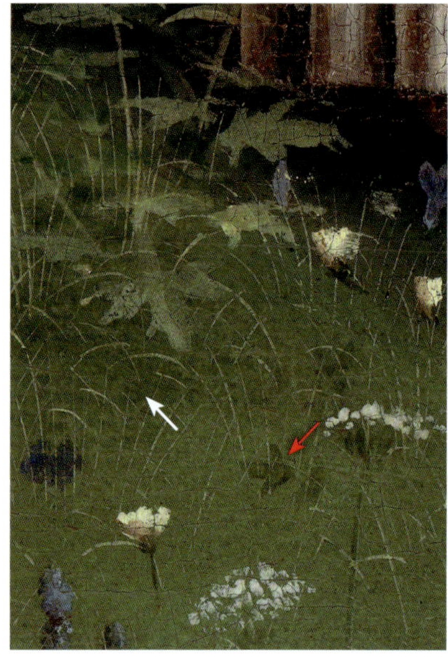
2.21b

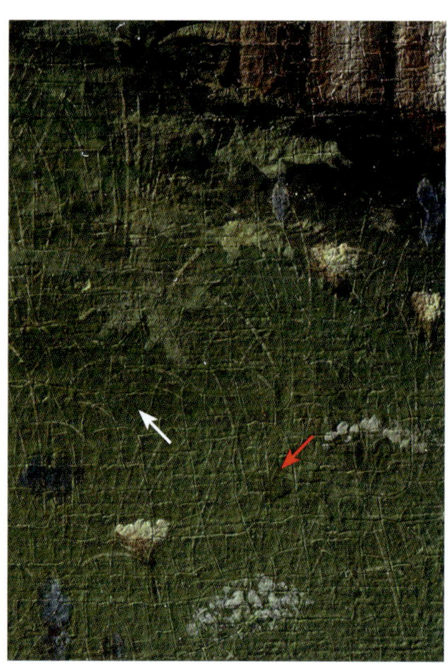
2.21c

Fig. 2.21a–c. *Adoration of the Lamb*, detail (a); green glazes from the first stage left uncovered, visible on the surface (white arrow), and localized green glaze added in the second stage (red arrow); VIS (b); raking light (c).

onto the new meadow without grass,[57] while the section above it was executed over already painted grass, as shown in the infrared photograph (fig. 2.30). The column was thus apparently not going to be so high and the shaft would have been simpler and would only have measured half its current height. Even so, the idea of a taller column probably emerged quickly, since the stylistic and technical characteristics appear to be the same for its full height. Lines were also scored to mark the limits of the enlargement of the fountain's section. The water with the gemstones at the foot of the basin may likewise have been enlarged at this point, as it is partially painted over the grass in the same way as the upper section of the column.

The column was painted over a brown base layer without as yet paying attention to the rings, even where the shaft has been extended over the meadow for which grass had already been painted. Dark brown, light yellow and ochre touches were then applied to shape the rings and simulate light reflecting on the metal.[58]

Soils in the wings

First stage The shutters also feature areas with clearly visible grass on the ground or on top of the crags and in the uniform green expanses in the distance. For the most part, however, the soil in the shutters consists mainly of rocky or sandy paths, although it appears that for certain of these paintings a first stage also existed where it had vegetation. There are several indications, for example, that the soil beneath the horses in the *Knights of Christ* was originally conceived as green. Small paint losses in the upper layers show an underlying green layer of this kind,[59] which has no reason to be present beneath the brown tonality of the current soil (fig. 2.31). The uniform presence of this green layer – most likely based on verdigris – is confirmed by the MA-XRF copper map.

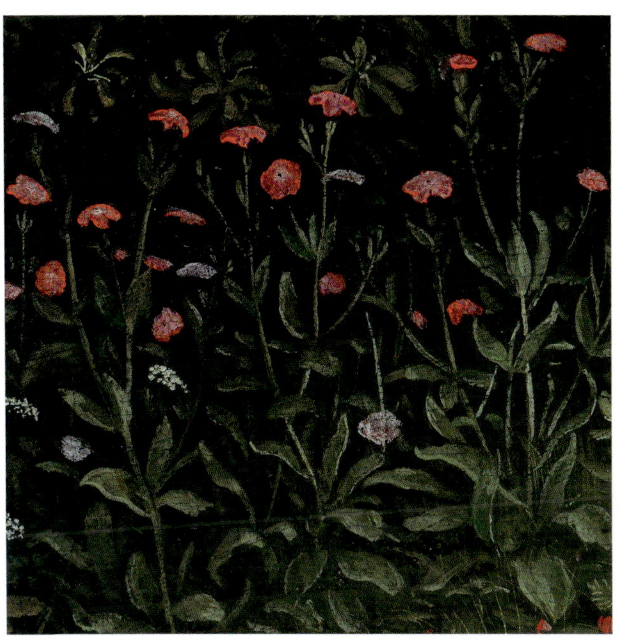

2.22a

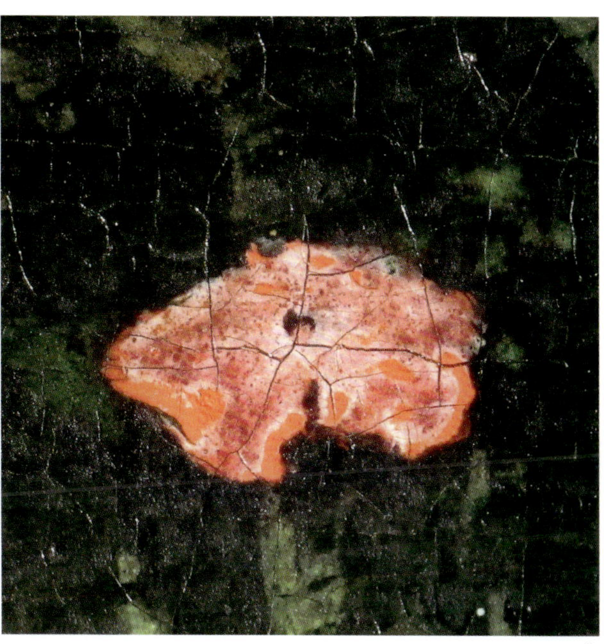

2.22b

Fig. 2.22a–b. *Adoration of the Lamb*, detail: working wet-in-wet to depict the rose campion.

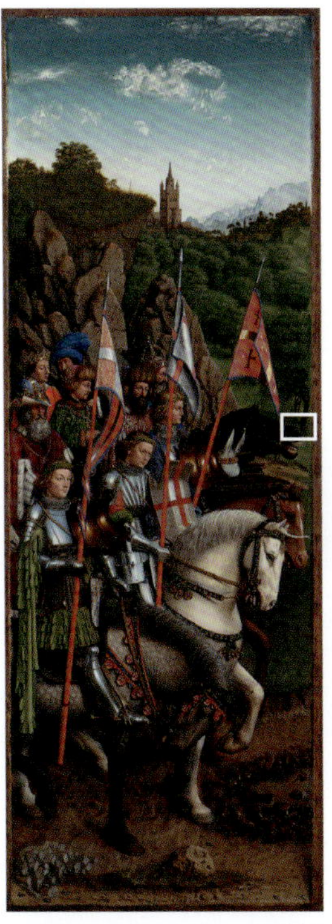

2.23a

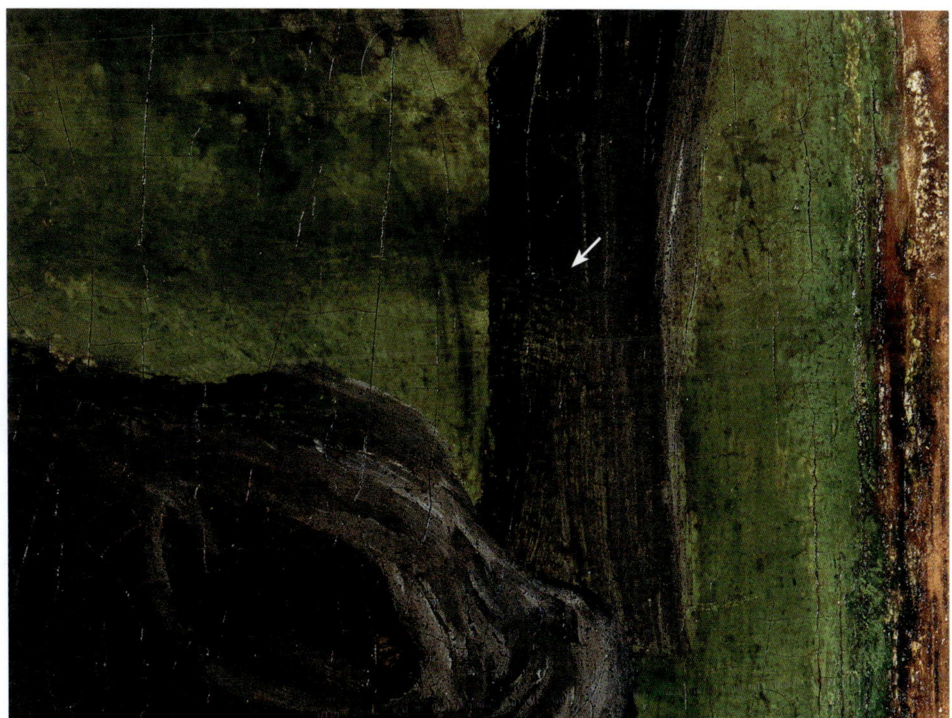

2.23b

Fig. 2.23a–b. *Knights of Christ*, detail: fingerprints.

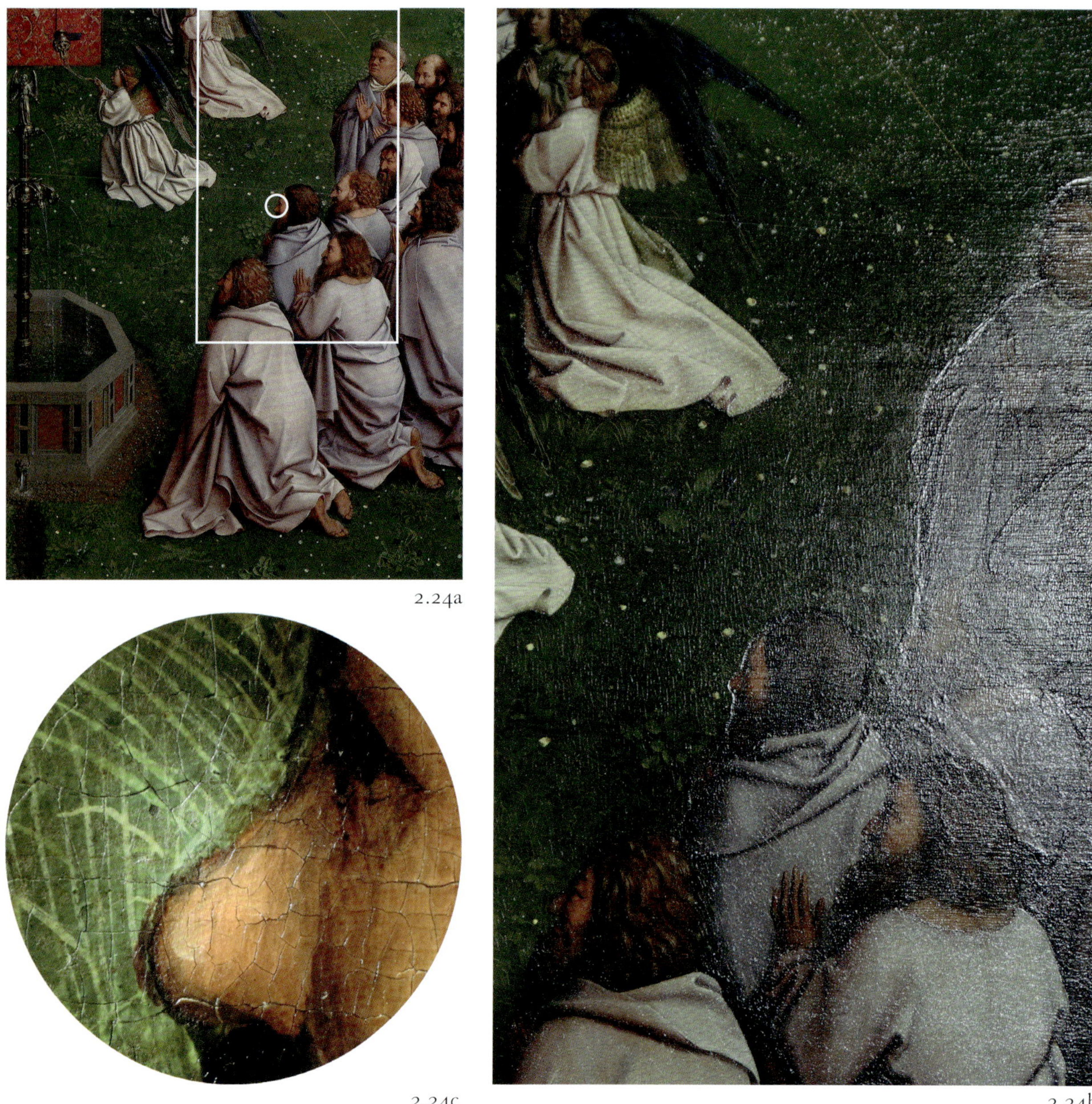

2.24a

2.24c

2.24b

Fig. 2.24. *Adoration of the Lamb*, detail (a); the ridge marking the limits of the second meadow skirts the outlines of the angels, prophets and apostles – photograph in reflected light (b); microphotograph (c).

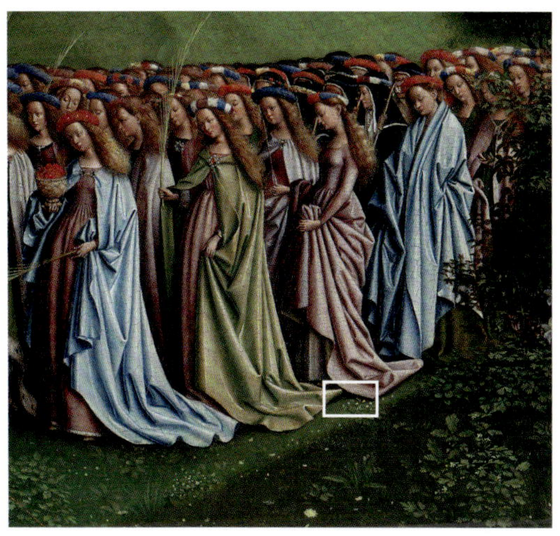

2.25a

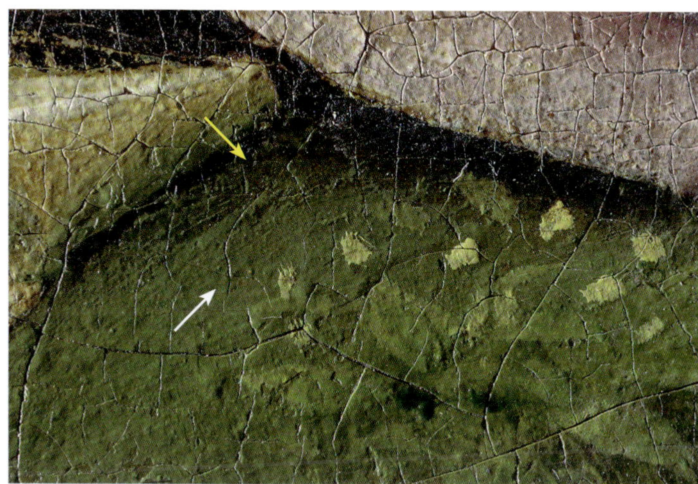

2.25b

Fig. 2.25. *Adoration of the Lamb*, detail (a); transition zone between first-stage (yellow arrow) and second-stage meadow (white arrow).

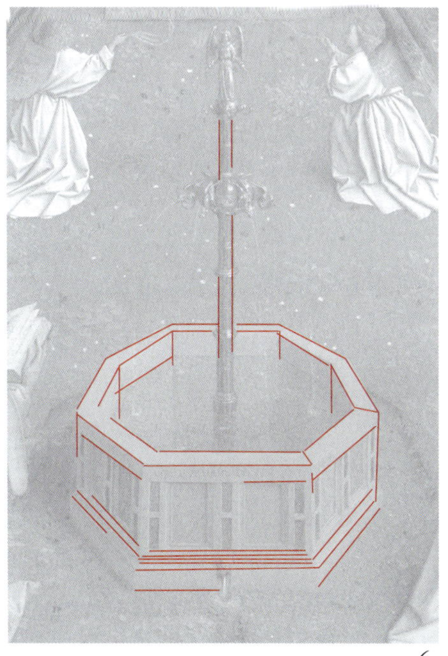

2.26a

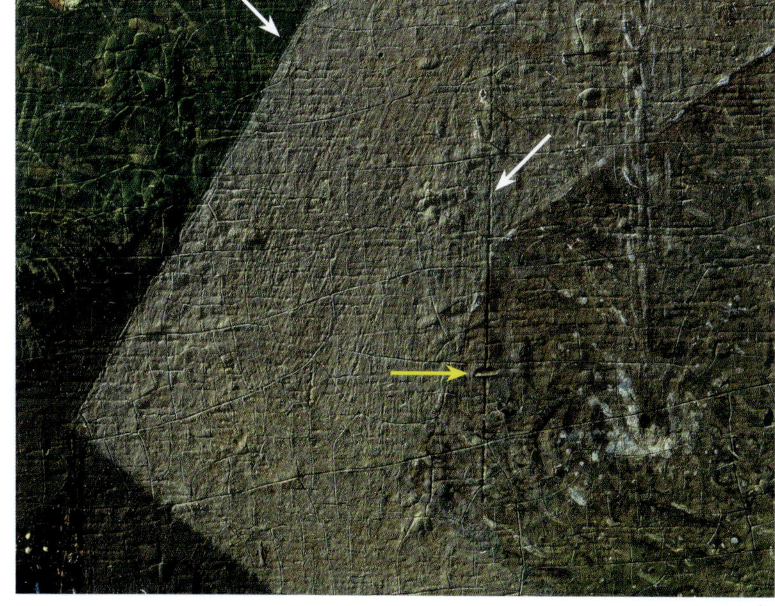

2.26b

Fig. 2.26a–b. *Adoration of the Lamb*, the fountain, diagram of scored lines (a); scored lines (white arrows) and scored guide marks, possibly using a compass (yellow arrow) – photograph taken in raking light (b).

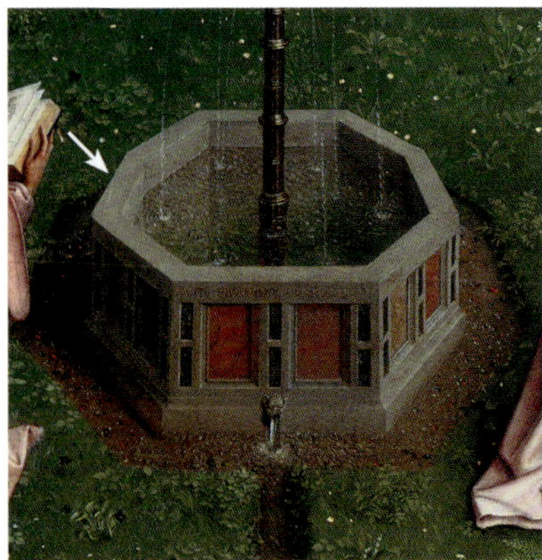

2.27a

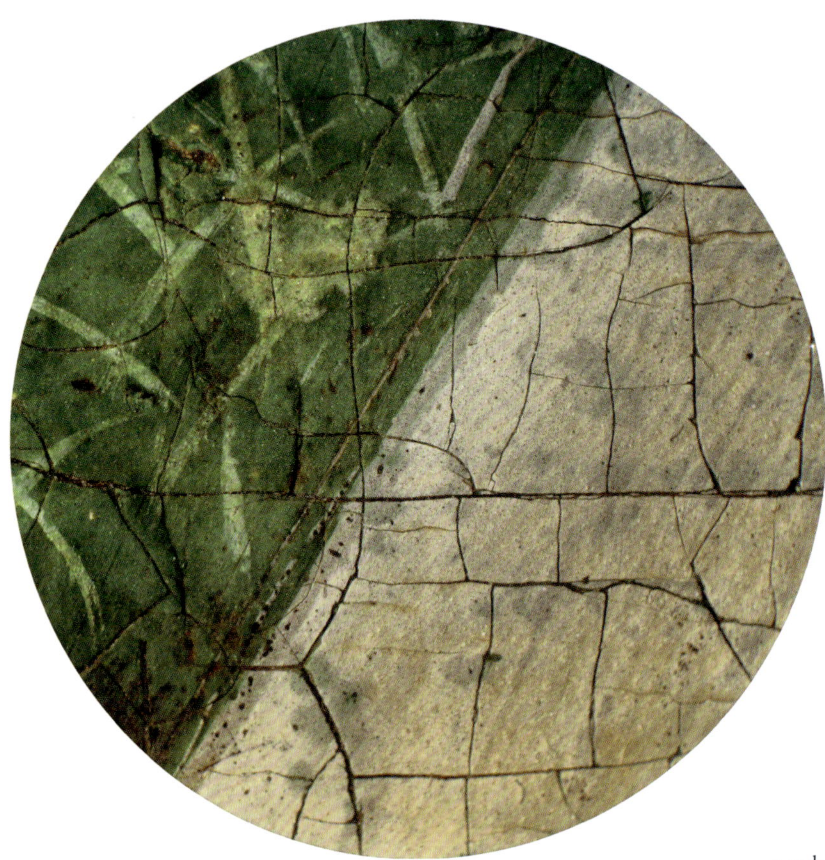

2.27b

Fig. 2.27a–b. *Adoration of the Lamb*, detail (a); line incised in the green paint layer marking the position of the basin – microphotograph (b).

Second stage Adjustments to the horses' legs in the *Knights* – also reported in previous studies[60] – are contemporary with these changes to the soil. The positioning of the legs, as we see them now, occurred during the second stage, when the green soil was changed to brown. A few corresponding indications have also been detected in the soil of the *Pilgrims*.[61] The possible adjustment of the nature of the soil in this painting was accompanied by changes in the position of the feet of figures behind the giant St Christopher. Present in a previous stage, they were covered by the tufts of grass we see now.[62] It therefore appears that modifications to the soil were also made in the wings after initial painting.

Rocks in the wings

First stage The vertical crags in the shutters were executed over a brown or grey base tone. The division into parallel strata was done by juxtaposing lighter expanses of varying size with brown lines that suggest deep fissures in the rock or slight differences in level. The red surface tones, lastly, were evoked by a few swiftly applied touches (CVE-21).

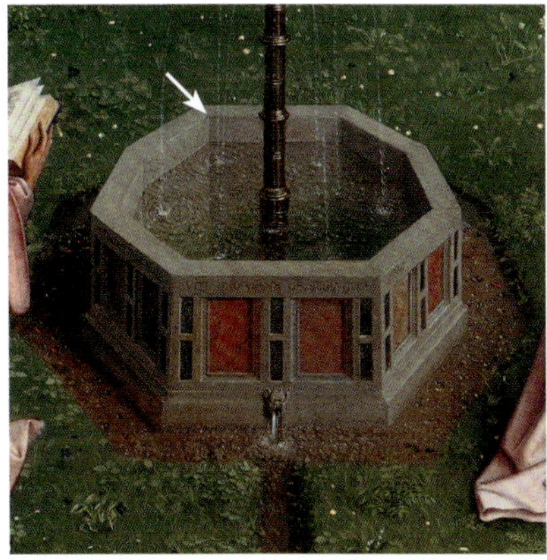

2.28a

Fig. 2.28a–b. *Adoration of the Lamb*, detail (a); compass marks – microphotograph (b).

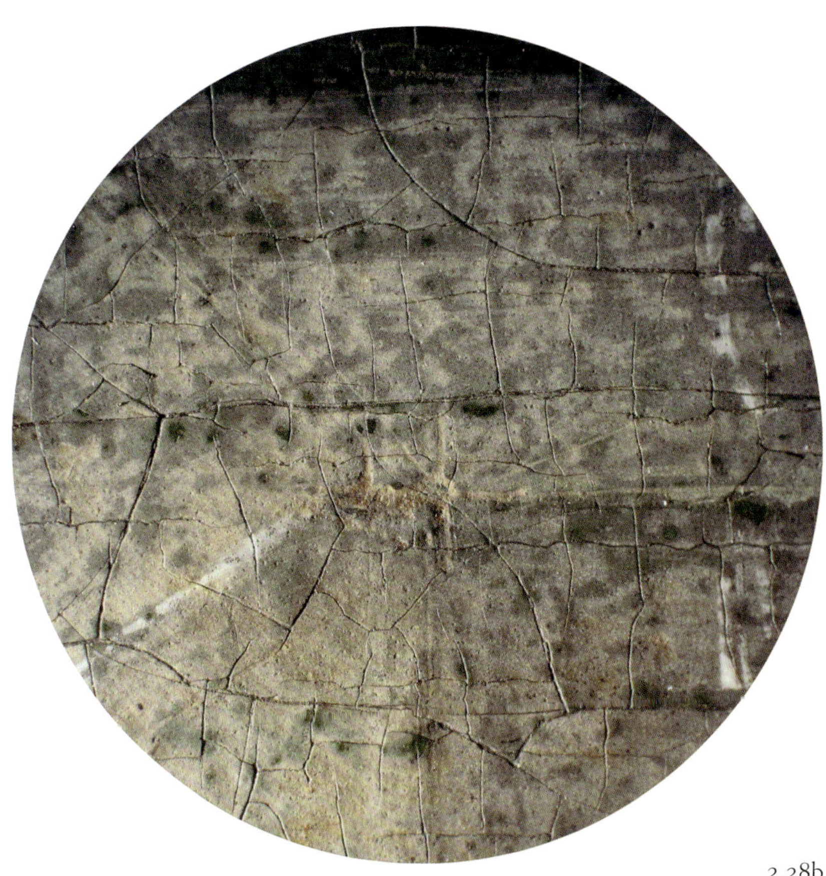

2.28b

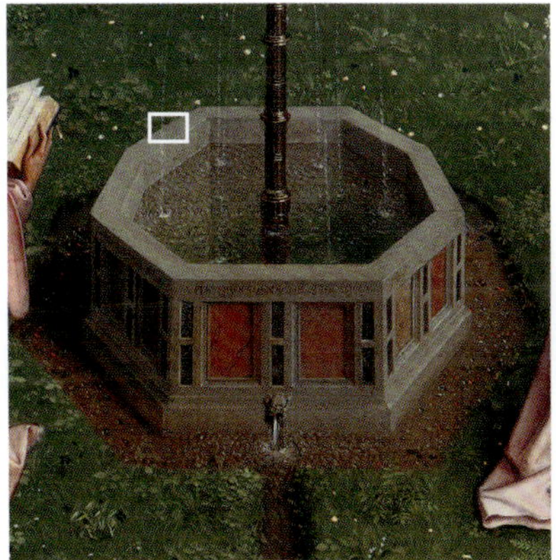

2.29a

Fig. 2.29a–b. *Adoration of the Lamb*, detail (a); the stone basin was painted essentially in two layers: a preliminary darker grey layer (yellow arrow) and an ochre-grey upper layer (white arrow) – microphotograph, during restoration (b).

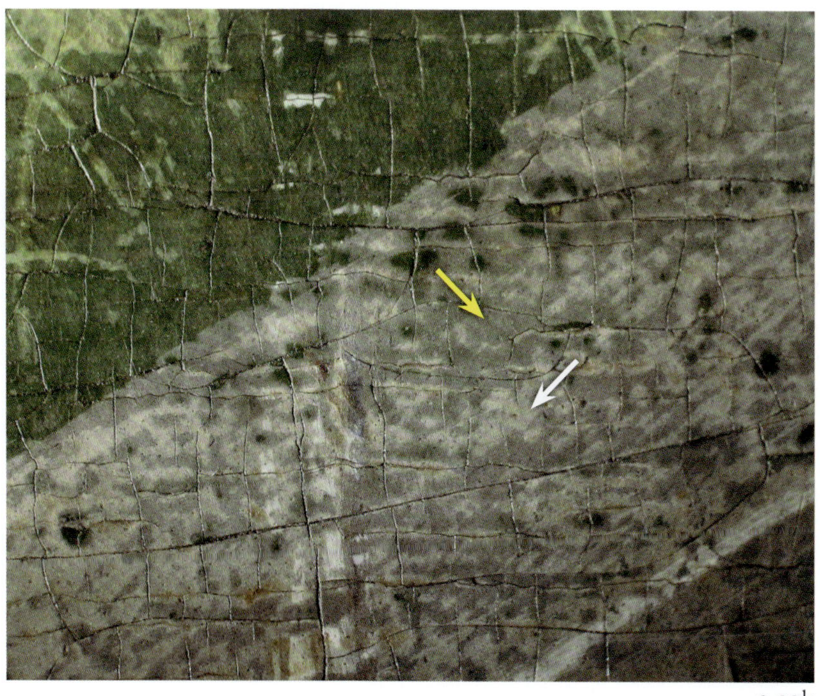

2.29b

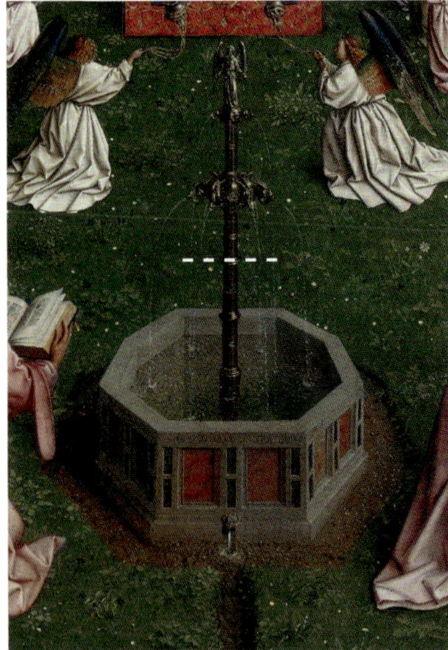
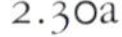

2.30a

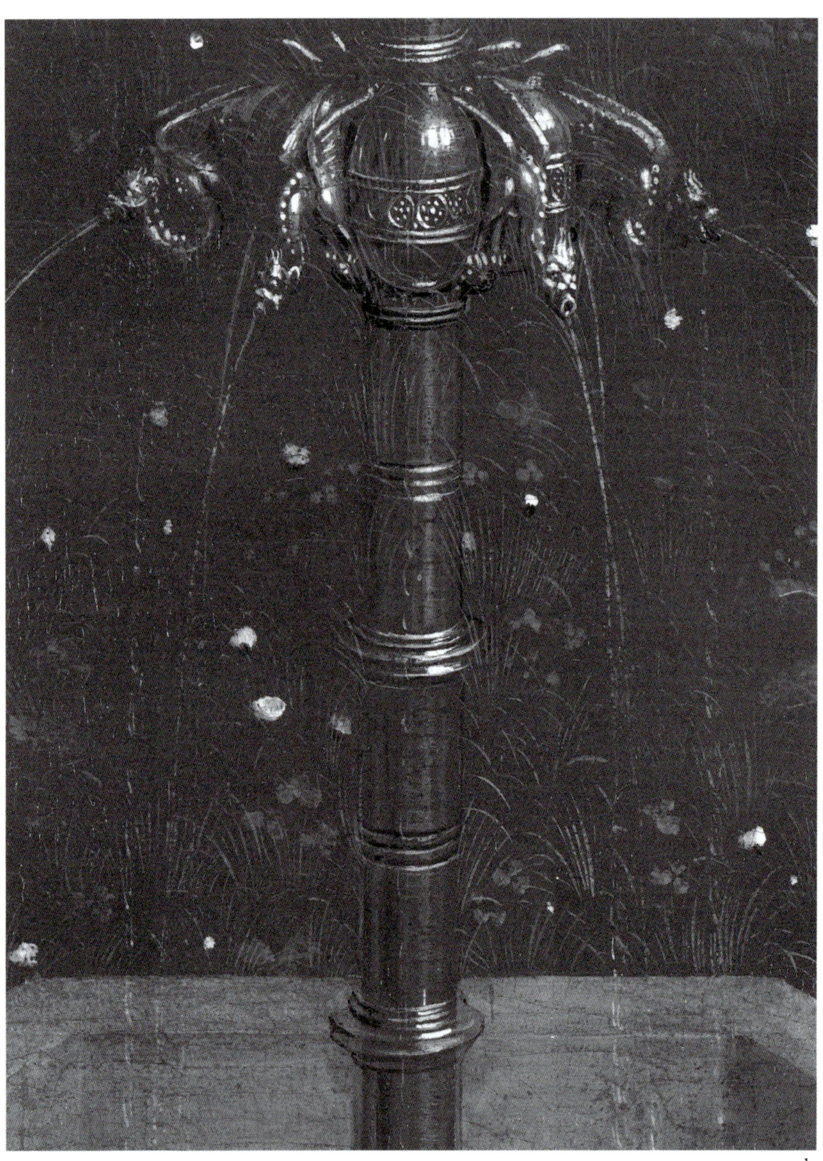

2.30b

Fig. 2.30a–b. *Adoration of the Lamb*, painted stalks of grass are present only under the upper part of the metal column. The diagram shows the limit of the first version of the column (dotted line) (a); the painted stalks of grass are visible in the IR macrophotograph (b).

Where the soils in the wings were originally grassier, the peaks of the crags were rockier than they are today. The grassy areas at the top of the crags were painted during the second stage: the rocky passages planned in the first stage were more arid and lacking in vegetation. The infrared reflectograms of the *Knights of Christ* and the *Hermits* suggest rocky plateaus below the grassy zones at the top, traversed in the middle by a change in level in the crag (fig. 2.32a, CVE-16 and CVE-22). In the *Knights*, a sample taken from the summit of the crag, as well as careful observation of the left edge (fig. 2.32c–d), does indeed show a first, greyish-ochre paint layer, which must have corresponded with the painting of the rocks before the grass was laid over them.

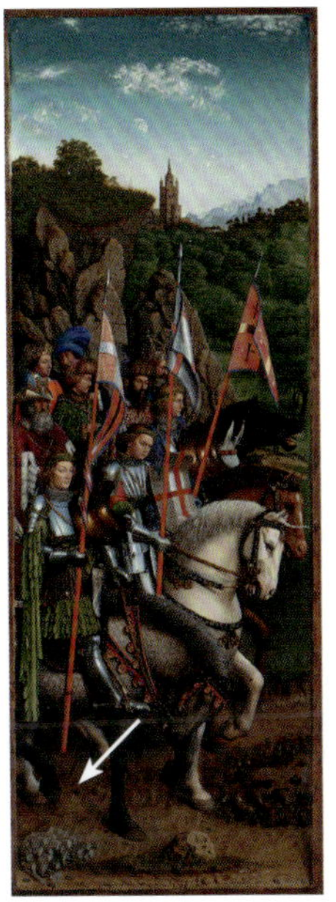

2.31a

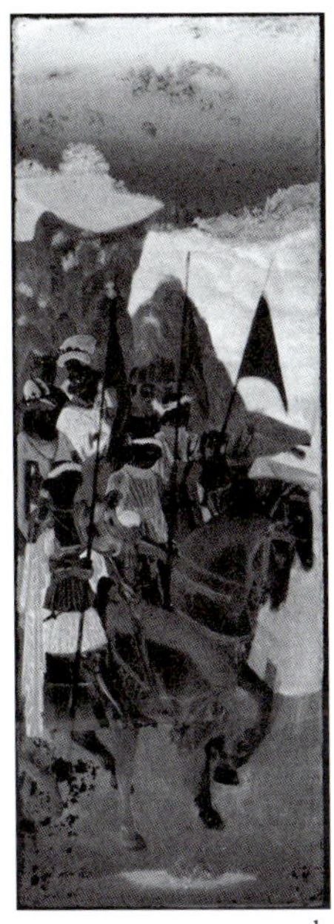

2.31b

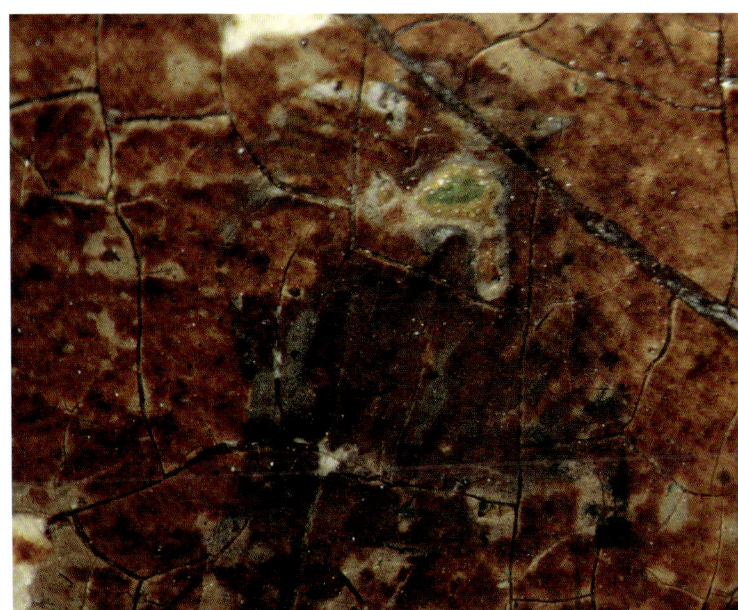

2.31c

Fig. 2.31a–c. *Knights of Christ* (a); the presence of a green layer underlying the brown soil is confirmed by the MA-XRF Cu-K map (b) and visible in small losses (c).

Second and third stages The situation in this zone of the *Knights* is, however, complex. There are two levels of meadow above the grey layer,[63] the first of which only covered the summit of the rocky plateau, while the second also adds a grassy overhang along the left edge, which does not create any perspective effect (fig. 2.32a–b).[64] The second level of meadow, which belongs to the same level as the grassy overhang, also conceals two painted birds (fig. 2.33).

The sky and the horizon

The skies in the central panel and the wings were built up through a significant number of layers: a base of indigo and lead white followed by three layers of azurite mixed with lead white[65] and a fifth and final layer of ultramarine and lead white (fig. 2.45). We will return in a moment to the ultramarine and lead-white layer, which is only found in the central panel and mostly runs around the edges of the currently visible architecture.

The sky is painted with a gradation from white horizon to blue upper sky. Existing samples taken from the sky in each of the four panels show that these shades had already been introduced as of the first pictorial layer, since the lower part of the sky was begun solely in lead white and the upper part with a mixture of lead white and indigo. This progressive variation in colour is confirmed in the subsequent layers. We can see this in the MA-XRF copper map, which detects a greater presence of this element – and hence of azurite – towards the top of the sky in each of the four panels. Was it necessary to apply four pictorial layers, each repeating the same shades in the gradation of the sky, to achieve the desired result? The economy of means we find in Jan van Eyck's art[66] argues against such complexity, even if no samples have been taken from the skies in other paintings by him.[67] This stratigraphy is more likely explained by the superimposition of several interventions.

An area of the sky in the *Knights* shows damage to the paint layer that is not visible on the surface but beneath it, in the X-radiograph and infrared reflectogram (CVE-15).[68] A joint appears to have opened up, requiring local gluing. The sky in the zone immediately surrounding this damaged area consists of a first indigo-based layer followed by three layers of azurite. Investigations carried out during the present restoration treatment allowed it to be further determined that there is a lacuna deep in this stratigraphy in the first layer of azurite, which is missing at that point.[69] This degraded zone only includes the final two azurite-based layers. In the corresponding location on the reverse of the painting, namely in the panel with Joos Vijd, a network of wider cracks on either side of the joint forms what is probably a trace of an intervention in the preparatory layers,[70] beneath the pictorial layer which appears to us to be original. In other words, it is a very early problem, which required the reworking of the sky at a date prior to or contemporary with Jan's intervention. This possibly indicates that the first azurite layer belongs to the first stage.[71]

Study of the central panel helps us to locate the two upper azurite layers. In certain places, we observe in raking light and with the naked eye a ridge in the paint surface crossing the sky along the horizon. This ridge demarcates[72] the limit of a white layer of the sky skirting the large masses of vegetation and architecture[73] but sometimes also passes beneath trees and the tops of certain painted buildings (fig. 2.34). The latter observation would not be surprising, were it not that this white layer masks other buildings that were already painted during the first stage. Details of this painted architecture are visible in the MA-XRF maps and in abrasions or micro-losses (fig. 2.35). The white layer, which is at the same level as the third layer of azurite higher up in the sky, covers them close to the horizon (fig. 2.45). We can therefore deduce that the third azurite layer belongs to the second stage. The intermediate – and hence second – azurite layer is situated between the first stage and the second stage and might belong to either level. We think, however, that it passes beneath the first-stage architecture and hence that it belongs to the initial project, even in the absence of a sample to confirm this.

On the other hand, a certain inconsistency has been introduced between the wings and the central panel by the supplementary ultramarine and lead-white-based layer, applied uniformly across the central panel and circumscribing the architecture (fig. 2.36) or even overlapping details already painted (fig. 2.37). The presence of this fifth blue layer raises questions: it breaks the greenish blue tone provided by the azurite that dominates the skies in the shutters. The question of the ultramarine layer's originality provoked discussion during the conservation campaign and has yet to be settled.[74] It remains a delicate matter, moreover, because the dove appears to belong to this stratum, even if the situation might be more complex, as we will see in a moment. It should be added that this ultramarine layer was located beneath the overpaint in the sky that was removed during the 2016–19 restoration campaign and which dated in any case to before 1557.[75] This mid-sixteenth-century overpaint, lastly, not only covered the ultramarine-based sky but also filled losses that were already present in this ultramarine-based stratum.[76]

Fig. 2.32a–d. *Knights of Christ*: IRR detail (a); VIS detail (b); visualization of the grey paint layer in a lacuna corresponding with the crags of the first stage (yellow arrow (c); cross-section 09/19 (white arrow) showing the layer build-up as follows: ground, underdrawing and priming (1, 2, 3); crags of the first stage (4); second-stage meadow (5, 6, 7); third-stage meadow (8, 9); non-original varnishes (10–14) (d).

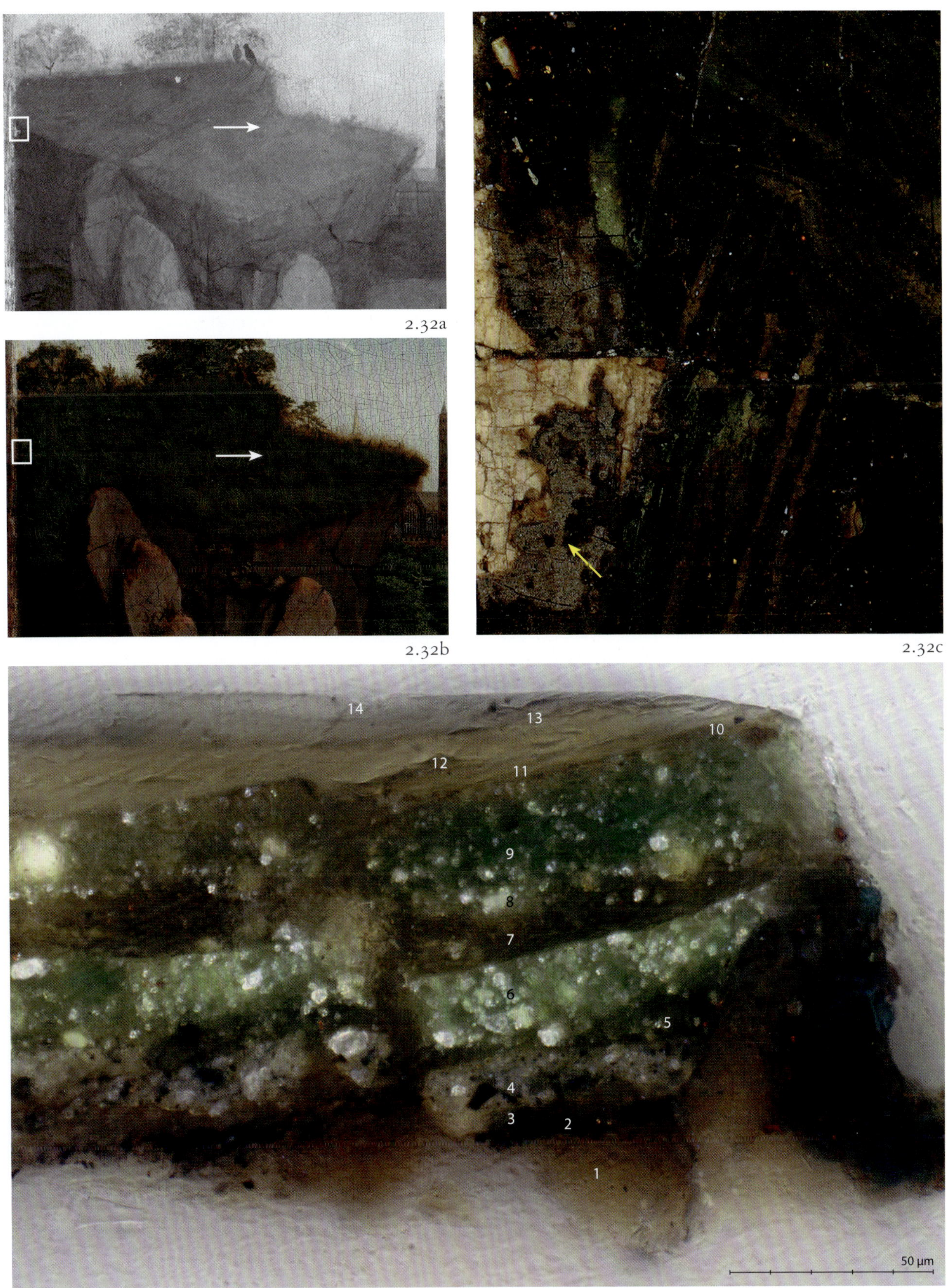

2.32a

2.32b

2.32c

2.32d

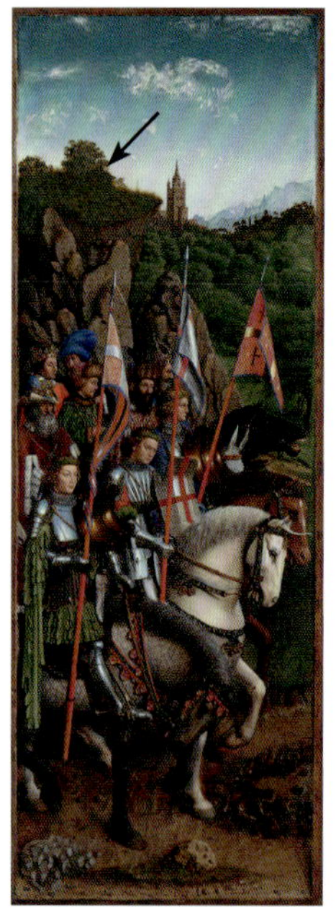

2.33a

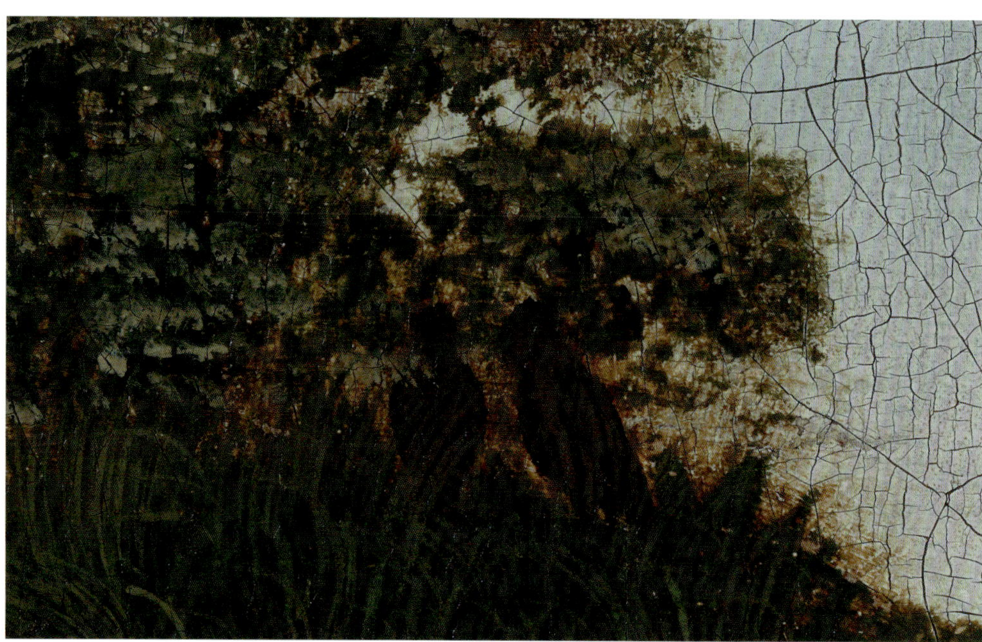

2.33b

Fig. 2.33a–b. *Knights of Christ*, detail: two painted birds hidden by the meadow (probably third stage).

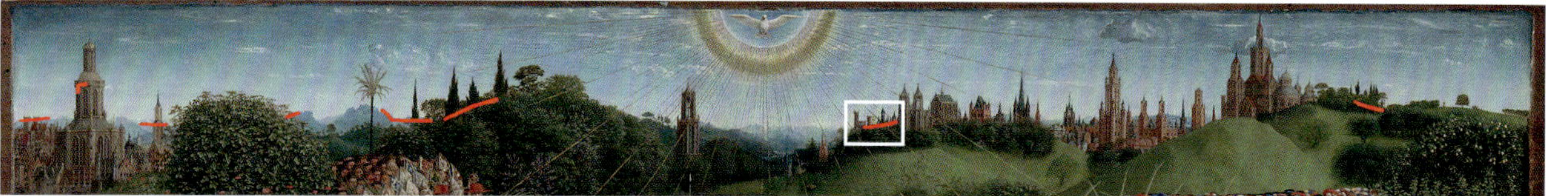

2.34a

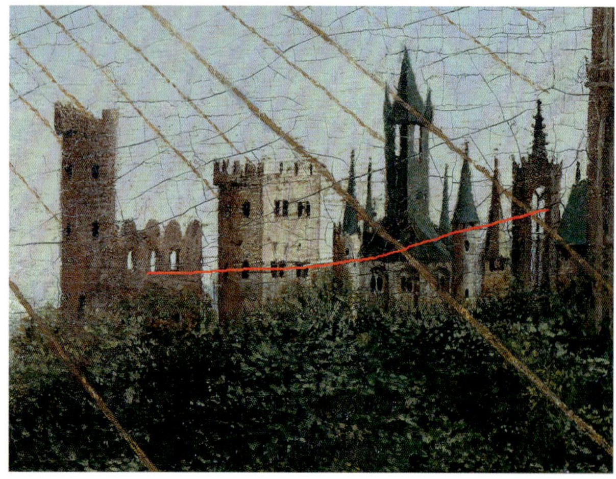

2.34b

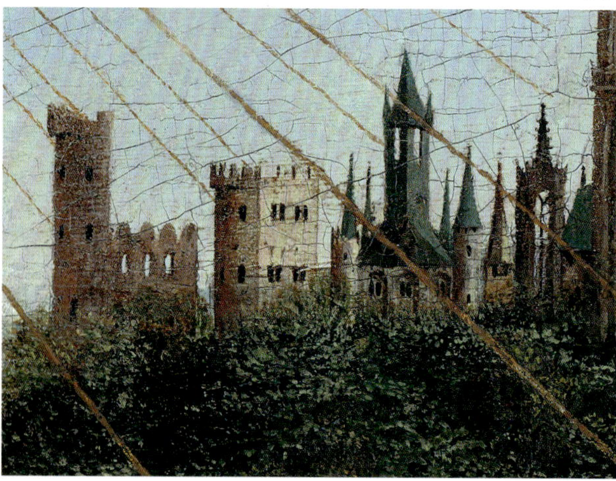

2.34c

Fig. 2.34a–c. *Adoration of the Lamb*. A ridge in the paint surface along the horizon crosses some of the hills and buildings. The diagrams show where it is visible in raking light (red line) (a–b); detail VIS (c).

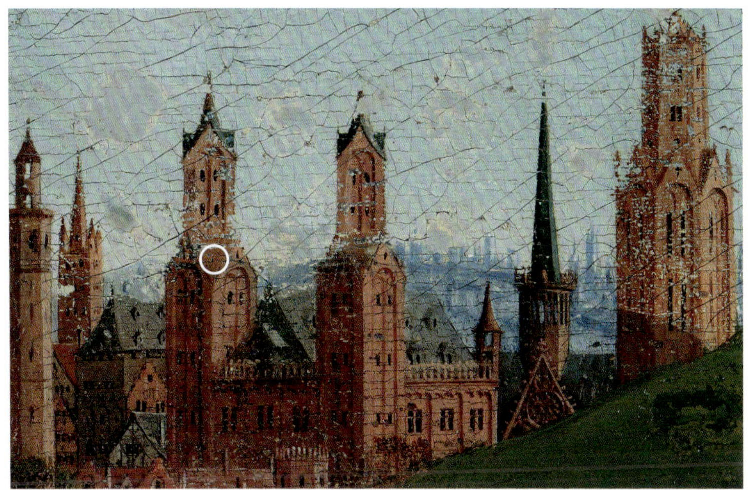

2.35a

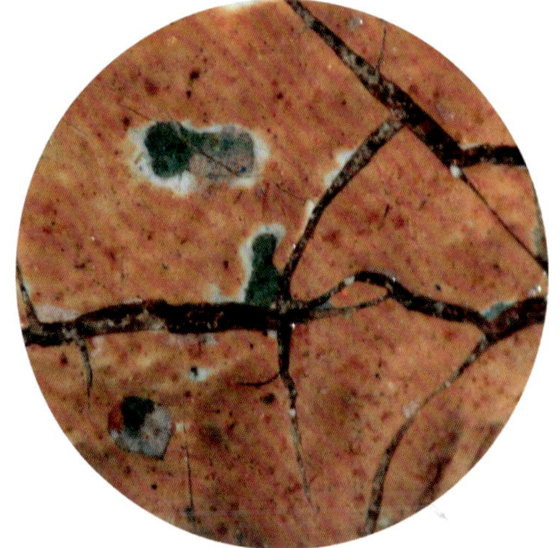

2.35b

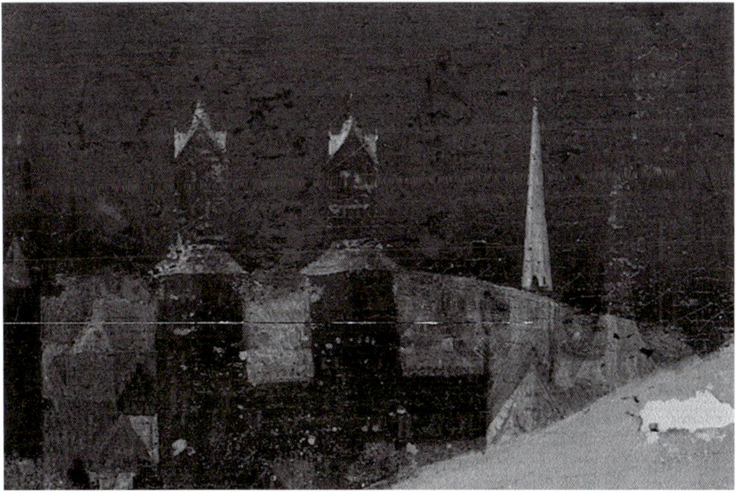

2.35c

Fig. 2.35a–c. *Adoration of the Lamb*, detail: buildings of the second stage (a) (Coremans group 6; see fig. 2.38); blue roofs of the underlying first stage are visible in the losses – microphotograph (b); and in the MA-XRF Cu-K map (c).

These losses are angular in shape, suggesting that the ultramarine layer mixed with lead white had time to dry, become hard and crack. Even though a pictorial layer rich in lead white polymerizes relatively quickly, the process still takes several years – or even decades. We can therefore deduce that a certain amount of time elapsed between the execution of the ultramarine sky and that of the sixteenth-century overpaint. It may thus be assumed that the application of this ultramarine sky, if not Eyckian,[77] dates from the second half of the fifteenth century, or the very beginning of the sixteenth century at the latest.

Architecture

The superimposition of the two first stages can be seen in the architecture on the horizon of the central panel and the *Knights of Christ* panel. Coremans had

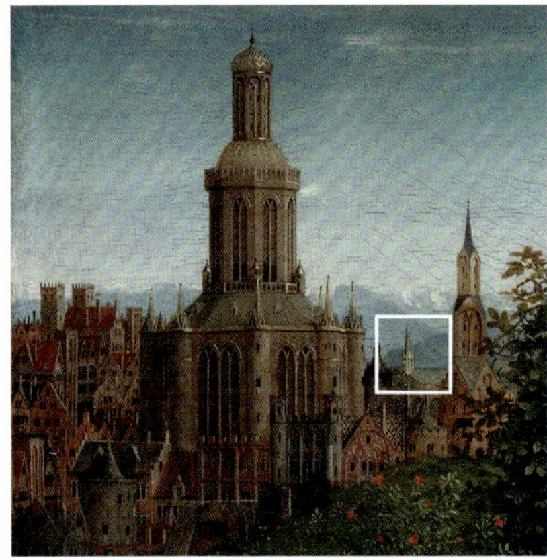
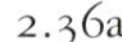

2.36a

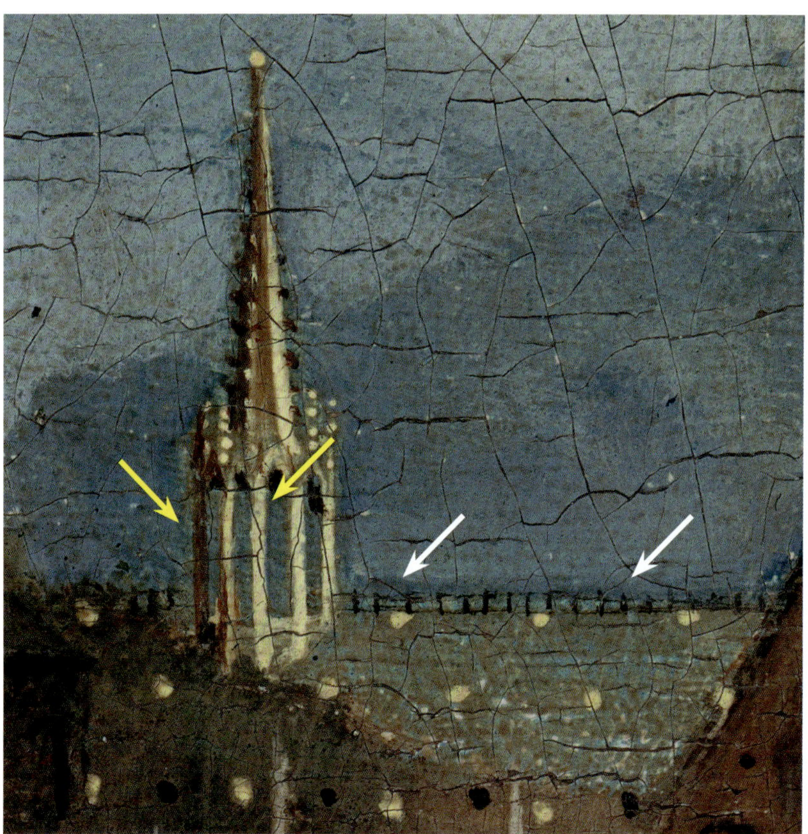

2.36b

Fig. 2.36a–b. *Adoration of the Lamb*, detail (a); the ultramarine layer of a mountain skirts the architecture and is painted on top of small details such as the crest of a roof (white arrows), while leaving a narrow strip around the tower, as well as the openings in the tower uncovered; in those places the azurite underlayer is visible (yellow arrows) (b). The ultramarine layer in the mountains belongs to the same stratum as the ultramarine layer in the sky.

already identified Eyckian architectural elements and additions.[78] His analysis was partly flawed, as he was unknowingly comparing the pictorial quality of buildings overpainted in the sixteenth century (the tower of Utrecht cathedral) with others that did not display the same overpainting (most notably the group of buildings on the far left, referred to as 'Coremans group 1', figs. 2.38, 2.39 and CVE-1).[79] However, even after the recent removal of overpaints from these zones, it is undeniable that different levels of intervention overlap and are juxtaposed on the horizon.

Based on the X-radiographs, Coremans believed that only for the two groups in the central panel with large buildings (groups 1 and 7, and possibly also the lower part of group 6; fig. 2.38) were reserves left while the first layers of sky and the distant blue mountains were painted,[80] and hence that they were planned from the outset (CVE 1 and CVE 10). The new infrared reflectogram and MA-XRF maps seem to indicate that groups 5 and 6 were also planned from a very early stage, since a first painted version exists below the buildings now visible.[81]

First stage The large main building in group 1 already existed, surrounded by houses, but with different architectural details – different windows and smaller towers, for example. The upper part also underwent subsequent changes.[82] Some roofs, as well as a stepped gable to the right of the main building, had been

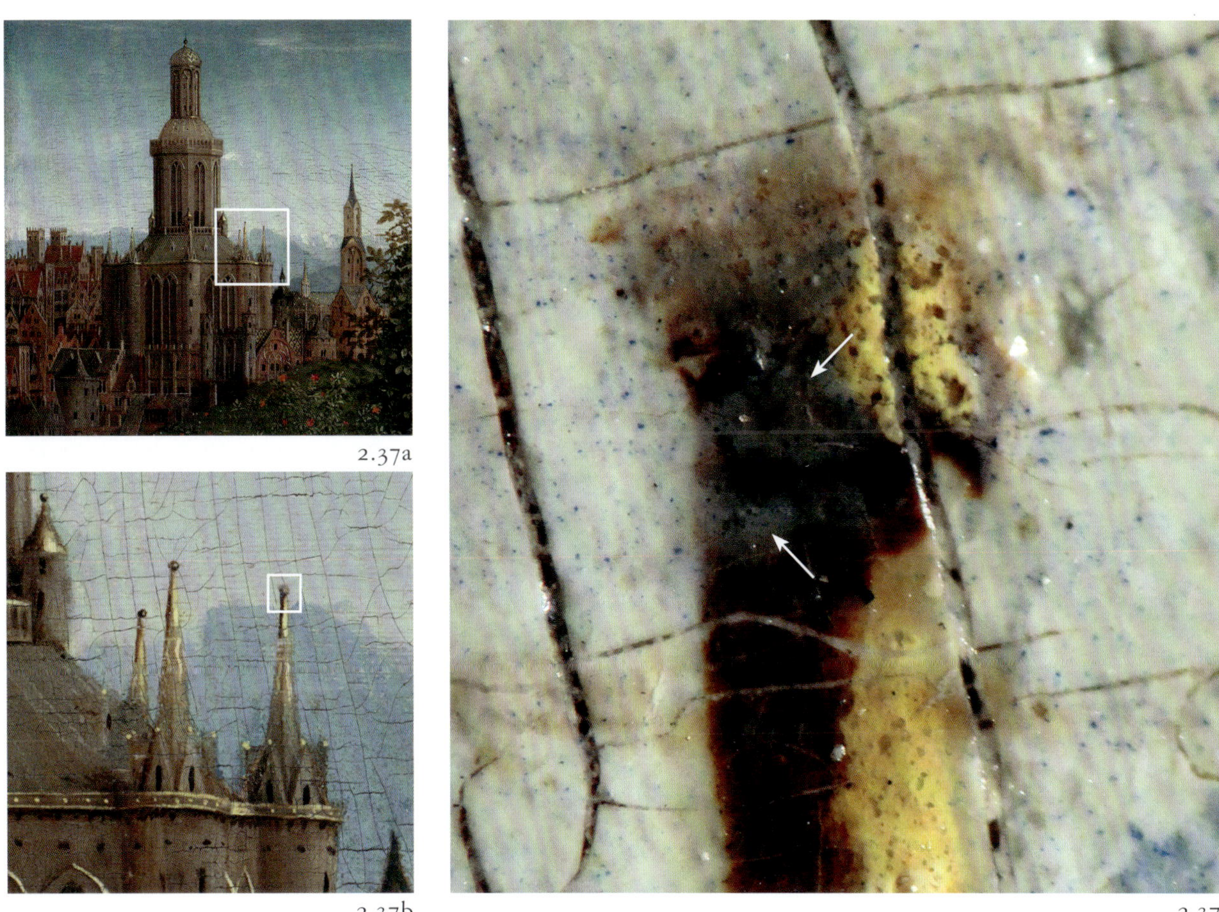

Fig. 2.37a–c. *Adoration of the Lamb*, details (a–b) (Coremans group 1; see fig. 2.38): the ultramarine-containing sky overlaps fine details of the architecture (white arrows), among which a highlight on a spire; microphotograph (c).

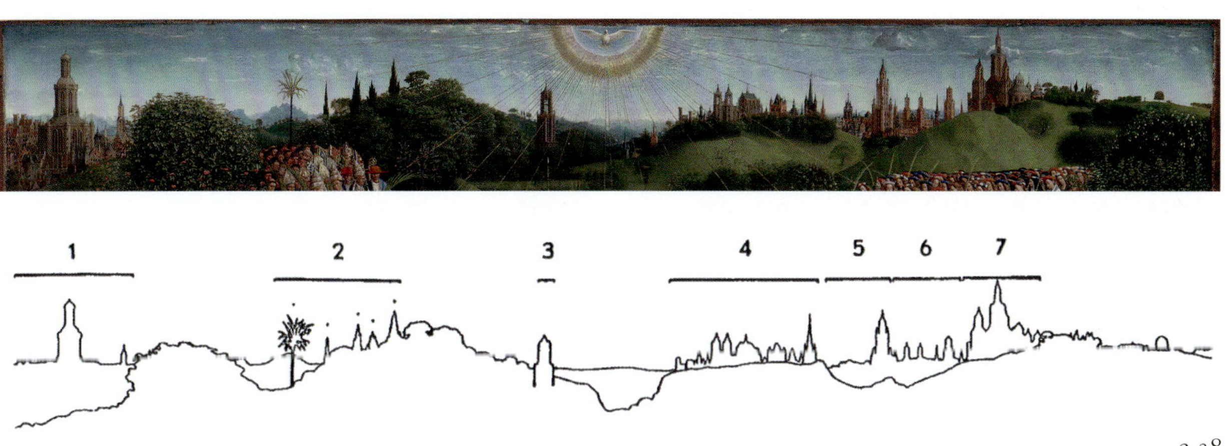

Fig. 2.38. *Adoration of the Lamb*: Coremans's diagram numbering groups of buildings.

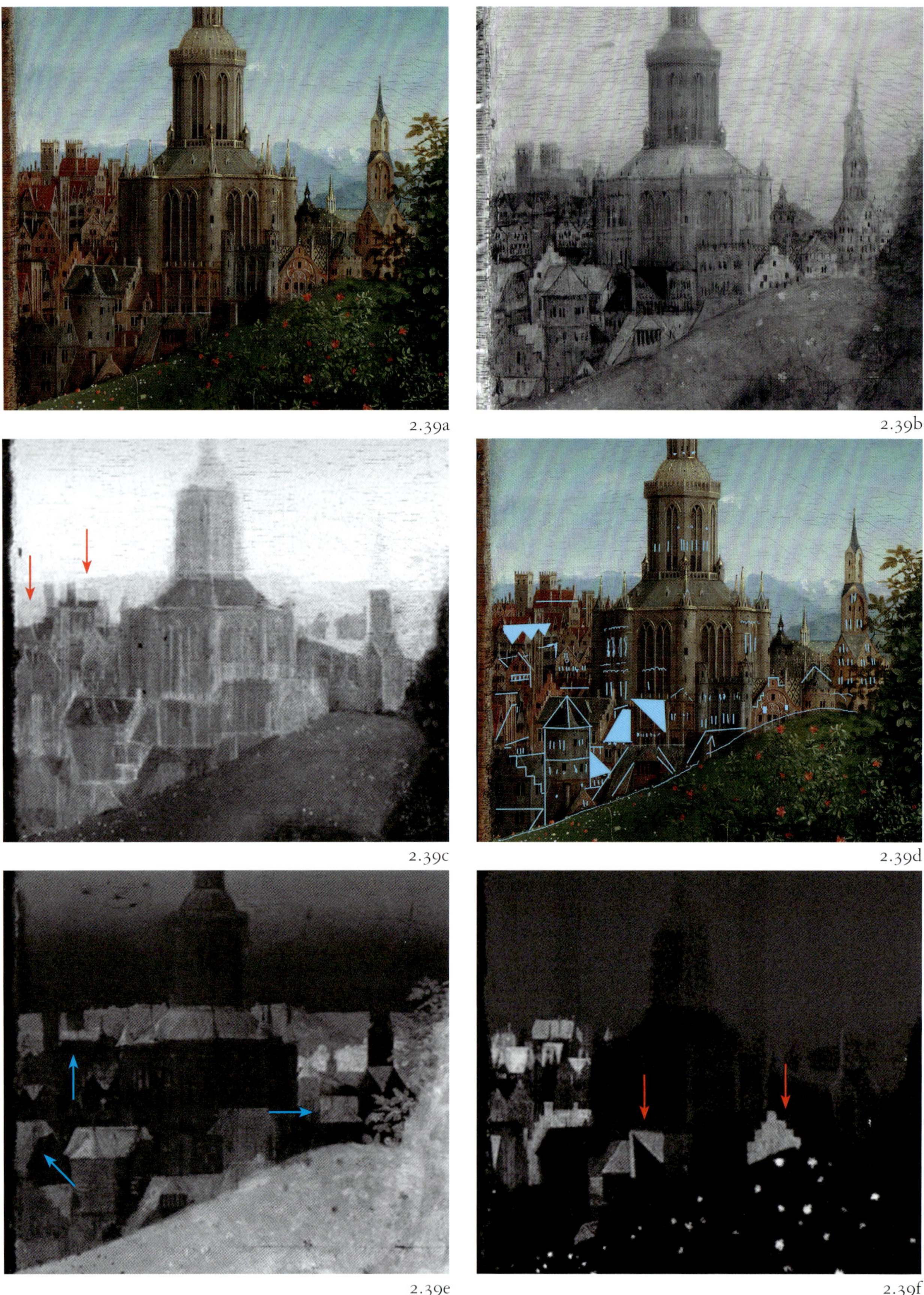

2.39a

2.39b

2.39c

2.39d

2.39e

2.39f

Fig. 2.39a–f. *Adoration of the Lamb*: differences in group 1 between the first and second stages – VIS (a); first stage visible in IRR (b); MA-XRF Pb-L map, some of the mountains were initially painted leaving a reserve for the first-stage roofs (red arrows), and the sky, too, was painted leaving a reserve for the first-stage architecture (c); VIS diagram with first-stage visible in IRR (d); roofs of the first stage, painted in azurite-containing blue visible in MA-XRF Cu-K map (blue arrows) (e); roofs and stepped gable of the first-stage (red arrows), painted in vermilion-containing red visible in MA-XRF Hg-L map (f).

executed at this stage in red paint containing vermilion (fig. 2.39f), others in azurite (fig. 2.39e). Similarly, the MA-XRF copper and lead maps, as well as the X-radiographs (CVE-1), show that some of the mountains were initially painted with a mixture of azurite and lead white (fig. 2.39c and e), with space reserved for the first-stage roofs.[83] The first-stage buildings in groups 4, 5 and 6 can also be seen through the small losses in the roofs of the houses painted later (fig. 2.35) as well as through certain buildings that have become more transparent over time (CVE-11). We can also see via abrasions and losses that the initial windows, visible in the infrared macrophotograph and reflectogram, were actually painted on top of a first paint layer, confirming that they are generally not part of the underdrawing (fig. 2.40).

The central area of the horizon, which includes the tower of Utrecht cathedral and the new buildings discovered during the recent restoration campaign (fig. 1.21) was only occupied by hills. Observation of the X-radiographs, but especially the MA-XRF maps, now enables us to see that the Utrecht tower was indeed painted over a landscape with wooded hills that had already been painted to an advanced degree or even finished, given that we can make out painted trees wich were covered by the tower (fig. 2.41). Part of the light blue hill from the initial concept can still be seen to the left of the tower. It is clear that in the first stage there was less architecture but more wooded hills in the central part of the horizon of the *Adoration of the Lamb.*

The buildings making up group 7, lastly, also had a somewhat different appearance at first, although the large volumes more or less correspond with what we see today (CVE-10). Some conical roofs were painted blue-grey (fig. 2.42) and the colour of these first roofs, based on azurite, is also visible in small losses in the upper layers. The same roofs also appear in the infrared reflectogram, as do a whole series of windows that differ from the ones we see now (CVE-11).

A similar reworking of the architecture is found in the *Knights of Christ* panel. A reserve in the sky marks the contours of a first stage comprising already painted architecture, smaller in size and topped with two pointed roofs with yellow highlights (fig. 2.43). One of the first-stage roofs was not reworked and can still be seen, protruding beyond the crag.

Second stage The horizon in the central panel was substantially altered following the first painted stage, which was largely completed. The second stage mostly corresponds with what we see now, although certain elements were later reworked once again.

The tower of Utrecht cathedral, the newly discovered buildings in the opening of the landscape above the lamb, as well as the buildings in groups 1, 4, 5 and 6 are painted with a profusion of details that seem to us characteristic of Jan van Eyck, rendered with deft touches, distributed coherently, never superfluous, pointing towards studies in situ of the architecture and even an understanding of construction methods. It is most likely Ghent's St Bavo's Abbey that is depicted, with well-integrated corner towers (CVE-8).[84] In the newly discovered 'city' (groups 5 and 6), the smallest detail is represented with great economy of brushwork. Two touches were all that was needed, for instance, to represent the entire volume of

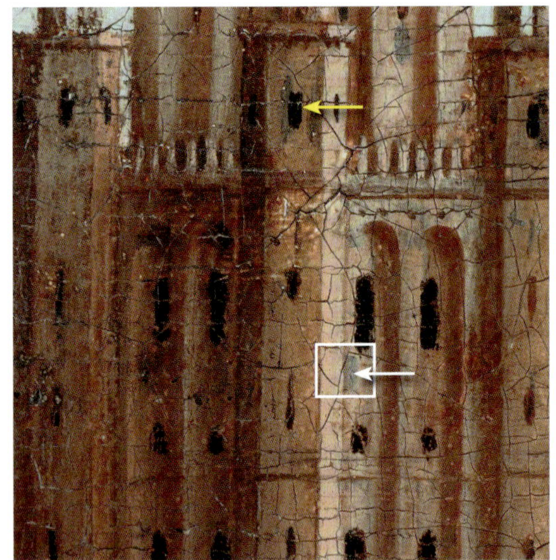

2.40a

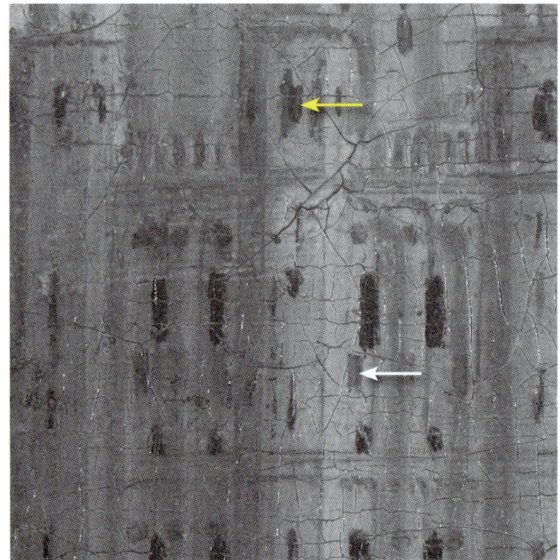

2.40b

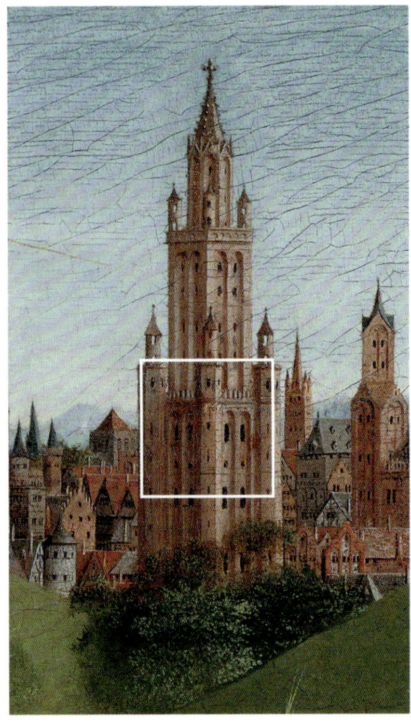

2.40c

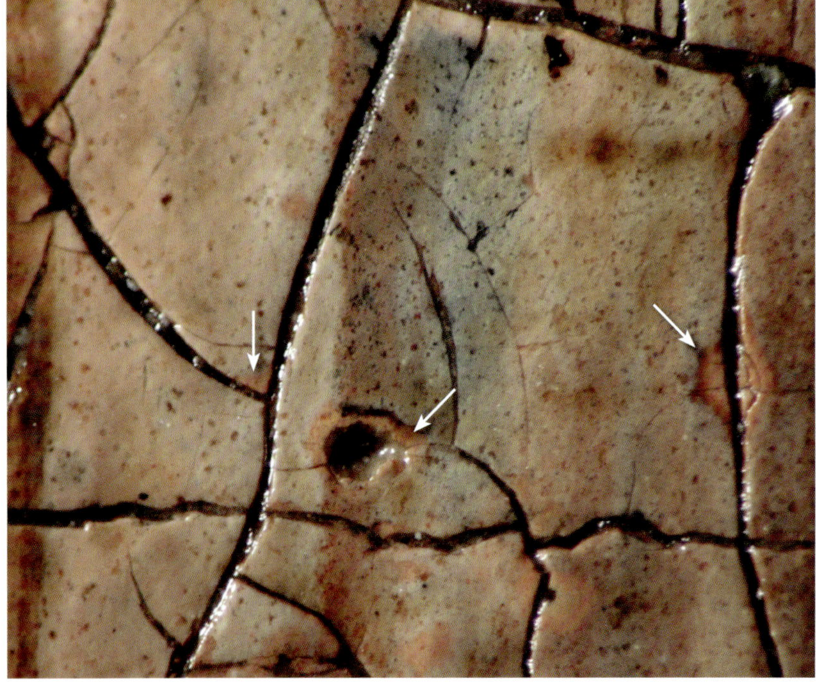

2.40d

Fig. 2.40a–d. *Adoration of the Lamb*, detail (a and c) (Coremans group 5; see fig. 2.38); windows visible in IR (b) (arrows); these first-stage windows were painted on top of an ochre-pink paint layer (arrows) and covered by the second-stage architecture (d).

Fig. 2.41a–c. *Adoration of the Lamb*: hills and trees, including cypresses, of the first stage, hidden by the Utrecht tower and still visible today – MA-XRF Cu-K map (a); MA-XRF Pb-L map (b); VIS (c).

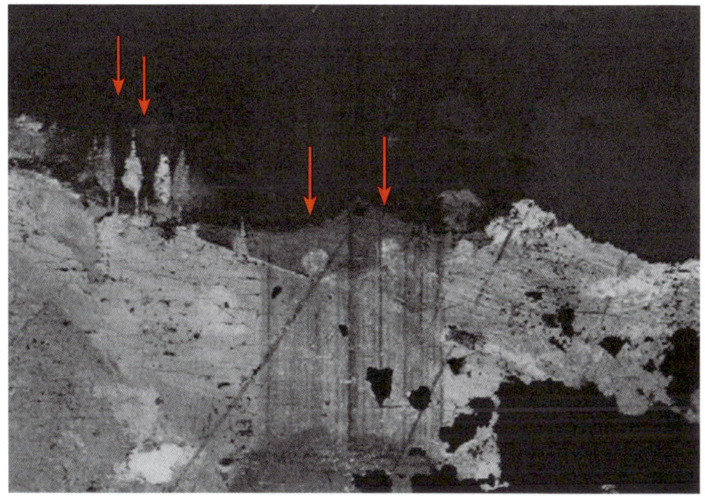

2.41a

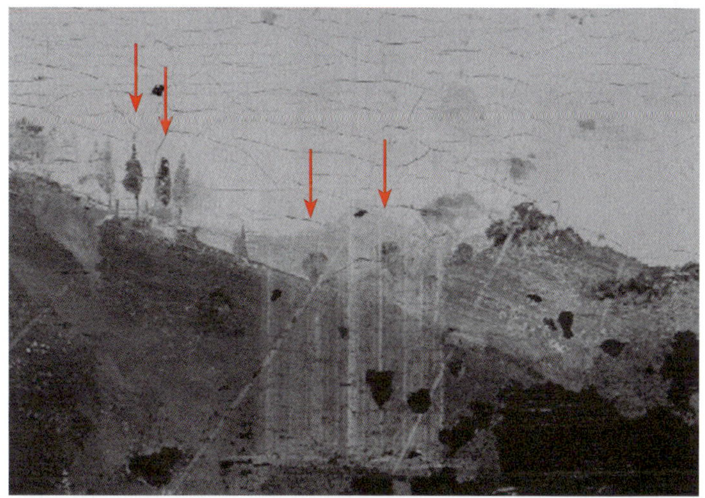

2.41b

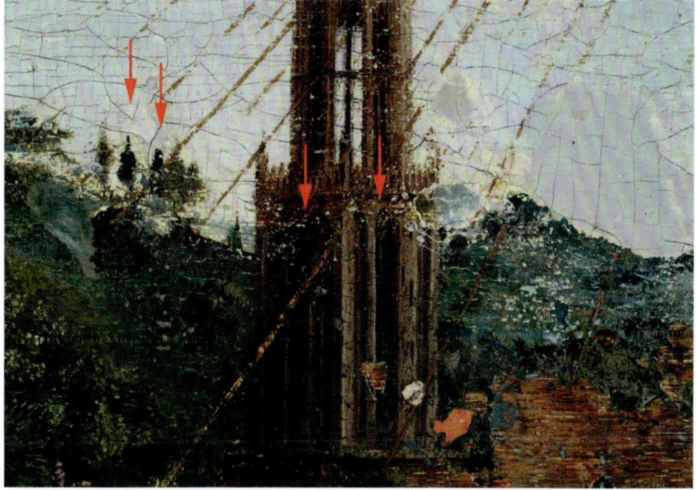

2.41c

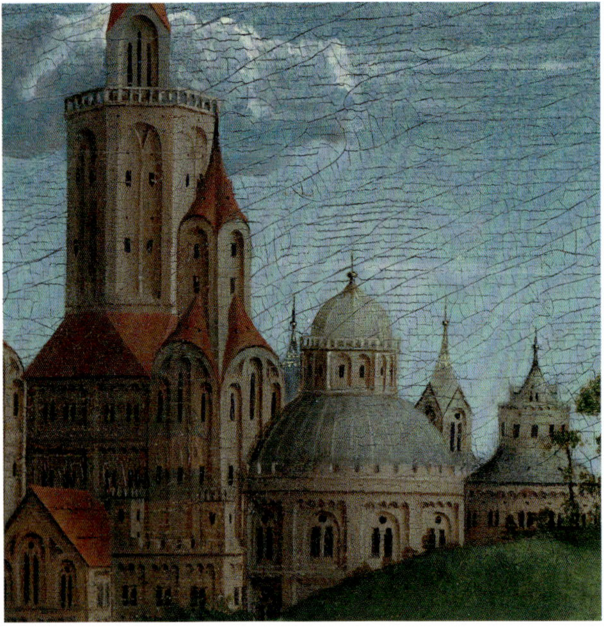

2.42a

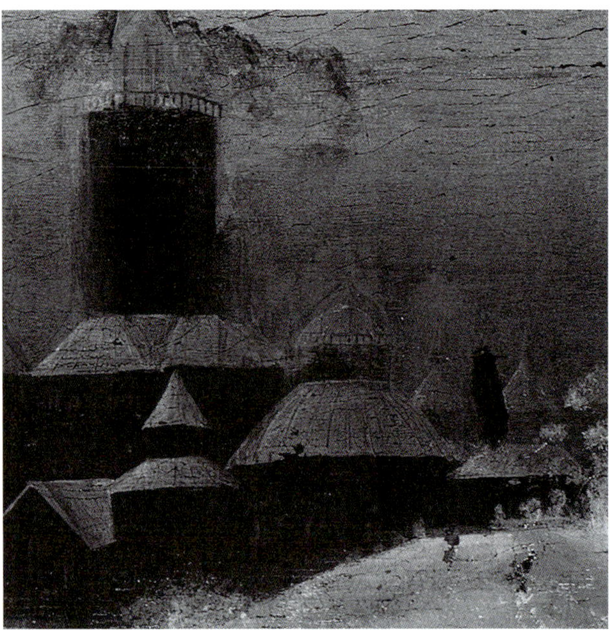

2.42b

Fig. 2.42a–b. *Adoration of the Lamb*, detail (a); conical roofs painted blue-grey in the first stage, now hidden but visible in the MA-XRF Cu-K map (b).

a dormer window emerging from a roof (fig. 2.44). The judicious placement of highlights gives shape to architectural details and helps distinguish a wide variety of materials – stone, brick and roofs covered with glazed tiles or copper. It is not impossible, however, that Jan retained certain elements of the architecture from the initial project and incorporated them into his alterations.

These second-stage buildings were sometimes painted directly over those of the first stage or onto a light intermediate layer corresponding, as we have seen, with the final azurite-based layer of the sky (fig. 2.45). This overlap led to differences in material density between the lower parts of the buildings, painted on a dark underlayer corresponding to the mountains or buildings of the first stage, and the upper parts, painted over this light, second-stage sky. This is the case for the tops of the main building and the bell tower to the left of the large fig tree in Coremans group 1, for the tower of Utrecht cathedral, and for the majority of the architecture in the right half of the composition.

Third stage Other changes have been made, which cover the second-stage painting, mostly by making it heavier in appearance. They include windows accentuated by touches of opaque dark paint and roofs repainted without nuance. In the large building of group 7 in particular, the pointed roofs stick out from the rest (fig. 2.42a). These are painted in a fairly opaque red paint and seem stuck on rather than truly attached to the body of the building, as we mentioned in the case of St Bavo's Abbey. The black lines representing the openings in the walls of this weaker architecture are repetitive shapes, far removed from the deft touches found elsewhere. This intervention appears to have been done by a painter who only reworked this zone locally. The hexagonal tower and round building, for example,

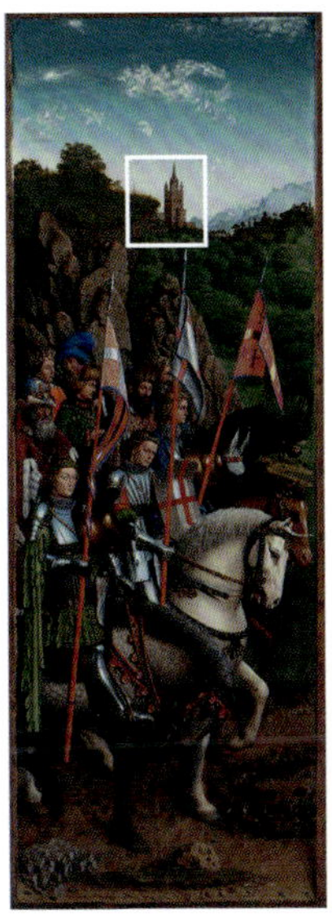

2.43a

2.43b

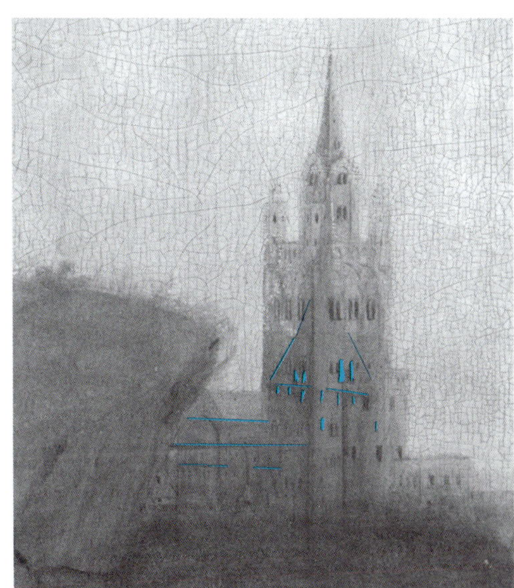

2.43c

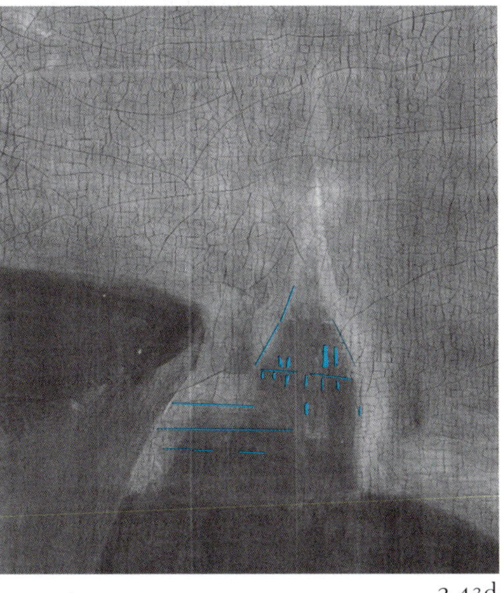

2.43d

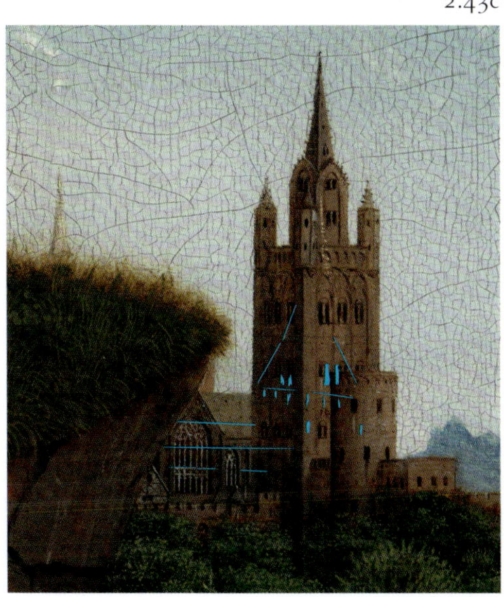

2.43e

Fig. 2.43a–e. *Knights of Christ*: first-stage building covered by second-stage architecture – VIS (a); IRR (b); diagram with details visible in IRR (c); RX diagram with details visible in IRR (d); VIS diagram with details visible in IRR (e).

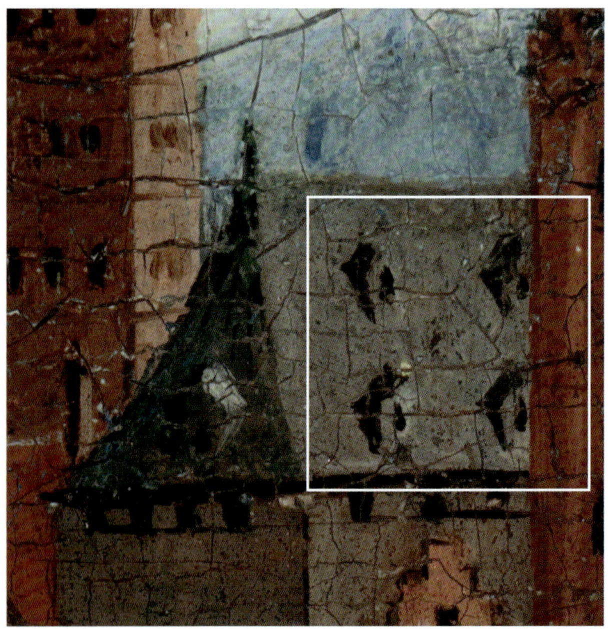

2.44a

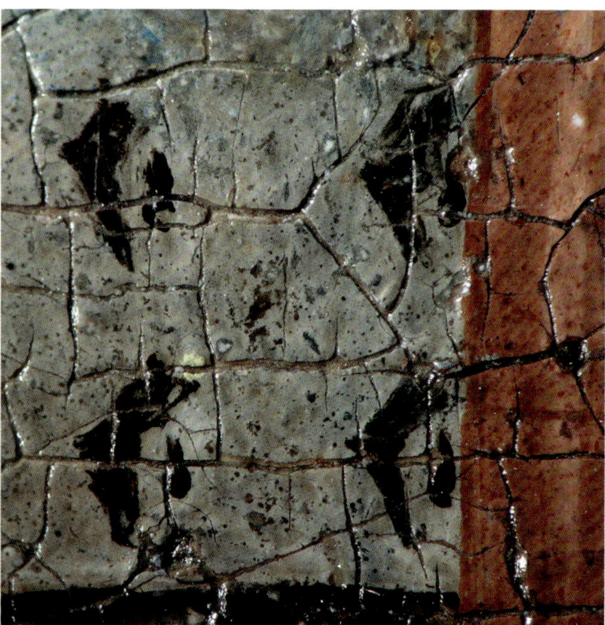

2.44b

Fig. 2.44a–b. *Adoration of the Lamb*, detail: two touches of paint suffice to represent the volume of dormer windows.

are more refined in quality, even if a reworking on the left side of the domed roof betrays the intervention of a weaker hand (CVE-12).

This painter, who strikes us as less skilful, tried to reproduce what he observed in the arrangement of the original architecture. And when he did make noteworthy changes, he sought to integrate them into the ensemble already painted by adding numerous, scattered touches, not only in the architecture on the horizon but also in the vegetation where the landscape intersects with the sky. In this way, architectural elements from three stages seem to coexist on the horizon of the central panel.

The city in the distance of the central panel (group 6) belongs to the stage of the ultramarine sky and is itself painted with ultramarine. It was done after the stage-1 and 2 buildings had already been painted (fig. 2.46). A similar reworking of the city in the distance in the *Pilgrims* (CVE-29), painted between a summarily

Fig. 2.45. Diagram of the paint layers of the sky and concordance with two levels of painted architecture.

Ultramarine
Architecture 2nd stage
Azurite 3
Azurite 2
Architecture 1st stage
Azurite 1
Indigo

2.45

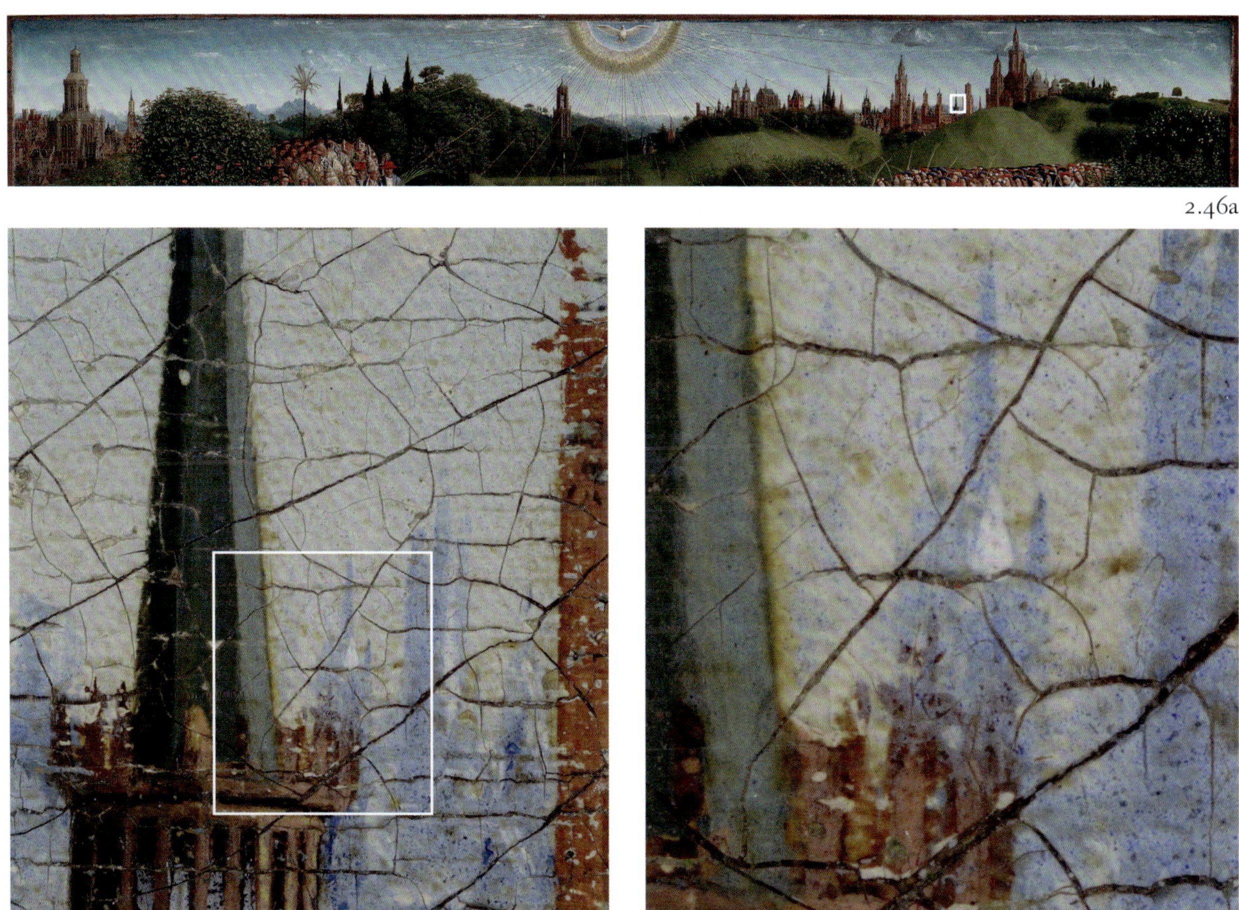

2.46a

2.46b

2.46c

Fig. 2.46a–c. *Adoration of the Lamb*: the ultramarine layer (sky and architecture of distant city) skirts and slightly overlaps the painted architecture.

executed dark blue foreground and mountains in the distance,[85] covers a first landscape[86] done in lighter and warmer tints and can be made out between the brushstrokes of the urban landscape we see today. Some buildings in the distance seem to have been planned from the underdrawing stage: the infrared reflectogram of this area appears to confirm this (CVE-29), unless what we see is – as elsewhere – the painted realization of a first city. The silhouettes of the buildings are summarily rendered and the light touches to suggest stretches of wall or roof lit by the sun are placed randomly, without introducing volume or perspective, contrary to what is seen in the majority of the buildings in the central panel. Similarly, the dark-blue foreground is painted without nuance. It reprises the idea of the first level in the stratigraphy of the underlying landscape painted in green, but without introducing variations. However, the dark-blue stripe and the architecture pass below the trees placed in front, whether it be the cypress, the palm or the small trees closer to the city skyline. The painter who executed this city retouched and enlarged the vegetation painted in front of it to further integrate his addition. The infrared macrophotograph and the reflectogram show a difference in the distribution of black pigments in the branching of the cypress in front of the city, suggesting that these were reworked (CVE-29).

The horizon of the *Knights of Christ* was then also modified after a first painting that might have been completed. The blue mountains and dark-brown vegetation are similarly painted with few nuances: we will return to them in chapter 4.

Fig. 2.47a–b. *Hermits*: first-stage tree trunks in the MA-XRF Pb-L map (a) covered with second-stage green foliage – VIS (b).

Trees

First and second stages Some adjustments to the landscapes were already noted by Coremans and Van Asperen de Boer, particularly in the thickets of trees.[87] The infrared images show a larger number of trunks than we see today and their volume already seems to have been well established, as the position of knots in the wood (CVE-2), for instance, was already indicated.[88] In some cases the trees had even been painted, as in the *Hermits* and *Pilgrims*, where a certain modelling is visible in the X-radiograph and the MA-XRF maps (Ca-K/Pb-L/Fe-K/Zn-K) (fig. 2.47, CVE-24 and CVE-27), implying a first pictorial layer at least. These more numerous first-stage trunks were then partly concealed by foliage in the shutters or, in the *Adoration*, completely masked by flower beds painted on the second-stage meadow. To give an example, a small tree planned for the first stage in the central panel was ultimately replaced by a herbaceous plant (CVE-2).[89] The mass of foliage to the left of the confessors in the central panel, which now consists of a large fig tree, rose bushes and pomegranate trees, must have looked more like a thicket of trees with the base of the trunks visible, similar to the existing ash and almond trees[90] to the right of the same group. The infrared reflectogram reveals what this first idea looked like, with visible trunks (CVE-2).[91] The infrared reflectogram made during the treatment also shows the presence of two large trees – likewise with visible trunks – beneath the tower of Utrecht cathedral (fig. 2.48). They are now hidden by the smaller bushes of the second-stage meadow. It is hard to make out whether these trees were also painted: the MA-XRF maps do not confirm this and the zone in question is also one of the most damaged parts of the panel.

All these trees with visible trunks, which were intended to provide a certain continuity between the central panel and the shutters, appear to belong to the first stage, given that, in the central panel, they were covered by the second meadow and the flowers dotting it. It is hard to determine the extent to which these trees with visible trunks were painted or not.

Coremans also noted that some trees[92] in the landscape on the right of the *Knights of Christ* conceal an initial landscape organized in three receding planes.[93] This landscape was already painted, since it is visible in the X-radiograph and the lead, copper and iron MA-XRF maps, in which a path can be made out meandering across this preliminary landscape (CVE-20). A sample taken from an area of meadow shows a superimposition of six green paint layers, including a glaze above three yellow-green layers. The glaze has itself been covered with an opaque layer and then again with a green glaze, as seen in the meadow of the central panel, which tends to confirm that the first landscape had already been painted to an advanced stage or even completed.

Fig. 2.48a–b. *Adoration of the Lamb*, detail (a); two first-stage trees can be made out between the tower of Utrecht cathedral and the altar in the IRR (b); see also CVE.

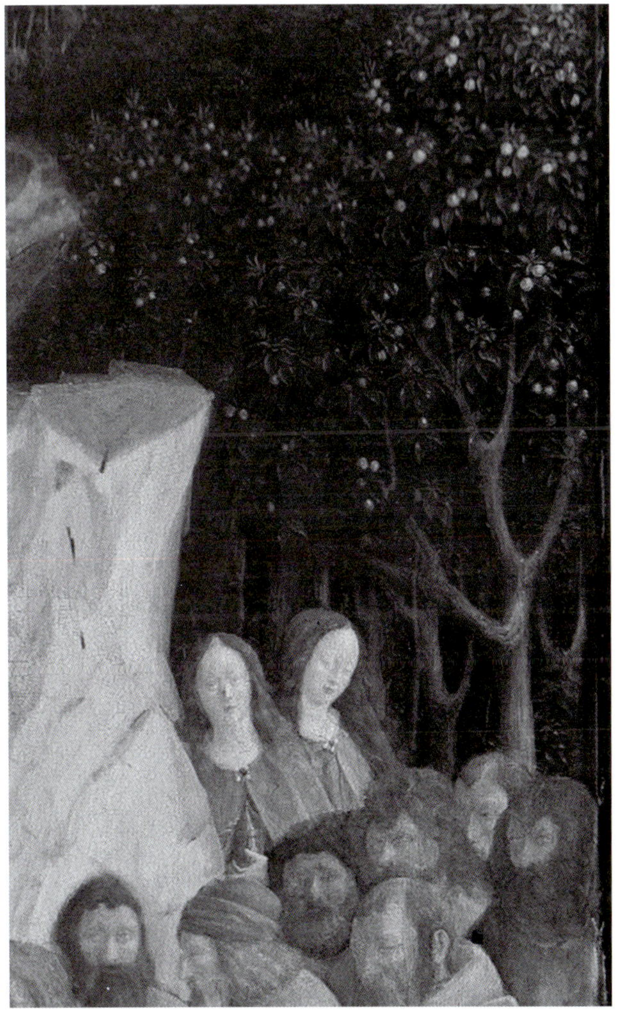
2.47a

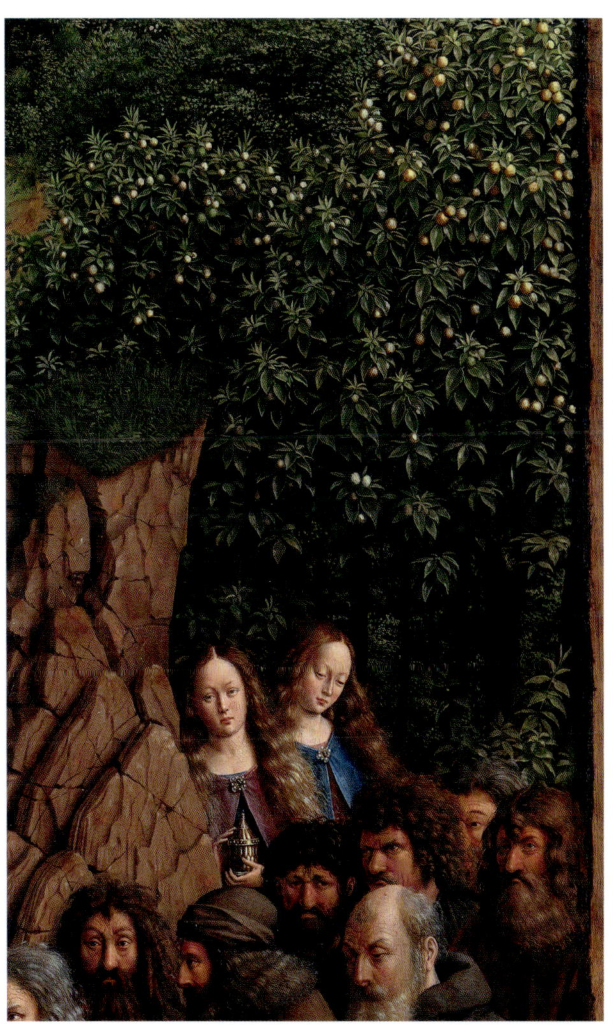
2.47b

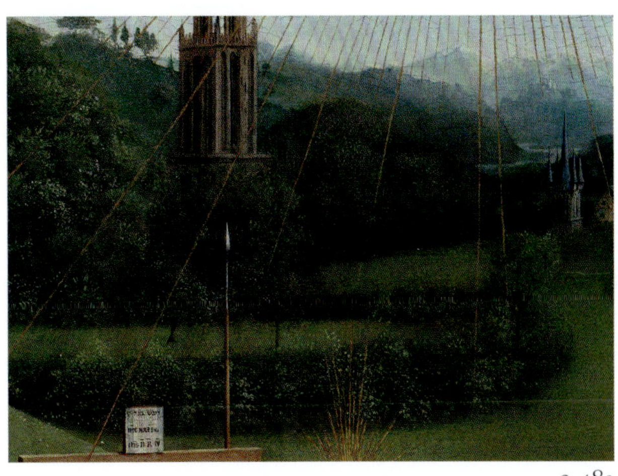
2.48a

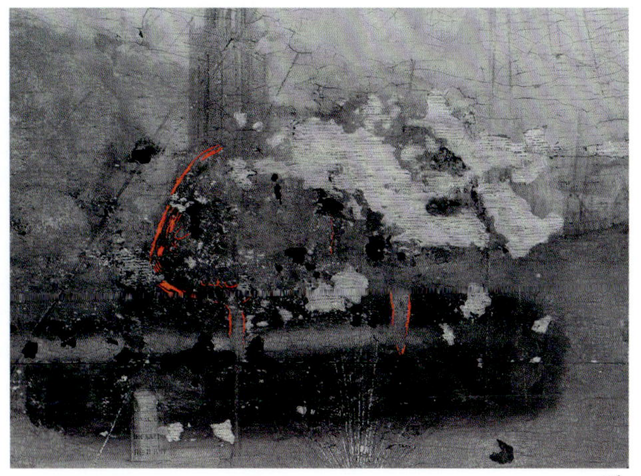
2.48b

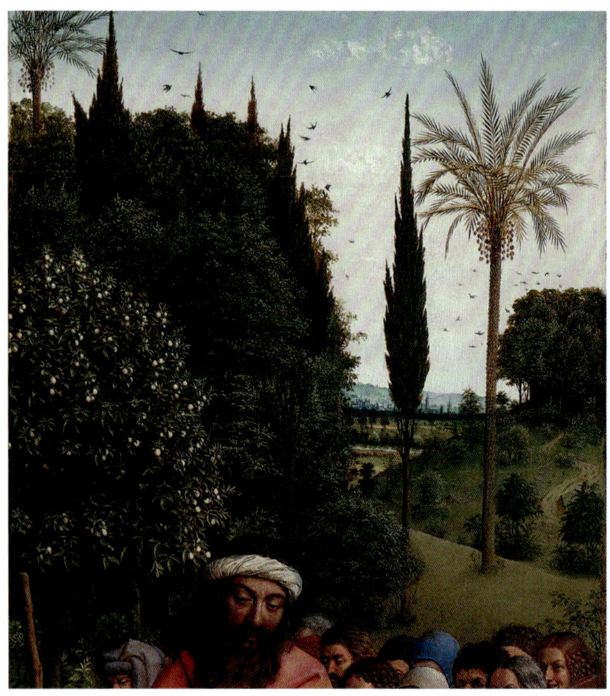

2.49a

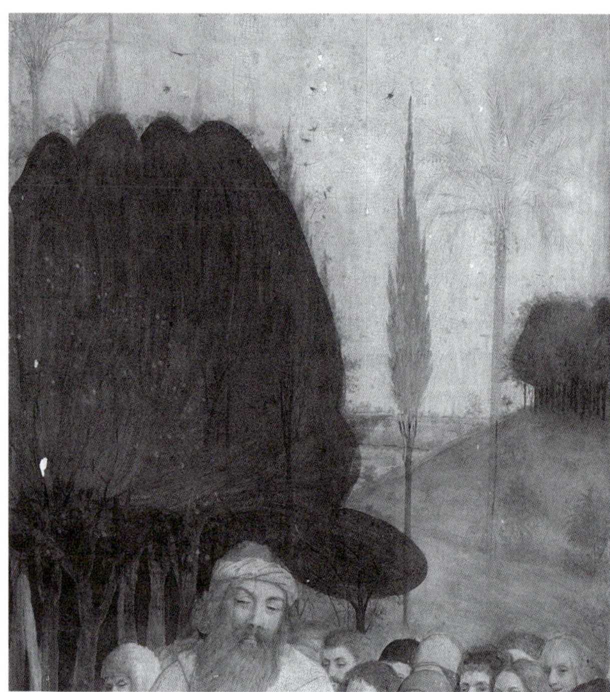

2.49b

Fig. 2.49a–b. *Pilgrims*: plain black areas serve as dark bases for thickets of trees – VIS (a); IRR (b).

Zones with thickets of trees requiring a dark base were constructed using a similar process in the central panel and wings. First of all, plain areas of black were brushed on quickly.[94] These are clearly visible in the infrared reflectograms of the *Pilgrims* and *Hermits* (figs. 2.49 and 2.50). The limits of this rather thick pictorial material can even be made out by the naked eye through the pictorial layers (CVE-26) or where it has not been covered along the edges of the paintings (fig. 2.50). Uniform tones like this below the thickets or patches of vegetation do not stand out as clearly in the infrared reflectogram of the central panel, but they were nonetheless undeniably applied in order to position zones with thickets of trees on either side of the groups of confessors and virgin martyrs. The difference in rendering probably relates to the typology of the wooded zones: less dark for thickets and darker for deep forest.

The application of large flat, monochrome areas in preliminary layers is a common practice in Jan van Eyck.[95] The technique seems to have been applied before Jan, possibly even by Hubert, as the black base of the spring would appear to suggest. Zones of dense vegetation in which an area of flat black was laid down vigorously before the green foliage was painted can be found, for example, in the *St Christopher* in the *Antwerp–Baltimore Quadriptych*, done around 1380–1400 (fig. 2.51).[96]

The foliage of the trees was then painted over these flat black areas, while the leaves that stand out against the sky were not painted directly onto the light layer of the sky but over an intermediate translucent brown layer (fig. 2.52). Strictly speaking, these are not rapidly brushed flat areas like the black base tones, but brown dabs[97] of varying thickness, which already correspond more or less with the

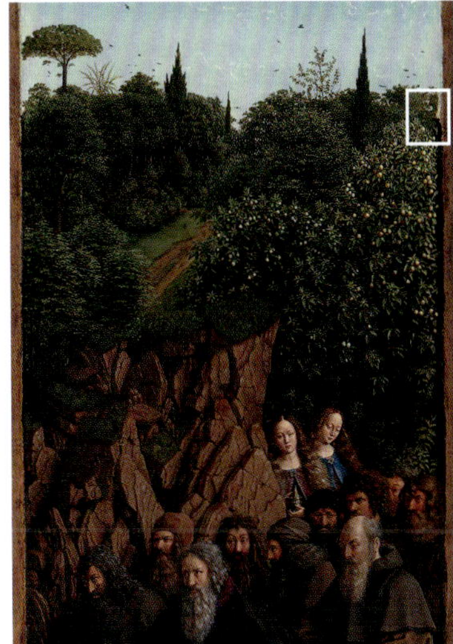

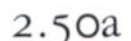

2.50a

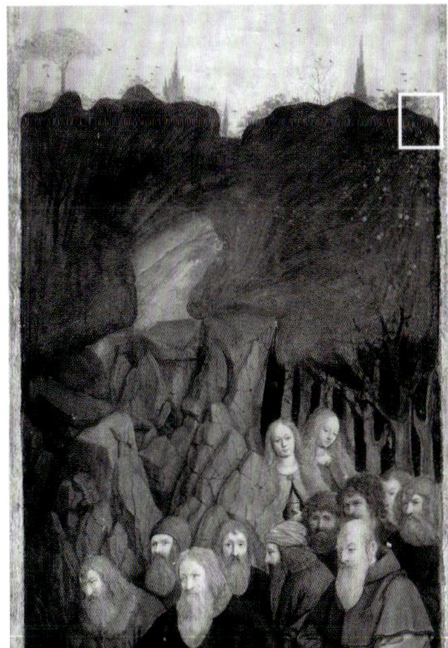

2.50b

2.50c

Fig. 2.50a–c. *Hermits*: plain black areas left uncovered along the borders of the panels – VIS (a); IRR (b); detail VIS (c).

shape of the foliage to be added in green on top. An intermediate brown layer of this kind also seems to have been used to create the leaves of the cherry tree visible in the window of the *Arnolfini Portrait*[98] or in the vegetation of the *Virgin at the Fountain*.[99]

The trees in the *Adoration of the Lamb*, especially the cypresses and the leaves that stand out against the skies, are painted in green over those brown layers, which ensure the transition between the dark masses of the trees and the light area of the sky by introducing a kind of aerial perspective. MA-XRF maps show the presence of copper, iron and zinc in these brown glazes. These elements were systematically found in all the brown layers used as transition between masses of vegetation and the sky (figs. 2.52 and 2.53). Applying the green foliage directly, without such a transition, over the areas of flat black and over the sky, would have

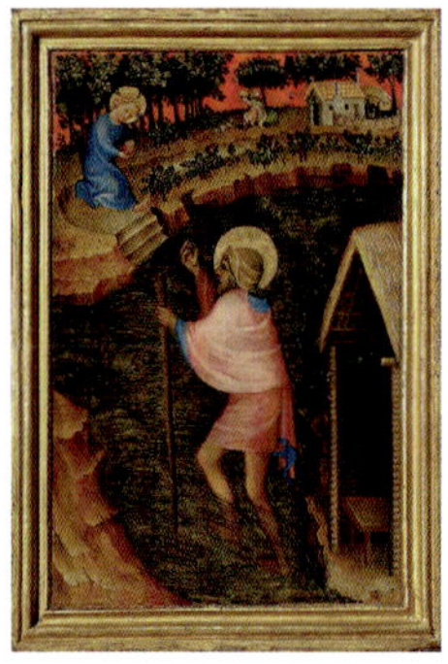

2.51a

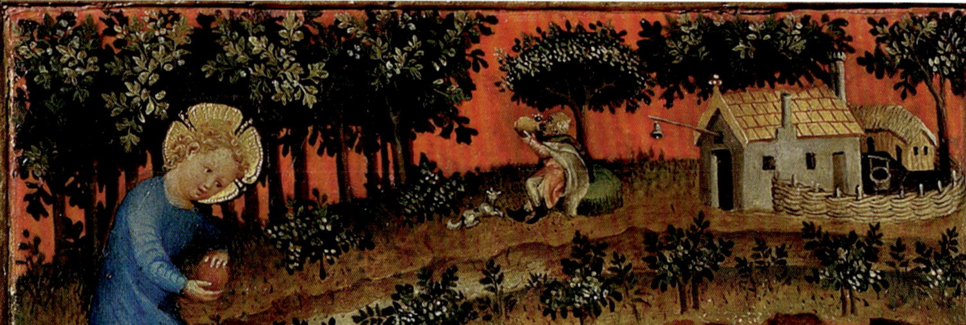

2.51b

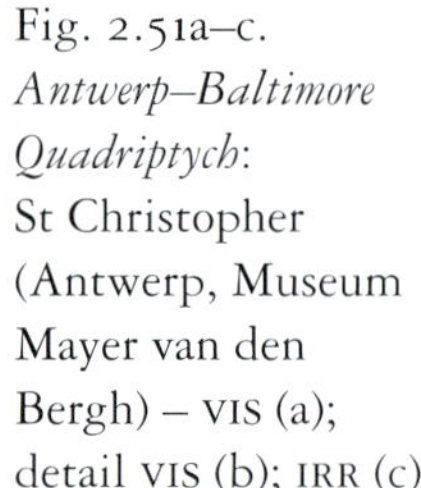

Fig. 2.51a–c.
Antwerp–Baltimore Quadriptych:
St Christopher
(Antwerp, Museum Mayer van den Bergh) – VIS (a);
detail VIS (b); IRR (c).

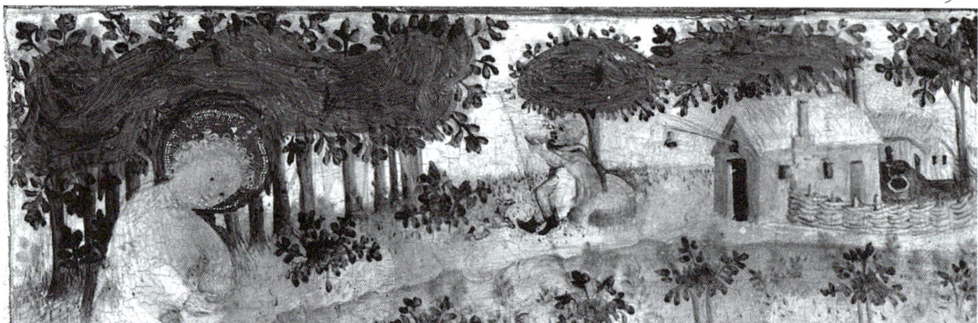

2.51c

resulted in overly strong contrasts that would probably have disturbed any formal continuity. A similar practice is already found in pre-Eyckian works, such as the *Tower retable with Scenes from the Infancy of Christ* in the Museum Mayer van den Bergh, Antwerp.[100]

The flat areas of black were laid down after completing at least one layer of the sky.[101] The brown layer of the vegetation was painted over the final azurite layer. The lead-white-rich layers constituting the sky were applied with wide brushstrokes that imprinted streaks in the pictorial material. This striated effect is accentuated by the fluid brown glaze, which settled more thickly in the hollows of the striations (CVE-26).[102] Use has been made of the black underlayer itself in the final appearance to convey the density of the wood: it serves as a base for the yellow-green leaves painted with rapid touches (CVE-25). The flat areas of black in the central panel are also exploited using a sgraffito technique, in which the green paint layer of foliage overlying areas of unmodulated black was scraped with a stylus or the back of the brush while fresh to expose the underlayer. The stems of the pomegranate tree to the left of the confessors were rendered this way before the leaves themselves were painted (fig. 2.54).

All these technical characteristics, the application of large areas of unmodulated colour in the first layers, use of a glaze over a striated underlayer and the sgraffito technique applied in the fresh paint layer, are found in Jan's repertoire,[103] although they may also have been practised by his brother. They exist in pre-Eyckian paintings, too, for that matter.[104] Considering that the final layer of sky in the shutters belongs to the second stage, however, the trees painted on top of the sky

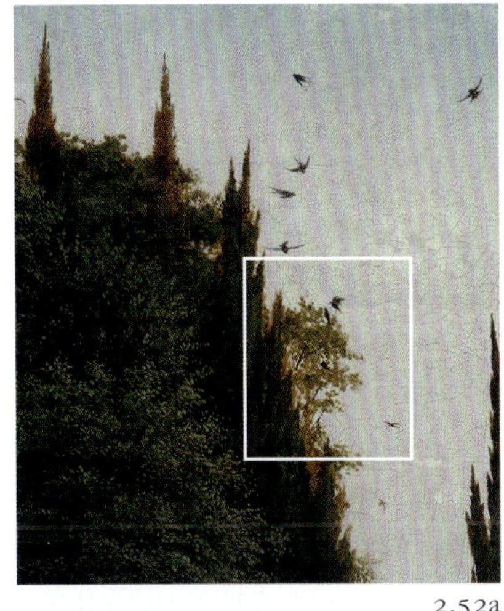

2.52a

2.52b

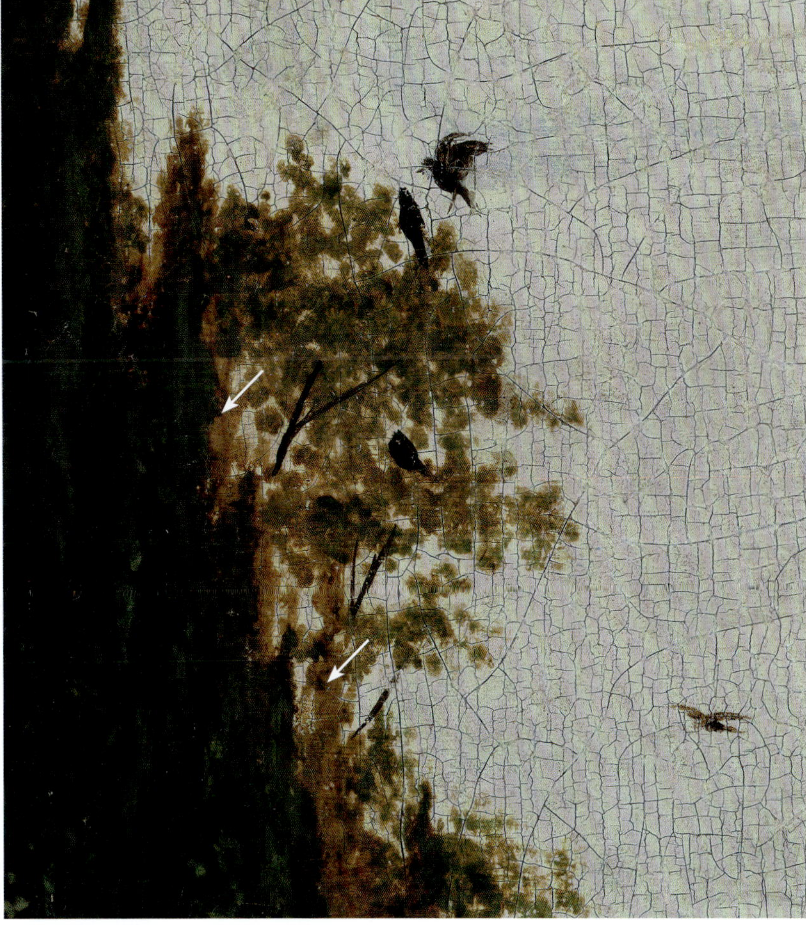

2.52c

Fig. 2.52a–c. *Pilgrims* detail (a): brown glazes producing a strong zinc signal (MA-XRF Zn-K) (b); brown glazes (white arrows) VIS (c).

must be contemporary with or later than that stage. A sample taken from the small palm tree on the left in the *Pilgrims* shows that it is painted on a sky already comprising the four layers found in the skies of the wings. On the other hand, the first paint layers might belong to the first stage.

Coremans noted, based on X-radiographs, that during the execution of the sky no space was reserved for some trees of Mediterranean origin – namely the palm tree and the four relatively large cypresses on the horizon of the central panel. The umbrella pines, palm trees, cypresses and orange trees in the *Pilgrims* and *Hermits* were not originally planned either.[105] Coremans therefore deemed them to be additions made by Jan van Eyck after his time in Spain (i.e. from 1430 onwards) to a more northern landscape attributable to Hubert. Jan van Eyck is known to have travelled to the Iberian Peninsula in 1428–29 (with the embassy sent by Philip the Good to Portugal in order to find a new bride for the duke), and perhaps already in 1426.[106] He spent at least ten months there and had ample time to familiarize himself with and sketch the gardens and vegetation of the Mediterranean region.[107] We have just

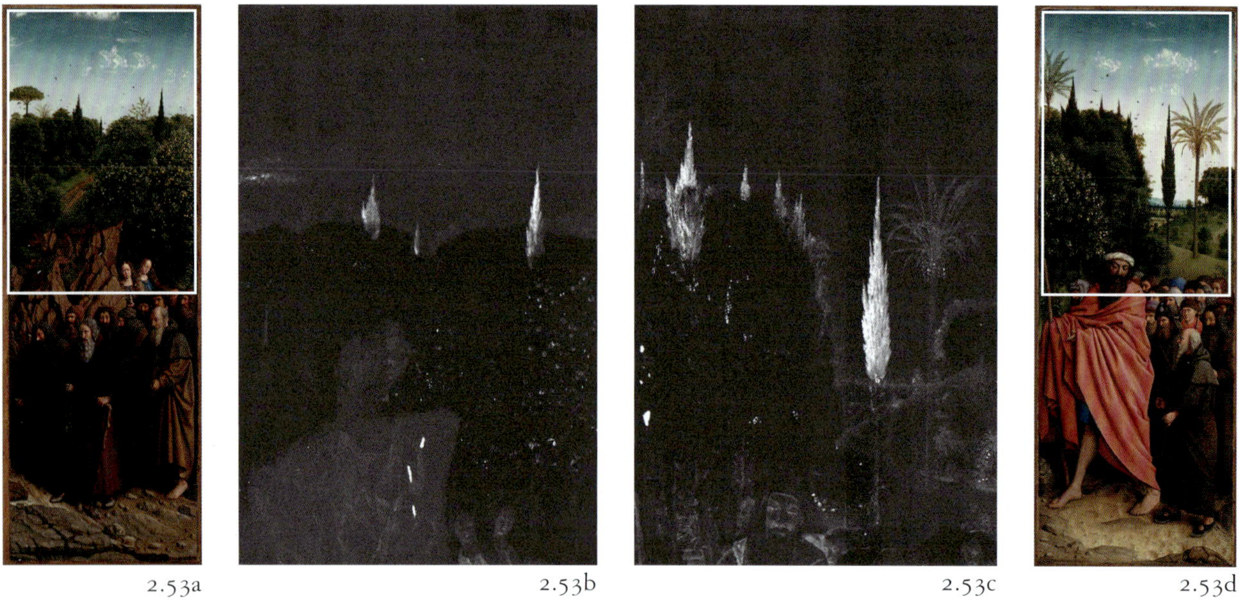

2.53a 2.53b 2.53c 2.53d

Fig. 2.53a–d. *Hermits* (a and b) and *Pilgrims* (c and d): strong zinc signals (MA-XRF Zn-K) (b–c) detected in the brown glazes of the vegetation along the horizon.

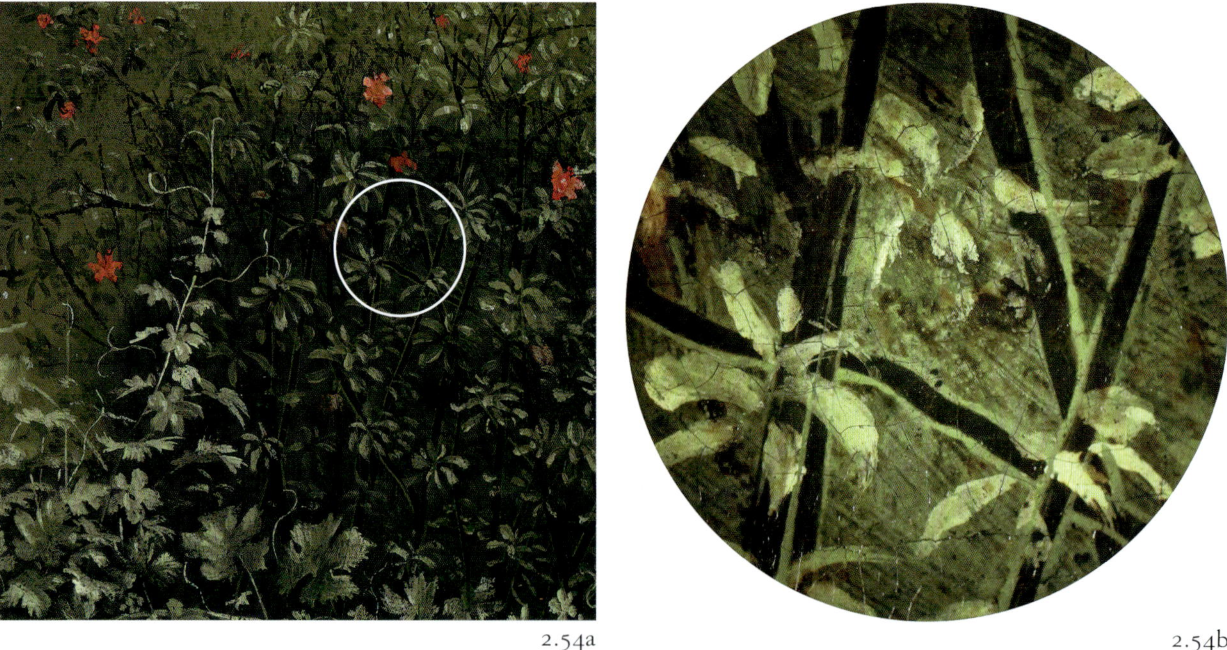

2.54a 2.54b

Fig. 2.54a–b. *Adoration of the Lamb*: the flat areas of black are also exploited using a sgraffito technique (microphotograph).

seen that the smallest of the palms in the *Pilgrims* panel was indeed painted late into the execution. The large central palm tree in this panel was itself added over the already painted hills: its trunk partially covers the overlapping branches of the thicket of trees on the right. The rendering of the typically rhomboid pattern of a date palm trunk, in both the large palm and – albeit more schematically – the small palm on the left, suggests a good knowledge of this species, which did not grow in northern Europe in the fifteenth century.[108]

These areas of vegetation in the central panel and wings were therefore altered at an already fairly advanced stage of painting. The way the thickets of trees were represented in the first stage seems in keeping with a more conventional conception of the medieval landscape, with rows of straight, woody trunks. The changes introduced highly varied vegetation, possibly represented less repetitively and hence with greater animation. They are particularly noticeable in the central panel, with the remarkably rendered flowerbeds and the addition of essentially Mediterranean trees, although it is important to note that cypresses were already painted on the first-stage hills before the tower of Utrecht cathedral was added (fig. 2.41). All these modifications are contemporary with the second meadow and the stone fountain, since the flowers that conceal the old trunks of the thickets of trees are contemporary with the second-stage meadow. It is more difficult, by contrast, to comment on the progress of the trees before Jan resumed the work and to determine the extent to which he was able to realize most of them or simply to insert finishing touches onto plain black areas that might already have been painted. The lack of comparative elements in Jan's work, and *a fortiori* in that of Hubert, makes the task even less straightforward.

Third stage A large amount of reworking that in our view is alien to Jan's manner is found across a substantial part of the vegetation.[109] These touches, done using a fairly opaque and grainy material,[110] were rather systematically applied to the surface of vegetation already painted. They consist merely of repetitive touches without any real connection to the foliage they are supposed to represent. To the right of the large palm tree in the thickets in the *Pilgrims* (fig. 2.55), these imprecise touches fill the black spaces of the underlayer and introduce separations within this mass of trees. Comprising a light brown-green paint, they produce a strong tin (Sn) signal in the MA-XRF maps.[111] The same desire to fill in the spaces left without foliage resulted in the systematic addition of similar touches in the *Hermits* (fig. 2.56), and they are also present in the bushes on either side of the path descending from the thicket in the *Pilgrims*, where they are superimposed on leaves that seem to have been built up mainly using green glazes. These touches are likewise found in many of the cypresses (fig. 2.57) and in the trunk of the large palm in the *Pilgrims*, as well as in the *Knights of Christ* in certain trees painted over the landscape, which initially featured a painted path.[112] The latter trees, too, appear to have been painted at first with green glazes and fewer highlights, and then covered with the same touches, which produce a strong tin signal in the MA-XRF map.

The central panel is not free from such stippled (fig. 2.58) or even more significant reworkings, as in the palm tree, the much more summary rendering of which[113] lacks the realistic features of the trunk of the large palm in the *Pilgrims*.

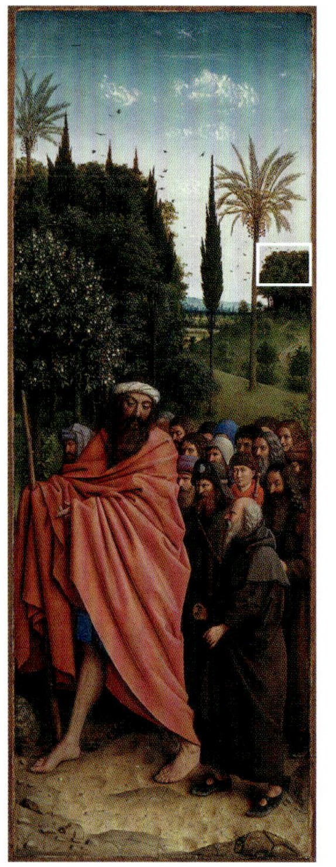
2.55a

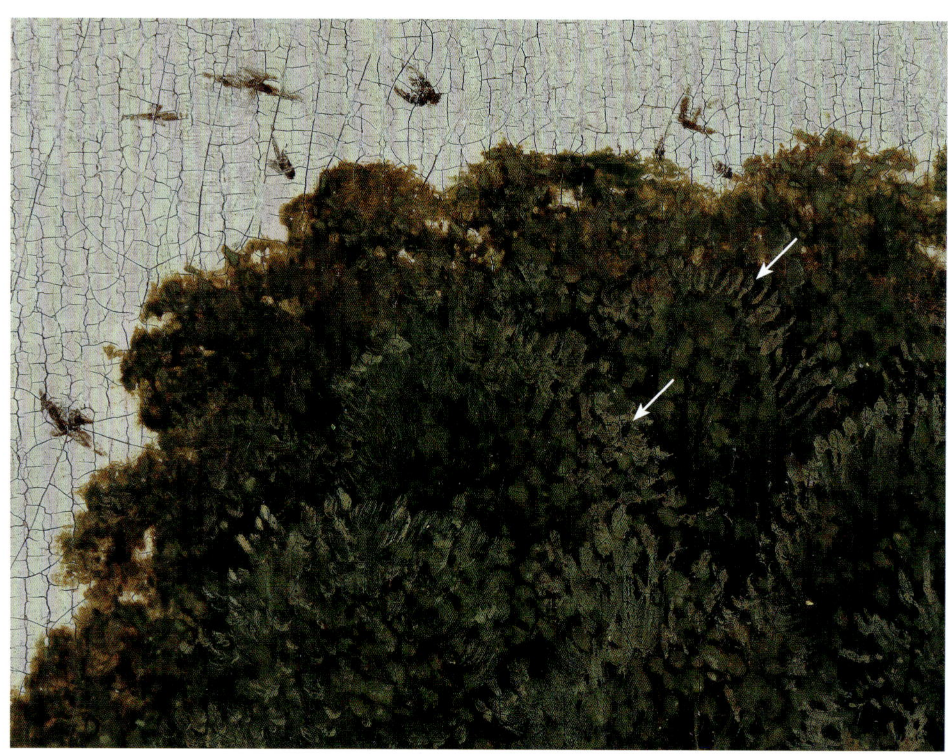
2.55b

Fig. 2.55a–b.
Pilgrims, detail:
third-stage touches.

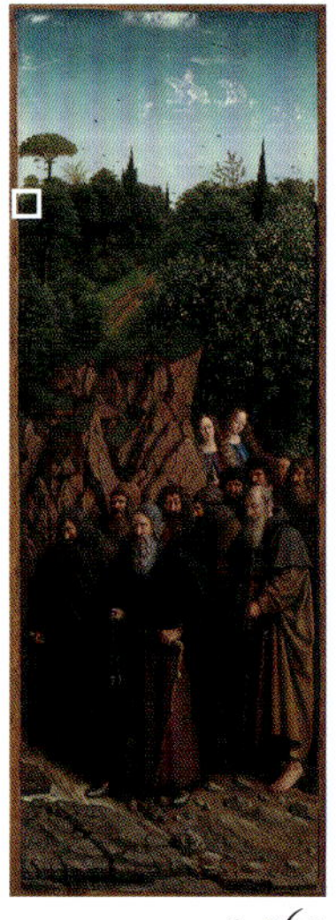
2.56a

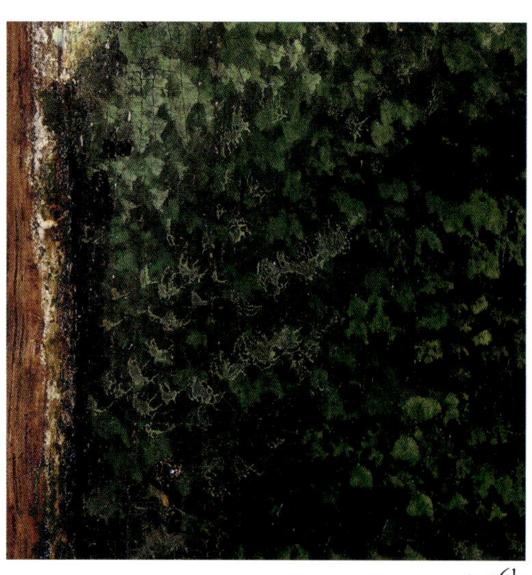
2.56b

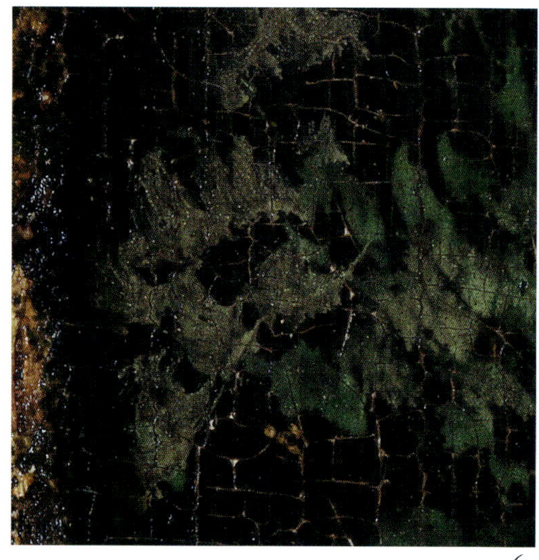
2.56c

Fig. 2.56a–c.
Hermits, details:
third-stage touches.

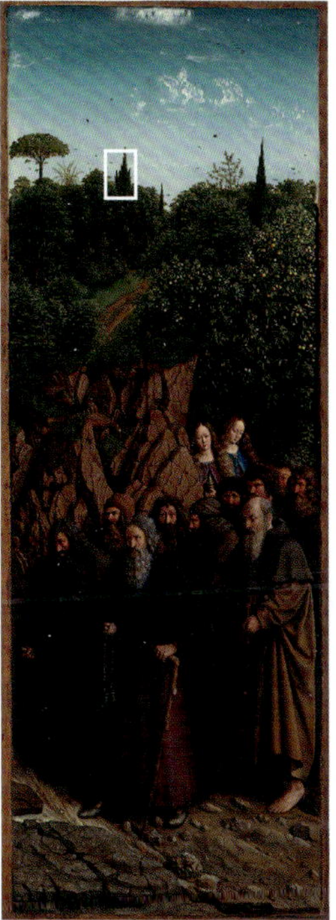
2.57a

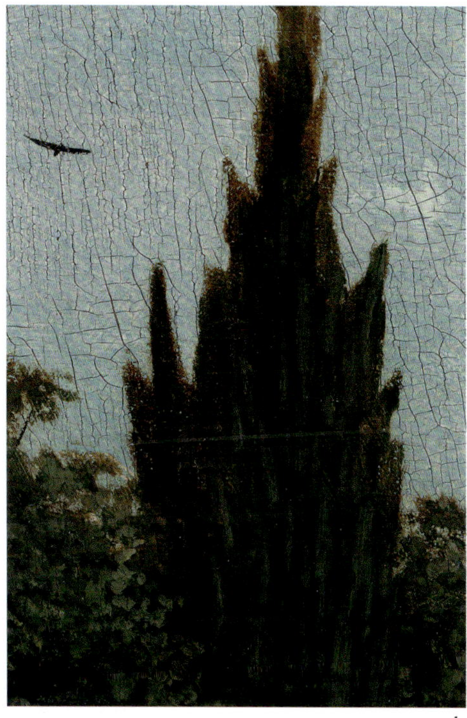
2.57b

2.57c

Fig. 2.57a–c. *Hermits*, details: third-stage touches.

The translucent brown layers against which the trees stand out from the horizon signal the presence of copper, iron and zinc in the MA-XRF maps of both the central panel and the shutters. An anomaly was found, however, in the large fig tree to the left of the confessors in the central panel (fig. 2.59). A strong zinc signal was detected in the rounded top of the tree – not in the now-visible brown leaves that stand out against the sky but slightly below it. It is indeed the original glazes that produce the zinc signal in the MA-XRF map.[114] During the third stage, these original glazes were partly masked by green leaves painted on top of the fig tree. The added leaves – brown over the sky and green at the top of the fig tree – allow a glimpse here and there of the underlying leaves, painted with deep-brown and green glazes.

All the surface interventions described above are superimposed over the second stage, making the reworked zones heavier rather than improving them. They seem to have been motivated by a desire to fill spaces that were originally more airy or else to rework the interfaces between the first and second stages, possibly to make them less obvious.

The large figures in the central panel

First and second stages The majority of decorative effects are found in the area of the central panel with the large figures and chiefly comprise the rendering of the fabrics worn by the philosophers, the patterns and textures of which were achieved

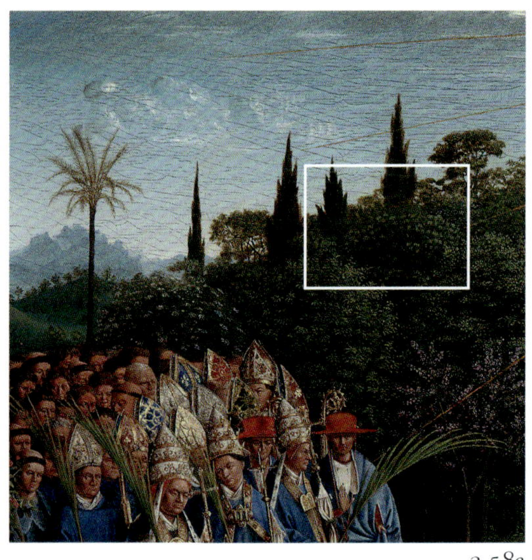

2.58a

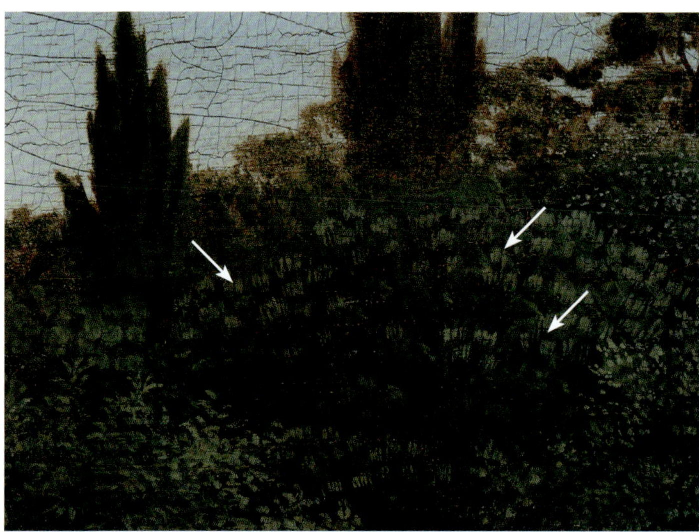

2.58b

Fig. 2.58a–b. *Adoration of the Lamb*, detail: third-stage touches.

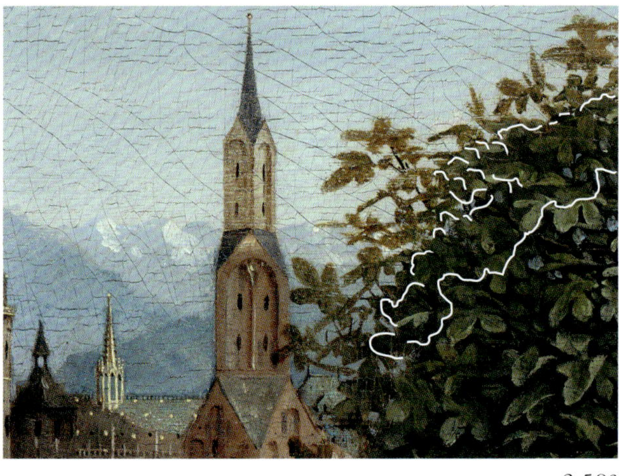

2.59a

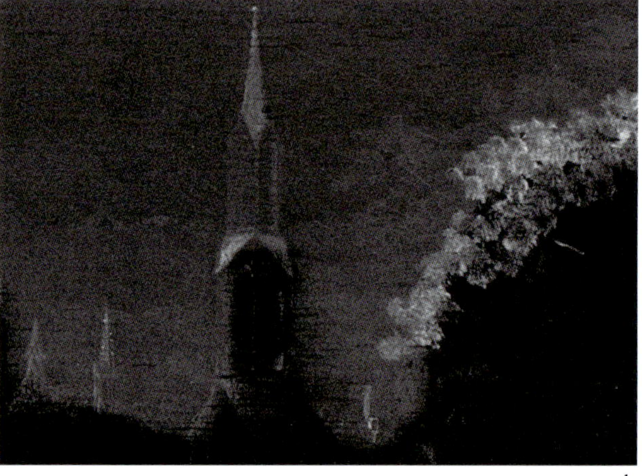

2.59b

Fig. 2.59a–b. *Adoration of the Lamb*, detail: diagram of third-stage touches on top of a partly hidden earlier stage with brown glazes outlined in white (a); brown glazes detected in the MA-XRF Zn-K map, during restoration (b).

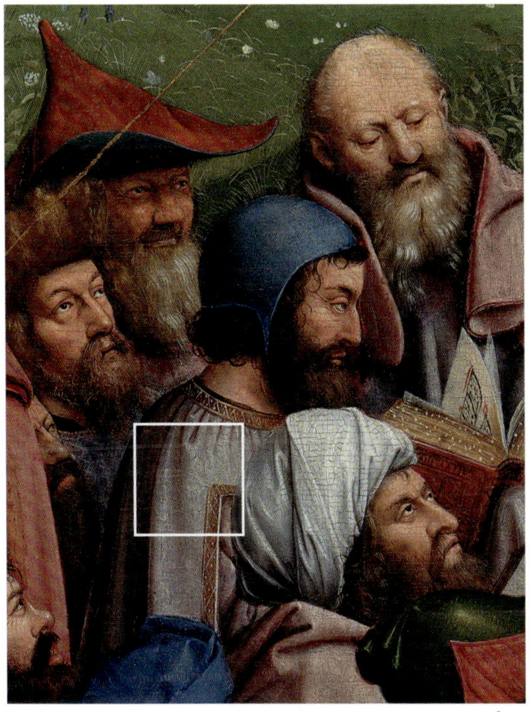

2.60a

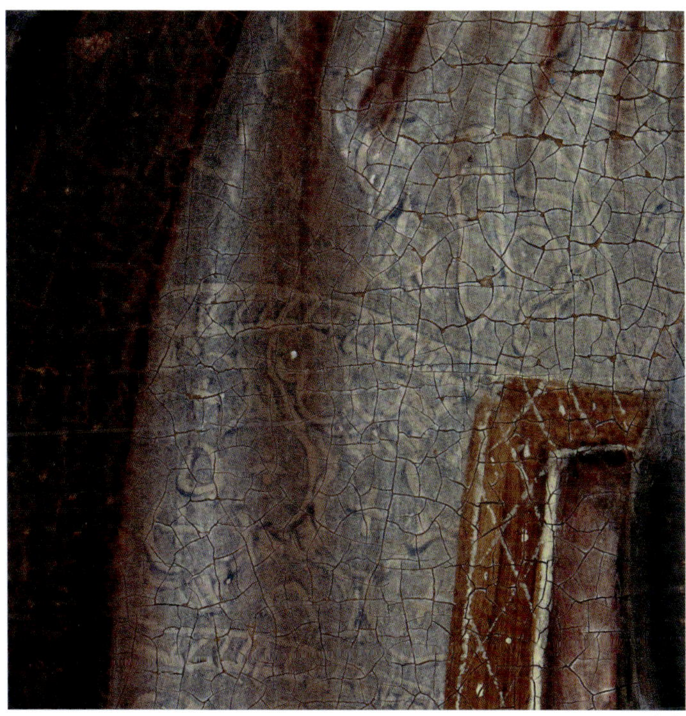

2.60b

Fig. 2.60a–b. *Adoration of the Lamb*, detail (a); decorative patterns realized by scoring the fresh glaze with the back of the brush in order to reveal the underlying paint layer (b).

by working wet-in-wet. There is a multiplicity of shapes and pictorial effects, from decorative motifs scored into the fresh paint (fig. 2.60), a pattern of tiny dots created with a stick or the back of the brush into the fresh glaze (fig. 2.61) to beading effects of the paint layer (fig. 2.62b). The lines or dots scored into the fresh paint to reveal the underlying paint layer are widely used in the large figures in the foreground to the left of the fountain. They were added in the fresh glazes to create patterns in the hats (fig. 2.62c) or to simulate the texture of the fabric in the red robe of the large figure in the lower left corner (fig. 2.61).[115] A similar practice, less frequent in the other parts of the lower register of the open altarpiece, was also detected in some places in the panels of the exterior, notably in the pages of the prophet Micah's book.[116] The process is specific to oil painting, because only an oily binder, which takes a certain time to dry (unlike all other painting systems, where the diluent is aqueous and drying is instant), offers the painter this possibility. The very fact of its use indicates a certain dexterity of handling.[117]

The use of additives[118] to accelerate the drying of the paint and the presence of drying crackle in certain fields of colour of the *Ghent Altarpiece* show that the Van Eyck brothers were fully aware of the technical problems intrinsic to oil painting.[119] What is more, we can safely assume that they were familiar with the demanding rules of the medium and the flaws that may result from not observing them. They actually used these flaws to good effect at times, including the beading effects that occur when a fresh layer is applied to a pictorial layer that is already dry on the surface or when the fat-on-lean rule is not respected.[120] We observed this in certain

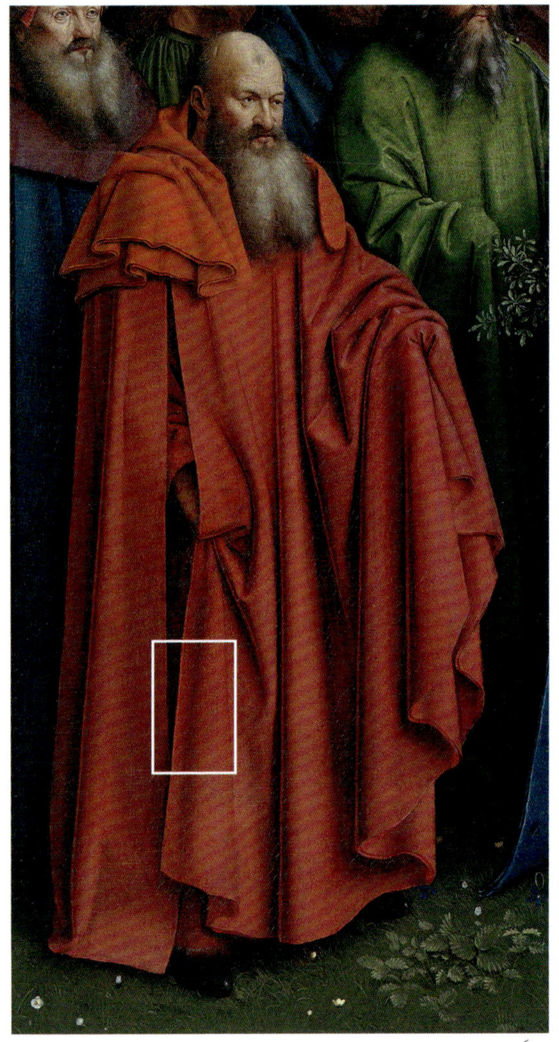

2.61a

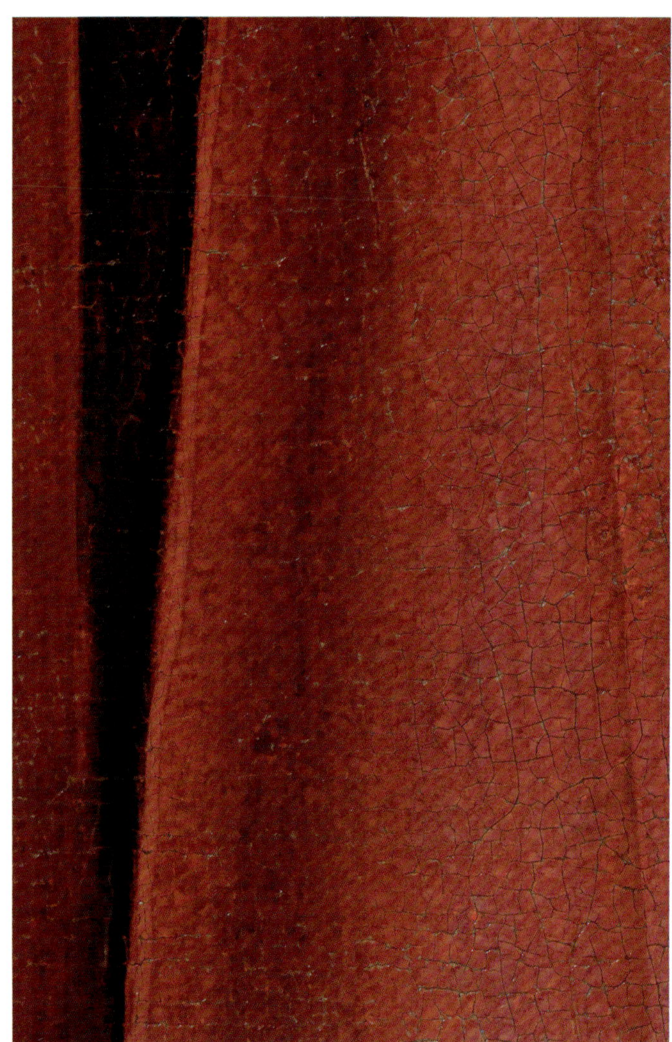

2.61b

Fig. 2.61a–b. *Adoration of the Lamb*, detail (a); a pattern of tiny dots created with a stick or the back of the brush into the fresh glaze to reveal the underlying paint layer (b).

Fig. 2.62a–c. *Adoration of the Lamb*, detail (a); beading effect of the paint layer (b); decorative pattern realized by scoring the fresh glaze with the back of the brush in order to reveal the underlying paint layer (c).

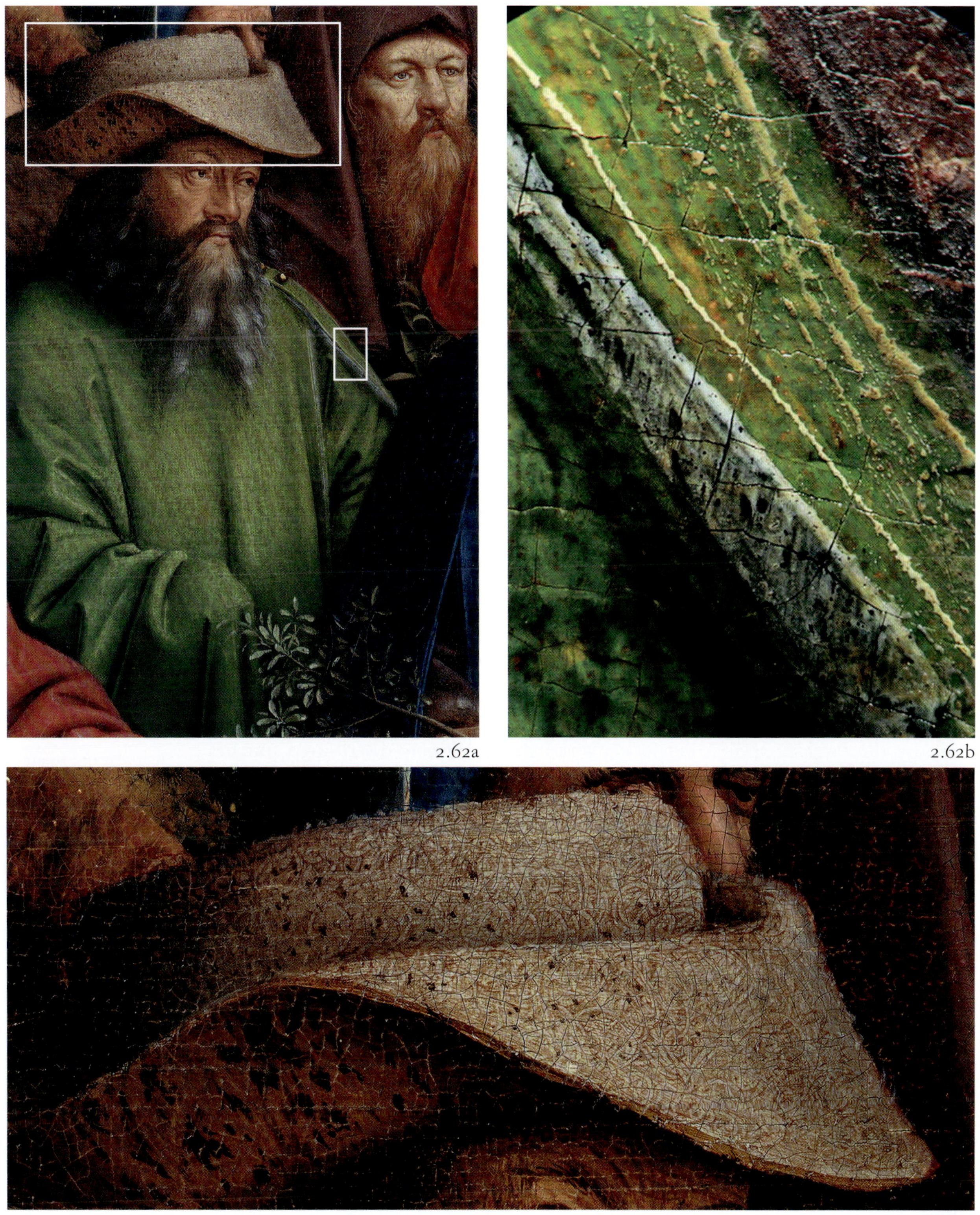

2.62a

2.62b

2.62c

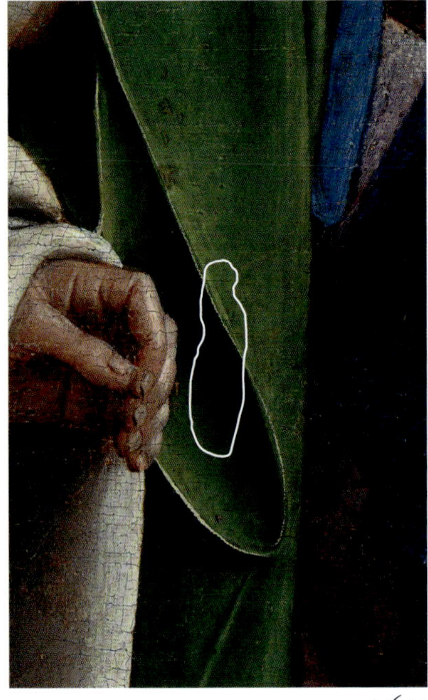
2.63a

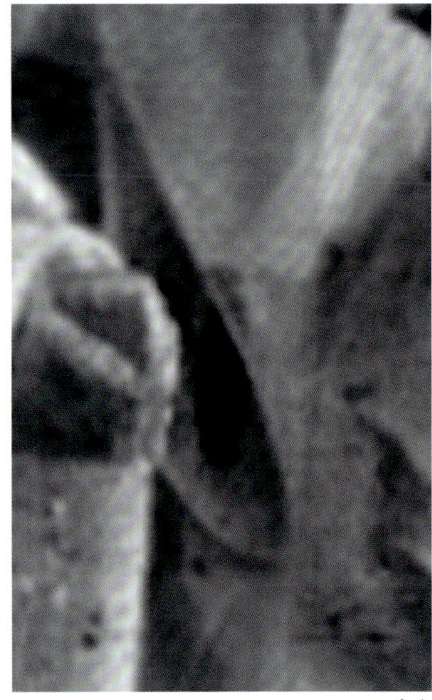
2.63b

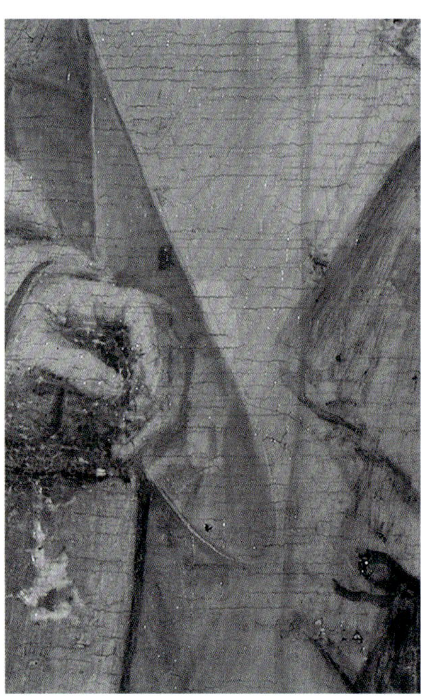
2.63c

Fig. 2.63a–c. *Adoration of the Lamb*, a lacuna embedded in the underlying paint layers, outlined in white (VIS diagram) (a), visible in the MA-XRF Pb-L map (b) and IRR (c).

local touches on the altarpiece exterior[121] and the same is true for the paintings of the lower register of the open altarpiece (fig. 2.62b).

Other material effects were achieved solely through touches of paint judiciously applied to simulate reflections on metal or semi-precious stones, as in the churchmen. Similarly, the coarse, thick or even shabby nature of the woollen fabrics of the robes worn by the *Pilgrims* and *Hermits* is conveyed through finely distributed touches that testify to excellent observation of the minutest details of each garment and the ability to render them in paint (CVE-31).

Techniques that exploit the properties of oil paint, such as working in the fresh paint and beading, were already practised by pre-Eyckian painters.[122] What does appear novel, however, is the translation of meticulous observation through the dynamic distribution of touches of paint to render palpable the nature of the represented materials.

Third-stage changes Modifications are found in the large figures in the foreground of the central panel, particularly where the kneeling figures meet the standing ones. To the left of the fountain, the first standing figures with green and pink draperies were emphasized to the detriment of three kneeling silhouettes, which had already been painted, perhaps even completely (CVE-4). This is slightly visible to the naked eye and more in the technical documents.[123] The kneeling figure in the blue cap wore a robe that was tied around the waist with a large belt, similar to that of the first figure to the immediate left of the fountain. The green drapery was added, concealing much of the original figure. A similar adjustment was made to the pink robe and chaperon of the figure above to partly obscure the heads of two kneeling men. The standing figures dressed in green and pink were thus enlarged to the detriment of these three kneeling figures, which are now barely visible. The effect is to create a clearer separation between the kneeling and standing men. A similar change can be seen in the group to the right of the fountain, where the red drapery of the pope standing behind the kneeling apostles has been rigidly plastered over the back of one of the kneeling figures (CVE-14). Were these changes made simply to adjust the articulation of the foreground or to mask possible damage? The question can be posed in relation to a zone near the left hand of 'Virgil' (clad in white, with laurel wreath), in which there is a lacuna embedded in the underlying paint layers (fig. 2.63).[124]

Coarse touches have been added, lastly, to some of the figures in the foreground of the central panel at the interface between the meadow and the figures, probably to 'improve' the juxtaposition of the first and second stages. They occur particularly at the point where the second-stage meadow skirts the large figures, thickening the pictorial layer. Some touches add stiff hair (fig. 2.64) or heavy highlights to the top of certain skulls (fig. 2.65).

The large figures in the wings

The flesh tones of St Christopher in the *Pilgrims* panel appear to have been reworked. In an already painted first stage, the eyes were positioned differently, the saint looked over his shoulder and his nostrils were more visible (CVE-28 and MA-XRF Pb-L). The giant's hair was extended over his right shoulder, concealing the top of a figure's head behind him. The obscured head shows a strong signal of iron in the MA-XRF map as it was painted brown – probably like the hair of the young boy in the red cloak holding a stick in the crowd of pilgrims. Eyckian features such as highlights emerging from the shadows[125] can be found at the base of St Christopher's nose, while other, coarser touches belonging to the third stage have been added to

Fig. 2.64a–b. *Adoration of the Lamb*, detail: third-stage retouchings.

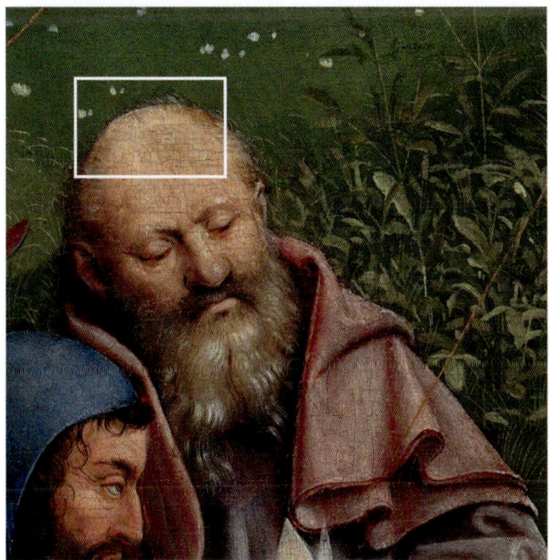

2.64a

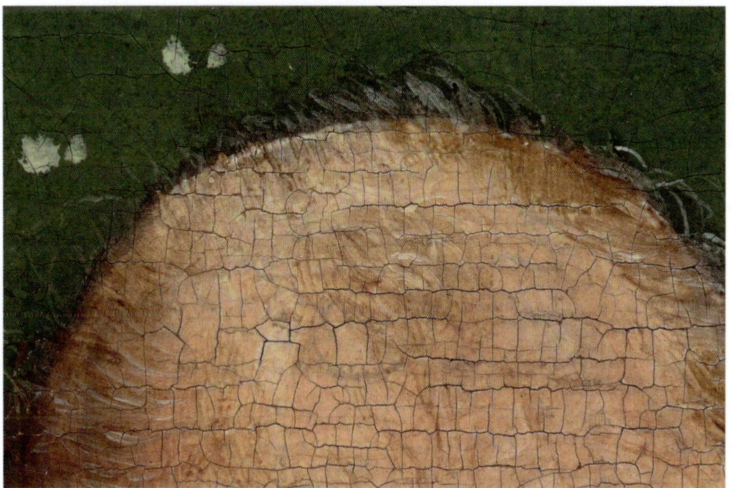

2.64b

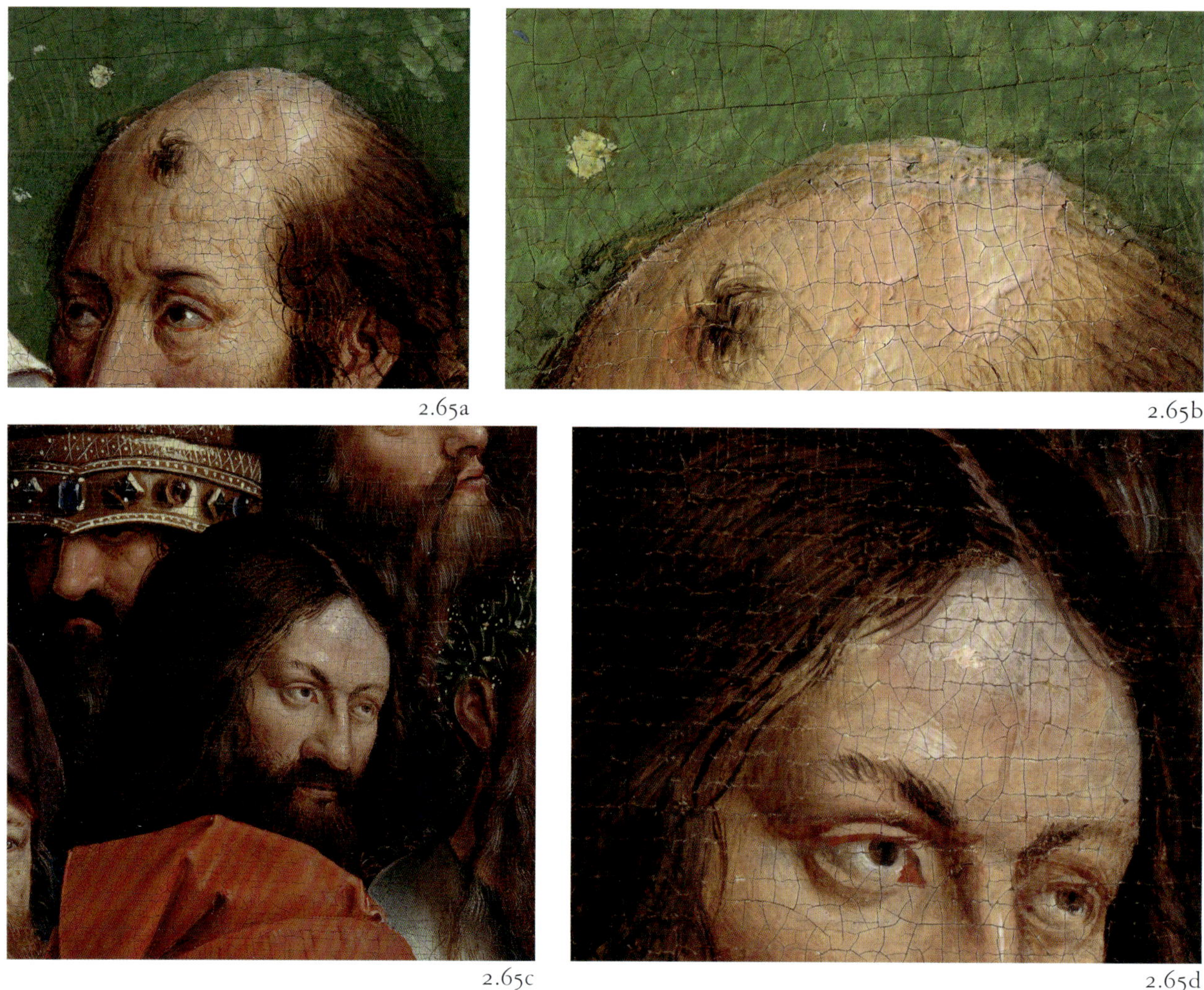

2.65a 2.65b 2.65c 2.65d

Fig. 2.65a–d. *Adoration of the Lamb*, detail: heavy highlights applied to some of the heads.

his white turban. The latter resemble the enlargement of some shapes in the body of the lamb and on the altar, which we will mention in a moment.

Significant elements were modified in the *Knights of Christ* panel in the group of four figures on the left at the foot of the large rock and also in the legs and hooves, eyes, ears, muzzles, manes and gear of the horses and in the standards carried by the knights.[126] The MA-XRF maps and X-radiograph confirm that these adjustments were made primarily during the painting process. We have already mentioned the initial position of the horses' hooves in the first stage, in which the ground differed from the current brown soil.[127] These changes appear to have been made in the second stage to horses painted in the first stage.[128]

Certain other changes, by contrast, belong to the third stage. This is particularly the case for the knight with the bushy grey beard, whose purple, ermine-trimmed cloak was painted over a brocade garment, the patterns of which were painted and show up in the MA-XRF map of iron and zinc (fig. 2.66).[129] A cross-section

Fig. 2.66a–b. *Knights of Christ*, third-stage purple cloak (a) painted over a brocade garment visible in the MA-XRF Fe-K map (b).

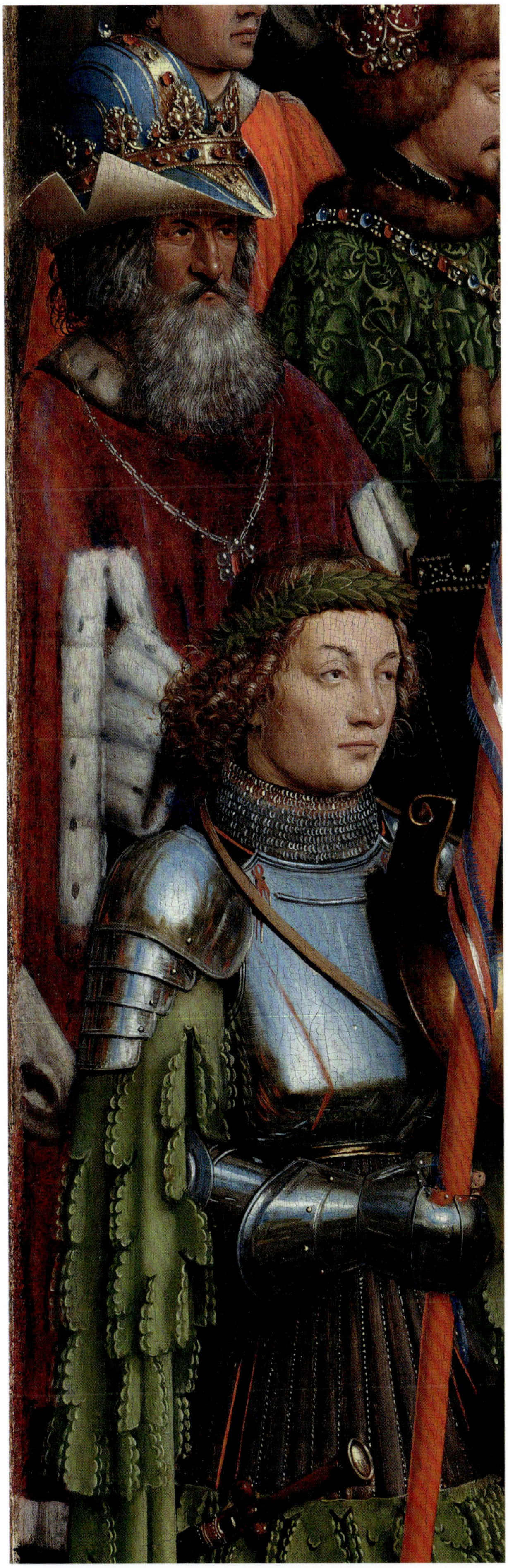

2.66a

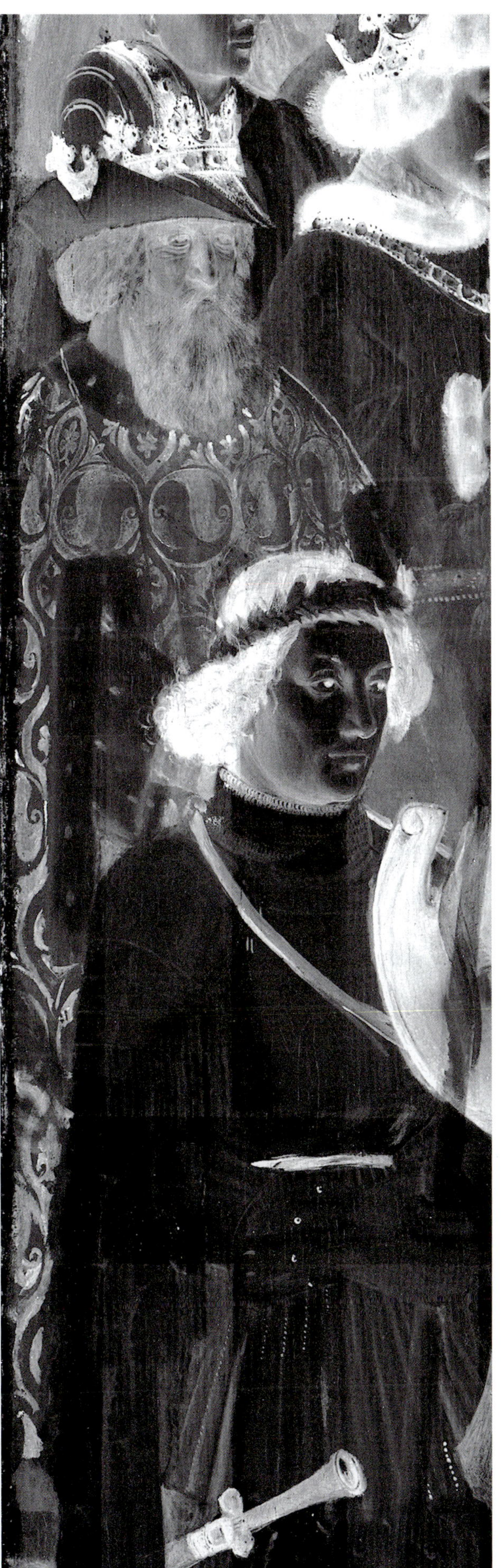

2.66b

reveals the stratigraphy of the corresponding pictorial layers.[130] The brocade was overpainted with the purple garment we now see, which alters the long green sleeve of the harnessed knight, but does not seem entirely to cover the bottom part of the original brocade robe (CVE-19 and fig. 4.18). It may appear surprising that the brocade pattern would have been overpainted with a rather uniform layer like this,[131] lacking any decorative pattern. The intention may have been to create a less elaborate background, so that the muzzle of the horse painted down the left edge would stand out more. This muzzle was meant as a continuation of the partially represented head of the second white horse on the right of the *Just Judges* (fig. 4.17). Painted over the purple robe, its anatomy is noticeably less well observed than those of the other horses' heads.[132]

Other layers added to figures in this zone[133] raise similar questions, including the shapeless retouching that masks part of the crown of the knight in green brocade (CVE-17);[134] the bright red robe of the figure upper left (CVE-18), which was painted over a deep-red glaze; the hair of the same figure, which covers an already painted ear and a red cap worn below the crown; and, perhaps, also the ultramarine chaperon of the figure referred to as 'Six',[135] which covers an azurite chaperon adorned with a crown (fig. 3.9).[136]

The Lamb

The sixteenth-century overpainting[137] of the lamb was partially taken away in the 1950s to reveal the original ears and has now been completely removed.[138] This allowed the recovery of the animal's eyes with horizontal slit pupils typical of prey animals (fig. 1.8c).[139] The body of the lamb was painted in a thin white layer with brown lines to suggest separate tufts of hair, followed by scattered white touches to evoke woolly curls, all this together evoking the thickness of the fleece.

The recent restoration campaign also revealed that the lamb's body has been enlarged compared to its original, less solid form. This can be made out in raking light (fig. 2.67) and in the infrared images and MA-XRF maps, especially the copper map (fig. 2.68), and was recently presented in a study combining multispectral images and MA-XRF maps.[140] The enlargement of the lamb's body actually overlaps the surrounding second-stage meadow (figs. 2.67 and 2.68). The green layer of this second meadow seems to have skirted carefully around the original form of the lamb, creating a ridge along that form, as is also the case around the large figures of the apostles and prophets. The animal's body was enlarged using a thick white layer, especially in its hindquarters, along the upper edge of the spine and the top of the head (figs. 2.69 and 2.70). These additions were made with brushstrokes that suggest tufts of white hair at the back, but without distinguishing the hairs as elsewhere in the body. The touches in question recall those we already noted on top of the apostles' and philosophers' skulls (fig. 2.65). There is also a brown, translucent shadow enlarging the left side of the body. The enlargement of the lamb's body thus appears to belong to the third stage. The shape visible in the infrared reflectogram follows probably more closely the original shape, which seems more realistic (figs. 2.70 and 2.71).

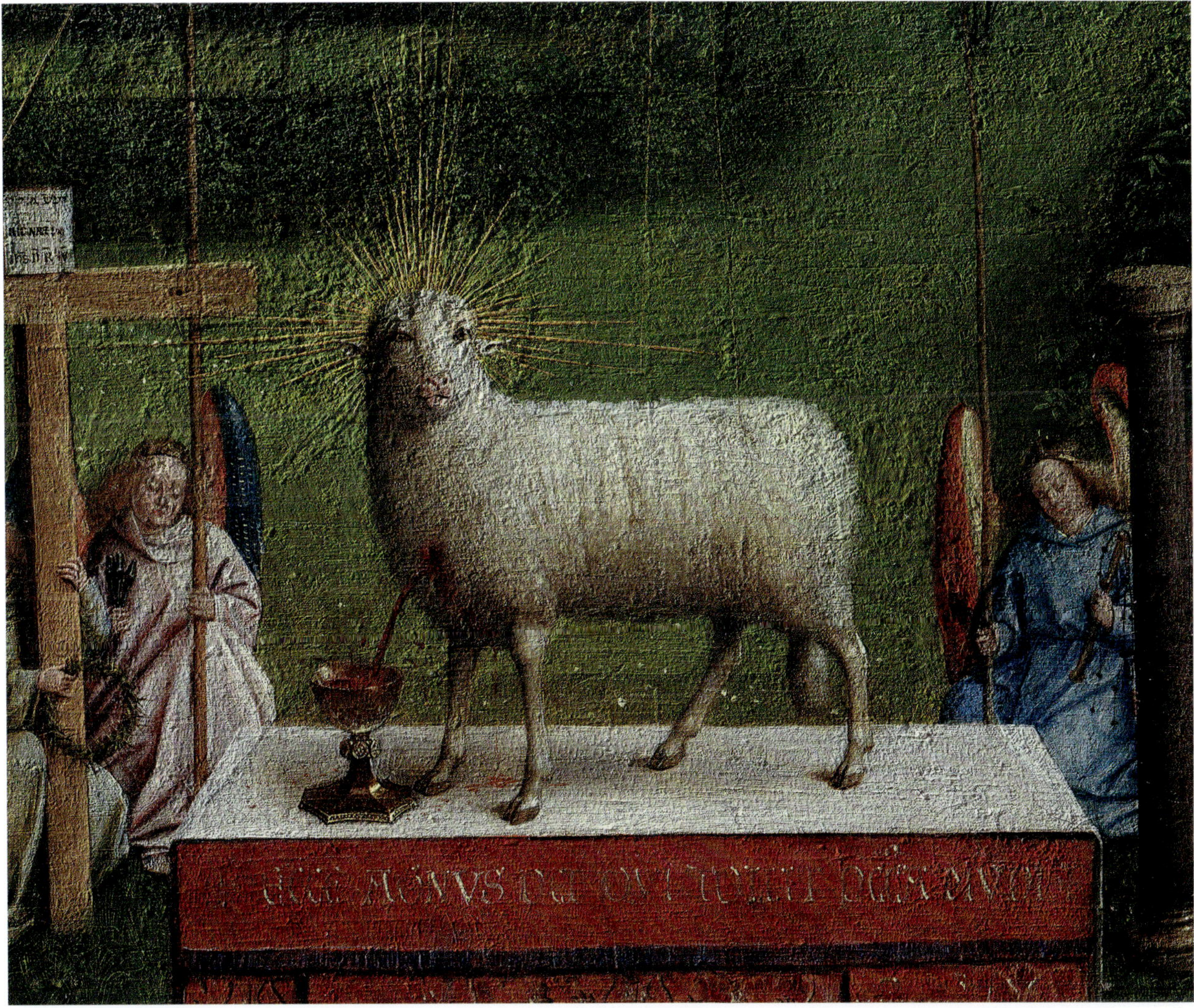

2.67

Fig. 2.67. *Adoration of the Lamb*, detail: enlarged body of the lamb overlapping the second-stage meadow noticeable in raking light (after treatment).

The lamb's gilded rays are located above the additions in the animal's head and along its neck and hence also belong to the third stage. Observation of this zone in raking light reveals a demarcation around the head of an irregular halo-shaped form extended in height (fig. 2.72). This irregular halo is also visible in the MA-XRF lead and tin maps, as well as in the X-radiograph. Perhaps it indicates a change to mask something that was originally planned or else it may be the trace of an intervention to address damage caused by the presence here of a dowel pin in the support.[141] None of the currently available scientific imaging techniques – not even MA-XRF – enables us to determine whether a halo or other rays were worked out in the first or second stage. However, rays do appear to have been intended in the underdrawing – the infrared reflectogram allows some of them to be detected (fig. 2.73).

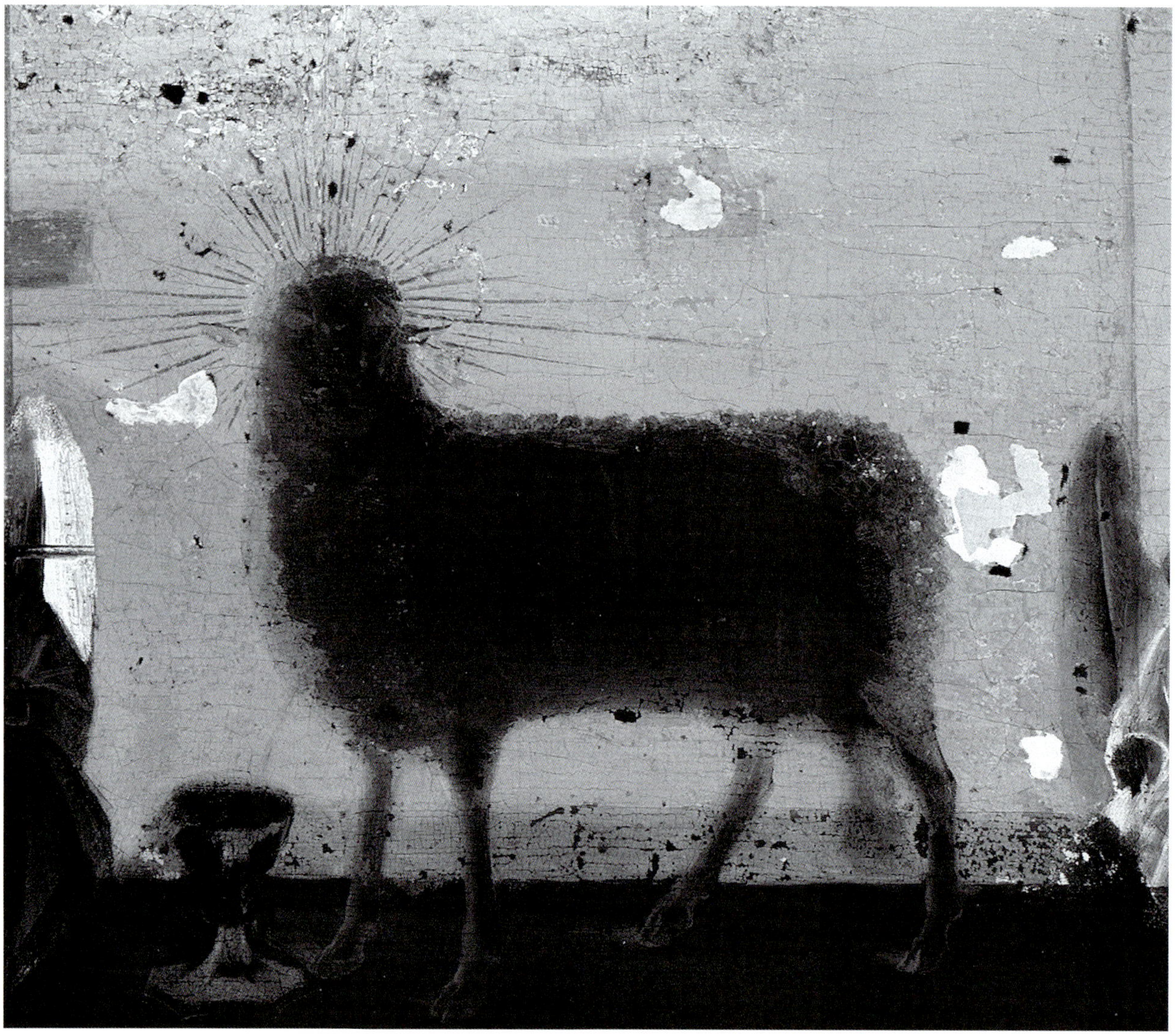

2.68

Fig. 2.68 *Adoration of the Lamb*, MA-XRF Cu-K map (during restoration) showing the enlargements of the lamb's body overlapping the second meadow.

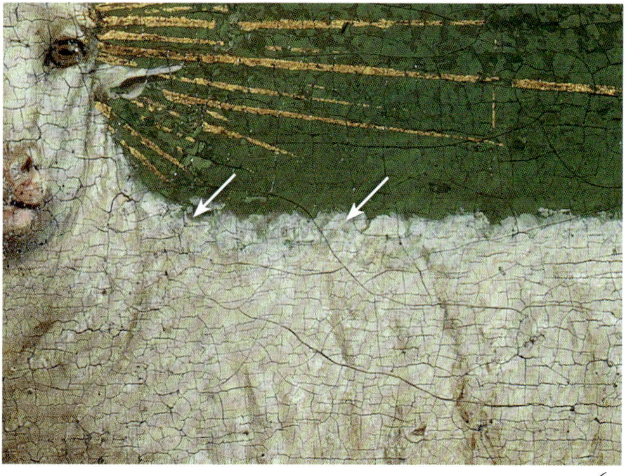

2.69

Fig. 2.69 *Adoration of the Lamb*, detail: third-stage enlargement of the lamb's body (white arrows).

Fig. 2.70a–c. *Adoration of the Lamb*: third-stage enlargement of the lamb's body – VIS (a); IRR (b); digital simulation without the enlargements (c).

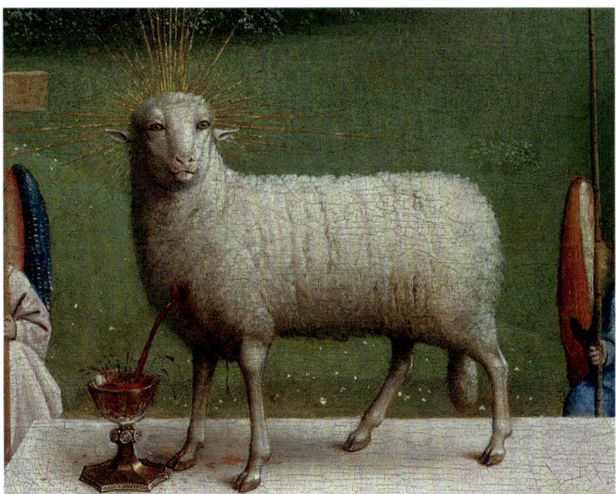

2.70a

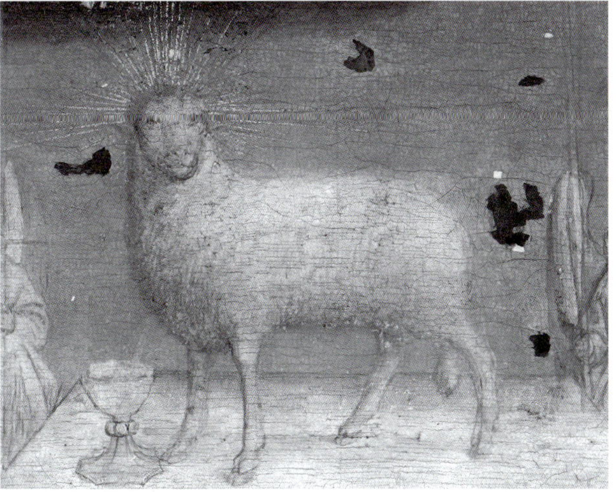

2.70b

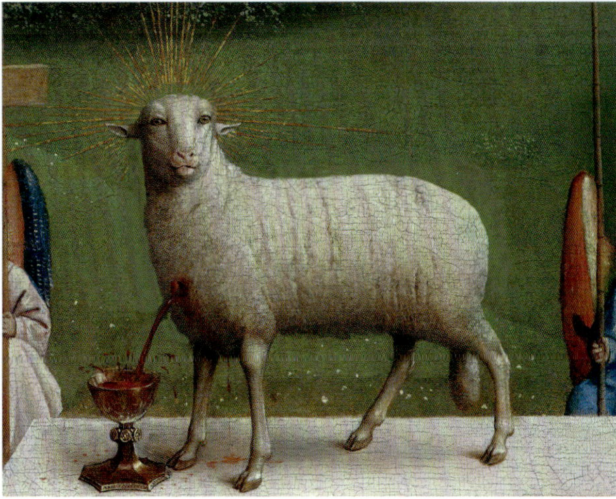

2.70c

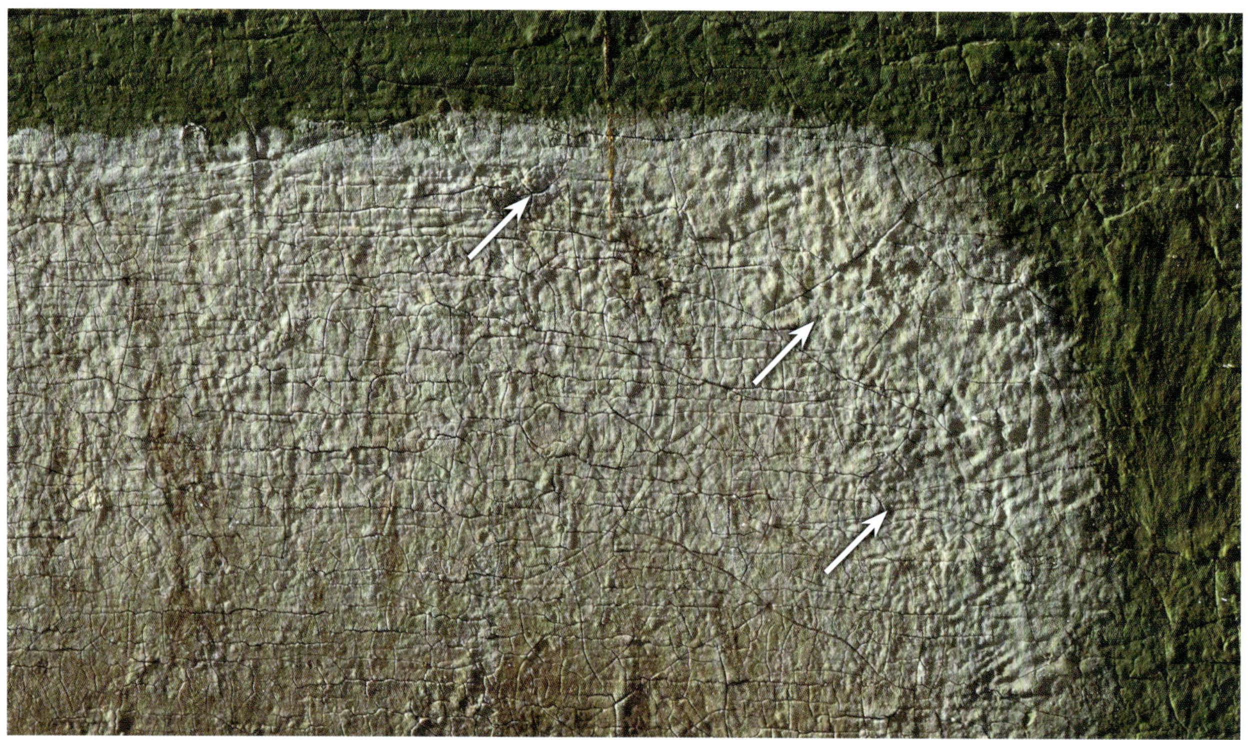

2.71

Fig. 2.71. *Adoration of the Lamb*, detail: third-stage enlargement of the lamb's body (white arrows) seen in raking light.

Another significant change was observed in the altar,[142] where a preliminary version had once again been painted during the first stage. This first version of the altar had a deeper top (CVE-9) and the perspective was different. It was skirted by the second-stage meadow, creating a ridge in the paint layer visible in raking light. The perspective of the altar table was later adjusted, reducing its depth, by the placement of a strip of green painted meadow, and the sides were adapted. These interventions seem to have occurred after the second-stage meadow had been painted. All the indications are, therefore, that the position of the altar was adjusted at the same time that the body of the lamb was enlarged.

The dove, the halo and the rays

The issue of the dove, the halo and the rays is a complex one: various stages of elaboration can be detected, especially in the rays, even after removal of the sixteenth-century overpaint, which included an additional level of gilded rays. The first-stage rays were established by the preparatory drawing (approximately 28 rays[143]) and then scored into the ground and isolating layer (fig. 2.74a). Their lengths vary[144] so as to form a symmetrical star pattern (fig. 2.74b). The drawn and scored rays are not interrupted beneath the body of the dove, and the dove does not show any preparatory drawing in the infrared reflectogram (CVE-6). These rays were abandoned in the second stage.[145] No trace of gilding, nor even of a mordant,

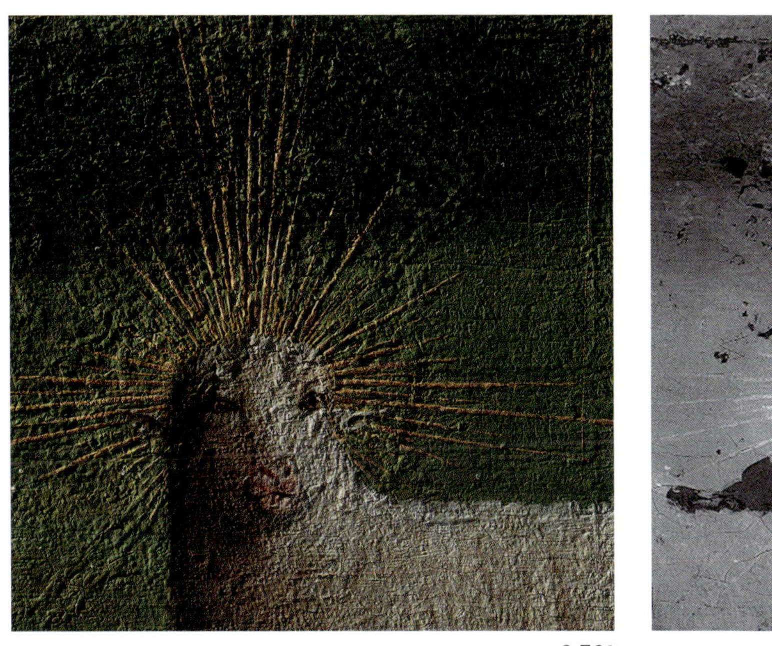

2.72a

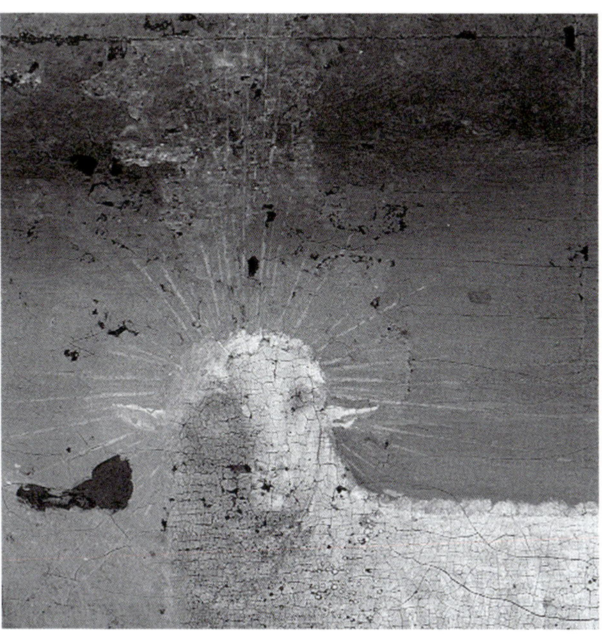

2.72b

Fig. 2.72. *Adoration of the Lamb*, detail: damaged area around the head of the lamb seen in raking light (a) and in the MA-XRF Pb-L map (during restoration) (b).

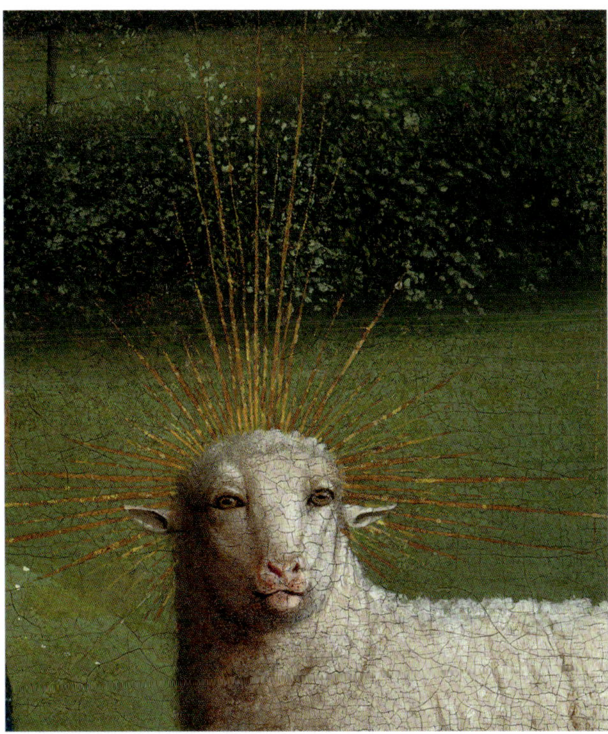

2.73a

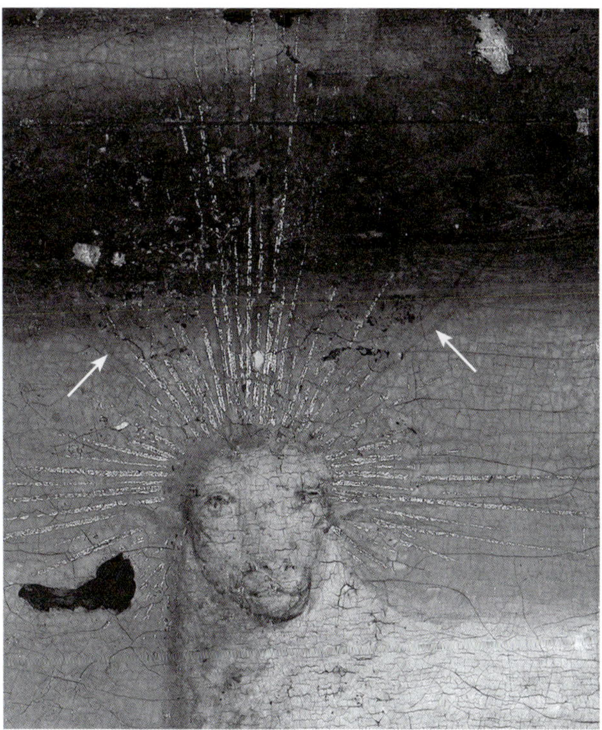

2.73b

Fig. 2.73. *Adoration of the Lamb*: presence of rays at underdrawing stage (white arrows) – VIS (a); IRR (b).

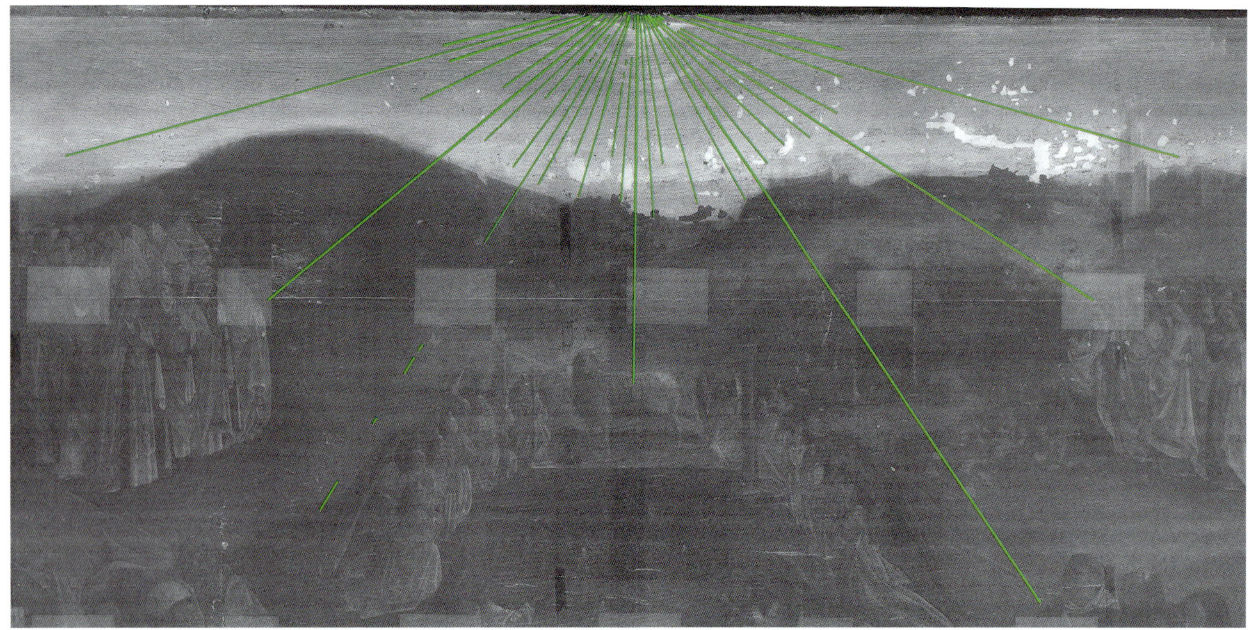

2.74a

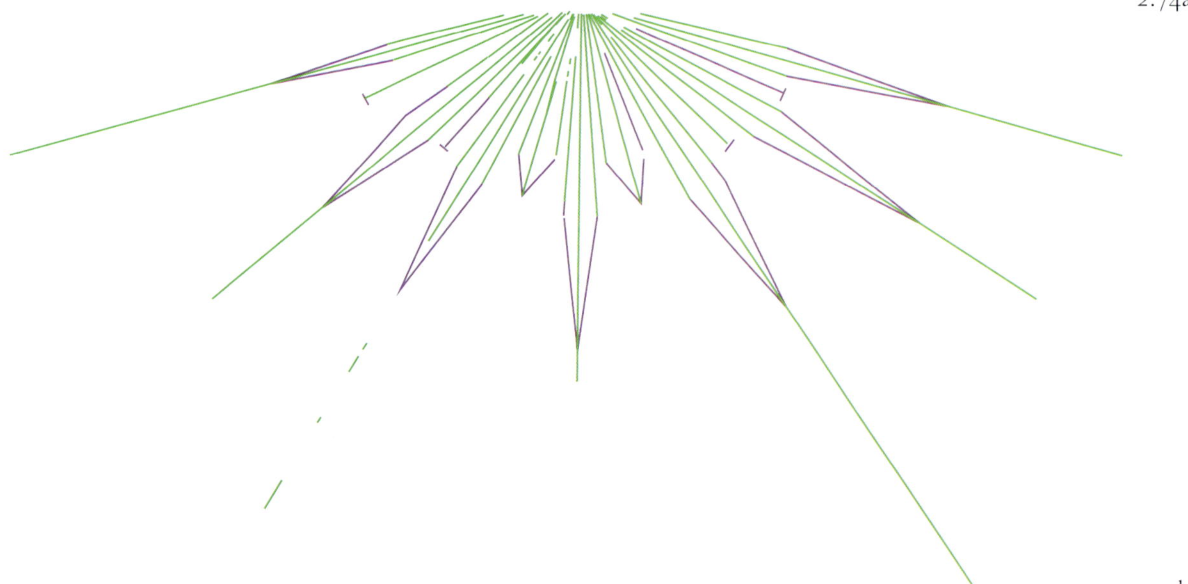

2.74b

Fig. 2.74a–b. Diagram of rays scored into the ground (green lines), visible in the XR (a); the incised rays of variable length form a symmetrical star pattern (schematically illustrated with purple lines) (b).

was detected on top of any of the three azurite-based paint layers in the sky of the central panel.[146] It was only after the ultramarine layer of the sky and halo had been painted in the third stage that the gilded rays were finally executed. This set of gilded rays differs from the original drawing: they are much more numerous (129) and the original star-shaped pattern has been abandoned. If the decision finally to add gilded rays was non-Eyckian, the original idea might still have been known, as the reliefs impressed in the paint layer along the scored but not painted rays could perhaps be seen before the ultramarine layer was applied, just as we can still today distinguish some of them in raking light.

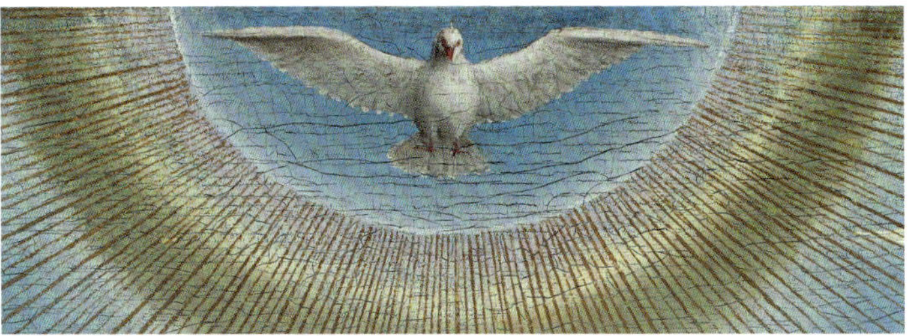
2.75a

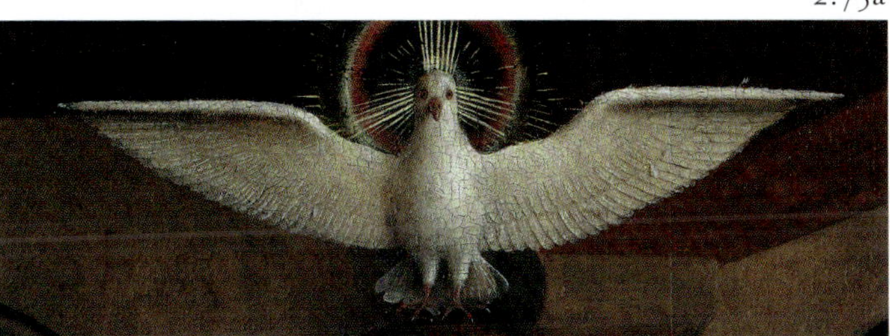
2.75b

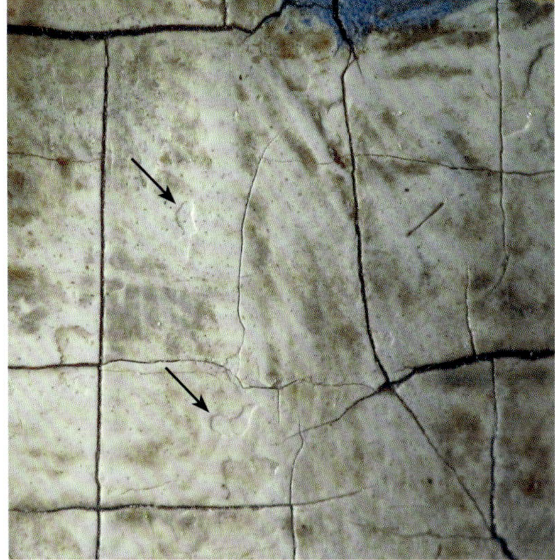
2.75c

Fig. 2.75a–c. Comparison of the dove in the *Adoration of the Lamb*, detail (a), and in the *Virgin Annunciate* on the exterior, detail (b); losses in the thick white top layer of the dove in the *Adoration of the Lamb*, microphotograph (c).

It thus appears that the idea of providing the sky with gilded rays was abandoned in the second stage. On the other hand, no trace of clouds or birds was found at the level of the azurite-based layers of the central panel, in contrast with the skies of the wings, where they can be seen on the surface. Could the sky of the central panel have been painted in the second stage without clouds, birds or rays? This hypothesis seems plausible when we consider that a halo, or even a dove, which were not apparently planned in the underdrawing, were added at this time: the halo we see now belongs to the same stratum as the ultramarine sky, and it is also hard to ascribe the present dove to Jan van Eyck (figs. 2.75a, 2.75b and 4.19).[147] Some scholars have raised the possibility that no dove was present in the original concept.[148] No one has suggested the presence of a preliminary dove or halo that would have been subsequently concealed by the corresponding elements we see today.

Samples taken from the dove indicate that it was painted in two layers and even three in certain places.[149] Small losses can be seen under the stereomicroscope in the white pictorial layer applied thickly to certain parts of the dove (fig. 2.75). An underlying white layer is visible through these losses. Each colour of the halo consists of two layers, both of which contain a mixture of ultramarine to which other pigments have been added to create the different nuances of the halo (fig. 2.76). The two ultramarine-based layers are located on top of the four layers of sky, the first of which is based on indigo and the following three on azurite. One of the questions that arises relates to the first of the two ultramarine-containing layers. Does it belong to the stratum of the ultramarine sky, which we consider to be non-Eyckian? If so, this would make the dove non-Eyckian. Or does it belong to an earlier stratum, applied locally by Jan in order to distinguish the area around the dove, using some ultramarine, from the remainder of the sky based on azurite? Careful observation of this important zone does indeed lead us to wonder whether

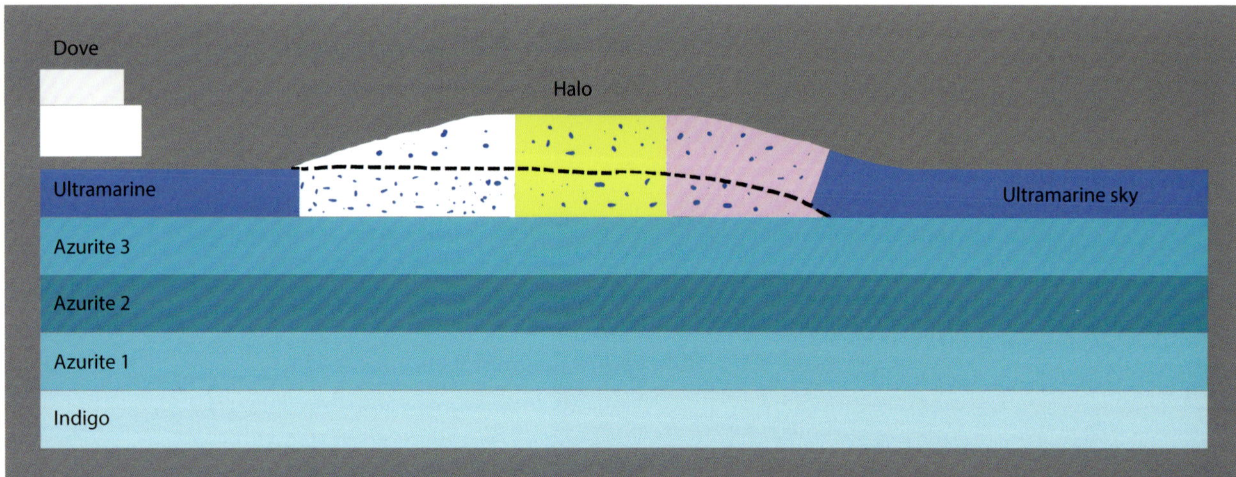

2.76

Fig. 2.76. Diagram – Hypothetical build-up of the paint layers in the halo and the dove.

there is not a difference between the ultramarine of the sky and that used below the dove and inside the halo around the dove. The laboratory analysis does not, however, allow us to conclude one way or another.

Yet another question concerns the pictorial layers of the dove. There is no evidence to state with any certainty that there is a dove below the present one.[150] But could the lower layer be Jan van Eyck's work? Analysis of the additives, and in particular of the powdered glass found in many of the altarpiece's paint layers, reveals the presence of particularly large wood-ash glass particles in the upper layers (up to 90 µm), whereas no glass particles have been detected in the lower, sometimes more greyish layer found in three of five cross-sections made in 1951. It should also be noted that in the only sample taken from the body of the lamb powdered glass was not detected.[151] The glass detected in the upper layer of the dove corresponds with a type found very frequently in the pictorial layers of fifteenth-century Flemish paintings. As it differs somewath from the glass found in the second stage paint samples,[152] it might even postdate the Van Eycks. The first layer of the dove could belong to the second stage.

Conclusion

It is apparent after the recent treatment that three stages can be identified in the development of the lower tier of the altarpiece interior. The first of these stages is barely visible now, as it has been concealed by the subsequent interventions. In addition to the construction of the supports and the completion of the preparatory layers, a large proportion of the first layers of paint date from this stage, not only in the skies and the vegetation of the central panel and the wings, but also in the positioning of the principal human and animal silhouettes. A different conception was planned for the central axis of the *Adoration* panel, with a simple spring in the ground and a sky without a dove but with rays, albeit few in number, all in a less varied landscape. This stage appears to have remained unfinished and only few elements of it are now visible, given the extent to which they were covered by the second-stage intervention.

The second stage followed much of the first-stage composition, but introduced significant changes to the central panel by adding an imposing fountain above the spring and possibly a dove and halo. It also abandoned the idea of rays in the sky. Elsewhere, the main changes relate to the adjustment of the architecture on the horizon, which is more numerous in this stage, the addition of more abundant and varied vegetation, and the finalization of the human figures, with occasionally significant adjustments of form and colour.

Touches of varying size, lastly, were added to all the paintings, in order to 'improve' the perspective, particularly along the central axis of the *Adoration* panel, to ensure continuity between the different shutters and undoubtedly also to satisfy a certain *horror vacui*. All the indications are that these touches post-date the second stage, over which they have been placed. These additions include the current sky of the central panel, as well as the current dove and halo.

The three different stages observed here were distinguished because they are superimposed in many places, but in some areas they are also juxtaposed.

Notes

1 Jones, Augustyniak, Dubois 2020. See also the Introduction to this volume.

2 The date of Hubert's death is known from his epitaph. Duverger 1945, pp. 15–28; Martens 2019, pp. 125–26; Paviot 2020, p. 60.

3 The *Just Judges* were stolen in 1934.

4 Panofsky 1953, pp. 207–22. Panofsky refers to earlier authors in note 208/3.

5 Fraiture 2017.

6 The present study has benefited from the comments and observations of all the conservators who took part in the treatment of the four paintings; see the Introduction to this volume.

7 Postec, Steyaert 2020.

8 Coremans 1953; Van Asperen de Boer 1979. Without seeking to be exhaustive, we will refer to other publications on the pictorial technique of the polyptych in the notes that follow.

9 Van Asperen de Boer 1979, p. 195, n. 71; Metzger, Steyaert 2009, p. 167; Steyaert 2012, p. 121.

10 See chapter 4.

11 Coremans 1953, pp. 12–15; Glatigny et al. 2010, pp. 172–232.

12 See chapter 3, section 'Ground'.

13 Postec, Steyaert 2020, pp. 196–99; Postec 2012, pp. 148–49.

14 Some are visible to the naked eye, and they show up in the IRRs as grey lines or in the XRs as black lines, due to the absence of pictorial material.

15 Postec, Steyaert 2020, pp. 196–98.

16 It should be noted, though, that bristles are fairly easy to identify in the IRRs of the altarpiece exterior but not in those of the paintings of the lower register of the altarpiece interior, as the latter are far more detailed, making it harder to distinguish possible bristles.

17 A technical detail not found in the panels of the altarpiece exterior.

18 The textile is impregnated with the chalk-glue mixture of the ground – both non-radio-opaque materials – which explains why the imprint of the cloth is hard to see in the XRs.

19 Verougstraete 2015, pp. 68–71. Examples of pre-Eyckian paintings

with textile strips glued to the panel: Melchior Broederlam, shutters of the *Crucifixion Altarpiece*, Dijon, Musée des Beaux-Arts, inv. 1420, see Currie 2009, p. 33; *Coronation of the Virgin* and *Annunciation*, Antwerp, Royal Museum of Fine Arts, inv. 516, see Verougstraete 2015, pp. 325–26; *Diest Last Judgement*, Brussels, Royal Museums of Fine Arts of Belgium, inv. 4658, see Dubois et al. 2009, p. 61; *St Maurice Shrine*, Namur, Musée provincial des Arts anciens du Namurois, inv. 150, see Deneffe, Peters, Fremout 2009, p. 364; see also 'Preparation of the picture support' in Von Baum et al. 2014, pp. 31–35; Serrat 2019, p. 71.

20 Verougstraete 2015, pp. 412–16.

21 Skaug 2006; Kühnen, Hern 2016.

22 This hypothesis was suggested by Jean-Albert Glatigny (oral communication). Two of the shutters – the *Knights of Christ* and the *Hermits* – show evidence of very early repairs (in the sky of the *Knights of Christ* and in the brown robe of the figure on the left of the *Hermits*), which we will discuss in detail in a moment. It is difficult to determine whether these repairs and the application of the canvas strip in the central panel occurred at the same time. The canvas does appear to have been placed on the central panel before the ground was applied, while some paint layers of the wings had already been executed at the time of the repairs.

23 Van Asperen de Boer 1979; Périer-D'Ieteren 2017.

24 As we will see in chapter 4, the execution of these preparatory layers most likely predates Jan's intervention.

25 Van Asperen de Boer 1979, pp. 178–201.

26 Postec, Steyaert 2020, p. 200.

27 Postec, Steyaert 2020, pp. 200–216.

28 Coremans, 1953, p. 110 and pl. XXXVI; Van Asperen de Boer 1979, p. 199, figs. 66a and b.

29 Coremans counted 29 scored rays (Coremans 1953, p. 110). It is difficult to count the rays drawn with a liquid medium in the IRRs, as they are not always distinguishable from the gilded rays, because the mordant also absorbs infrared. Even so, 27 rays drawn with a liquid medium can be counted in the area directly around the dove.

30 If this is the case, the purpose of these lines, scored with a blunt tool – a kind of stylus or metalpoint – differs from that of the lines drawn in a dry medium that were detected in the panels of the altarpiece exterior, where we think that metalpoint could have been used to lay down the initial drawing, before being strengthened and completed in brush with a liquid medium. Postec, Steyaert 2020, pp. 200–206.

31 This point will be discussed in more detail in the section 'The dove, the halo and the rays'.

32 Contrary to what is stated in Martens 2019, p. 128.

33 Van Asperen de Boer 1979, p. 194.

34 Postec, Steyaert 2020, pp. 207–21.

35 Postec, Steyaert 2020, p. 200 and n. 33.

36 See the analyses in chapter 3, section 'Underdrawing'.

37 Jan van Eyck, *St Barbara*, 1437, Antwerp, Royal Museum of Fine Arts, inv. 410. Van Asperen de Boer 1992; Billinge, Verougstraete, Van Schoute 2000; Postec, Sanyova 2016. The presence of washes has been noted in several works by Jan van Eyck; see Postec, Steyaert 2020, p. 245, n. 53.

38 See chapter 3, section 'Priming'.

39 See chapter 3, section 'Priming'.

40 Coremans 1953, p. 110, and pl. XXXVII-4; Van Asperen de Boer 1979, p. 203, pl. 69.

41 Postec, Steyaert 2020, p. 220; Billinge et al. 1997b; Von Baum et al. 2014, pp. 47–57.

42 Van Asperen de Boer 1979, pp. 194 and 201.

43 The nature of the copper pigment, verdigris, was confirmed by analysis. See chapter 3, section 'Green'.

44 Cross-section 10/82.

45 Kirby 2012, p. 272; Spring 2017, p. 17.

46 This oval shape, the lower part of which bulges out towards the bottom of the panel, conceivably follows the shape of the preparatory drawing, which established the position of the spring (the black paint prevents the drawing from being visible in the IRR).

47 *God Placing Adam in the Garden of Eden*, miniature from Guyart des Moulins, *Bible historiale*, Paris, Bibliothèque de

l'Arsenal, MS 5057, fol. 8; see Meiss 1974, pp. 339–42.

48 Limbourg Brothers, *La Rencontre des Mages*, in *Les Très Riches Heures du duc de Berry*, Chantilly, Musée Condé, MS 65, fol. 51.

49 Light pictorial layer consisting of lead white, ochre, verdigris, chalk and lead-tin yellow.

50 High-resolution MA-XRF maps could not be made of the entire surface of the painting.

51 As we will see in due course, however, the present altar is the result of an enlargement that might be non-Eyckian.

52 The IRR of the *Fountain of Life* in the Museo Nacional del Prado (follower of Van Eyck, 1440–50, inv. P1511) shows several segments in the preparatory drawing of the octagonal fountain (Pérez Preciado 2018, p. 47, ill. 35). The arcs here appear to be clearly linked to the basin. They might be construction lines for the drawing of octagonal shapes, or perhaps the basin was initially round. There is no trace of a similar dark underlayer or bulge in the IRR, nor is there any grass around the fountain.

53 Van den Bremt, Van Crombrugge 2020, pp. 252–53.

54 The scored lines used to position the stone basin became visible to the naked eye when the thick layers of varnish and retouches were removed. There was no generalized overpainting in this area, merely a few localized retouches and oxidized varnishes.

55 Similar lines are also found in the paintings of the altarpiece exterior, see Postec, Steyaert 2020, pp. 206 and 218. For other examples with compass marks in Netherlandish painting, see: Metzger, Steyaert 2009, pp. 172–73 and n. 41; Steyaert 2012, pp. 132–33.

56 Due to abrasion of the light-brown layer, the grey underlayer is exposed in numerous places.

57 We know this was the new meadow, as lines were scored in the fresh paint of this fresh green pictorial layer in order to mark the position of the column.

58 It cannot be ruled out, in our view, that the brown glaze, the highlights and other accents along the edges of the column and which overlap the surrounding meadow are a non-Eyckian intervention.

59 The green underlayer is also visible in the barb along the right and bottom edges.

60 Van Asperen de Boer 1979, pp. 178–80.

61 Even though we could only make out this underlying green layer by the naked eye along the right edge in the *Pilgrims*.

62 Unless the patch of grass dates from the third stage, which would mean the change occurred at a later date.

63 This stratigraphy is confirmed by cross-section 09/19, observations made by stereomicroscope and analysis of the MA-XRF maps, XR and IRR.

64 Philippot, Sneyers 1953, p. 83, mentioned 'surpeints anciens dans la végétation au-dessus des rochers'.

65 Only two layers of azurite and lead white were detected in a few cross-sections, e.g. 12/03, but these were generally the result of samples taken from the edges of the panels, making the interpretation less reliable.

66 Campbell 2017, p. 258; Postec, Steyaert 2020, pp. 33, 43, 49.

67 Given the relatively simple stratigraphy of these passages, the sky is generally not the preferred place from which to take paint samples. We found two examples in which the sky comprises two layers containing azurite: Petrus Christus, *The Lamentation* (Brussels, Royal Museums of Fine Arts of Belgium, inv. 564), Kockaert 1995, p. 190; Jan Gossaert, *The Adoration of the Magi* (London, The National Gallery, NG2790), Billinge et al. 1997a, pp. 92–93. In a third example, the sky is built up in two layers, one based on azurite and the other on ultramarine: follower of Rogier van der Weyden, *Pieta* (London, The National Gallery, NG6265), Billinge et al. 1997a, p. 77.

68 We also note that a similar problem is located in the robe of one of the hermits in the right wing. See chapter 3, section 'Zinc vitriol'.

69 The first indigo-based layer is also missing. These investigations were performed using samples taken from and alongside the damage, in a zone displaying other, more recent losses.

70 Other indications, visible in the XR and the IRR of the *Joos Vijd* panel, might indicate early damage: stains, indications of density differences along the joint at the corresponding site, as well as in the arch.

71 As we will see, this is not the only indication, see p. 69 and note 83 below.

72 The ridge is split in places in the XR, suggesting that this might be two different stages of execution, unless the more weakly contrasting zones in the XR correspond with differences in thickness within the same layer, which is rich in lead white. It is hard to interpret the XR of the horizon, as the sky is composed of different layers of paint, each containing lead white and each of which might deviate a little – but differently in each case – from the horizon line or the outlines of the planned buildings. What is more, there are also several hills and mountains in this zone, some of them painted on top of each other, all of which also contain lead white. Regarding 'borders forming a ridge', see also Van Asperen de Boer 1979, n. 76.

73 This is what Coremans called 'un double changement de composition', Coremans, Loose, Thissen 1953, p. 112.

74 It should be noted that no varnish appears to be present between the final layer of azurite and the ultramarine layer (no intermediate varnish was detected in any of the samples in which we believe a third-stage layer to be present). The application of the ultramarine layer might have been preceded by cleaning. There is no evidence, however, that Flemish painters systematically varnished their paintings. A few rare traces of possibly original varnish or intermediate layers have been found on medieval paintings (Sauerberg et al. 2009, pp. 244–46; Dunkerton, Morrison, Roy 2017, pp. 275–78). However, certain sources – albeit Italian – suggest that distant blues were not necessarily varnished (Glanville 1995, p. 14; Postec 2006, pp. 229–31).

75 This ultramarine-based level is repeated in Coxcie's 1557 copy, and might correspond with Blondeel and Van Scorel's documented intervention (see Dubois 2017). For the dating of the overpaint removed from the sky, see also chapter 3, section 'Soda-ash glass'.

76 One of those losses is present at the right side of the bell tower, in the sky and a leaf of the large fig tree. The retouching of the leaf in this loss might be contemporary with the application of the thick layer of sky that was removed during the 2016–19 restoration treatment.

77 As stated in the 'Note to the Reader', we use 'Eyckian' to refer to everything that could have been executed by Hubert or Jan, and 'non Eyckian' for everything not executed by the two brothers, which does not exclude the intervention of a contemporary painter.

78 Coremans, Loose, Thissen 1953, p. 112.

79 For the sake of clarity, we have retained the numbering of the building groups used by Coremans, Loose, Thissen 1953, p. 111.

80 Coremans, Loose, Thissen 1953, p. 112.

81 Van Asperen de Boer noted changes in the architecture that he situated essentially between the preparatory drawing and the painting, although he detected the presence of dark layers beneath the tower of Utrecht cathedral, which he interpreted more as a first 'dark undermodelling'. Van Asperen de Boer 1979, pp. 187–88.

82 Coremans, Loose, Thissen 1953, p. 112.

83 This is an additional indication that the first layer of azurite in the sky belongs to the initial concept.

84 See chapter 1 (fig. 1.21).

85 The light-blue mountains in the background of this city could belong to the initial concept. They are similar to the small area of light-blue mountain visible to the left of the tower of Utrecht cathedral.

86 In IRR, some forms do not correspond with the current landscape, particularly to the left of the cypress. These forms probably correspond with the initially planned landscape and indicate the possible presence of fields.

87 Coremans, Loose, Thissen 1953, p. 118; Van Asperen de Boer 1979, pp. 182–83.

88 Van Asperen de Boer 1979, p. 197.

89 Identified as angular Solomon's seal, scented Solomon's seal; see Van den Bremt, Van Crombrugge 2020, pp. 210–11.

90 Van den Bremt, Van Crombrugge 2020, pp. 160–61, 218–19.

91 These are also visible in the copper, calcium and iron MA-XRF maps.

92 Possibly hazel; Van den Bremt, Van Crombrugge 2020, pp. 146–47.

93 Coremans, Loose, Thissen 1953, pp. 106–07.

94 Van Asperen de Boer 1979, p. 183. This layer recalls the black shape of the spring. For the composition of this layer, see chapter 3, section 'Zinc vitriol'.

95 Postec, Steyaert 2020, pp. 222–23 and 247 nn. 86–87.

96 Anonymous, Antwerp, Museum Mayer van den Bergh, inv. 1; Mund et al. 2003, pp. 254–87, esp. pp. 267–74 and p. 265 (IRR of the *St Christopher* panel); Kemperdick, Lammertse 2012, pp. 114–18.

97 See chapter 3 (sections 'Green' and 'Zinc vitriol') for the possible composition of these brown/brown-green layers.

98 Jan van Eyck, *Arnolfini Portrait*, London, National Gallery, 1434, NG186. The zones of brown around the vegetation in other paintings from this period have occasionally been interpreted as altered green glazes (Billinge et al. 1997a, p. 80, plate 49). In this phase of the study, however, there is no evidence that the brown colour arose from a change in a pigment, even though verdigris is present in these layers. This well-drying pigment may also have been introduced as an additive to speed up the drying of layers comprising poorly or non-drying yellow-brown organic colourants, the possible presence of which is discussed in chapter 3, section 'Zinc vitriol'.

99 Jan van Eyck, *The Virgin at the Fountain*, Antwerp, Royal Museum of Fine Arts, inv. 411. See the macrophotographs, VIS on the 'Closer to Van Eyck' website: http://closertovaneyck.kikirpa.be (the black spot visible in the IRR in the vegetation to the right of the Virgin corresponds to a loss).

100 Illustrations in Deneffe, Peters, Fremout 2009, p. 96, ill. 10a and b. http://balat.kikirpa.be/object/115812 (photograph no. Z006990).

101 As a reminder: the sky consists of an indigo and lead-white-based layer and three layers based on azurite and lead white. A sample (C12/15) taken from the *Pilgrims* shows that the areas of flat black were painted after at least one preliminary layer of sky (containing, as elsewhere, only lead white near the horizon) had been applied.

102 Verougstraete 1987, pp. 21–27. Verougstraete, Van Schoute 1995, pp. 195–98; Stroo et al. 1999, pp. 149–50, pl. 22f.

103 See Postec, Steyaert 2020, p. 230, and chapter 3.

104 See chapter 3.

105 Coremans, Loose, Thissen 1953, pp. 112 and 118.

106 Paviot 2020, pp. 70–71 (also for further references); Fransen 2017.

107 Dumoulyn, Buylaert 2020, p. 104; Van den Bremt, Van Crombrugge 2020, pp. 38, 53–59.

108 Van den Bremt, Van Crombrugge 2020, pp. 196–97.

109 Already reported in Philippot 1953, p. 78 and pl. XLVIII; Philippot, Sneyers 1953, p. 83 and pl. LVIII.

110 The grainy character of the touches is not sufficiently characteristic to classify them as later reworkings, but it is true that touches where the style does not strike us as Eyckian possess this grainy appearance, which is not found in the Van Eycks' smoother pictorial matter.

111 The presence of tin – probably indicating the use of lead-tin yellow – is not limited to the touches that we date to the third stage: the yellow pigment is also present in the Eyckian vegetation, although the grainy touches applied systematically and with no real connection to the represented vegetation give a particularly strong tin signal in the MA-XRF Sn-L map.

112 Coremans, Loose, Thissen 1953, pp. 106–07.

113 A cross-section 10/92 from the trunk of the palm in the central panel clearly shows that it was painted over an ultramarine-based mountain, contemporary with the ultramarine sky, which was itself painted over a preliminary azurite-based mountain.

114 The presence of zinc detected in many places in the original is discussed in chapter 3.

115 The practice has already been detected in a red drapery by Jan van Eyck in *Leal Souvenir*, signed and dated 1432, National Gallery, London; Campbell 1998a, p. 218. The technique is also found in the *Lamentation* by Petrus Christus, Royal

Museums of Fine Arts of Belgium, Brussels; Verougstraete, Van Schoute 1995, p. 198; Stroo et al. 1999, p. 149, pl. 22c.

116 Postec, Steyaert 2020, p. 230.

117 The practice also exists in pre-Eyckian painting. It can be found, for instance, in the *Scenes from the Life of the Virgin*, known as the 'Kortessem Panel', in the Royal Museums of Fine Arts of Belgium, c. 1400, inv. 4883, Deneffe, Peters, Fremout 2009, pp. 226–29; or in the *Antwerp–Baltimore Quadriptych*, see note 96, Mund et al. 2003, p. 272. Other works by Jan van Eyck present the same technique of scored lines, including the *Arnolfini Portrait*, see note 98; Campbell 1998a p. 184; Dunkerton, Billinge 2005, pp. 48 and 57. See also note 115.

118 See chapter 3 , especially section 'Paint additives'.

119 In the central panel: the blue draperies of the confessors and the philosopher on the foreground, in the red draperies of the Popes and churchmen and the philosopher in the lower left corner; the purple drapery in the *Hermits*. Other painters who pioneered this technique, such as Leonardo da Vinci, encountered similar problems. See Dunkerton 2011, pp. 18–20.

120 Increasing the proportion of oily binder as the work progresses. Mayer 1973, p. 165; Van Loon, Noble, Burnstock 2012, p. 225. These observations are also based on years of practice and teaching of the pictorial techniques of the Flemish Primitives.

121 Postec, Steyaert 2020, p. 231.

122 See, e.g., beading in St Joseph's beard in *The Nativity* of the *Antwerp–Baltimore Quadriptych*; see note 96, Mund et al. 2003, p. 276, ill. 19 and http://balat.kikirpa.be/object/90530 (photo Z006027).

123 IR photograph, IRR, XR and MA-XRF maps for Pb-L, Cu-K, Hg-L, Fe-K.

124 The lacuna is visible in the IRR, XR, MA-XRF Pb-L and Ca-K maps, but not on the surface or in the MA-XRF Cu-K map. Other lacunae or accidents were noted in the sky of the *Knights of Christ*, in the robe of one of the *Hermits* and in the robe of the apostle in the foreground. All these lacunae and their repair do not necessarily date from the same intervention. More systematic analysis of all the scientific images and layering them might allow further alterations of this type to be detected.

125 Highlights like this in the shadows were detected in many of the draperies in the panels of the altarpiece exterior during the 2012–16 restoration campaign. Depuydt-Elbaum et al. 2020, p. 139, fig. 4a.29–30; Dubois 2020a, p. 19, fig. 1.10; Postec, Steyaert 2020, p. 228, fig. 5a.31a.

126 Van Asperen de Boer 1979, p. 178.

127 See the section 'Meadow and fountain', above.

128 The XR shows that the legs of the first-stage white horse already had painted hairs.

129 We are grateful to Geert Van der Snickt for drawing our attention to the presence of this painted brocade.

130 Cross-section 09/34b. There are base layers painted in pinkish-purple tones, over which the brocade pattern was painted in dark, brownish red, with highlights containing lead-tin yellow.

131 The currently visible purple garment was painted in three layers. The first is an opaque vermilion-based layer followed by a red glaze and finally blue, ultramarine-based shadows indicating the folds, or white highlights in the light zones.

132 See chapter 4. The added muzzle does not appear in Coxcie's 1557 copy of the *Knights of Christ* (Royal Museums of Fine Arts of Belgium, Brussels, inv. 1460; see Dubois 2017 regarding the copy), but it is found in the copy in the Royal Museum of Fine Arts Antwerp (inv. 417) dating from the end of the sixteenth or the seventeenth century (for this copy, see Kemperdick 2014, p. 49). Drawn lines corresponding to the contours of the muzzle can, however, be seen in the IRR of the copy by Coxcie (we are grateful to Véronique Bucken for providing us these documents), who ultimately decided not to paint it. Similar adjustments between the underdrawing of the Coxcie copy and the version as painted can be found elsewhere, too. See Dubois 2017, pp. 98–102.

133 These are zones from which the sixteenth-century overpaint has been removed (see chapter 1, fig. 1.12).

134 The drawing of the front part of the crown can be seen in the IRR (Van Asperen de Boer 1979, p. 180) and the

painting of it in the XR and MA-XRF iron and zinc maps.

135 Coremans, Loose, Thissen. 1953, p. 106, note 21 and pl. XXVI; Van Asperen de Boer 1979, p. 180.

136 The underlying chaperon, which is slightly smaller than the current one and which leaves a reserve for the crown, gives a high signal of copper, corresponding with verdigris or azurite blue, and of lead in the MA-XRF Cu-K and Pb-L maps. The painted crown, meanwhile, is readily legible in the IR photograph, XR and MA-XRF iron map. See chapter 3, fig. 3.9.

137 This is the sixteenth-century overpaint that was further removed during the current restoration campaign; see chapter 1.

138 See fig. 1.8.

139 Depoorter 2020, p. 52.

140 Van der Snickt et al. 2020, pp. 3–7. The authors have not been able to determine, however, whether or not these changes are Eyckian.

141 A dowel pin also caused damage to the *Interior View* in the altarpiece exterior; Ketels, Glatigny, Augustyniak 2020, p. 48; p. 50, fig. 2.3 and n. 19. Damage related to the presence of a dowel was also noted in the *Virgin Annunciate*, just above the wing of the dove.

142 Van Asperen de Boer 1979, p. 194.

143 See note 29.

144 Van Asperen de Boer 1979, p. 199.

145 Coremans (1953, p. 111) concluded that the system of 'rayons gravés' had been abandoned.

146 If any rays had existed beneath the ultramarine layer, it is highly likely that the conservators would have found traces of them during the very many hours required to remove the sixteenth-century overpaint over the entire sky. The ultramarine layer presented enough small losses – or was sufficiently translucent in places – to offer a view of the underlying layers.

147 See chapter 4.

148 Beenken 1933, p. 68; Beenken 1933–34, pp. 27–28; Panofsky 1953, pp. 218, 225; Van Asperen de Boer 1979, pp. 195–97, 200, 212; Dubois, Sanyova, Vanwijnsberghe 2017, pp. 71–73.

149 These samples were taken from the dove at the edge of its silhouette. See chapter 3, section 'Wood ash with some fern ash'. It is not impossible that a first, smaller version of the bird is present beneath the current one. One of the cross-sections was already described by Coremans, Loose, Thissen 1953, p. 108, pl. XXXVII–2.

150 Another detail worth noting is the presence of fragments of gilding below the upper white pictorial layer of the dove (Van Asperen de Boer 1979, p. 196). Old gilding around the dove was removed during the restoration campaign in the 1950s along with the clouds over the halo. Some fragments might remain of this gilded background, which has now been removed, a few of these fragments are clearly trapped between two white paint layers of the dove.

151 See chapter 3 (section 'Powdered glass') on the laboratory analysis regarding the addition of powdered glass to the pictorial layers.

152 See chapter 3, section 'Paint additives'.

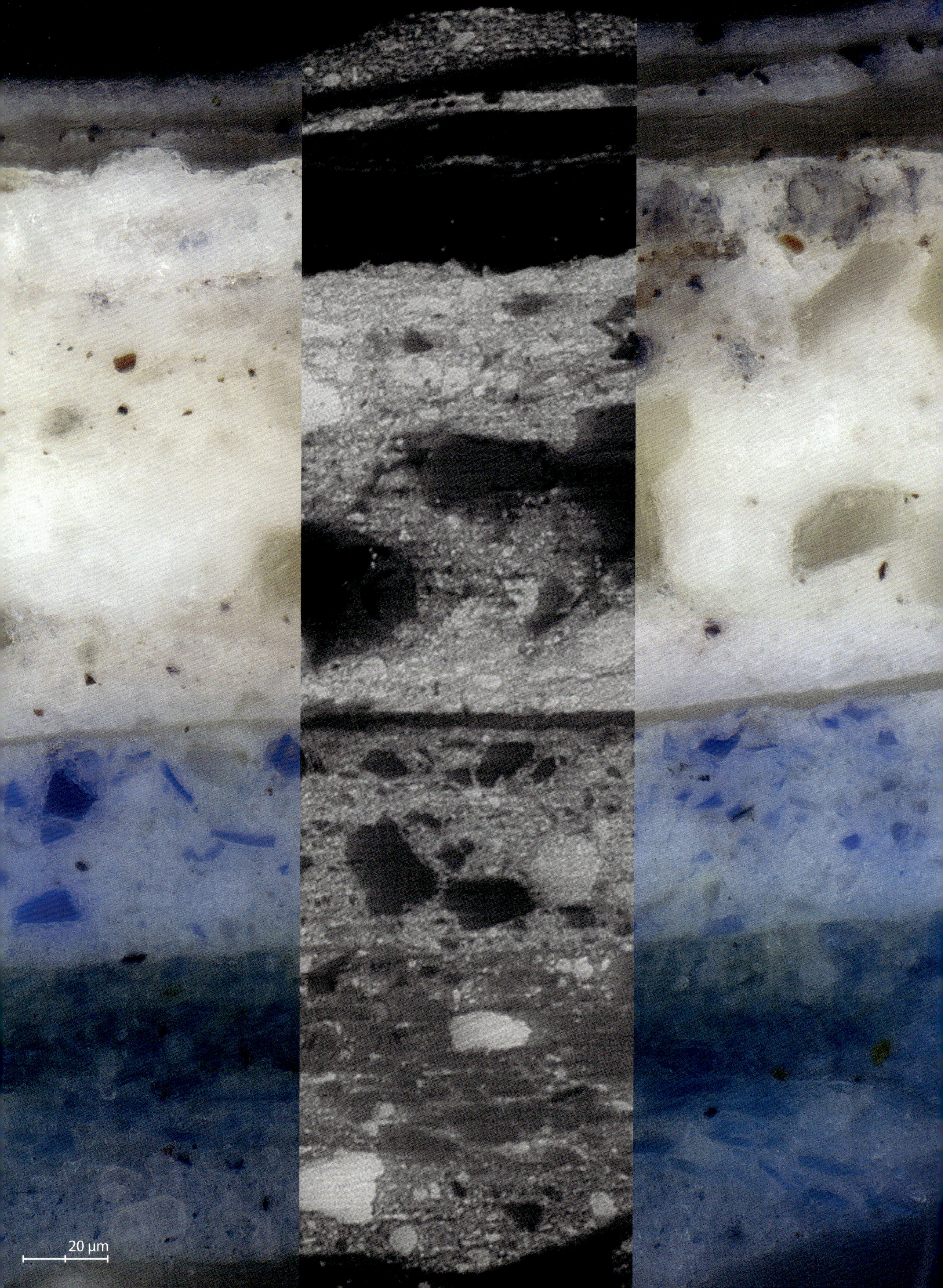
20 µm

3
The Challenges of a Complex Stratigraphy from a Chemical Point of View

Jana Sanyova, Geert Van der Snickt and Francisco Mederos-Henry

With contributions by Cécile Glaude, Frederik Vanmeert, Steven De Meyer, Stijn Legrand and Koen Janssens

Introduction

The technical virtuosity and highly prized status of one of the world's most important large-scale artworks make the *Ghent Altarpiece* stand as a reference for the study of the technique of early Netherlandish painting and of Hubert and Jan van Eyck in particular.

The materials and techniques of Jan van Eyck and his contemporaries have been thoroughly investigated and are relatively well understood. Since the first and well-known scientific study conducted in the early 1950s by Paul Coremans and his team,[1] our understanding of fifteenth-century painting studio practice has been considerably enlarged. In the following decades, the numerous technical studies of Jan van Eyck's paintings in Berlin, Bruges, London and Washington generated supplementary insights that facilitated the interpretation of data obtained during the current investigations of the *Ghent Altarpiece*.[2] Also, recent research on pigments and additives and their complex interactions with binders enables us to contextualize our findings. For instance, the intensive use of powdered glass and zinc sulphate as additives in the *Ghent Altarpiece* panels, further discussed below, ties in well with recent findings in other early Netherlandish paintings.[3]

The large size of the polyptych presented a challenge to its material investigation. The more than twenty-five square metres of painted surface with a very turbulent material history provide unprecedented opportunities for an in-depth study during the time-consuming, meticulous work on its restoration. Indeed, studying the painting technique requires linking visual observations, supported by X-radiography (XR), infrared reflectography (IRR) or ultraviolet (UV) photography, with the insights obtained from chemical analysis. The latter is performed with a wide range of instruments and methods, which are subject to continuous innovation, even during the course of the treatment. For instance, macro X-ray fluorescence (MA-XRF) was used for the first time for large-scale elemental mapping during the first restoration phase,[4] while, in the second phase, the main novelty was the

(facing page) *Adoration of the Lamb*: cross-section of the dove (10/18) under VIS, combined with back-scattered electron SEM image (see also 3.18f–g).

introduction of macro X-ray powder diffraction (MA-XRPD). The latter technique proved highly valuable as it allowed identification of crystalline pigments and degradation products at the paint surface, especially in the non-sampled areas, as exemplified further in this chapter.

Nonetheless, a refined understanding of complex paint stratigraphies such as those observed in the *Ghent Altarpiece* requires a comprehensive insight into the layer sequence and the composition of individual layers. This necessitates the chemical characterization of cross-sectioned paint samples at micro- and nano-scale. In this context, samples extracted during previous restoration campaigns and preserved in KIK-IRPA's sample database have proved highly informative even if not always sufficient or suitable to answer current research questions. Additional micro-sampling was thus needed. Apart from classic cross-sections including the entire paint layer build-up, the overpaints removed by conservators were collected and used for the careful documentation of the historic moment marked by the present restoration campaign. This sample set, in both embedded and non-embedded form, was thoroughly characterized using a wide diversity of analytical techniques, such as scanning electron microscopy with energy dispersive X-ray spectroscopy (SEM-EDX), micro-Fourier transform infrared spectroscopy (FTIR), micro-Raman spectroscopy (MRS), high performance liquid chromatography (HPLC) and pyrolysis-gas chromatography–mass spectrometry (Py-GCMS). A smaller selection of highly relevant samples was also analysed using advanced techniques such as time-of-flight secondary ion mass spectrometry (TOF-SIMS), liquid chromatography-tandem mass-spectrometry (LC-MS/MS), synchrotron radiation-based X-ray powder diffraction (SR-XRPD), X-ray fluorescence (SR-XRF) and X-ray absorption near-edge structure (SR-XANES).[5] This extensive micro-sample investigation campaign provided many answers and confirmations to hypotheses proposed by the interdisciplinary team of experts involved in the recent restoration campaigns, but quite often it raised many new, challenging questions.

This chapter offers a general, state-of-the-art overview of the latest findings on Eyckian materials and painting techniques by cross-interpretation of the diverse results obtained during the first two restoration phases of the *Ghent Altarpiece* (2012–19). It also outlines the most recent achievements as well as the remaining challenges related to the material understanding of the Van Eycks' polyptych.

Layer build-up

The cross-sections, prepared from the sample set taken during the 1950–51 treatment of the altarpiece before removal of the overpaint, often revealed a very complex stratigraphy with a number of layers both larger and more variable than usually encountered in cross-sections of early Netherlandish paintings. A certain variability was also observed in other paintings by Jan van Eyck (e.g. the *Annunciation* in the National Gallery of Art, Washington, and the *Arnolfini Portrait* in the National Gallery, London[6]) but seemed to correspond to the modelling, shading and/or changes in the composition. However, in the *Ghent Altarpiece* the unusual number of layers (sometimes up to ten under the first identifiable varnish) could also have had an additional reason, as discussed in chapters 2 and 4: at least two painters may have been involved in the creative process, not necessarily working together. As stated in the quatrain on the exterior frames,[7] the altarpiece was presented in 1432, started by Hubert and finalized by his brother Jan van Eyck. Very little is known about how work on such sizeable altarpieces was undertaken and organized. We do not know when work on the *Ghent Altarpiece* started, nor whether the Van Eyck brothers worked alone or with assistants, and – in the latter case – if there would have been a difference in painting technique between different hands. We also ignore what would have been the impact of the double authorship on the paint layer structure. Trying to distinguish between the contributions of both brothers is anything but straightforward. Whereas several paintings signed by Jan have been carefully examined, the only work that can be linked to Hubert is the *Ghent Altarpiece* itself. What is more, the presence of non-Eyckian interventions with paint materials very similar to those used by the Van Eyck brothers makes the understanding of the layer build-up an even greater challenge.

Preparatory layers

As described in numerous studies[8] on early Netherlandish painting technology and Van Eyck's technique in particular, the preparatory layers commonly consist of a sizing of the wooden support followed by a chalk ground and a carbon black underdrawing and completed with an oil-based isolation layer that renders the absorbing ground impervious. This isolation layer is sometimes tinted to function simultaneously as a priming. The aforementioned variability of strata in the different cross-sections taken from the *Ghent Altarpiece* is even found in the preparatory phase of the painting process.

Ground

An off-white, chalk-based ground is evenly spread on all (undoubtedly sized) oak panels. The number of layers and their thickness is not homogeneous over the various sampled locations. Observation with the optical and electron microscope allowed us to distinguish between two and five layers, each ranging from 30 to 50 µm in thickness. The entire chalk ground system is between 80 and 200 µm thick. The ground is composed of natural calcium carbonate or chalk, characterized by the presence of fossilized coccoliths.[9] The presence of some gypsum as an impurity, probably resulting from the sulphation (weathering) of the calcium carbonate, was revealed in one sample analysed by SR-XANES in the upper part of the ground.[10] The binder of the ground is an animal glue, as is common in medieval panel painting. A further chromatographic characterization of the animal origin of this glue became possible thanks to the local accumulation of the fluid ground material during its application in a slit between the (ill-fitting) frames and panels of the *Just Judges*[11] and the *Knights of Christ*. This created an opportunity for sampling during the unframing of the panels, prior to their restoration. Three samples of

Group	Characteristics of the priming oil-based layers	Panels in which these layers are encountered
A	Composed of one or two translucent layers (overall thickness 10–15 µm) containing particles of calcium carbonate, lead white, carbon black. Sometimes a few red particles such as red earth, vermilion or minium are present (mainly under the green and blue areas).	**Interior: lower register** (*Knights of Christ, Adoration of the Lamb, Hermits* and *Pilgrims*) **Interior: upper register** (*Singing Angels, Virgin Enthroned, Deity Enthroned, St John the Baptist Enthroned* and the *Angel Musicians*)*
B	Quite thick (10–30 µm), greyish, semi-translucent layer containing particles of bone white, calcite, lead white and variable proportions of coal black. Sometimes a few particles of vermilion or red earth are encountered.	**Exterior: upper register** (*Archangel Annunciate, City View, Interior with Lavabo* and *Virgin Annunciate*) **Interior: upper register** (*Adam*)*
C	Very thin (1–3 µm), unpigmented transparent layer, in a few cases not visible (absorbed?) or exceptionally located below the underdrawing.	**Exterior: lower register** (panels *Joos Vijd, John the Baptist, John the Evangelist* and *Elisabeth Borluut*)
* Based on the preliminary study of the cross-sections taken in 1950–51		

3.1

Fig. 3.1. Summary of the main differences observed in the priming layers in the *Ghent Altarpiece* panels.

the ground were thus analysed with LC-MS/MS after trypsin digestion. The results obtained indicate that the collagen originated from sheep, probably recovered from a parchment made of sheepskin as recommended in historical documentary sources dealing with the preparation of animal glue.[12]

Underdrawing

Although a visual study supported by infrared reflectography images is a better approach for assessing the underdrawing methods, the paint material analysis of these black layers in the cross-sections yielded additional insights. As discussed in chapter 2, the underdrawing was carried out in several steps using various materials and techniques, including incisions in the preparation, liquid aqueous media and a dry drawing material, such as coal and charcoal or a metallic stylus. Contours and hatching were completed with washes to reinforce the modelling of shadow areas.[13] The samples, taken in areas showing liquid or dry drawing materials in infrared reflectography, invariably revealed the presence of carbon black, either finely ground or as quite large particles (5–20 µm), mixed with calcium carbonate and impurities containing silica, aluminium, sulphur and chlorine. This composition in combination with the angular shape of the black particles indicates the use of coal, and, in view of the chlorine content, more probably sea-coal.[14] The evidence of organic thiol-based compounds and gypsum, revealed with SR-XANES in one sample from the prophet Zechariah's drapery, also supports this identification (fig. 3.16). Interestingly, this cross-section, taken in an area with overlapping underdrawing lines, shows three superimposed black layers. The lower one is thin and discontinuous and probably done in a dry material, whereas the two upper layers, probably applied as liquids, have an overall thickness of up to 40 µm (fig. 3.16b). This exceptional thickness facilitated the ATR-FTIR (Attenuated total reflection – Fourier transform infrared spectroscopy) identification of proteins used as a binder, thus confirming the underdrawing's aqueous character.

Priming

As in many early Northern European paintings, including early Netherlandish as well as some pre-Eyckian paintings,[15] a (semi)-translucent oil-based, highly UV-fluorescent layer was systematically found on top of the underdrawing in the Ghent panels. Such layers are often described in the modern technical literature as 'priming',[16] but also as 'isolation', 'impermeabilization' or 'intermediate' layers.[17] 'Priming' seems to be the most appropriate term, as it derives from its ancient variants *primuersel*, *pourmuersel*, *imprimis* or *emprimure*, described in the historical documentary sources.[18] The priming layers observed in the samples from the *Ghent Altarpiece* are typically rich in binder, characterized by a diffuse and homogeneous distribution of lead, and various particles of cerussite, hydrocerussite, calcium carbonate (from chalk and/or probably another source of calcite, such as marble, calcined bones or carbonated slaked lime) or calcium phosphates (from calcined bones). Beside calcium and lead compounds, related to the pretreatment of the binder, variable amounts of coal black and a few particles of a red pigment (vermilion, minium or red earth) were also occasionally found. The composition of this isolation layer and its thickness varies significantly (between 1 and 30 μm) in the cross-sections, with the thickest layers containing bone white. The layer was applied over the entire ground surface but does not seem to present the same aspect in all samples: sometimes it appears to be more pigmented. Comparative study of the priming layers in the available cross-sections reveals similarities in composition and appearance of these layers in the different panels. Within the corpus of cross-sections showing a priming, three main categories emerge, as summarized in the table shown in figure 3.1.

GROUP A (Interior: lower and upper register) includes the panels of the *Knights of Christ*, the *Adoration of the Lamb*, the *Hermits* and the *Pilgrims* with a priming layer composed of one or two thin strata (10–15 μm) (fig. 3.2). When two layers are found, the upper one is more pigmented, but both contain particles of calcium

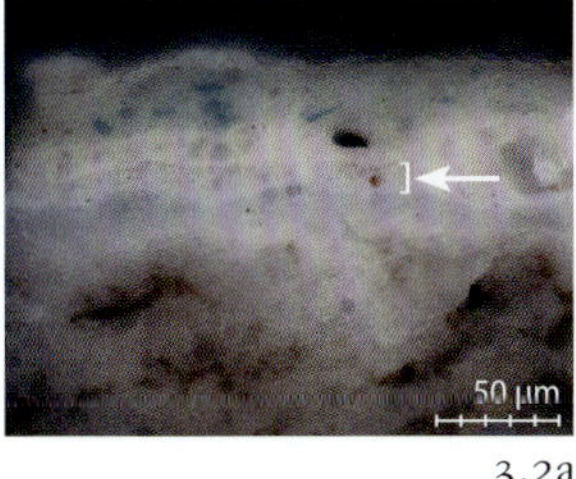

3.2a

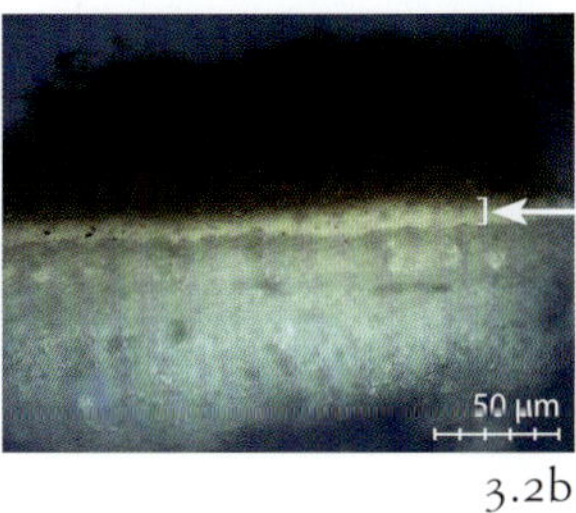

3.2b

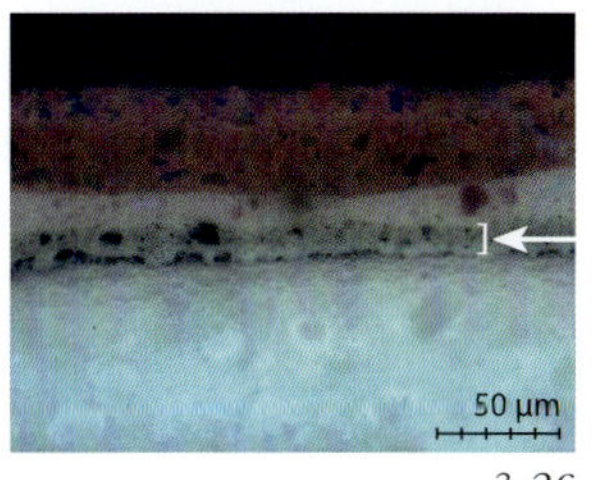

3.2c

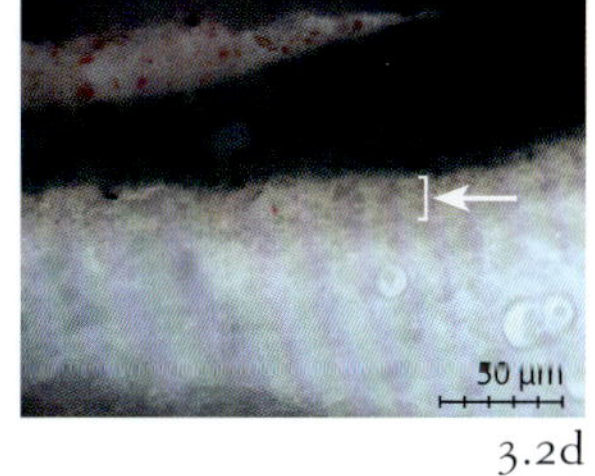

3.2d

Fig. 3.2a–d. Paint cross-sections under UV light showing the priming layers of **group A**: *Knights of Christ*, sky (9/9) (a); *Adoration of the Lamb*, meadow under the fountain (10/82) (b); *Adoration of the Lamb*, philosopher's violet drapery (10/75) (c); *Pilgrims*, sky (12/08) (d). Arrows indicate the priming layer in a–d.

carbonate[19] and carbon black. In several cross-sections, mainly those extracted from green or blue areas, a few red particles identified as vermilion, red lead or a red earth were found as well. A priming layer with similar characteristics was detected in the panels of the upper interior register, the *Singing Angels*, the *Virgin*, *Deity* and *St John the Baptist Enthroned*, and the *Angel Musicians* in a preliminary examination of the old samples. Interestingly, the preliminary analysis of a sample from the *Adam* panel suggests that it rather belongs to group B (see below) than to group A.[20]

This group A in priming could relate to the flesh-like, beige *primuursel*, discussed by Karel van Mander in his *Schilder-boeck* (1604). The author concludes that this was the standard mixture of materials (or standard painting technique if he does not mention the pigments) of his fifteenth- and sixteenth-century predecessors, explicitly including Jan van Eyck.[21]

GROUP B (exterior: upper register) includes the *Archangel*, the *City View*, the *Interior View* and the *Virgin Annunciate* (fig. 3.3). The layer is significantly thicker, up to 30 µm, more pigmented and therefore less translucent, but the drawing is still visible. In certain areas the priming layer serves as an underpainting. In particular, the blue and pinkish glazes of the wing of the *Archangel* or the rose glaze in the prophet Zechariah's drapery (figs. 3.3b and 3.16) were applied directly on top of the greyish priming layer.[22] Here, the layer holds particles of calcined bone, hydrocerussite, cerussite, calcite, variable proportions of coal black and, only in the *Virgin Annunciate* panel, some vermilion and red earth.

The finding of calcined bone in the priming of five *Ghent Altarpiece* panels was surprising, as technical studies rarely report this material in West European panel paintings. To the best of our knowledge, only two other cases of similar priming were reported in early Northern European painting. One is Memling's large-size ensemble of *God the Father with Singing and Music-Making Angels* (Royal Museum of Fine Arts Antwerp, inv. 778–780)[23] and the second is the Norwegian frontal *Tresfjord* produced in the second quarter of the fourteenth century.[24] Calcined bone was also found in the gilded pastiglia letters on the frame of the *Crucifixion* (Metropolitan Museum of Art, New York, acc. 33.92ab) attributed to Jan van Eyck and a workshop assistant,[25] as well as in the gilding mordant and in the tin foil adhesive of the pre-Eyckian *Scenes from the Life of the Virgin* (Royal Museums of Fine Arts of Belgium, Brussels, inv. 4883) dated around 1400.[26]

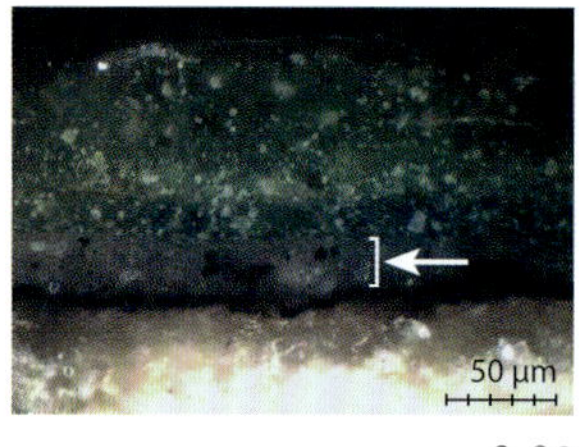

3.3a

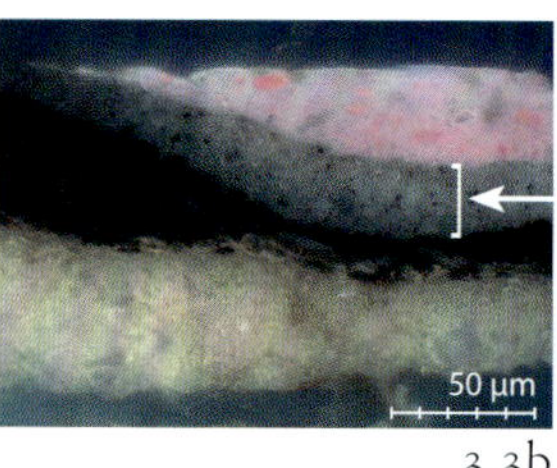

3.3b

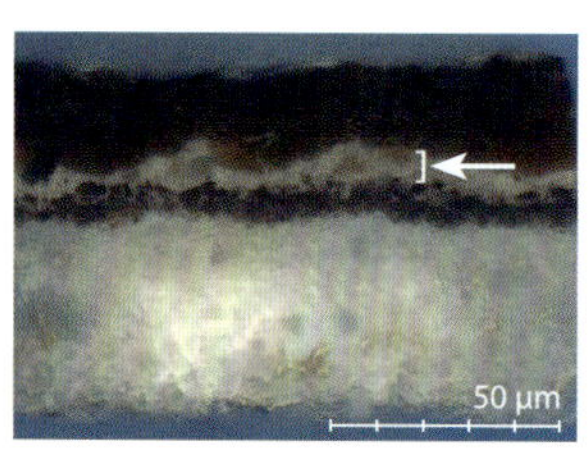

3.3c

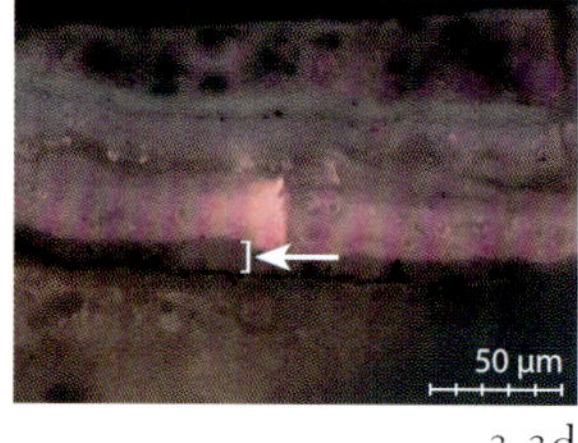

3.3d

Fig. 3.3a–d. Paint cross-sections under VIS (a) and UV (b, c, d) light showing the priming layers of **group B**: *Archangel*, green book (13/5) and Zechariah's pink drapery (13/20), respectively (a, b); *City View*, brown wooden ceiling (14/1) (c); *Virgin Annunciate*, Micah's mantle (16/40) (d). Arrows indicate the priming layer in a–d.

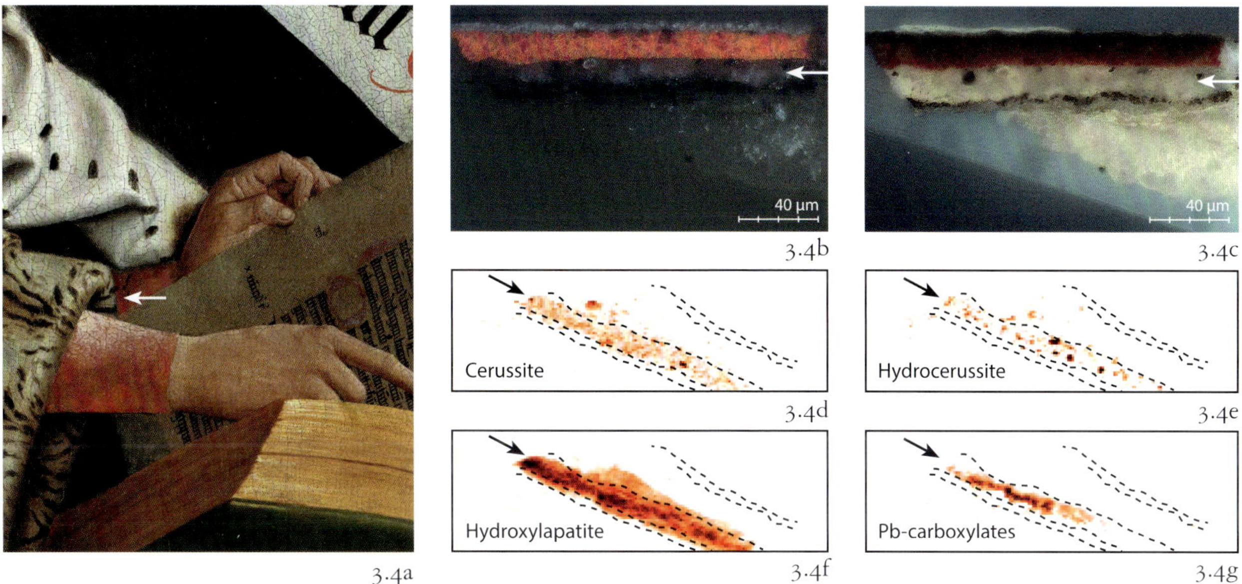

Fig. 3.4a–g. *Archangel*: detail of the prophet Zechariah's red sleeve. Location of sampling (a), paint cross-section (13/22) in VIS (b) and in UV light (c). Spatial distributions of cerussite (d), hydrocerussite (e), hydroxylapatite (f) and lead carboxylates (g) within the cross-section visualized using SR-µ-XRPD. Arrows indicate the priming layer in b–g.

In medieval recipe books for artists, burnt bone is usually recommended for the preparation of a suitable surface for metalpoint drawing.[27] However, it is also proposed as an additive for improving the drying of oil. Two fifteenth-century German manuscripts, the Strasbourg and the Tegernsee manuscripts,[28] include bone white in recipes for preparing an oil-based paint medium, a gold varnish and a mordant for gilding. But the most relevant recipe for priming is found in the fourteenth-century Icelandic manuscript known as Likneskjusmiå: '… you should grind burnt bone with oil and this is called underwhite. It should be spread on the whiting with a paintbrush on those places where you intend to apply other colours …'.[29] This description fits quite well with what is observed in the upper register of the exterior Ghent panels where the priming is simultaneously fulfilling the role of underpaint.

The chemical composition of this particular kind of priming was studied in the sample taken from the sleeve of the prophet Zechariah's drapery using synchrotron radiation-based (SR) analysis.[30] The SR-µ-XRPD mapping of the cross-section from this area (fig. 3.4) demonstrated the presence of a relatively high concentration of hydroxyapatite, from calcined bone, evenly dispersed in the priming.

A small fraction of calcite was also found, most likely part of the calcined bone or stemming from the addition of chalk or carbonated quicklime. The latter is indeed recommended in a fourteenth-century manuscript for the preparation of a sun-thickened leaded oil.[31] The addition of highly alkaline quicklime to oil containing lead white would catalyse the saponification of triglycerides and the formation of metal carboxylates which accelerate oil drying. Lime, calcined bone and also zinc vitriol, would act as secondary (auxiliary) driers, reinforcing the drying property of oils containing lead- or manganese-based primary driers.[32]

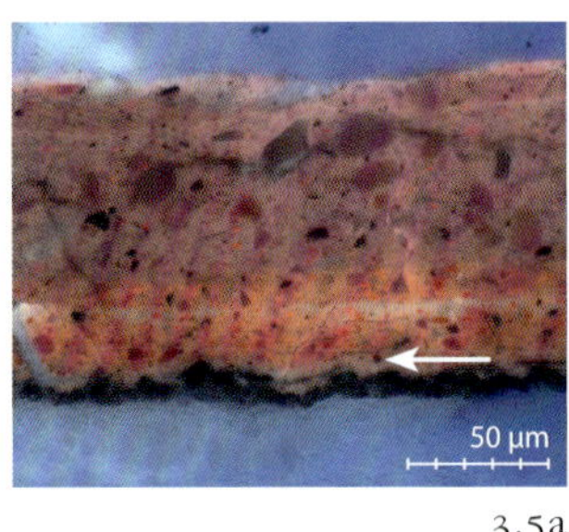

3.5a

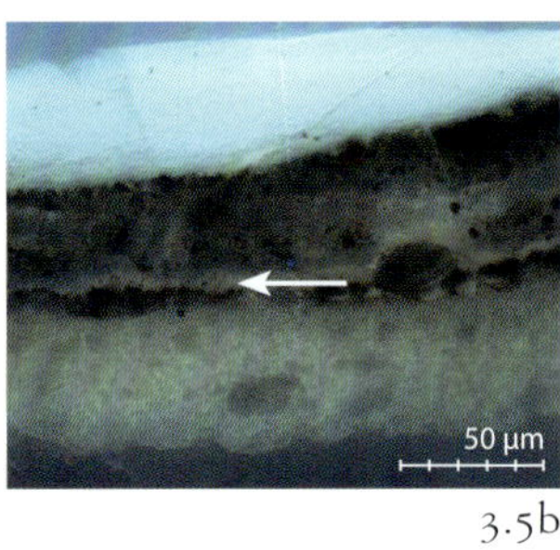

3.5b

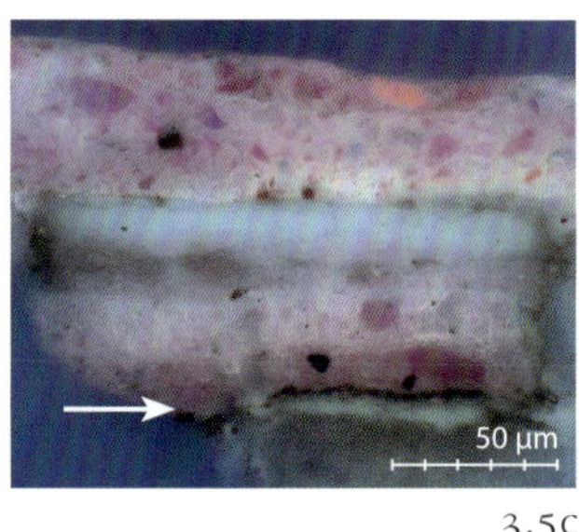

3.5c

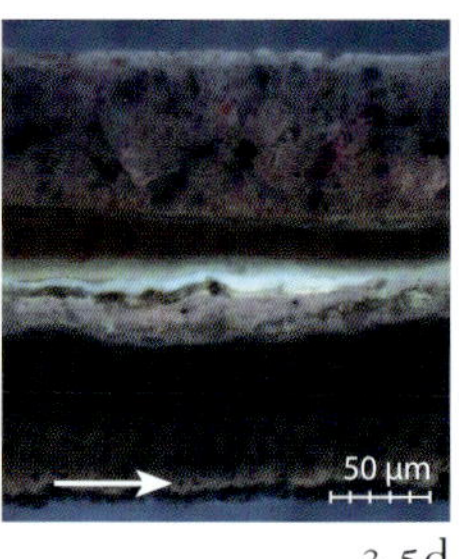

3.5d

Fig. 3.5a–d. Paint cross-sections under UV light showing the priming layers of **group C**: *Joos Vijd*, red drapery (17/39) (a); *St John the Evangelist*'s drapery (19/9) (b); *Elisabeth Borluut*, pink drapery in a light area (20/25) and in a shadow area (20/32), respectively (c, d). Arrows indicate the priming layer in a–d.

Finally, SEM-EDX mapping has shown that lead is homogeneously dispersed in the binder and sometimes associated with discrete particles of lead white. SR-µ-XRPD (fig. 3.4) also revealed the presence of two lead carbonates, basic hydrocerussite ($2PbCO_3.Pb(OH)_2$) and neutral cerussite ($PbCO_3$). At the moment, it is not clear to what extent these lead carbonates were added to the starting mixture, or were formed by remineralization of lead carboxylates; both hypotheses are conceivable. As demonstrated by Cotte, lead carboxylates could have been formed during boiling of the oil or 'maturation' by sun-thickening and it is well known that lead carboxylates are also spontaneously formed during the ageing of a paint film by the interaction of the binder and lead white.[33]

In GROUP C are placed all the panels of the lower register of the exterior shutters: *Joos Vijd*, *John the Baptist*, *John the Evangelist* and *Elisabeth Borluut*. The isolation layer in these paintings is very thin (ranging from 1 to 3 µm), rather unpigmented (containing only a small amount of chalk), and thus completely transparent. Thanks to its strong fluorescence, it can readily be recognized when the cross-sections are observed in a microscope under UV illumination (fig. 3.5c). As it is almost unpigmented, it might have penetrated into the underlying layers. It is thus hardly detectable in such cases.[34]

Paint layers

Palette overview

The Eyckian palette used for the *Ghent Altarpiece* was not extensive; it included around twenty pigments commonly found in fifteenth- and sixteenth-century Northern European painting.[35] In general, most of these pigments were correctly identified in the previous studies of samples taken from the polyptych in 1950–51.[36]

The list of materials previously found in the panels' original paint layers was complemented with pigments and additives. Thus coal black, bistre, kermes lake, orpiment, bone white, white vitriol or colourless powdered glass were added to the existing list which included lead white, chalk, carbon black, azurite, ultramarine, indigo, verdigris, malachite, lead-tin yellow, yellow ochres, vermilion, red earth and red lead (minium) (fig. 3.6).

Fig. 3.6. Pigments identified in the *Ghent Altarpiece* panels studied between 2012 and 2019.

Colour	Pigment	Appearance in the *Ghent Altarpiece*
White	Lead white	Only opaque white pigment used, rarely used alone, more often for modelling
Blue	Azurite	Main blue pigment
	Ultramarine	Less frequent than azurite in blue and violet areas
	Indigo (likely from dyers' wool)	Used only in underlayers
Green	Verdigris	Standard green pigment, frequently used in mixtures with yellow, brown, sometimes blue or red pigments
	Malachite	One single detection with MA-XRD; could be a later addition
Yellow	Lead-tin yellow type I	Frequently used for bright yellow tones and in green mixtures
	Yellow ochre (goethite-based)	Frequently used for ochre colours
	Siena lepidocrocite-based	Used in brown mixtures
	Yellow lake	Mainly used in mixtures with verdigris
	Orpiment	Very rarely found, only some particles in green underlayers
Red	Vermilion and cinnabar	Frequently used in underlayers for red lakes
	Red earth (hematite-based earth pigments)	Not used alone, found in small amounts in red glazes, in painted brocade motifs, green verdigris-containing layers, grey underlayers of sky, sometimes in priming
	Kermes lakes (containing traces of lac-dye)	Standard red pigment, alone or in mixture with blue or black
	Red lead	Not found in paint layers, only in priming and mordants
Black and brown	Coal (sulphur-rich, containing some chlorine)	Main black pigment, used in underdrawing and shadowing
	Charcoal	Used to a much lesser extent than coal
	Bistre from soot	Detected in a few brown paint layers
	Brown ferruginous earth (containing peat?)	Used in dark brown glazes
Additives (less than 3%) and extenders	Powdered potash-lime glass	Used in red and green glazes and in the black lettering of frames
	White vitriol (zinc sulphate)	Frequently used in small amounts, mainly in red, brown and green layers
	Quartz	Used in red, pink and green glazes, in priming and in blue, rose and brown opaque layers, also present as ultramarine impurities
	Bone white (hydroxylapatite-based)	Extender in type B priming layers, likely as an additive in brown and green layers
	Chalk (calcium carbonate)	Extender of ground and priming, as an additive in red, green, brown glazes, grey

3.6

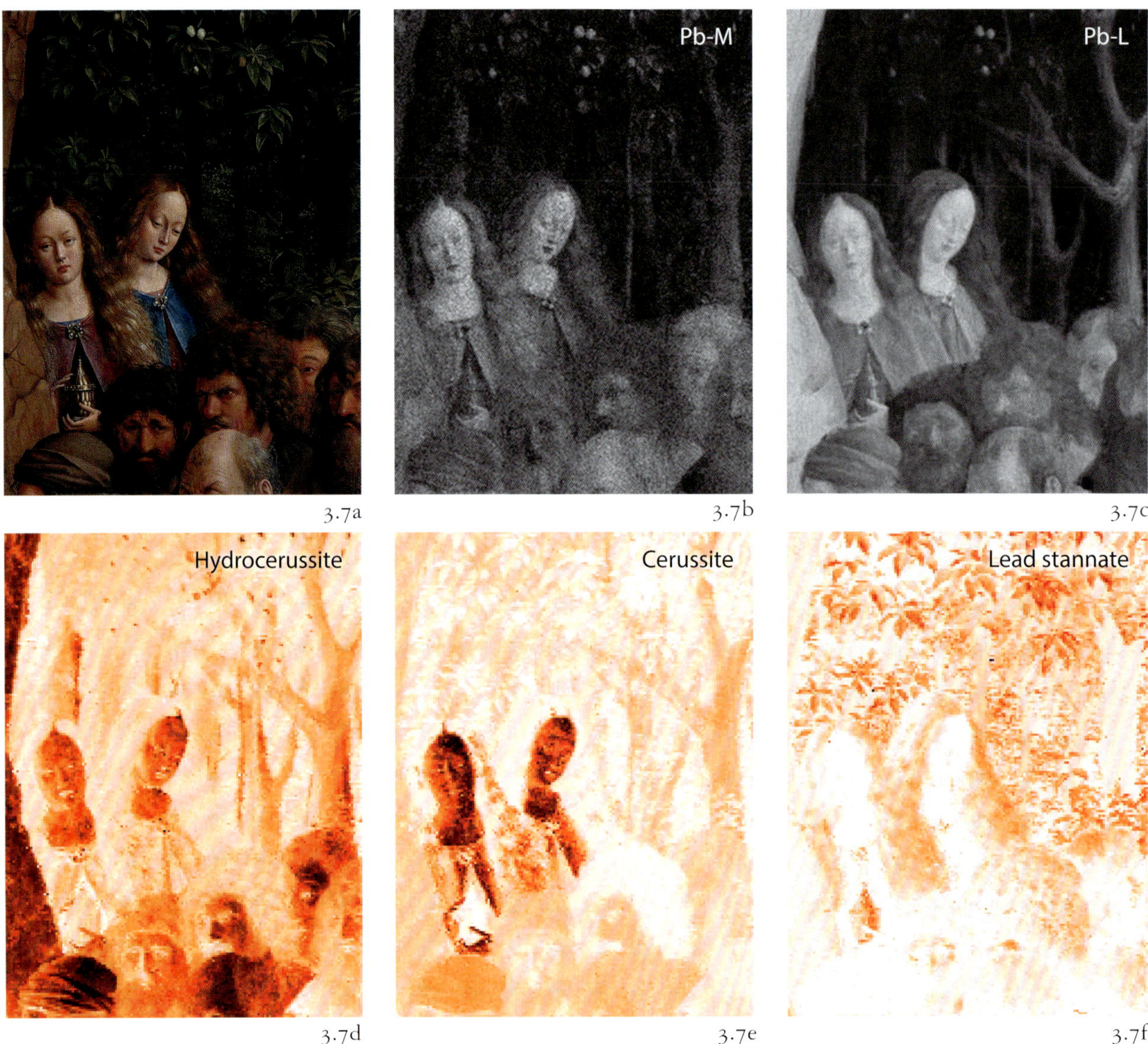

Fig. 3.7a–f. *Hermits*: detail of two women (a); MA-XRF distribution maps of Pb-M (b) and Pb-L (c); MA-XRPD distribution maps of hydrocerussite (d), cerussite (e) and lead stannate (f).

From visual observation and MA-XRF elemental scanning of the panels in their entirety combined with the stratigraphic analysis of samples, it is evident that some of these pigments, such as lead white, azurite, verdigris, lead-tin yellow, earth pigments containing iron oxides of various colours, vermilion and red lakes, were widely used. Ultramarine was reserved for smaller areas, at least in the original layers, for it was more extensively used in the non-Eyckian interventions. Indigo, orpiment, minium and bone white were detected exclusively in underlying layers that were meant to be covered. Malachite was identified with MA-XRPD only in the green cloth of a knight in the *Knights of Christ* panel, while it was never detected in the green microsamples available for analysis.[37] The lack of a malachite-containing microsample made it impossible to determine whether the pigment was present in the original layers or was added later during an early intervention.

White

Lead white (basic lead carbonate) is one of the most widely used pigments in the polyptych. It was added in all opaque layers and is present in quite low proportion in both the (semi-)transparent and the priming layers.[38] It was also used in later interventions. Historically, lead white was produced artificially by the corrosion of metallic lead in vinegar, leading to the formation of lead acetate, which is transformed into lead carbonate by carbon dioxide. The resulting material is mainly composed of two crystalline phases of lead carbonate, hydrocerussite (HC, $2PbCO_3 \cdot Pb(OH)_2$) and cerussite (C, $PbCO_3$). The synthesis and purification methods applied during pigment processing impact not only the pigment's physico-chemical properties and quality grade but also the HC/(HC+C) ratio value. Given that it can be measured with X-ray diffraction techniques, this relation can thus be used to categorize different types of white lead found in paintings.[39]

Considering the above, the MA-XRPD[40] mapping of the Ghent panels in the areas containing lead white allowed some interesting observations to be made. For example, in the background of the *Hermits* panel, the lead white used for the female figures contains a higher proportion of cerussite than the one found in the group of male figures and mountain rocks in the background, which are richer in hydrocerussite (fig. 3.7). This result suggests that (at least) two different types of lead white were used. It is not unthinkable, therefore, that the female figures and the groups of hermits were not painted at the same time and thus not necessarily by the same artist, unless the use of two different types of lead white was a deliberate choice of the painter of this scene. However, this problem is more complex than just the determination of the quality grade of lead white using the HC/(HC+C) ratio. Frequent detection of plumbonacrite, a third lead carbonate that can be ascribed to the carbonation of lead oxide (massicot or litharge) and lead carboxylates formed by the interaction of an oily binder and lead pigment, complicates the interpretation of the HC/(HC+C) ratio.[41]

MA-XRF scanning allows us to extract two distribution images for the element lead (Pb) from the data cube, the Pb-L and Pb-M emission lines, each providing different information. The map of the high-energy Pb-L emission lines reveals the distribution of lead from underlying layers, showing their cracks and losses, while the Pb-M map corresponds to the lead from the paint surface. The combination of these two chemical maps allows us to examine the Eyckian painting technique with some depth-selectivity. As shown in the illustration (fig. 3.7), all faces and the rocky mountain were underpainted with lead white and the modelling with final colours was realized in the upper layer.

Blue

Azurite The use of azurite as the main pigment in the blue areas in the altarpiece panels was largely confirmed by the MA-XRF copper maps. This pigment was employed either alone or in admixture with red lakes to create shades of violet. Inspection of cross-sections demonstrates its occurrence, both in the final paint

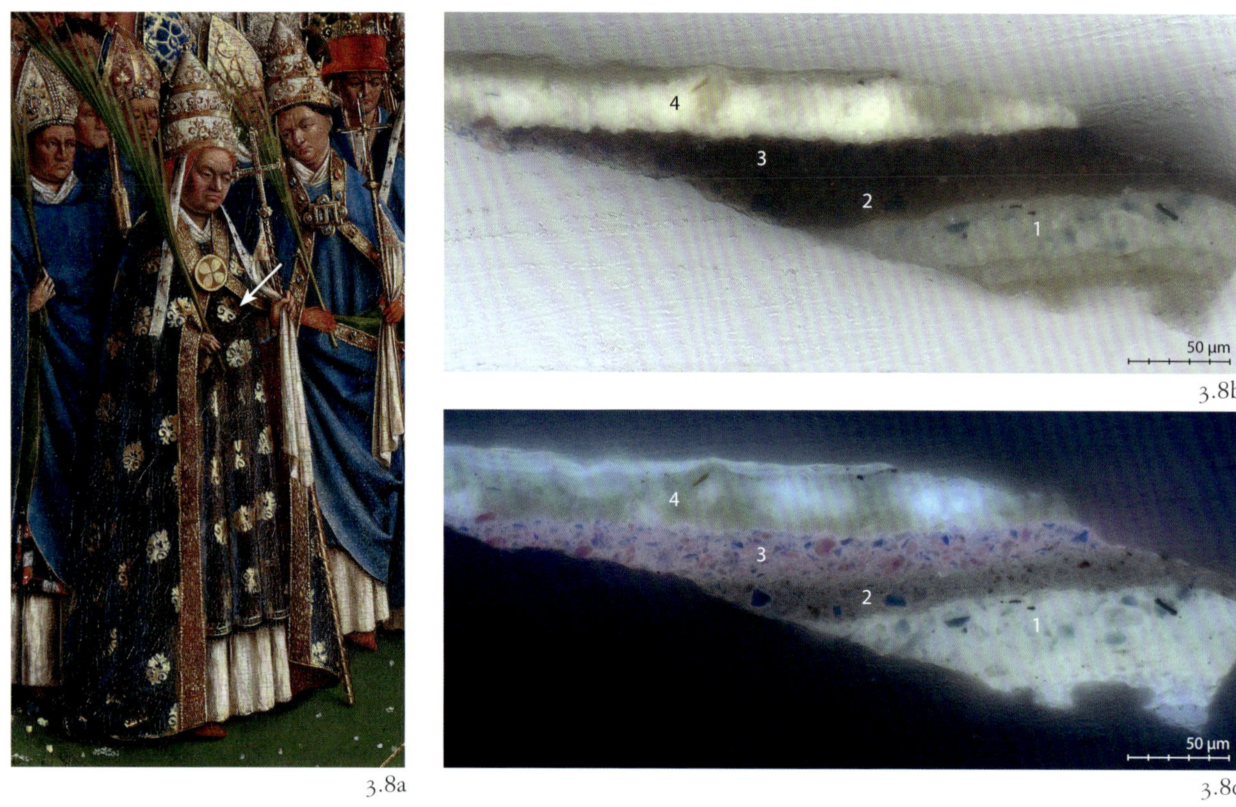

3.8a 3.8b 3.8c

Fig. 3.8a–c. *Adoration of the Lamb*: detail of a velvet cloth of gold of a confessor. The white arrow indicates the sampling location (a); paint cross-sections (10/76) under VIS (b) and UV (c) light showing the layer structure: azurite-containing underlayer (1), followed by ultramarine-containing brownish (2) and purple (3) glaze layers. The golden motifs were painted with lead-tin yellow type I (4).

layers and in the underlayers (figs. 3.8 and 3.10). The pigment is commonly intermixed with lead white, as observed in the skies, where it was applied in two or three layers over an underlayer containing indigo and combined with incremental proportions of lead white towards the horizon.

In the draperies, it was more often found underlying the ultramarine blue or violet glazes. For instance, quite coarser azurite (ca. 20 µm particle size) was found as an underlayer of purple and brownish glazes in the illusionistic representation of the *changeant* or shot[42] velvet cloth of gold fabric of one confessor in the *Adoration of the Lamb* (fig. 3.8).

Ultramarine In contrast to azurite, the ultramarine blue (coloured by lazurite $[(Na,Ca)_8[(S,Cl,SO_4,OH)_2|(Al_6Si_6O_{24})]]$, a blue mineral extracted from lapis lazuli) is much less frequently found in original layers, with a notable exception for the *Adoration of the Lamb*, where it was used for the drapery and headwear of many figures. In the exterior panels, ultramarine was found only in small areas on the upper register: such as the jewels of the *Archangel* and *Virgin Annunciate* panels, the Archangel's wings, the Cumaean Sibyl's underdress, the lines on the Erythraean

Sibyl's and Zechariah's headwear. The same goes for the interior shutters, where ultramarine was only used in several small areas. In the *Knights of Christ* panel, the jewels of the crowns and horse harnessing and the left knight's helmet painted with an ultramarine blue are considered to be original. However, the ultramarine areas on this panel, such as the purplish velvet drapery covering the painted brocade of the knight on the extreme left (fig. 2.66), the large headgear of a knight in the background covering a smaller, azurite-containing headgear with a crown (fig. 3.9), and the mountains painted on top of the sky are probably later interventions. A small amount of ultramarine was also detected in the mixture with red lake in the dark purplish red of St Anthony's drapery (fig. 3.15).

A great deal of ultramarine was found in the *Adoration of the Lamb*, where understanding the layer structure was most problematic. Consequently, the potential differentiation of various ultramarine types was thought to be useful as a supporting argument for the recognition of Eyckian and non-Eyckian interventions.[43] Two criteria for differentiating between them were explored: the distribution of the different sizes of ultramarine particles and their elemental and mineralogical impurities. Although it is too early to draw final conclusions, a few tendencies have been observed. For instance, the Eyckian ultramarine is more finely ground

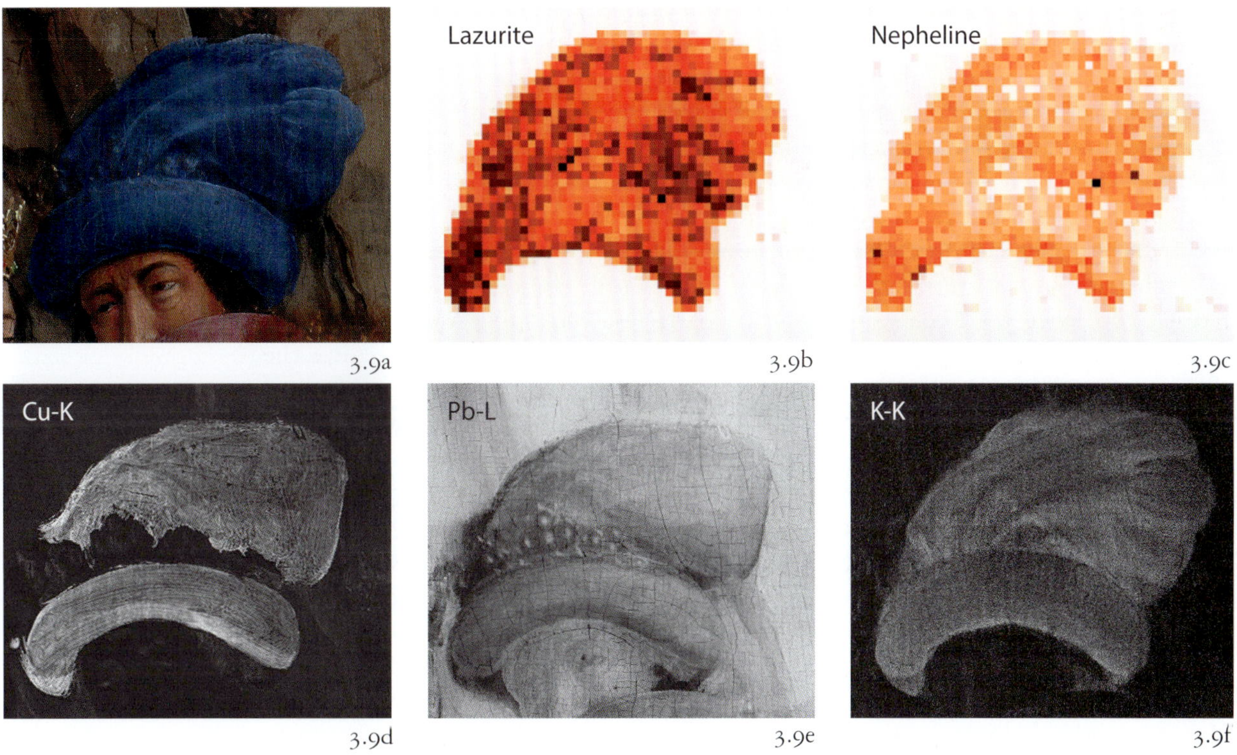

Fig. 3.9a–f. *Knights of Christ*: detail of the knight with a blue headgear (a). The azurite-containing headgear of the first stage is represented by the MA-XRF maps of copper (Cu-K, d) and lead (Pb-L, e), while the later ultramarine-containing headgear of the second stage is represented by MA-XRF maps of potassium (K-K, f). The ultramarine of the upper headgear is rich in lazurite and in nepheline as shown by their MA-XRPD distribution maps (b) and (c) respectively.

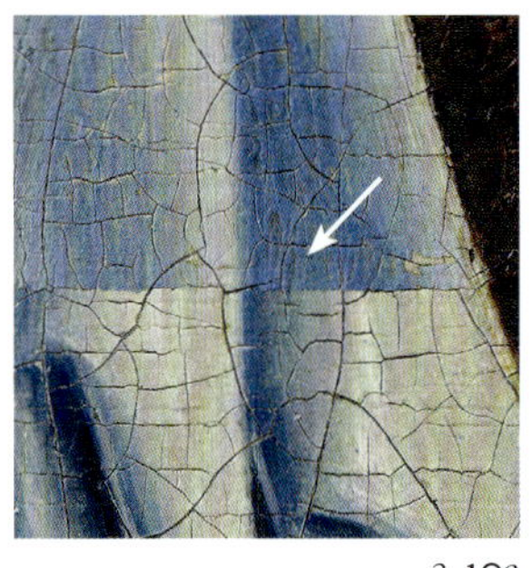

3.10a

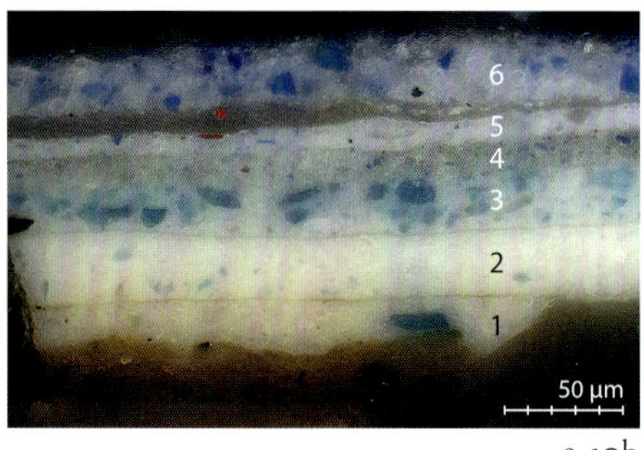

3.10b

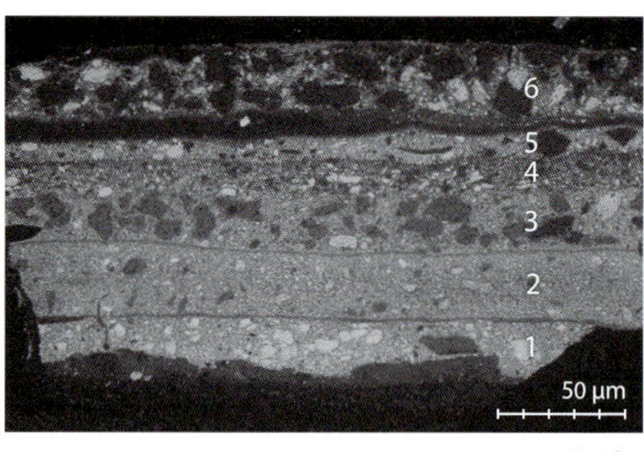

3.10c

Fig. 3.10a–c. *Adoration of the Lamb*: detail of the ultramarine-containing drapery of St Dorothy, during overpaint removal (a). The paint cross-section (10/K) under VIS light (b) and back-scattered electron SEM image (c) shows the following layer structure: three azurite-containing layers (1, 2, 3) coated with two ultramarine-containing layers (4, 5). The uppermost, ultramarine-containing blue layer (6) corresponds to the overpaint removed during the treatment.

(2–5 µm in light blue areas and up to 15 µm in the shadows). Such fine granulometry is systematically observed in other works by Van Eyck, too.[44] In contrast, the non-Eyckian pigment is coarser (some particles reaching up to 40 µm in diameter). As far as the impurities are concerned, the Eyckian ultramarine holds more sodium-containing compounds and more diopside ($CaMgSi_2O_6$), whereas the non-Eyckian ultramarine seems to be richer in potassium-containing colourless grains, such as nepheline [(Na,K)AlSiO4], which is particularly present in the blue headgear of a knight in the background in the *Knights of Christ* panel (fig. 3.9c).

A direct comparison of these elements became possible with samples taken from areas in which ultramarine was used in both the original paint layers and the overpaints. A first example is a cross-section taken from the drapery of St Dorothy, one of the women carrying a basket of flowers in the group of female martyrs on the right side of the *Adoration of the Lamb* (fig. 3.10). The cross-section presents a thick top layer with coarse ultramarine particles, corresponding to the now-removed overpaint that was applied over two thin Eyckian layers containing the aforementioned finely-grained ultramarine. Interestingly, the lead white admixed with ultramarine shows the same trend in particle size. Indeed, this white pigment is roughly ground in the overpaint while it is very fine and seems to have been purified in the lower original paint layers. An exception is to be found in the rather coarse lead white found in the more yellowish bottom underlayer.

It is not unthinkable that the bottommost, azurite-containing layers (fig. 3.10b–c, layers 1, 2 and 3) form a (semi-)finished paint level composed of a coarser lay-in underlayer (layer 1) on top of which a fine light blue (layer 2) and a deep dark blue (layer 3), shadowing layer were applied. In that case, the overlying ultramarine layers (layers 4 and 5) could be regarded as one single paint system and thus might have been added during the execution of the later, second stage. The topmost overpaint, then, contains the lower quality of lead white and a coarser grade of ultramarine well recognizable in the backscattering image (fig. 3.10c, layer 6). This layer corresponds to the blue paint removed during the restoration treatment, which is still visible in the upper part of fig. 3.10a.

The nature of the binding medium for the Eyckian ultramarine blue is another important issue related to this pigment. Based on various microchemical staining tests performed on a sample taken from the *Virgin Enthroned* drapery, Coremans and Kockaert concluded that ultramarine in the *Ghent Altarpiece* was applied using an aqueous medium.[45] This conclusion had already been questioned several years ago, when progress in understanding of pigment–binder interactions is led to the reinterpretation of the old analysis results.[46] The ATR-FTIR analysis performed on the ultramarine-containing layer of a sample from the Erythraean Sibyl's turban (fig. 3.11) shows the absence of characteristic signals attributable to proteins (e.g. amide I and II bands). Instead, it displayed the thorough presence of weddellite, a calcium oxalate ($CaC_2O_4{\cdot}2H_2O$). These results are consistent with the published observation on the alteration of oil-based binders in other works by Van Eyck.[47]

Indigo As mentioned above, indigo was systematically found in the underlayers of the sky in the interior lower register. Apart from that, indigo was sometimes added together with ultramarine to the verdigris-based green paint layers in very small quantities in order to achieve the subtle bluish-green nuance of the prie-dieu at the right side of the *Virgin Annunciate* as well as in the book of the prophet Zechariah, above the *Archangel*. The pigment was extensively used (e.g. the sky covers a rather large surface) but was never found in the upper paint layers. It is thus likely that this pigment originates from a locally produced and less expensive variety called *florée*, which was prepared from dyer's woad (*Isatis tinctoria* L.) rather than from the expensive, imported Asian indigo (*Indigofera tintoria* L.).[48] In the Middle Ages, *florée* was known for its tendency to fade, and in some cities it was prohibited by the guild statutes for works of the highest quality, such as altarpieces.[49] Nevertheless, the use of indigo was recommended by the author of the Strasbourg Manuscript for producing and shading grey oil paint, either alone or with soot-brown,[50] and has also been detected in brown glazes in late medieval Cologne panel paintings.[51]

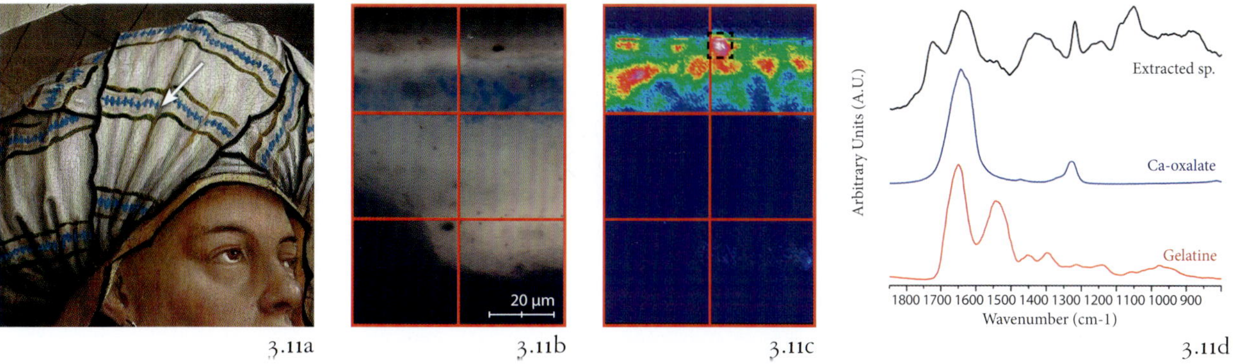

3.11a 3.11b 3.11c 3.11d

Fig. 3.11 a–d. *City View*: detail of the Erythraean Sibyl's turban sampling location (white arrow) (a). The paint cross-section (14/03) under VIS light (b) shows a detail of the area analysed by ATR-FTIR. Results obtained show the distribution of metal oxalates (c) in the topmost, ultramarine-containing layer. The FTIR spectrum (black) extracted from this layer (dotted black square, c) shows characteristic calcium oxalate vibrations. Calcium oxalate (blue) and gelatine (red) reference spectra are included for comparison (d).

Green

The green pigment identified in all green areas is the organo-copper pigment verdigris. The identification of verdigris is not straightforward, as its chemical composition is not well defined.[52] Produced by the corrosion of metallic copper or its alloys exposed to the vapour of various organic acids (mainly acetic acid), the composition of this pigment is indeed variable. It can include different copper salts (acetates, chlorides, citrates, carbonates, formates, oxalates), of which copper acetate is considered the main reference molecule.[53] Its composition is not influenced only by the raw materials used, but also by the purification process (often in vinegar) and the formulation of the paint mixture (binder, additives, etc.). Because of its chemical composition, it reacts with the carboxylic acid moieties in oils and resins resulting in green carboxylates and resinates, which catalyses the autoxidation of oil. Because of its resulting drying properties and its aesthetic qualities, verdigris was the green pigment preferred by early Netherlandish painters.

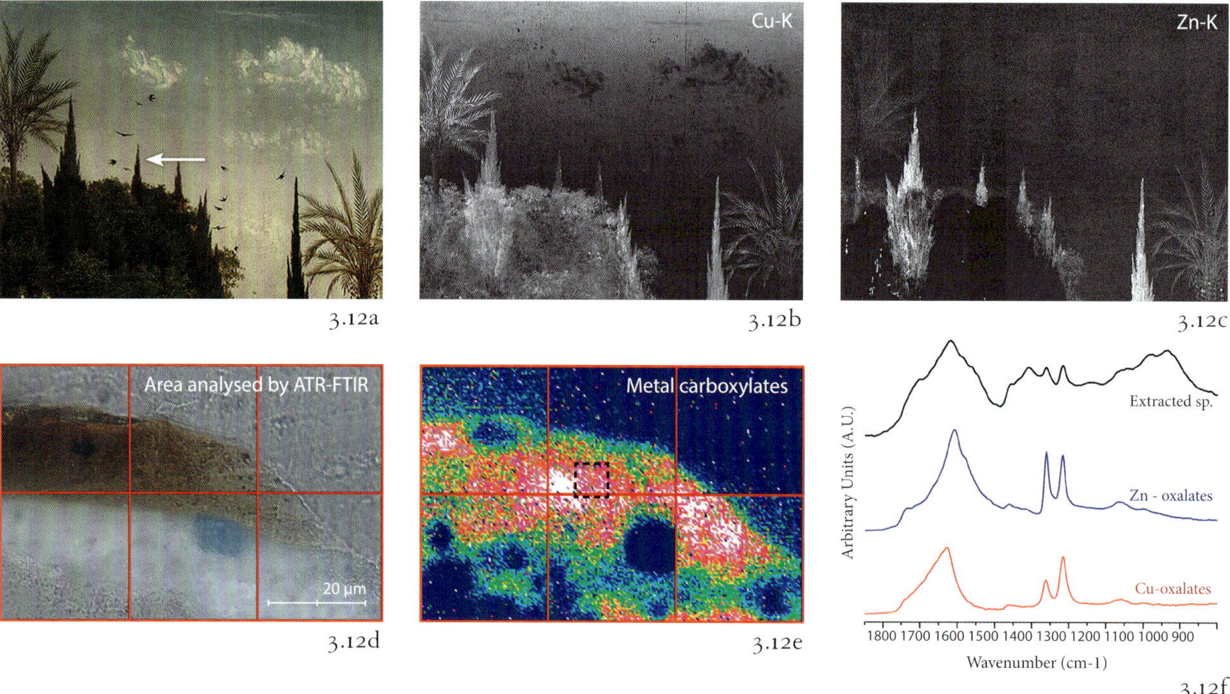

Fig. 3.12a–f. *Pilgrims*: detail of the cypresses and palm tree behind horizon (a) corresponding to the area imaged by means of MA-XRF. The white arrow indicates sampling location (a). MA-XRF images showing the elemental distribution of copper (Cu-K) (b) and zinc (Zn-K) (c). The paint cross-section (12/13) (d) from the brownish cypress contains two layers: the light blue lower one corresponds to the sky layer and the brownish upper one is related to the cypress. The ATR-FTIR spatial distribution map shows the presence of metal carboxylates (e), in both layers. Moreover, copper and zinc oxalates were also detected in the brownish upper layer (dotted black square (e) as shown in the extracted FTIR spectrum (black). Zinc (blue) and copper (red) oxalates reference spectra are included for comparison (f).

In the *Ghent Altarpiece*, verdigris is present in all green areas, including the vegetation and draperies, and was used in all superimposed layers. It was often mixed with minor amounts of other pigments in the modelled underlayer and used pure in the green glazes. Sometimes, a thin yellow glaze was recognizable over the green one, probably to enhance and saturate the colour with a yellow dye, possibly saffron or barberry, as recommended by the Strasbourg Manuscript.[54]

Verdigris is nearly always found in admixture with small amounts of other pigments, additives and/or dyes that are often difficult to identify. It is clear in many cases that these were added intentionally, as was the case with the aforementioned ultramarine or indigo blue, but also with lead white, lead-tin yellow, yellow and brown ochres, orpiment, carbon black, yellow lakes or glass and quartz. Copper chlorides, however, which were also quite systematically found in the *Ghent Altarpiece*'s green samples, were not a deliberate addition. These compounds were more probably formed as a by-product of the production of verdigris prepared following one of the recipes using sodium chloride (salt). That ingredient was used to slow down the corrosion of copper by the organic acid (e.g. acetic acid), allowing the latter to penetrate deeper into the copper plate. Besides copper chlorides, copper oxalates and copper formates were also detected in the verdigris replicated from historical recipes.[55] Their presence in the historical samples should therefore not be automatically considered to result from the interaction of binder and verdigris, as is often proposed also for the copper carboxylates. Nevertheless, this phenomenon is still not well understood and needs to be further investigated.[56] In the *Ghent Altarpiece* panels, copper carboxylates, copper formates and copper oxalates (moolooite) were identified in several green zones by ATR-FTIR and/or MA-XRPD. Through MA-XRPD results it was observed that moolooite is present in higher concentration in the green-brownish vegetation areas where the lead-tin yellow or a zinc-containing additive were codetected.[57] This was, for instance, the case in the green areas with vegetation along the horizon (cypresses, shrubs and trees) in the *Adoration of the Lamb*, the *Knights of Christ,* the *Hermits* and the *Pilgrims* (fig. 3.12a). The phenomenon can be illustrated by the MA-XRF results for copper and zinc of one such area on the left side of the *Pilgrims* panel (fig. 3.12b–c), correlated with the ATR-FTIR mapping results of a cross-section sample taken in the cypress. Results obtained with the latter technique revealed metal carboxylates in both layers constituting the pictorial system (fig. 3.12e): lead carboxylates in the lower, light blue sky layer; and copper and zinc carboxylates and oxalates in the zinc-containing brownish transparent upper layer, related to the cypress tree painted over the horizon (fig. 3.12d–e).

It is worth mentioning that no copper oxalates (moolooite, $Cu(C_2O_4)\cdot nH_2O$, $n<1$) were identified by MA-XRPD in the azurite-containing areas ($(Cu_3(CO_3)_2(OH)_2)$). However, these metal oxalates were found in the green-yellowish malachite-containing ($(Cu_2(CO_3)(OH)_2)$) drapery of a rider in the *Knights of Christ* (fig. 3.13), but in significantly smaller amounts than in the verdigris-containing greens. Interestingly, this was the only green region, probably from the Eyckian stage, where the pigment malachite was positively identified during the present campaign.[58] Unfortunately, as mentioned above, no samples concerning this area were available. Thus, the position of malachite in the paint layer structure and the

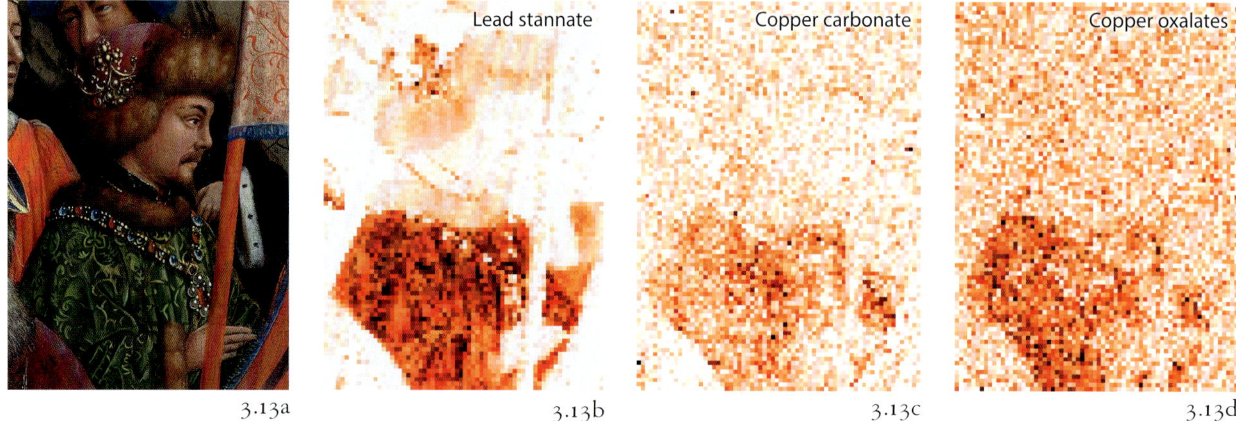

Fig. 3.13a–d. *Knights of Christ*: detail of the knight with a green brocade (a), containing lead-tin yellow and malachite as demonstrated by MA-XRPD maps of lead stannate (b) and copper carbonate (c), respectively. The same area contains mooloite as revealed by the ma-xrpd map of copper oxalates (d).

presence of other non-crystalline compounds are unknown. We therefore cannot rule out the possibility that malachite was mixed or superimposed with a non-crystalline verdigris and that moolooite is associated to the latter pigment rather than to the former.

Organic red and brown

In the green areas, verdigris was often in admixture with organic brown-yellow or brown-black pigments. These pigments, together with red and yellow lakes, hold pride of place in the Van Eyck brothers' palette used for the *Ghent Altarpiece*. As they form a translucent layer when mixed with oil, their use cannot be dissociated from the Eyckian painting technique, which is characterized by the superimposition of translucent layers. However, the organic pigments are also the most problematic to identify and their detection and localization are often merely assumed on the basis of visual observation of a colour and/or the identification of additives or extenders. These pigments share the common feature that they are poor driers and thus do not offer an appropriate paint consistency. Accordingly, they need to be associated with a drying agent and/or an extender. Their organic constituents can only be identified using chromatographic methods, such as HPLC for the dyestuffs and GC-MS for the specific markers in the soot-brown (e.g. guaiacol and syringol derivates).

Carbon-based brown and black A soot-dark brown pigment, called bistre, was identified with Py-GCMS in two dark brown paints inside the frame of the *Just Judges*. The recovered paint, supposed to be an Eyckian material, flowed and solidified into a gap between the panel and the frame. One sample originated from a dark brown area, presumably featuring rocks, the other from the green-brownish

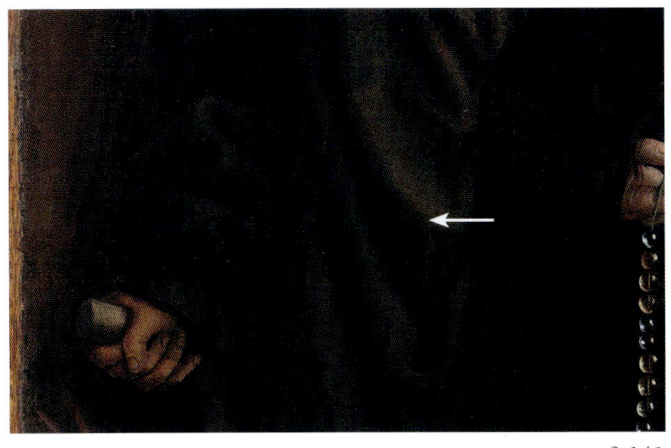

3.14a

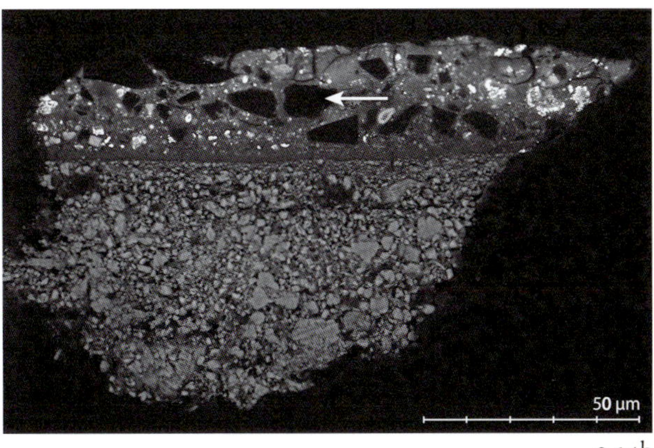

3.14b

Fig. 3.14a–b. *Hermits*: detail of the far-left hermit's brown garment – sampling location (a). Back-scattered electron SEM image of the paint cross-section (11/K) (b) shows large coal-black pigment particles.

vegetation on the left side of the painting.[59] Bistre is a dark brownish carbon-based pigment extracted from chimney wood soot, referred to as *caligo* and *fuligo* in the manuscript of Jehan le Begue or *gelutert rus* in the Strasbourg Manuscript.[60] Despite its hydrophobic, slightly resinous character, bistre is more often recommended for watercolour and for washes and ink drawings. However, it has been identified in medieval paintings from Cologne, in a brown oil-based paint containing also verdigris and ochre, similar to what has been found in the *Ghent Altarpiece* panels.[61] Bistre was cheap and easy to make but remains difficult to identify. It is therefore likely that it was more frequently used in fifteenth-century paintings than reported in technical studies.[62]

Coal black is another carbon-based pigment frequently detected in the *Ghent Altarpiece* samples. It is recognizable in cross-sections thanks to the sharp edges of its particles typical for a ground mineral rock, and shows a high concentration of sulphur with chlorine, calcium, aluminium and silicon-containing impurities. As already mentioned, it was used in the liquid underdrawing (fig. 3.16) and was frequently detected in the priming layers, where it was finely ground (figs. 3.2, 3.3 and 3.5). In the paint layer, coal was systematically observed in dark brown areas, such as the drapery of the far-left Hermit (fig. 3.14b), as well as in the black underpaint of the dark green vegetation areas in the central panel and the interior shutters. Likewise, coal black was added in some dark green and dark red glazes. In short, it is the most used black pigment in the panels studied so far.

Charcoal, which could sometimes be mistaken for coal, is only sporadically present in the *Ghent Altarpiece* samples. No bone black has been detected.

Red lakes Among the red pigments, lakes are dominant in the *Ghent Altarpiece* panels, as they are present in all nuances of red, pink, violet and some dark brown colours. The range of colours that can be obtained by the superposition of red lake-containing glazes over opaque underlayers or even, in the case of the outer *Annunciation* panels, over the tinted priming layer, is quite large indeed. For instance, at least seven colour nuances are created with red lake pigments in the draperies and headdresses of the figures in the foreground of the *Adoration of the Lamb*.

Red lakes are pigments consisting of an organic dyestuff precipitated onto a translucent substrate of, usually, amorphous hydrated alumina or a combination of calcium and aluminium salts, so that their identification requires analytical methods for both organic and inorganic compounds. While the inorganic substrate and the additives of the glaze could be analysed and localized in the cross-sections, the identification of the organic dyes was often compromised by contamination of old overpaints having a similar composition and/or by the complexity and non-availability of sample material in a sufficient amount for chromatography.[63] HPLC analysis of two samples of the Eyckian pink glaze from the outer panels and two samples from the interior panels nevertheless evidenced the use of Kermes lake (*Kermes vermilio* Planchon). Besides kermesic acid, small amounts of laccaic acids from the *Kerria lacca* Kerr[64] and pseudopurpurin and purprine originating from the *Rubia tinctorum* L. were also detected by HPLC. The Eyckian use of madder lake (*Rubia tinctorum* L.) is still a matter of discussion, as the sample of St Christopher's bright red drapery in which it was found was taken from the barb of the *Pilgrims* panel and thus might have been contaminated with overpaint.[65]

The identification of a small amount of flavokermesic and ellagic acids in the samples from St Christopher's (*Pilgrims*) and St Anthony's (*Hermits*) mantles suggests that at least one of the red lakes present in these multi-layered samples was prepared from silk, dyed with the extract from the scale insect *Kermes vermilio* Planchon.[66] Furthermore, ATR-FTIR mapping of the cross-section from St Anthony's dark purple drapery has revealed the presence of proteins in the lake substrates (fig. 3.15c). These proteins originated from sheep wool, as indicated by the LC-MS/MS analyses performed on this sample.[67]

The revealing of Kermes or madder lakes manufactured from wool shearings in the *Ghent Altarpiece* samples, in both the original and overpaint layers, is consistent with the numerous studies on recipes mentioned in the documentary sources dating from the fifteenth and sixteenth centuries as well as the identification of lakes found in paintings from the same period.[68] A connection between the dyeing industry and red lake manufacture has been widely demonstrated and it is now commonly accepted that the kermes and madder lakes used in the fifteenth and sixteenth centuries were indeed derived from wool shearings or silk dyed with these colourants. From the study of the original red glazes, it seems evident that at least two (probably more) varieties of lakes were used. One was prepared from wool shearings that were boiled in a highly alkaline solutions giving a gelatinous coloured mass, which was then washed and neutralized by the addition of alum. The particles of such lakes are large and irregular in shape, and contain small amounts of alumina and residual wool proteins from the shearings. The second variety was also prepared by the recovery of the dyestuff from textiles (silk or wool), but this textile material was filtered out after the extraction and is only present in the substrate in very small amounts. The lake is precipitated from the solution by the addition of potash alum. The substrate of this type of lake is composed of hydrated alumina and its particles have sharper edges. This second variety is sometimes found in thin surface layers applied over thick glazes containing the lakes from wool shearings.

The number of transparent layers accumulated in the areas with red glazes is variable. In general, the shadows contain more strata (typically 3 to 4 layers) than

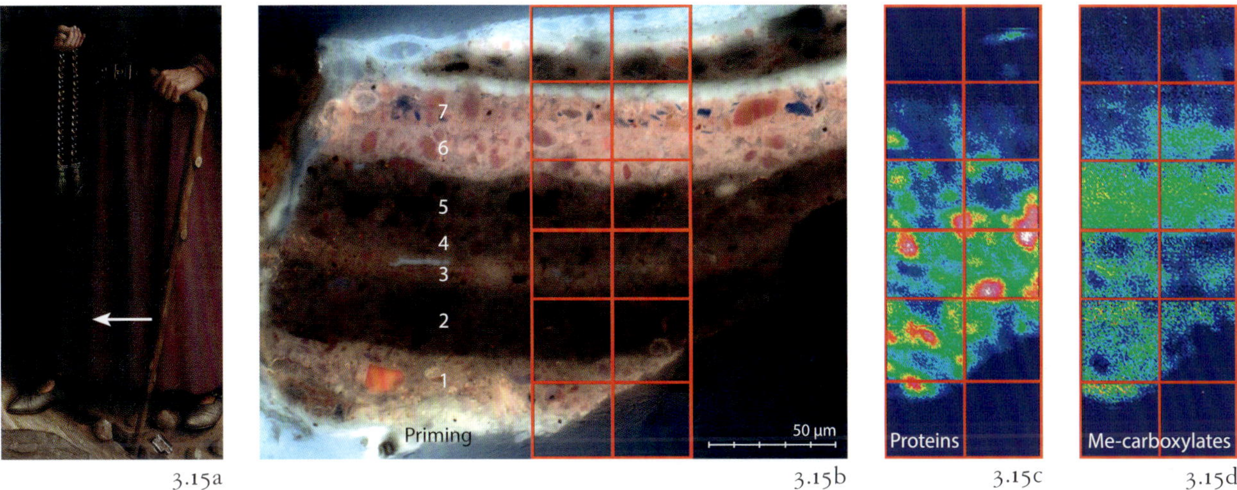

Fig. 3.15a–d. *Hermits*: detail of St Anthony's purple garment sampling location (indicated by white arrow) (a). The paint cross-section (11/12) under UV illumination (b) shows the squares matrix representing the ATR-FTIR analysed area. The enabled analysis visualization of the spatial distribution of proteins (c) and metal carboxylates (d) in the cross-sections.

lighter areas (2, sometimes 3 layers). In some cases this number is even higher, as can be seen in St Anthony's dark purple mantle in the *Hermits* panel (fig. 3.15b). The paint structure in this area shows seven red glazes containing the expensive kermes lake. This extensive and seemingly redundant pictorial construction might be an indication that the work was executed in two stages.

Interestingly, some differences can be observed between the upper two and lower five layers. For instance, the dark purple colour was obtained by the addition of coarser coal black in the lower layers whereas, in the uppermost layer, ultramarine was employed instead. Likewise, the lake from wool shearings was detected mainly in the lower layers as indicated by a strong protein signal observed in the ATR-FTIR mapping (fig. 3.15c). In the upper layers, the lake(s) seem(s) to be prepared from dyed silk. It seems likely that lower paint layers were applied in a single stage of the creative process while the two upper layers were added in a later stage.

On the exterior of the shutters, lakes were used to a large extent for *Joos Vijd*'s red and *Elisabeth Borluut*'s pink drapery in the lower register, and in the *Archangel*'s wings, in the Erythraean Sibyl's drapery and in the prophets Zechariah's and Micah's clothes, in the upper register. It is worth noting that the layer structure in the red and pink areas of the upper register is much simpler than in those of the lower register, clearly denoting different painting techniques. The red and pink glazes in the upper register were applied in one or two layers, directly on the grey priming (fig. 3.16b), whereas those in the donor portraits, which are more vivid, present a much more complex layer structure with three or four glazes applied on an opaque underlayer. The underlayer of the bright red robe of *Joos Vijd* is cinnabar-based, while that of the pink drapery of *Elisabeth Borluut* is red lake-based. Another difference between the painting methods in the upper and lower exterior panels consists in the use of additives: in the donor portraits the glazes contain powdered glass, while zinc sulphate was detected with SR-XANES in the pink

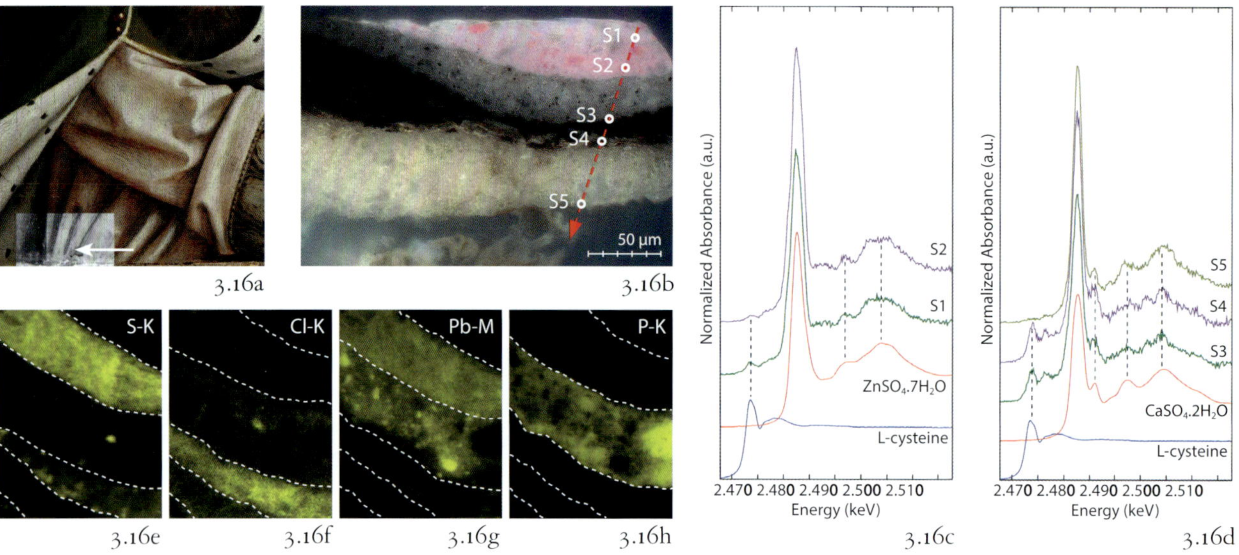

3.16a 3.16b 3.16c 3.16d 3.16e 3.16f 3.16g 3.16h

Fig. 3.16a–d. *Archangel*: detail of the prophet Zechariah's pink drapery. The white arrow indicates the sampling location on the IRR detail showing the underdrawing lines (a), paint cross-section (13/20) in UV illumination (b). SR-XANES S-K edge spectra originating from the top pink layers (points S1 and S2) (c), and from the underdrawing (S3, S4) and the ground (S5) (d), compared with the references for the thiol functional group (L-cysteine) and sulphate function ($ZnSO_4.7H_2O$ and $CaSO_4.2H_2O$) (c, d). Distributions of sulphur (S-K, e), chlorine (Cl-K, f), lead (Pb-M, g) and phosphorus (P-K, h) within the cross-section visualized using SR-µ-XRF.

glazes applied to depict the prophet Zechariah's clothes (fig. 3.16c–d).[69] It should be stressed that these two additives, which were expected to accelerate the drying of oil[70] (together with others detected in the *Ghent Altarpiece* samples, such as calcined bone, chalk, copper vitriol, quartz and small amounts of 'good' drying pigments, such as verdigris or lead white), play an important role in the understanding of the Eyckian paint formulation and behaviour during the grinding, application, drying and ageing processes. For this reason they were investigated with particular attention, as explained below.

Paint additives

The brushstrokes of Jan van Eyck are characterized as quick and precise,[71] and it is clear that his paint mixture needed to have an appropriate consistency, neither too viscous nor too liquid. Besides the binder and pigments, painters had at their disposal a number of materials to modify the paint's rheological and drying properties. They were usually added in small amounts to modify the oil binder, such as zinc or copper vitriol, calcined bone, lime or litharge. However, they could also be added in quite a large proportion like chalk, quartz, starch or powdered glass. Various modifiers were encountered and systematically identified in the *Ghent Altarpiece* paint samples, but only two of them, glass particles and zinc vitriol, have so far been studied in greater detail.

Powdered glass

Powdered glass has been found at the Eyckian level in the red and pink glazes of the two donor portraits and in the black paint of the letters of the quatrain on the exterior grisaille panels. In the interior panels studied so far, very small glass particles have been found in several of the Eyckian vegetation greens. Likewise, larger glass particles of slightly different composition were identified in the *Adoration of the Lamb*, in the white paint layers of the dove and in the mordants for some of the gilded rays surrounding it.

It should be noted that, ever since the 1950s, questions have been raised about the dove because of its poor pictorial quality, uncommon for Van Eyck's work. Consequently, it has been hypothesized that it was added later by another painter, when the altarpiece was finished, as discussed in chapters 2 and 4. Colourless glass powder has also been found in later fifteenth- and sixteenth-century interventions. At these levels, the glass additive was used even more extensively than in the Eyckian stage. These findings correspond well with the evolution of painting practice in the late fifteenth and early sixteenth centuries. Indeed, glass powders are recommended in the technical documentation of this period as siccative agents in preparation of boiled oil and as an additive for grinding poorly drying pigments such as red lake, indigo and lamp black in oil.[72] However, this function is debatable and has been widely discussed in recent scientific communications.[73]

In the medieval and renaissance periods, glass was manufactured by melting sand or quartz pebbles with one or more alkali-rich fluxes, which had important effects on its chemical composition. In Northern Europe, the flux could have been composed of various types of potassium-rich wood or plant ashes, while sodium-rich coastal halophytic plants were employed in the Mediterranean area.[74] A systematic study of the elemental composition of the glass particles found in London's National Gallery paintings by Marika Spring has shown that calco-potassic glass made with potassium-rich wood or fern ash was more common in Netherlandish paintings. Within this group of paintings, various compositional categories of glass were identified, mainly based on the proportions of calcium and potassium oxides (CaO/K_2O): (a) wood ash (CaO/K_2O between 1 and 2); (b) wood ash with some fern ash (CaO/K_2O below 1); (c) wood ash–lime (CaO/K_2O above 3.5); and (d) wood ash-lime with high lime/low alkali content (CaO/K_2O between 5 and 8).[75] Similar glass families were found in the samples taken from the *Ghent Altarpiece*. The correlation between the category of glass and the stratigraphic position of the layer in which the glass particles were found permitted us to propose a hypothesis on the chronology of their use. The results are summarized in the table (fig. 3.17), followed by a short discussion of each category.

Wood ash

The particles made of wood ash-type glass were found in many samples at the Eyckian level, although not systematically. The use of powdered glass at the original level was indeed quite moderate in comparison with the overpaints. It

Chronology	Type of glass	Examples
Original Eyckian level, before 1432	Wood ash	Red and pink draperies in the donor portraits, red clothes of a figure in *Adoration*; green vegetation in *Adoration* and the *Knights*; red glaze or black letters on silvered frames of the panels *Knights of Christ*, *Archangel* and *Virgin Annunciate*, *Joos Vijd*, *St John the Evangelist*
Non-Eyckian addition (?)	Wood ash with some fern ash (?)	Dove and mordant for one of the gilded rays
Late 15th-century–early 16th-century overpaints, after 1470 (?)	Wood ash–lime (High lime low alkali – HLLA)	Specific varnishes in various areas of *Adoration* (blue clothes). Donors' clothes: fillings in paint losses, varnish
Late 15th-century–early 16th-century overpaints, between 1470 (?) and 1557	Wood ash	Red glaze in the *Archangel*'s wing
16th-century overpaints, before 1557	Soda ash	Red and pink glazes and fillings of losses in major 16th-century overpaints

3.17

Fig. 3.17. Types of glass particles found in the twelve restored panels of the *Ghent Altarpiece* and hypothetical chronology of their use.

was found in the red, green and black layers in only four out of the twelve restored panels and in four frames.

A low sodium and high potassium and calcium oxides composition was observed in all samples. The proportion of the two latter oxides ranges from 1 to 2 (CaO/K_2O ~1–2). The glass is equally rich in magnesium and phosphorus oxides.

In most cases, the glass was finely ground, with particle sizes varying from 3 to 15 µm, and down to even 2–5 µm in green glazes. Wood ash glass particles were used mainly in the red and pink glazes of the two donor portraits, *Joos Vijd* and *Elisabeth Borluut*, in the closed polyptych. A larger amount was found in the *Joos Vijd* panel, while a smaller proportion was encountered in the pink drapery of *Elisabeth Borluut*. It is interesting that the wood ash glass particles were rarely found in the red clothes of the figures depicted in the lower register of the open polyptych. They were found only in the red cloak of the bearded and bald prophet in the lower left group of the *Adoration of the Lamb*. In this panel, the wood ash glass particles were also detected in the verdigris-containing greens, and they were similarly found in the greens in two other restored panels of the open polyptych, the *Knights* and the *Pilgrims*. The black layers in which the powdered colourless glass was also found were all sampled from the lettering on the frames of the panels of the *Knights*, the *Virgin Annunciate* and the *Archangel*, and the *St John the Baptist*.

Interestingly, it was detected in one sample at the level of an overpaint on the Archangel Gabriel's wing, where the red glaze with wood ash glass particles was applied over an original red glaze covered by two varnishes. The top-most varnish contained the particles of wood ash lime (high lime, low alkali [HLLA]) glass. This type of glass frequently occurs in the paintings dated after 1470. Unlike other Eyckian red glazes from the upper register of the exterior, the original red glaze under this varnish does not contain any powdered glass.[76]

Wood ash with some fern ash

The type of glass containing wood ash with some fern ash was identified in the *Adoration of the Lamb*, in the thick upper white layer of the dove of the Holy Spirit, and in one sample taken from the gilding of the rays in the coloured halo around the dove. Four additional samples from the rays showed wood ash glass particles in the gilding mordant. The introduction of powdered glass to accelerate the drying of a mordant for gilding was a common studio practice,[77] but its presence in a paint containing well-drying lead white is more sporadic[78] and suggests that the glass may have been employed for a different purpose, for instance to modify the paint's optical properties and/or texture.

It should be noted here that establishing a clear difference between the wood-ash and the wood-ash-with-some-fern-ash glass types is not straightforward because of both the slight difference in the CaO/K_2O values for these glass types and the uncertainty associated with the EDX spot measurement. Likewise, the leaching of alkaline cations (e.g. sodium and potassium) from the glass particles in the course of their ageing process can artificially increase the value of the CaO/K_2O ratio. Nevertheless, the analyses carried out on all the samples taken in 1950–51 from the dove showed the same tendency: the CaO/K_2O ratio was below one in nearly all measured particles. The remarkably large size of the particles in the dove and in one mordant sample was also taken into consideration. Indeed, the size of most glass particles ranges between 10 and 60 µm, which is exceptional as the powdered glass in the Eyckian paintings is usually finely ground with particle sizes typically ranging between 5 and 15 µm.[79]

These results might suggest that the dove and some of the rays would have been added in one single painting stage. But given that this type of glass can be found in fifteenth-century painting (including Jan van Eyck's *Arnolfini Portrait*), the dove cannot be dismissed as a non-Eyckian intervention based on purely material grounds.[80] Furthermore, taking into consideration that a dove of the Holy Spirit was mentioned in 1458 as part of the tableau vivant representing the scene of the *Adoration of the Lamb* presented at the Joyous Entry of Philip the Good into the city of Ghent, it may be argued that the dove was present in the painting at that moment.[81] Likewise, as suggested in other chapters, the presence of another version of the dove, hidden by the currently visible version, cannot be excluded.[82]

Cross-sections prepared from three dove samples taken in the 1950–51 analysis campaign were reanalysed. The samples do not show a consistent stratigraphy; they present two or three white layers that seem to belong to the same intervention as there is no clear separation between the strata. In contrast, the white layers are clearly separated from an underlying blue paint system that consists of two layers of ultramarine applied over several layers of azurite. The sample taken from the

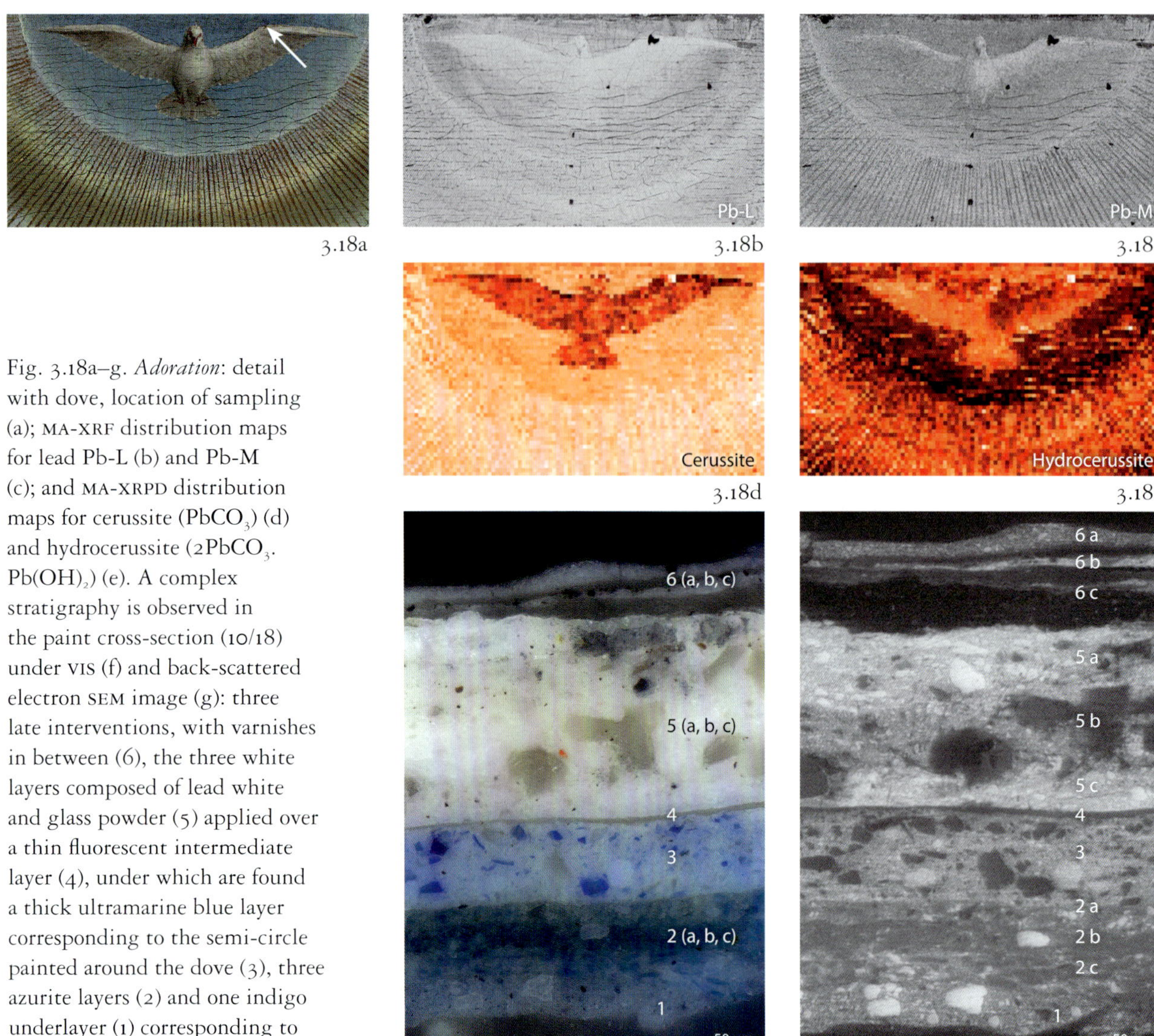

3.18a 3.18b 3.18c 3.18d 3.18e 3.18f 3.18g

Fig. 3.18a–g. *Adoration*: detail with dove, location of sampling (a); MA-XRF distribution maps for lead Pb-L (b) and Pb-M (c); and MA-XRPD distribution maps for cerussite ($PbCO_3$) (d) and hydrocerussite ($2PbCO_3 . Pb(OH)_2$) (e). A complex stratigraphy is observed in the paint cross-section (10/18) under VIS (f) and back-scattered electron SEM image (g): three late interventions, with varnishes in between (6), the three white layers composed of lead white and glass powder (5) applied over a thin fluorescent intermediate layer (4), under which are found a thick ultramarine blue layer corresponding to the semi-circle painted around the dove (3), three azurite layers (2) and one indigo underlayer (1) corresponding to the sky.

wing (fig. 3.18a) actually shows a thin fluorescent intermediate layer between the first white dove layer and the ultramarine blue layers (fig. 3.18f). This finding suggests that they were not painted during the same stage. The results of the MA-XRPD scanning of this area (fig. 3.18d–e) support this interpretation. Based on the various HC/(HC+C) calculated ratios, it is evident that the lead white used to paint the dove (HC/(HC+C) = 60%) is different from that used for the surrounding and underlying blue layers (HC/(HC+C) = 90%). It would seem therefore that the dove was separately painted on top of a fully finished blue sky, which shows a paint build-up similar to that of the rest of the sky on the *Adoration of the Lamb*. The fact that the dove consists of two or three layers belonging to the same intervention does not rule out the possibility that the current dove hides an earlier version not included in the examined cross-sections. Thus, up to this moment, none of the existing samples nor any of the non-invasively obtained findings can provide a definitive answer to the current dove's originality.

Wood ash with high lime and low alkali glass

The high-lime and low-alkali (HLLA) glass with a CaO/K_2O ratio between 5 and 8 was systematically detected in red glazes found in the first overpaints (e.g. *Joos Vijd*) and in many varnishes, located just below or on top of the first overpaint, indicating that they are very likely associated with the first overpaint campaign. The sodium oxide content was typically around 1.5–2 w%, and in some cases higher (3.8–5 w%). It is very likely that this value is overestimated, since the sodium might be partially derived from ultramarine. This type of calco-potassic glass only began to be commonly used in the Netherlands at the end of the fifteenth century,[83] and, according to Spring, it is very unlikely to have been used before 1470.[84] The identification of the HLLA-type of glass particles allowed us to propose the 1470 date as a provisory *terminus post quem* for this early interference with the polyptych.

Soda-ash glass

The most abundant use of glass particles was detected in the sixteenth-century overpaint, which has been discussed in detail in the earlier book on the first phase of the *Ghent Altarpiece* treatment.[85] The glass particles found at this level presented a relatively consistent composition showing a high sodium oxide content (between 8 and 13.5 w%) and low concentrations of potassium, magnesium and phosphorus oxides (2–3.3 w%, 1.8–2.7 w% and 0–1.1 w%, respectively), indicating the use of soda-ash Mediterranean glass. This type of glass is usually detected in Italian paintings and also in some German paintings dating from the end of the fifteenth century.[86] Soda-ash glass was imported from Italy until the beginning of the sixteenth century, when the first Italian glassmakers arrived in the Netherlands and started to produce it locally under the name of *façon-de-Venise* glass.[87]

This rather easily distinguishable type of glass turned out to be a very specific indicator for the major sixteenth-century overpainting campaign, that was carried out before 1557–58, the date of Michiel Coxcie's copy of the polyptych, in which these overpaints are reproduced. In this level, the powdered glass was used in even larger quantities than in the older levels. It is interesting to add that the earliest Netherlandish painting in which this type of glass particle has been found so far is Colijn de Coter's *St John the Baptist and Six Apostles* (Bayerische Staatsgemäldesammlungen, Alte Pinakothek, Munich, inv. WAF 163), presumed to have been painted around 1510.[88]

Zinc vitriol

As long ago as 1849, Mary Merrifield wrote: 'There is a good reason to suppose that white copperas (sulphate of zinc), which is mentioned as a dryer by Flemish and German writers of the fifteenth century, was the dryer of van Eyck. We owe this discovery to the research of Mr. Eastlake.'[89] This hypothesis was solely based on the study of medieval and Renaissance technical treatises, without any material proof. It took more than 160 years to confirm Eastlake's and Merrifield's assumption using scientific analysis. The first time the presence of zinc in the *Ghent Altarpiece* was mentioned in an analytical report was in 2010.[90] In the context of a preliminary study prior to the first restoration campaign, in-situ XRF spot analysis detected an 'intriguing' presence of zinc in the red draperies of the central panel. It was intriguing because the area was apparently not overpainted and, at that time, zinc was commonly taken to be an indicator of modern zinc pigments. In the following years, the re-analysis of two other Van Eyck paintings revealed the presence of zinc in the original paint layers, including a violet paint layer from the *Arnolfini Portrait* (The National Gallery, London, inv. NG186) and red and black layers in the *Portrait of Margaret van Eyck* (Groeningemuseum, Bruges, inv. 0000.GRO0162.I).[91] Besides the paintings by Van Eyck, zinc was found in many mid-fifteenth-century Cologne paintings.[92] This research, together with Marika Spring's recent article summarizing current knowledge on the use of white vitriol as an additive for oil painting,[93] supports Eastlake's assumption that white copperas was commonly used by Netherlandish and German painters. Similarly, traces of zinc have been mostly found in the red glazes and black paint layers in the *Ghent Altarpiece* panels. In addition, zinc was found in many brownish shadows in ochre areas, in certain green vegetation zones, in numerous dark brown colours such as the wooden ceiling beams in the exterior upper panels, and in bronze (or brass)-like objects, such as the chalice in front of the lamb, the column of the fountain in the *Adoration of the Lamb* and the lavabo in the *Interior View*. In the aforementioned cases, the presence of zinc was mainly demonstrated during the systematic MA-XRF screening of the panels. Furthermore, zinc was also detected and localized in the paint stratigraphy of the cross-sections by SEM-EDX.[94] Even though the chemical identity of the zinc compounds present in paint layers was quite difficult to determine, some interesting results have already been obtained by SR-XANES, which confirms the presence of zinc sulphate, and by ATR-FTIR, which makes it possible to detect the zinc carboxylates and oxalates.

In summary the current results suggest that the use of zinc vitriol as an additive was a common practice in the two first stages of execution. Interestingly, the elemental zinc distribution observed in the Eyckian paint layers in the *Pilgrims* and the *Hermits* panels, or the group of popes, the fountain and the vegetation above the horizon line in the *Adoration of the Lamb*, is richer in this element than other parts, such as the vegetation behind the group of confessors (fig. 3.19a–d). The later Netherlandish painters who altered the painting during the sixteenth century also used zinc driers, as it was detected in the old overpaints. Certain areas, such as the draperies of *Elisabeth Borluut* (fig. 3.19e–f) or the Cumaean Sibyl, scanned with MA-XRF during the removal of these overpaints, suggest that these layers are richer in zinc than the underlying Eyckian layers.

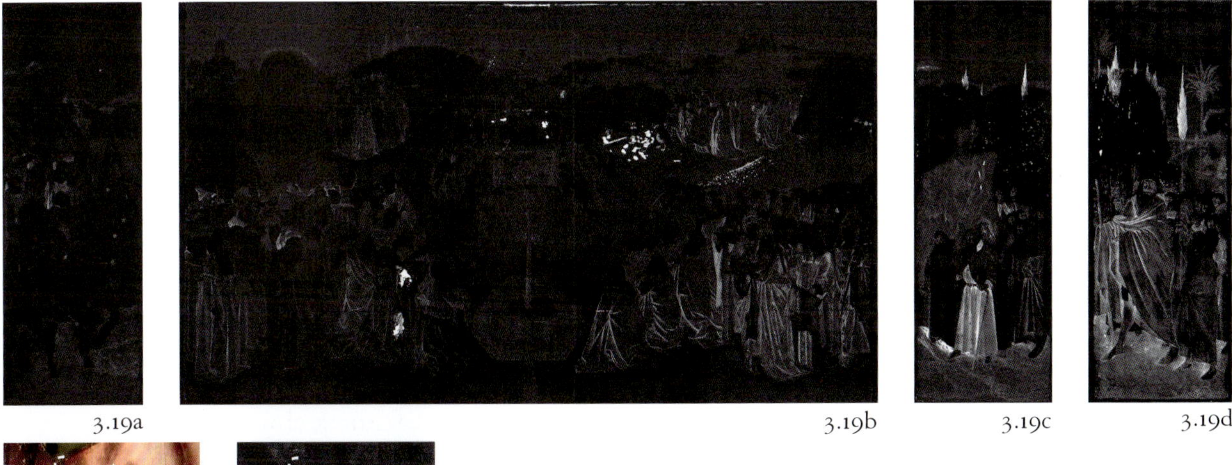

3.19a 3.19b 3.19c 3.19d

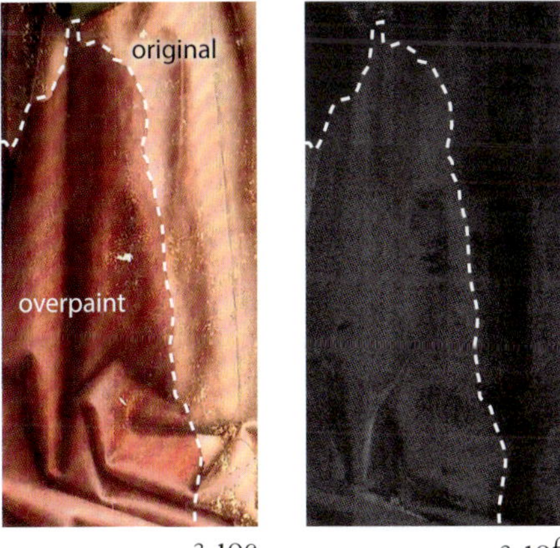

3.19e 3.19f

Fig. 3.19a–f. MA-XRF distribution elemental maps for zinc (Zn-K) in the *Knights of Christ* (a), *Adoration of the Lamb* (b), *Hermits* (c) and *Pilgrims* (d) panels. The most intense Zn signals are found on the right side of the *Adoration* (b) as well as in the *Hermits* (c) and *Pilgrims* (d) panels, in particular for the cypress trees behind the horizon line. Strong Zn-K signals observed in luminous and irregular spots correspond to paint losses in-filled with a modern zinc white (ZnO)-containing material. Detail of pink drapery of *Elisabeth Borluut* halfway through overpaint removal (e) and the corresponding MA-XRF Zn-K distribution map (f) showing a more intense Zn signal in the overpaint zone.

When and how was the drier introduced into the paint? Was it already incorporated into the binder or was it added to the pigment before the paint was made? Was it added on the grinding slab during paint production or was it mixed on the palette?[95] In the case of red lakes, a careful examination of the macro- and micro-analytical results suggests that the additive is related to the lake pigment rather than to the binder. For instance, in the MA-XRF Zn-K maps, the most intense signals are observed in the lake-containing red and pink clothes of the figures in the *Adoration of the Lamb*, in St Anthony's purple drapery in the *Hermits* (fig. 3.15) and in the drapery of St Christopher in the *Pilgrims*.[96] The signal is likewise intense when multiple, superimposed lake-containing layers are present. An example of the latter was evidenced by comparing MA-XRF results with three samples taken from St Christopher's drapery, in light, half-shadow and shadow zones in which respectively two, three and four red lake-containing layers were observed. In the light areas of the modelling, the lake is mixed with lead white and the intensity of zinc seems much lower, as shown by the MA-XRF Zn-K map. Conversely, the intensity of the MA-XRF zinc signal in the shadow zones is high.

MA-XRF maps also revealed a series of smooth-edged losses in St Anthony's dark purple mantle. As illustrated by the Pb-L and Zn-K MA-XRF map (fig. 3.20b–c),

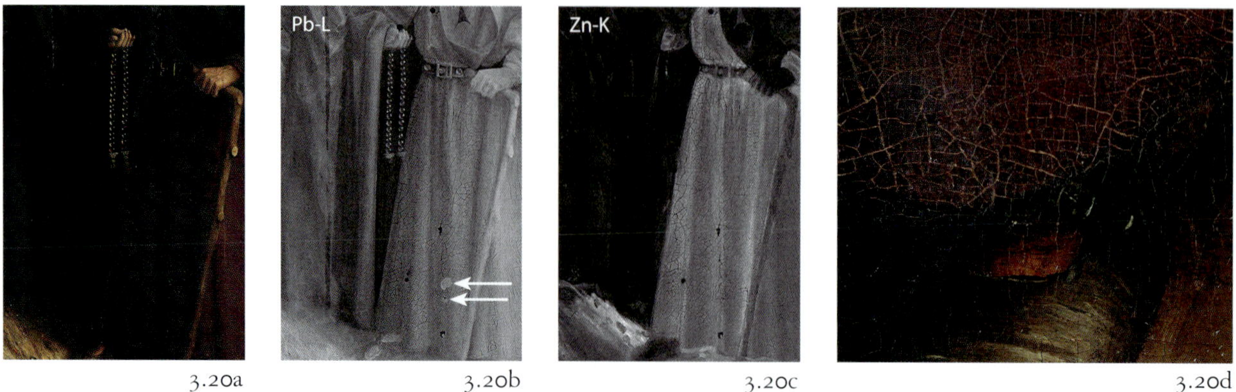

3.20a 3.20b 3.20c 3.20d

Fig. 3.20a–d. *Hermits*: detail of the brown mantle of the far-left hermit and the purple mantle of St Anthony corresponding to the area imaged by means of MA-XRF (a). Map of lead (Pb-L) (b) visualising lead-containing underlayers round repaired losses in the purple mantle of St Anthony (white arrows). Map of zinc (Zn-K) (c) shows that the zinc additive was used in the purple drapery only. Detail of St Anthony's drapery taken during the treatment illustrates the drying cracks (d).

these losses occurred at an early stage in the creative process. Indeed, they seem to have been infilled with a lead-containing material and retouched with a zinc-containing red lake. The reason for these losses could be a technological problem, for example an excess of drying agent(s), resulting in strong drying cracks which are still observable in this area (fig. 3.20d). The ATR-FTIR analysis of one sample taken in this area contributed to a better insight into the latter phenomenon. By this method, zinc and lead carboxylates were indeed found in all red lake-containing glazes. Their presence suggests the use of zinc- and lead-based driers that reacted with the oil binder.

A zinc drier was also typically used in the brownish areas presenting a transparent glaze layer (fig. 3.21) that consists of an organic brown colourant. The latter has not yet been identified but is assumed to be either a bituminous coal-based pigment – bistre, asphalt, aloe, pitch or similar materials retarding the drying of oil. The zinc additive was consistently introduced in such brown glazes, for instance in the shadowing of the earthy paths on which the figures of the *Knights*, *Hermits* and *Pilgrims* panels stand. Interestingly, it was also observed in more opaque dark brown and green mixtures containing pigments such as verdigris or brown ochre which, unlike the colourants, advance the hardening of the oil binder. This brownish transparent paint, seemingly prepared with a substantial concentration of zinc vitriol, was observed under the binocular microscope as well as in samples taken from the leaves, cypresses and palm trees painted above the horizon line in the *Pilgrims* and the central *Adoration of the Lamb* panels. It seems that they were not planned in the first stage, but were possibly added subsequently, as discussed in the previous chapter.[97]

Likewise, the fountain in the middle of the *Adoration of the Lamb* is considered to be a compositional modification introduced in the second stage. As suggested by the Zn-K and Fe-K MA-XRF distribution maps in this area, the central brownish column, rising from the dark green water of the fountain, is painted with brownish

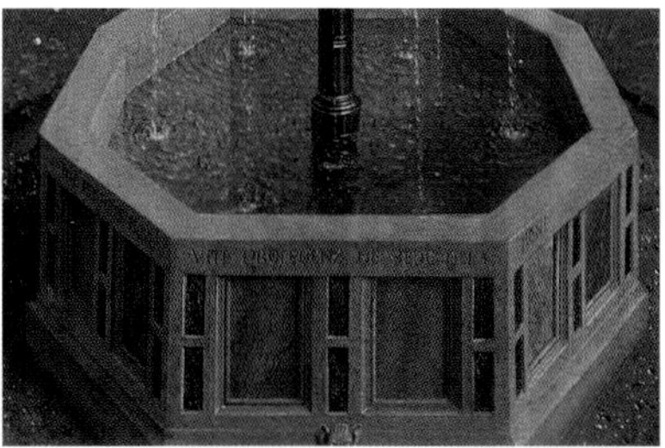

3.21a

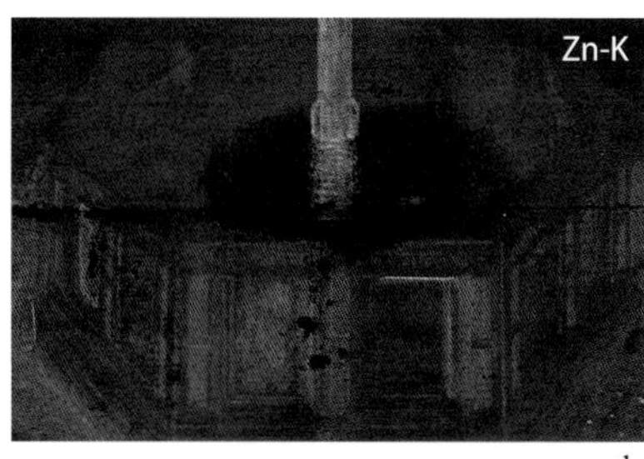

3.21b

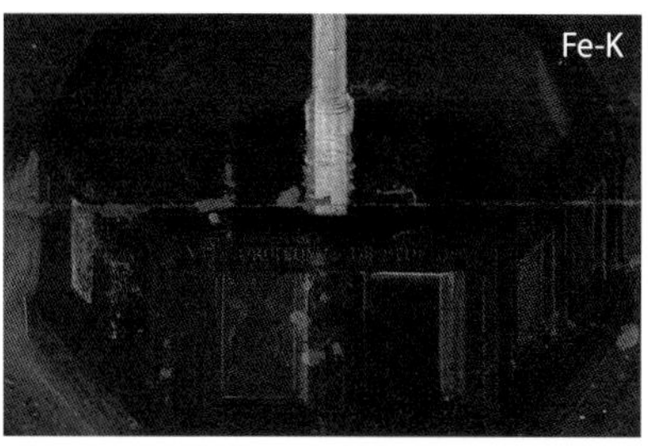

3.21c

Fig. 3.21a–c. *Adoration*: detail of the lower part of the fountain with sampling location (a). MA-XRF distribution elemental maps for zinc (Zn-K) (b) and iron (Fe-K) (c) showing that the central brownish column is painted with a mixture containing an iron-based pigment(s) with quite high amounts of zinc additive.

ochre-containing mixtures with quite high amounts of zinc additive (fig. 3.21a–c).

A sample taken from the area where the column is below the water level shows two thin, brown ochre-containing layers on top of the stratigraphy. Two other strata are visible under the brown layers: a bluish-green one applied over a black one (fig. 3.22a–b). Taking into account the hypothesis proposed in chapter 2, this black layer possibly corresponds to a dark hole in the meadow (a 'spring' painted in the first stage of the creative process).[98]

Surprisingly, SEM-EDX mapping suggests that zinc is not only present in the brown upper layers, but dispersed in all the strata in very low amounts (fig. 3.22c). ATR-FTIR microscopy indicated that this element is mostly present in the form of zinc carboxylates. Interestingly, copper and lead soaps, as well as copper oxalate and formate, were also detected throughout the sample's strata (fig. 3.22f), suggesting that the binder has thoroughly reacted with the pigments and driers employed to produce these paint layers.

Besides zinc, SEM-EDX analysis of the top brown layers indicated the presence of some lead, copper, calcium and phosphorus (fig. 3.22c), the latter being found in the form of phosphates as revealed by ATR-FTIR. Accordingly, these results suggest the presence of calcium phosphates in these layers, but further research is required to define their precise chemical identity. Such simultaneous addition is reminiscent of the recipes to accelerate drying mentioned in the Strasbourg Manuscript.[99] The zinc vitriol and the calcined bones can be added on the grinding slab ('... to all above mentioned colours you must add a little calcined bone or a little zinc vitriol – as much as a bean – in order to make the colour dry well') or in the preparation of the oil called *oleum preciosum*, described as 'very quick drying and [it] makes all colours lovely, clear and bright'.[100] Given that such a combination of compounds has also been detected in other *Ghent Altarpiece* samples, we consider it very likely that Van Eyck used one or both methods described by the German anonymous author.

As shown by the paint cross-sections analysed so far, zinc vitriol and powdered glass were not used together in the same layer. It was also very rare to find them in a sequence of layers that can be attributed to the same painting intervention.[101] However, both are frequently found in combination with other compounds such as verdigris, calcined bones or lead-based pigments which, in certain conditions of the

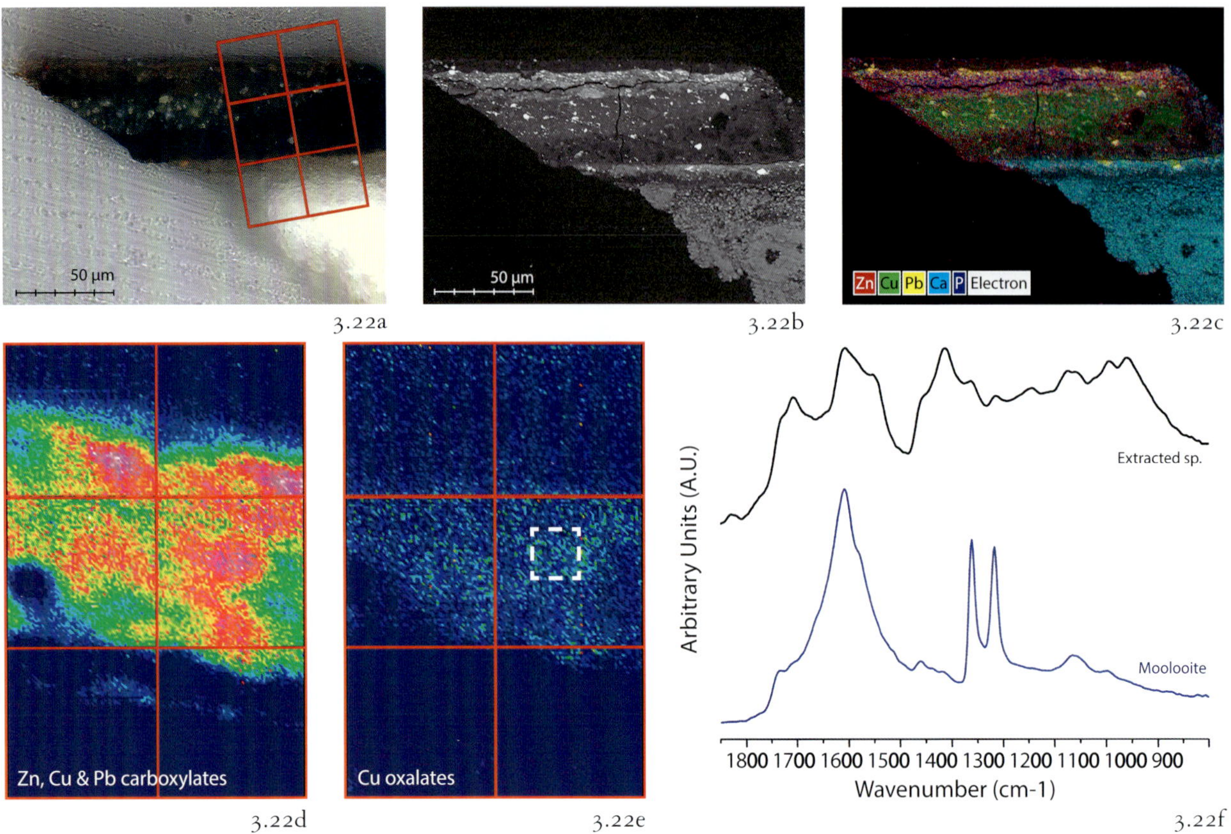

Fig. 3.22a–f. *Adoration*: paint cross-section from the column below the water surface (fig. 3.21) (10/83) under VIS light (a) and back-scattered electron SEM image (b). SEM-EDX spatial distributions (c) of copper (Cu-K, green), zinc (Zn-K, red), phosphorus (P-K, dark blue), lead (Pb-M, yellow) and calcium (Ca-K, cyan). ATR-FTIR analysis of the cross-section enabled us to obtain spatial distribution maps of metal carboxylates (d) and copper oxalates (e). An FTIR spectrum (red), extracted from the black layer (dotted white square, e), shows characteristic copper oxalate (moolooite) vibrations. Moolooite reference spectrum (blue) is included for comparison (f).

preparation of the paint mixture, can promote the formation of metal carboxylates, themselves enhancing the drying properties of oil.[102] These metallo-organic driers are nowadays classified into primary (or active fast) and secondary (or auxiliary), with lower catalytic activity, and it has been demonstrated that their combination allows a fast and 'thorough' drying without causing certain defects such as drying cracks or 'wrinkling'.[103] The examination of the Ghent samples makes us think that the Van Eyck brothers empirically mastered this subtle association and dosage of additives (Pb, Zn, Cu, Ca-P), producing a liquid paint with suitable handling properties which could quickly convert into a good-quality paint film.

Conclusions

The scientific investigation of the *Ghent Altarpiece* panels restored so far has allowed us to establish an already quite robust, general overview of the Eyckian materials and painting techniques.

Some of the results allow us to complement previous material studies of the polyptych, for instance with respect to the identification of a series of new pigments and additives (coal black, bistre, kermes lake, orpiment, bone white, white vitriol and colourless powdered glass), which enlarge the list of previously found paint materials in the original layers.

However, the ongoing scientific research has also allowed us to unravel novel details which should make it possible to refine our comprehension of the *Ghent Altarpiece*'s creation process. For example, the comparative study of the priming layers applied in different panels of the altarpiece has demonstrated material similarities between certain panels and enabled us to categorize them into three main groups. Similarly, the quantitative study of the glass particles in various paint levels permitted us to propose a hypothesis correlating the material composition of the different glass types found in the altarpiece and the chronology of execution of the paint layers containing them. Finally, the detection of various additives supposed to accelerate the drying of the oil binder, such as zinc sulphate, calcium phosphate, lead- and copper-based pigments, paves the way towards a better understanding of how these associations and minute dosages allowed this huge work of art to be painted.

Notes

1 Coremans 1953.

2 Coremans 1953; Van Asperen de Boer 1979; Brinkman et al. 1984/85, 1990; Billinge et al. 1997a; Campbell 1998a; Gifford 1999; Deneffe 2011; Gifford, Metzger, Delaney 2013; Gifford et al. 2017; Spring, Morrison 2017; Dunkerton, Morrison, Roy 2017.

3 Spring 2012; Spring 2017; Spring, Morrison 2017.

4 Van der Snickt et al. 2017; Sanyova et al. 2020.

5 The methods mentioned are described in the previous publication devoted to the first phase of restoration, Sanyova et al. 2020.

6 Gifford 1999; Gifford, Metzger, Delaney 2013; Billinge, Campbell 1995; Campbell, Foister, Roy 1997.

7 Jones, Augustyniak, Dubois 2020.

8 Coremans 1953; Brinkman et al. 1984/85; Faries 2006; Clark 2011; Vandivere 2013; Steyaert, Postec 2020.

9 During the 1950–51 campaign, scientists suggested that the study of coccoliths present in the altarpiece's chalk ground could help to differentiate studio practice, but that aspect was not further explored: Dubois, Deneffe 2019. In the next study of these old samples, the coccoliths revealed by SEM-EDX were identified as originating in Western Europe: Brinkman et al. 1984/85.

10 Sample from the prophet Zechariah's pink drapery was analysed at the European Synchrotron Radiation Facility (ESRF), Grenoble, as part of the HG41 project; Beamtime with SR-XRF, SR-XANES and SR-XRPD at ID 21 and ID 13.

11 The painting of the *Just Judges* was stolen, but its frame was not and it

remained with the other frames of the wing panels.

12 Neven 2016, pp. 121 and 160.

13 These techniques are described in detail on the basis of the IRR images in chapter 2 of this volume.

14 https://www.researchgate.net/publication/248517293_Chlorine_in_coal_A_review (accessed 12 November 2020).

15 Coremans 1953; Brinkman et al. 1984/85; Campbell 1988; Campbell, Foister, Roy 1997; Stroo 2009, pp. 122–23, 153–55, 270–71, 417–19.

16 Campbell, Foister, Roy 1997a,b, pp. 22, 71; Stege et al. 2007, pp. 74–75; Nadolny 2008; Faries 2011; Spring 2012; Spring 2017.

17 Ferreira 2006; Gifford, Metzger, Delaney 2013; Vandivere 2013, p.75; Van Baum et al. 2014, p. 49.

18 Nadolny 2008.

19 Chalk was detected in several samples with SEM-EDX thanks to the presence of fragments of coccoliths.

20 No reliable sample from the *Eve* panel was available to confirm whether or not it also belongs to this same group.

21 Van Mander (1604); see Vandivere 2013, p. 76.

22 It is interesting to note that the priming in the upper part of the *Archangel* panel with the prophet Zechariah is darker than that used in the part with the Archangel Gabriel.

23 The bone white-containing layer was not detected in all samples, which makes it uncertain that it was applied over the entire ground. Klaassen et al. 2021.

24 Plahter 2003.

25 https://www.metmuseum.org/blogs/collection-insights/2019/jan-van-eyck-frames-imaging-xray-xrf (accessed 12 November 2020).

26 Stroo 2009, pp. 270–71.

27 Bone white is also mentioned as an extender of the ground on a dry wall as an alternative to gypsum or chalk in the Montpellier *Liber diversarum artium* (Clark 2011, p. 143). Cennini mentions using the calcined bone in chapters 5–7; Cennini (ed. Thompson) 1960, pp. 4–5.

28 Neven 2016, pp. 121, 123 recipes 66, 68, pp. 161–162, 184, 189.

29 Plahter 1992; Nadolny 2001, pp. 426 and 445.

30 Measurements with SR-μ-XRPD were carried out at the ID13 (ESRF, Grenoble) in March 2014.

31 The addition of highly alkaline quicklime to the leaded oil is recommended by Archerius in 1398 for the preparation of a heat-bodied oil for tempering pigments: 'Si vous voulez appareiller oile pour destemper toutes manieres de couleurs. Prenes chaux vive avec autant de ceruse cofirne est de loile, puiz metez au soleil et ne le movez jusques a ung moyt ou plus tar quant plus y sera, et mieulx vaudra, puis le colez et gardez tres bien loile, et de celle oille gardee et ainsi preparee, povez destremper toutes couleurs ensemble et chacun par soy.' In *De diversis coloribus* no. 319; Merrifield 1849, p. 303.

32 Keller 1973; Bielman 1993.

33 Cotte et al. 2016.

34 A similar intermediate layer was observed in the National Gallery of Art *Annunciation*.

35 Campbell, Foister, Roy 1997; Campbell 1998a.

36 Coremans 1953; Brinkman et al. 1984/85; Brinkman et al. 1988/89.

37 The copper green pigment identified by Thissen as malachite in all green samples taken in 1950–51 is in fact verdigris.

38 It should be noted that the hydrocerussite and cerussite present in the priming layers could also have been formed by the remineralization of the lead soaps from a leaded oil, as described by Cotte et al. 2016.

39 Gonzalez et al. 2017.

40 This attempt to recognize various qualities of lead white, using SR-XRPD on several microsamples from the *Ghent Altarpiece* panels, showed the potential of such an approach. The long-term lead white evolution is the topic of an ongoing research led by the University of Antwerp's AXES group.

41 Gonzalez et al. 2017.

42 Vandivere, Clarke 2012.

43 For a further discussion of these interventions, see chapter 2, sections 'The sky and the horizon' and 'Architecture' and chapter 4.

44 Van Asperen de Boer 1974; Spring, Morrison 2017.

45 Coremans 1953; Campbell, Foister, Roy 1997; Campbell 1998a.

46 Spring, Morrison 2017; Spring 2017; Gifford et al. 2017.

47 Ibid.

48 The same biomarker, the indigotine molecule, is commonly used for the identification of both the European and the Asian plants, which cannot be differentiated on this basis.

49 Kirby 2006.

50 Borrodaile, Borrodaile 1966, p. 61.

51 Von Baum et al. 2014, pp. 137 and 336.

52 Eastaugh et al. 2004, p. 385; Buse et al. 2019.

53 Scott, Taniguchi, Koseto 2001; Buse et al. 2019.

54 Borrodaile, Borrodaile 1966; Neven 2016.

55 Scott, Taniguchi, Koseto 2001; Buse et al. 2019.

56 The mechanism of formation of metal oxalates in Southern Netherlandish oil paintings, including the *Ghent Altarpiece* panels, is currently under investigation in the MetOx project (BELSPO BR/165/A6/METOX) coordinated by KIK-IRPA.

57 The use of zinc-containing compounds is discussed in the section related to the additives.

58 During the study in 1950–51, all copper-based green pigments were described as malachite and all transparent green glazes as copper resinates (Coremans 1953, pp. 71–73). The updated analyses in 1988/89 have confirmed that copper resinate is present in the transparent layers, while malachite was not found. Consequently, the green pigment was described as "copper based" only (Brinkman et al. 1988/89).

59 Both samples were analysed with pyrolysis-gas chromatography–mass spectrometry (Py-GCMS) after their methylation with (tetramethyl) ammonium hydroxide (TMAH). The positive detection of bistre was based on the presence of methoxyphenol markers, deriving from pyrolyzed lignin, the guaiacol and syringol derivates (2-methoxyphenol and 1,3-dimethoxyphenol respectively) as well as polycyclic aromatic hydrocarbons (PAHs). Baumer et al. 2019.

60 Borrodaile 1966, p. 49; Merrifield 1967, pp. 24, 27.

61 Von Baum et al. 2014, p. 140.

62 Roldan et al. 2014; Baumer et al. 2019. Bistre is so finely dispersed in the washes obtained through the reconstruction of old recipes that it forms a thin discontinuous barely visible layer and it would be quite hard to find an area large enough to be suitable for sampling.

63 The samples containing an original red glaze were available in very low amounts and were nearly always contaminated by later interventions, as shown by the optical microscope observation of the cross-sections under UV light.

64 This was based on the detection of the kermesic acid and laccaic acid A and E.

65 Sanyova et al. 2020.

66 Kirby, Spring, Higgitt 2005.

67 The analysis was carried out and interpreted by Dr Stepanka Kuckova at the University of Chemistry and Technology, Prague.

68 Kirby 2008; Kirby et al. 2014.

69 See note 12.

70 Lutzenberger, Stege, Tilenschi 2010; Spring 2012; Spring 2017; Spring, Morrison 2017; Melo et al. 2020.

71 Campbell, Foister, Roy 1997a; Campbell 1998a; see also chapter 2 in this volume.

72 Pacheco's and Paduan manuscripts are cited by Merrifield (1849) 1967. pp. ccxxxix–ccxlii.

73 Lutzenberger, Stege, Tilenschi 2010; Spring 2012; Spring 2017; Melo et al. 2020.

74 Lutzenberger, Stege, Tilenschi 2010; Spring 2012.

75 Spring 2012; Spring 2017.

76 The glass-containing red overpaint detected in this sample from the Archangel's wing (13/37) was described as a second overpaint in the first phase of treatment: Sanyova et al. 2020. The updated comparative study of the glass powder compositions in the *Ghent Altarpiece* samples suggests that this glaze was applied before the overall sixteenth-century overpaint.

77 Lutzenberger, Stege, Tilenschi 2010; Spring 2012; Spring 2017.

78 Lutzenberger, Stege, Tilenschi 2010 has found the soda ash glass powder in the

flesh tone of a painting by Colijn de Coter dated before 1510. This type corresponds to the *cristallo* type of soda glass.

79 A similar case was observed in the *Tiefenbronn Altarpiece* by Lukas Moser (dated 1432) with a particle size up to 70 µm. However, the composition of this glass was different from that found in the dove. Two types of glass were found in the gilding mordant in Moser's altarpiece, one sodium-rich, Venetian soda ash glass (*vitrum blanchum*) and one with quite high content of sodium and potassium, considered as an intermediate mixed alkali type; see Lutzenberger, Stege, Tilenschi 2010.

80 Spring 2012.

81 Dubois, Sanyova, Vanwijnsberghe 2017.

82 The authenticity of the dove is discussed in the previous chapter 2, section 'The dove, the halo and the rays' and in chapter 4.

83 Janssens et al. 1998; Caen et al. 2006.

84 Spring 2017: HLLA-type glass was identified in ten out of nineteen Netherlandish paintings in the National Gallery, London, all dated after 1470.

85 Sanyova et al. 2020.

86 Lutzenberger, Stege, Tilenschi 2010; Spring 2012; Spring 2017.

87 Janssens et al. 1998.

88 Lutzenberger, Stege, Tilenschi 2010.

89 Merrifield 1849, p. ccxlii.

90 The project Lasting Support (1 April 2010–30 June 2011) was supported by The Getty Foundation. The analyses were carried out within the CHARISMA project by MOLAB.

91 Spring, Morrison 2017.

92 Stege, Tilenschi, Sanyova 2012; Spring et al. 2012; Von Baum et al. 2014, pp. 133–140.

93 Spring 2017.

94 As an additive, it is often present in minor concentrations that might easily fall below the minimum detection limit of the analytical method used, e.g. SEM-EDX. The detection limit of SEM-EDX is typically in the order of 200 parts per million (ppm) while the MA-XRF instrument used for the *Ghent Altarpiece* was able to visualize zinc concentrations at or just below 100 ppm; Alfeld et al. 2011.

95 Spring mentioned (2017) that zinc vitriol could have been used for the preparation of a special quick-drying oil, *oleum preciosum*, or added as a powder on the grinding slab according to the Strasbourg Manuscript. According to the Tegernsee Manuscript, it could also have been used as an ingredient in the manufacturing of a high-quality red lake, having better drying properties.

96 Care should be taken when an attempt is made to give semiquantitative significance to MA-XRF plots, as various unknown parameters can influence the resulting pixel intensities, such as the potential accumulation of Zn-based layers, their possible fragmented lateral distribution and heterogeneous paint layer thicknesses.

97 Chapter 2, section 'Trees'.

98 Chapter 2, section 'Meadow and fountain' and fig. 2.14.

99 Borrodaile, Borrodaile 1966, pp. 55, 61, 65.

100 Ibid., p. 55.

101 This was the case of the red mantle of a bald philosopher on the lower left in the *Adoration* panel, where two red layers with lake from wool shearings containing zinc vitriol (10/73, layers 5, 6) were covered with a third red glaze (10/73, layer 7) containing wood ash-type glass particles.

102 Cotte et al. 2016.

103 Bielman 1993.

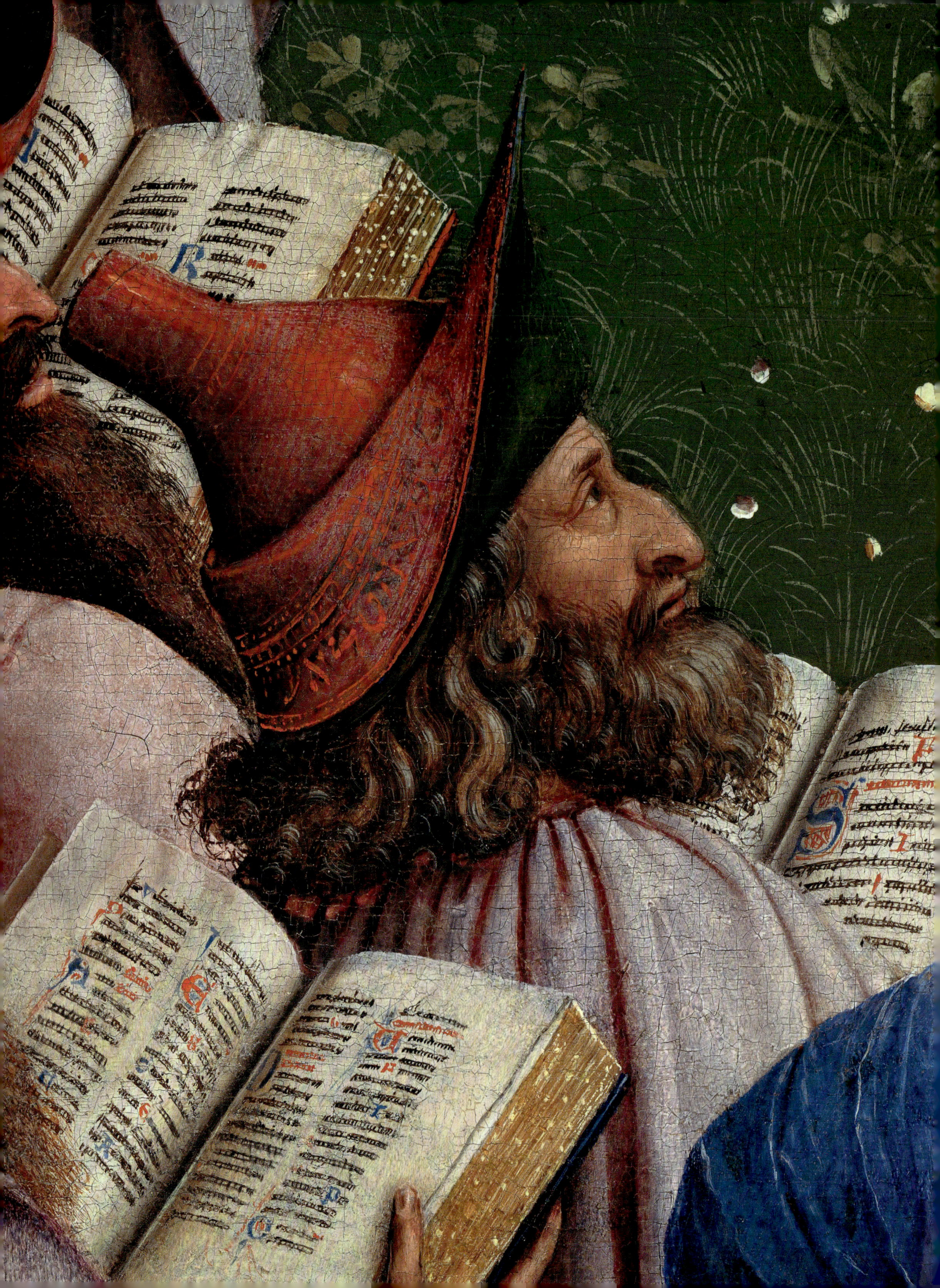

4
One Painter or Several? A Stylistic Study

Griet Steyaert and Marie Postec

Technical and scientific research has enabled us to distinguish three stages in the development of the lower register of the altarpiece interior. Are they evidence of a single painter adjusting his composition as the creative process unfolded?[1] Are they the work of Hubert and then of Jan, as the quatrain states? Or may we attribute the first stage to Hubert, the second to Jan and the third to assistants or even to a later painter? Neither the technical scientific investigation nor the chemical analysis are sufficient in themselves to attribute these successive interventions with certainty. A stylistic approach is thus still required in any attempt to establish whether different hands might be in evidence. The only known quantity in this equation with multiple variables is Jan van Eyck.

Eyckian interventions

Jan

Besides the *Ghent Altarpiece*, Jan van Eyck's oeuvre comprises nine paintings that are signed and dated between 1432 and 1439,[2] to which we may add a few widely accepted attributions.[3] These works are used here by way of comparison. Jan van Eyck's keen sense of observation and his extraordinary ability to represent what he observed enabled him to translate the many nuances of colour produced by the reflection of light on materials of every kind, thus making the world he painted tangible.[4] In the *Adoration of the Lamb*, the painter conveyed the many shades observed in the metal column of the fountain, in the same way as in the *Virgin at the Fountain*,[5] through more or less warm tones but also by touches of varying density – from an intense highlight rendered through a dense pictorial substance to filaments of diffuse reflection.[6] A dragon's head in the fountain of the *Adoration of the Lamb* closely resembles a similar detail of the chandelier in the *Arnolfini Portrait* (fig. 4.1a–b).[7] On top of a brown silhouette, Jan suggested reflections by applying a few yellow dots – tiny, but precisely distributed in accordance with the lighting of the represented location.

The veins and cavities specific to the various materials of the stone and marble basin in the *Adoration of the Lamb* are represented, as are two characteristic fragments of a chipped stone (fig. 4.2b). Similar details are also found in the *Virgin of Chancellor Rolin* and the *Virgin of Canon Van der Paele*,[8] right down to the chips in the stone,

(facing page) *Adoration of the Lamb*: head of a prophet attributed to Hubert van Eyck (see also fig. 4.5).

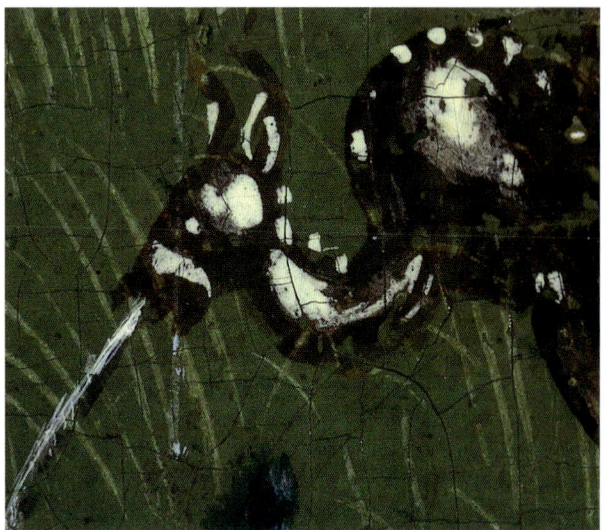

4.1a

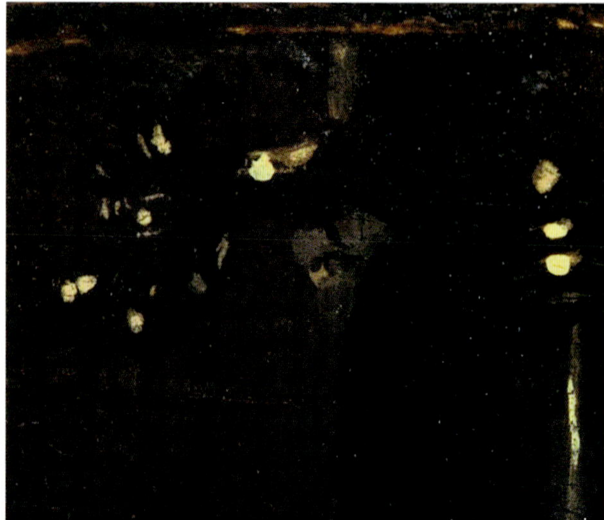

4.1b

Fig. 4.1a–b. Reflections on metal. Jan van Eyck: detail of the fountain, *Adoration of the Lamb* (a); detail of the chandelier, *Arnolfini Portrait*, 1434, London, The National Gallery, inv. NG186 (b).

indicated by two simple touches of paint, one brown, the other white (fig. 4.2a and c). The waves created by the water of the fountain as it falls into the basin in the *Adoration* are painted with nuanced strokes (fig. 4.3a). The water splashes back up at the point of impact to form suspended droplets, grouped together and then bursting, in precisely the same way as in the *Virgin at the Fountain* (fig. 4.3b). The rendering of tufts of grass and certain small flowers in the second-stage meadow of the *Adoration* is likewise comparable with what Jan painted at the feet of the *Virgin at the Fountain* and in the flowerbeds of the *Virgin of Chancellor Rolin*.[9] Through the very shape of the touches of paint and their precise distribution, through the orientation of his brush, and the gesture he made when applying the paint, he not only gave shape to the plants he painted, but also captured what distinguishes lily-of-the-valley, say, from buttercup, no matter how small the flecks of colour. This extraordinary ability to translate such refined observations into painting through swift yet never accidental brushstrokes is found throughout Jan van Eyck's work.[10] His touches combine precision with speed (seemingly contradictory characteristics), enabling him to vary his effects.

In his hands and faces, Jan did not simply paint the colour of the skin: he incorporated all the nuances created by veins, blood vessels and imperfections of the epidermis. The flesh tones of the prelates in the *Adoration* (fig. 4.4a) resemble those of St Donatian in the *Virgin of Canon Van der Paele* (fig. 4.4b) and the donor in the *Virgin of Chancellor Rolin* (fig. 4.4c). Stubble is indicated by bluish areas of skin, patches of red in the epidermis are finely distributed, brown lines suggest wrinkles that furrow the flesh. Two fingers of the left hand of the philosopher in the blue cloak are lit from behind (fig. 4.14b), just like Arnolfini's right thumb (fig. 4.14a)

All these characteristics associated with Jan van Eyck are found in the second stage.

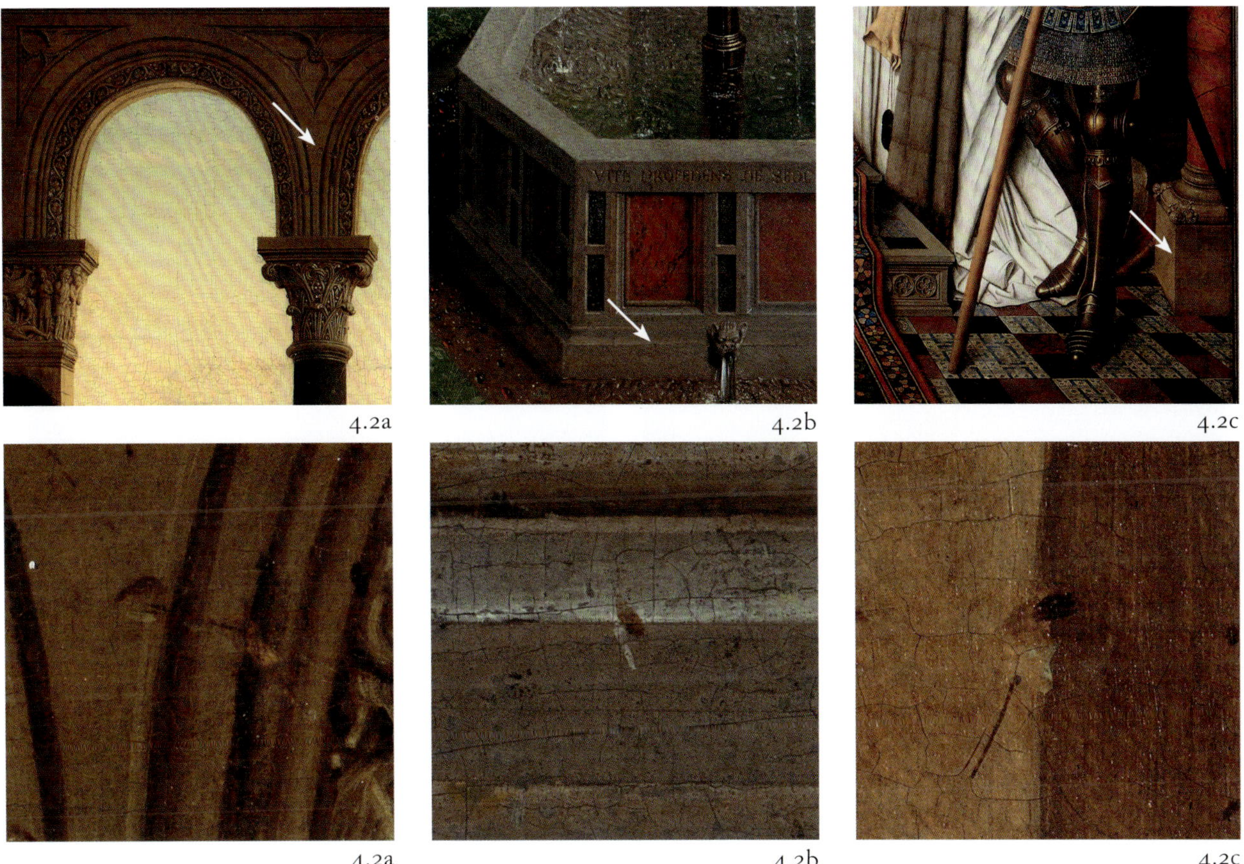

Fig. 4.2a–c. Chips in stone. Jan van Eyck: detail of the arcade, *Virgin of Chancellor Rolin*, Paris, Musée du Louvre, inv. 1271 (a); detail of the fountain, *Adoration of the Lamb* (b); detail of a plinth, *Virgin of Canon Van der Paele*, 1436, Bruges, Groeningemuseum, inv. 0000.GRO0161.I (c).

Hubert

Comparison of the first apostle to the right of the fountain (fig. 4.5b) with other figures reveals stylistic differences that can only be explained by the involvement of two painters. The difference between his profile[11] and that of the pilgrim next to St Christopher (fig. 4.6b) or the three-quarter view of St Anthony in the *Hermits* (fig. 4.6a) is telling, especially in the way the eyes are painted. In the first apostle (fig. 4.5b), the painter used a base tone for the entire area of the eye, with very little modulation. He indicated the boundary between the upper eyelid and the eye with a thick, dark line that unrealistically ends in a curl in the corner of the eye where the wrinkles begin. The base tone is the same for the eyes of St Anthony and the pilgrim (figs. 4.6a–b), but the volume of the eyeball is suggested by brown glazes that also mark the cavity below the arch of the eyebrow. The eyelids are suggested by grey touches that introduce subtle shades and their thickness is evoked by red lines, as found in the eyes of Giovanni Arnolfini (albeit light pink there rather than red).[12] The wrinkles around the eyes also illustrate these differences in vocabulary.

Technical analysis has shown that the second-stage meadow, which can be attributed to Jan, was painted at the same time as the fountain and that it meticulously skirts around several of the figures, including this first apostle.[13] Other works by Jan show that areas of grass were done before the figures,[14] suggesting that the first

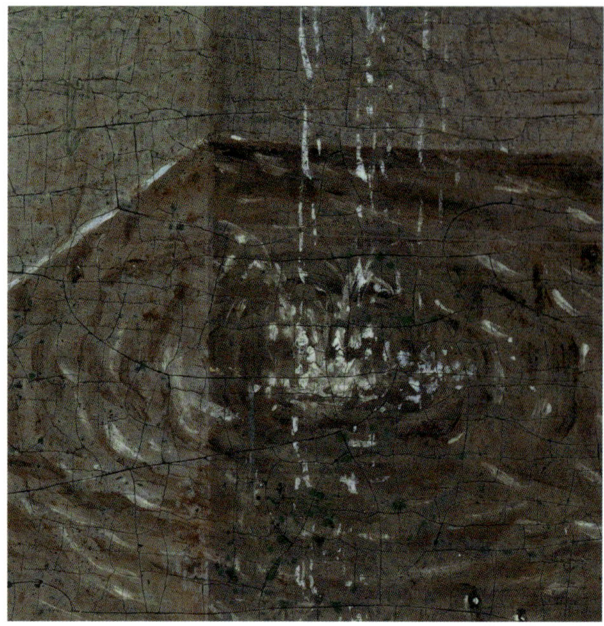

4.3a

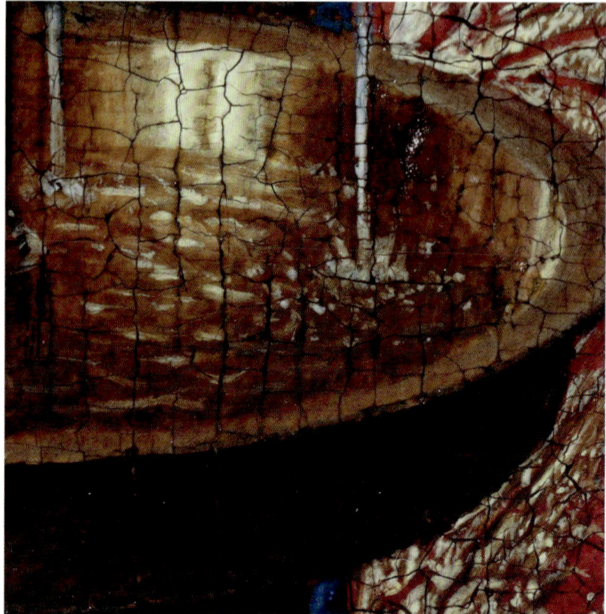

4.3b

Fig. 4.3a–b. Splashing water droplets and waves. Jan van Eyck: detail of the fountain, *Adoration of the Lamb* (a); detail of the fountain, *Virgin at the Fountain*, 1439, Antwerp, Royal Museum of Fine Arts, inv. 411 (b).

apostle in the *Adoration* had already been painted when Jan intervened and that he decided to retain him.[15] A sample[16] taken from the spot where the apostle's robe overlaps the first-stage meadow tells us that this meadow had been painted, right up to the glaze, before the figure was added. The figure and the first meadow may thus belong to the same stage. Bearing in mind the information provided by the quatrain, we may indeed conclude that this apostle could be Hubert's work, together with the first meadow and the spring, now concealed.[17]

The first apostle (fig. 4.5b) is not the only figure that may be attributed to Hubert: the one kneeling to his right in the front row and another a little further down (fig. 4.5a) belong to the same category of figures that we will refer to as 'less realistic', as do some of the faces of the first prophets to the left of the fountain.[18] The eye zone (fig. 4.5a) shows the same characteristics as those observed in the first apostle (fig. 4.5b). In the prophet with the red hat (fig. 4.5c), we find the same dark line between the upper eyelid and eyeball, terminating in a curl where the wrinkles begin. The face of the figure in the blue cap, partly hidden by the green drapery, also displays features that seem far removed from Jan's art (fig. 4.5d). In the figures painted by Hubert, wrinkles are schematically indicated rather than that they convey a precise topography of the creases in the skin. They lack relief, as does the volume of the cheek. The brown lines in the hermit and pilgrim painted by Jan are combined with light touches that perfectly suggest the irregularities in the folds of the flesh (fig. 4.6a–b). Moreover, the difference in colour in the skin between the wrinkles at the corner of the eye and those in the cheeks lends volume to the faces.

There are likewise disparities between the meadow next to the horses in the *Knights of Christ* and that of the *Adoration of the Lamb*. In the *Knights* panel, the grass is grouped into tufts that form a stylized motif, unlike the airy grass of the

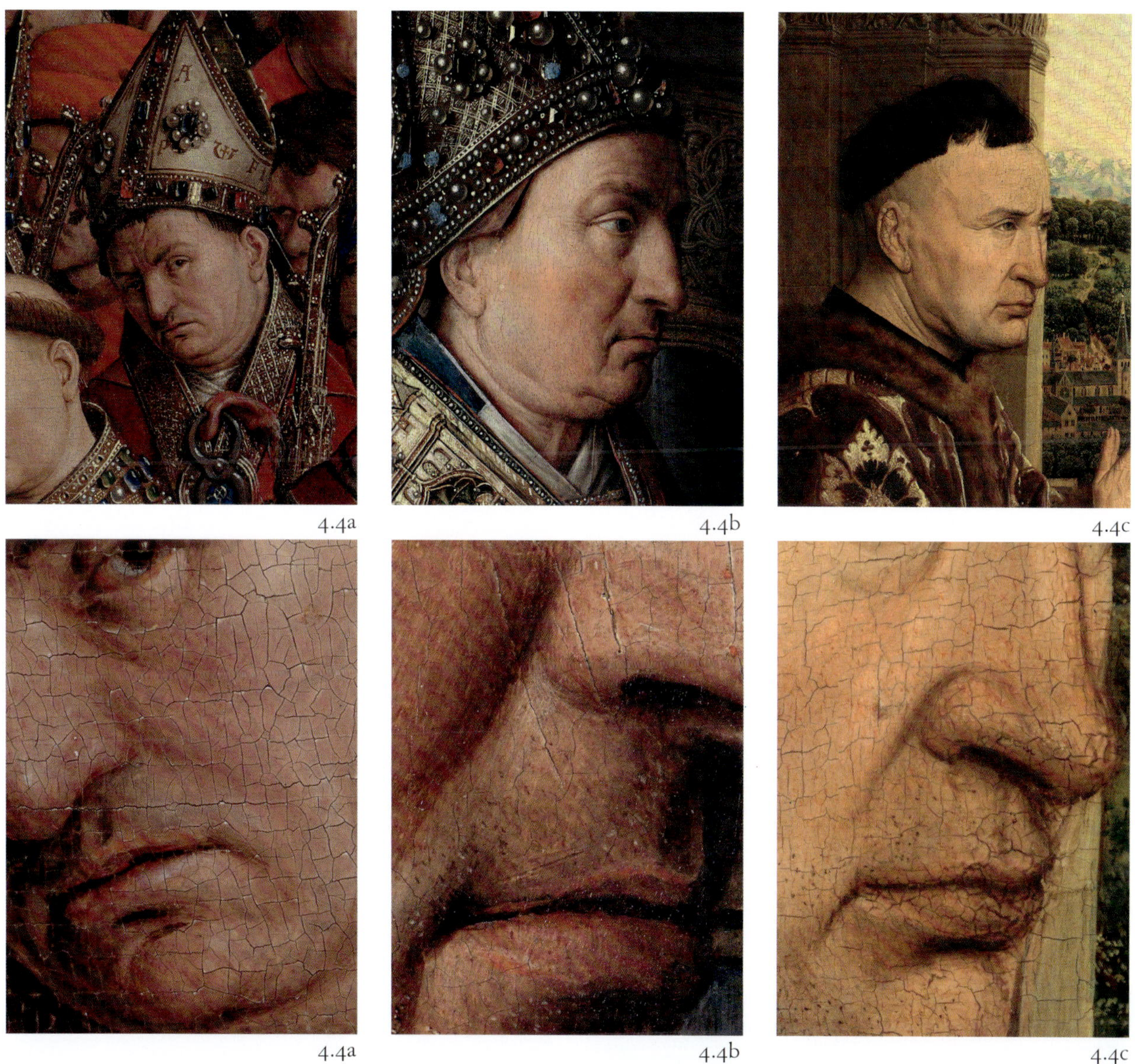

Fig. 4.4a–c. Rendering of flesh tones attributed to Jan van Eyck: *Adoration of the Lamb* (a); *Virgin of Canon Van der Paele*, 1436, Bruges, Groeningemuseum, inv. 0000.GRO0161.I (b); *Virgin of Chancellor Rolin*, Paris, Musée du Louvre, inv. 1271 (c).

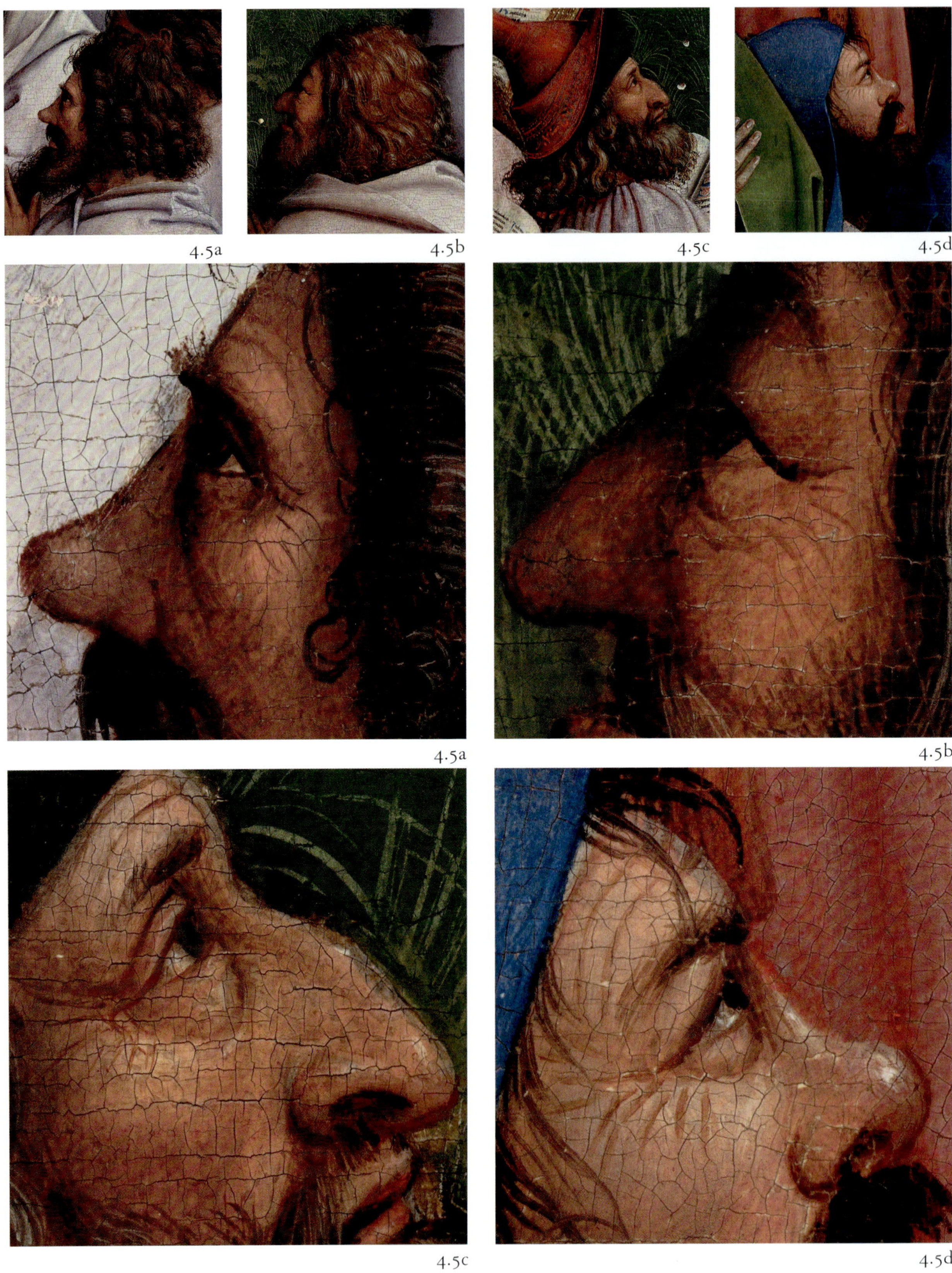

Fig. 4.5a–d. *Adoration of the Lamb*, heads attributed to Hubert van Eyck.

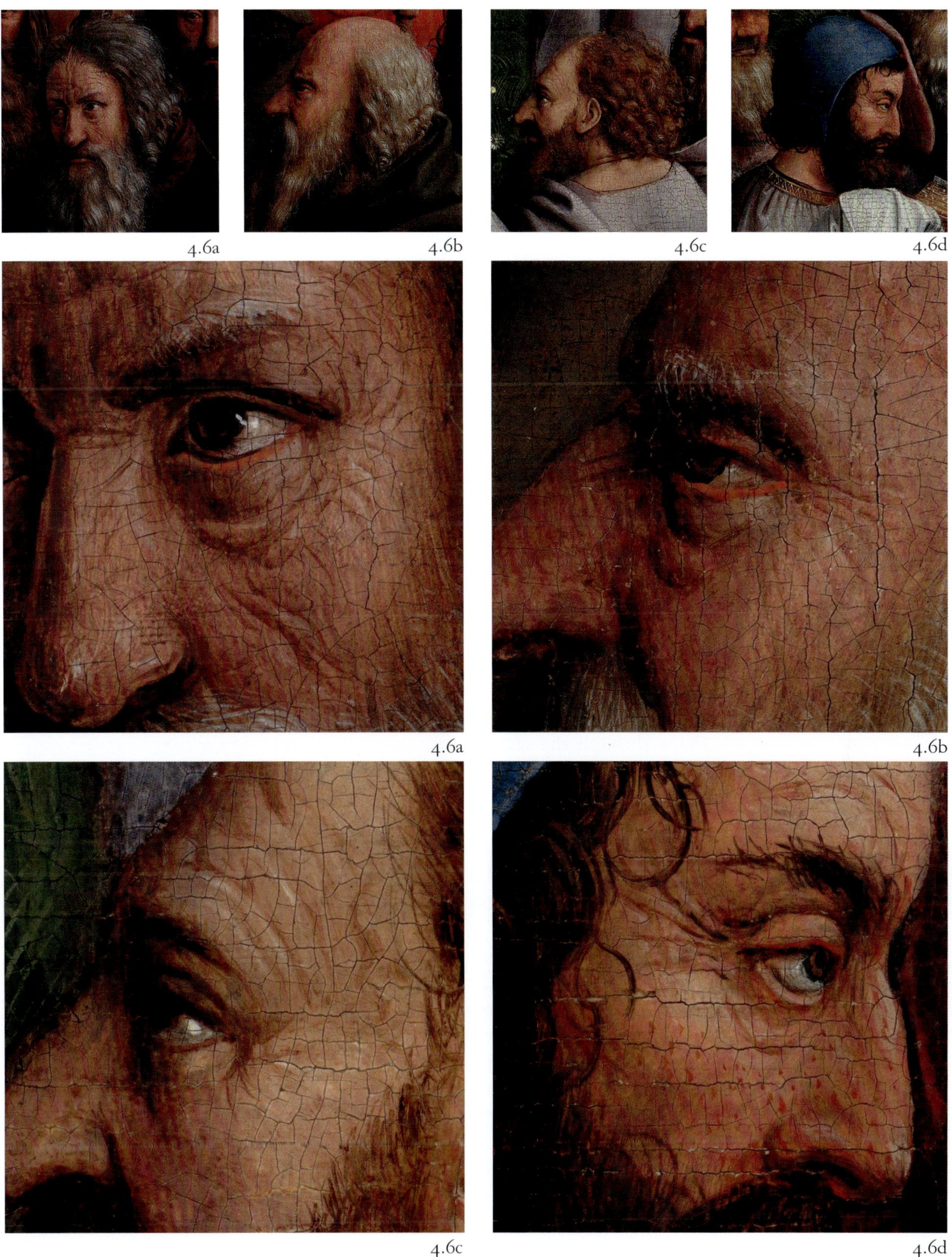

Fig. 4.6a–d. *Hermits*, head attributed to Jan van Eyck (a); *Pilgrims*, head attributed to Jan van Eyck (b); *Adoration of the Lamb*, heads attributed to Hubert and reworked by Jan van Eyck (c and d).

central panel. Analysis of a cross-section[19] shows that a second meadow has not been painted here over a first,[20] as is the case in the central panel, and that only two layers of green are present above a brown layer. This meadow zone in the *Knights* may thus be attributed to Hubert.

The differences are not limited to the richness of nuances and variety in the brushwork: Jan, who painted the hermit and the pilgrim (fig. 4.6a–b), was clearly more concerned with observing and recording reality and perhaps also better able to translate these refined observations into paint. Both artists used the same technical means, but there is a world of difference in their respective visual languages.

Sequence of pictorial execution

Based on the characteristics outlined above, the painted faces in the lower register may be roughly divided into two groups – one clearly more faithful to anatomical reality than the other. The less realistic faces are much fewer in number (fig. 4.7). Some authors mention the possible participation of Jan's or possibly Hubert's assistants and hence of two workshops.[21] It seems unlikely, however, that an assistant would have painted less realistic figures in such a central part of the composition or that Jan would have worked so meticulously around an assistant's contribution. The two groups mentioned above are coherent and, where differences exist within them, these were consciously introduced by each of the two brothers. Hubert and Jan both sought to vary the figures' faces, as well as taking account of the direction of the light in their execution. The figures to the left of the fountain are fully illuminated, while those on the right partially turn their backs to the light, which results in differences of colour.[22] Some of Hubert's heads, lastly, were probably reworked or retouched by Jan. The eye of one of the apostles, for example, was given a more natural shape through the addition of a white highlight and a few shadow lines (fig. 4.6c). The face of one of the prophets, meanwhile, in which traces of rosacea were not really integrated in the modelling, had the eyebrow and wrinkles retouched (fig. 4.6d).

All the less realistic heads are grouped in the centre of the composition, in two specific zones on either side of the fountain, close to the edges of the first lawn, which had already been painted (fig. 4.7). These are the very figures within each group that were most likely to be painted first in a fifteenth-century panel. Once the underdrawing had been completed, the logical elements to be painted first would have been large expanses such as the sky and the meadow, leaving a reserve for other parts of the composition, including the groups of figures.[23] These reserves were then filled in a logical order, working from the background to the foreground and superimposing figures further back in the group with the ones nearer the front, so that the pictorial layer of each figure slightly overlaps that of any others behind it.[24] Figures on the edge of the reserved space slightly overlap the edges of the first meadow.

Certain parts of a painting – especially in an ensemble as large as the *Ghent Altarpiece* – will have been completed while adjoining areas were still at the underdrawing stage or had only been given their first layers of paint. This is illustrated by unfinished works like the *St Barbara* in the Royal Museum of Fine Arts Antwerp.[25] Hubert appears to have followed this general pattern of working from the back to the front. Having painted the sky, the architecture on the horizon, the meadow and the spring, he started work on the large figures in the foreground. He began with those nearest to the spring at the centre of the composition and progressed outwards. At some point, his work was curtailed and subsequently resumed by Jan.[26] Hubert's contribution seems to have halted after the execution of the figures in the vicinity of the spring. The further away we move, the more we find characteristics of Jan's hand: in most of the philosophers to the left of the fountain, in the apostles located somewhat further away on the right, and in the figures of the churchmen.[27]

We have seen in the central area how the second-stage meadow skirts the first-stage altar, lamb and angels. Even if Hubert had laid down the basic foundation of these figures, the final result seems to be Jan's. While there are no securely dated works by Jan that include animals similar to the lamb, he often painted the fur lining of garments with the same accurate rendering of specific texture that we find here in the lamb's coat. The eyes, meanwhile, with their horizontal slit pupils typical of prey animals (fig. 1.8c),[28] may be compared with the eyes of the dog in the *Arnolfini Portrait* or the eye of the collared parakeet in the *Virgin of Canon Van der Paele*[29] (fig. 4.19), each of them painted with an amazing attention to the specific morphology of each species.

The virgin martyrs and confessors groups can also be attributed to Jan. The faces and hair of the female saints are very similar to those of St Catherine in the *Dresden Triptych* (fig. 4.8), although the lighting is different.[30] The fact that the second

Fig. 4.7. *Adoration of the Lamb*, diagram: heads attributed to Hubert (hatched in yellow) and to Jan van Eyck (hatched in red) and heads attributed to Hubert and reworked by Jan van Eyck (hatched in yellow and red).

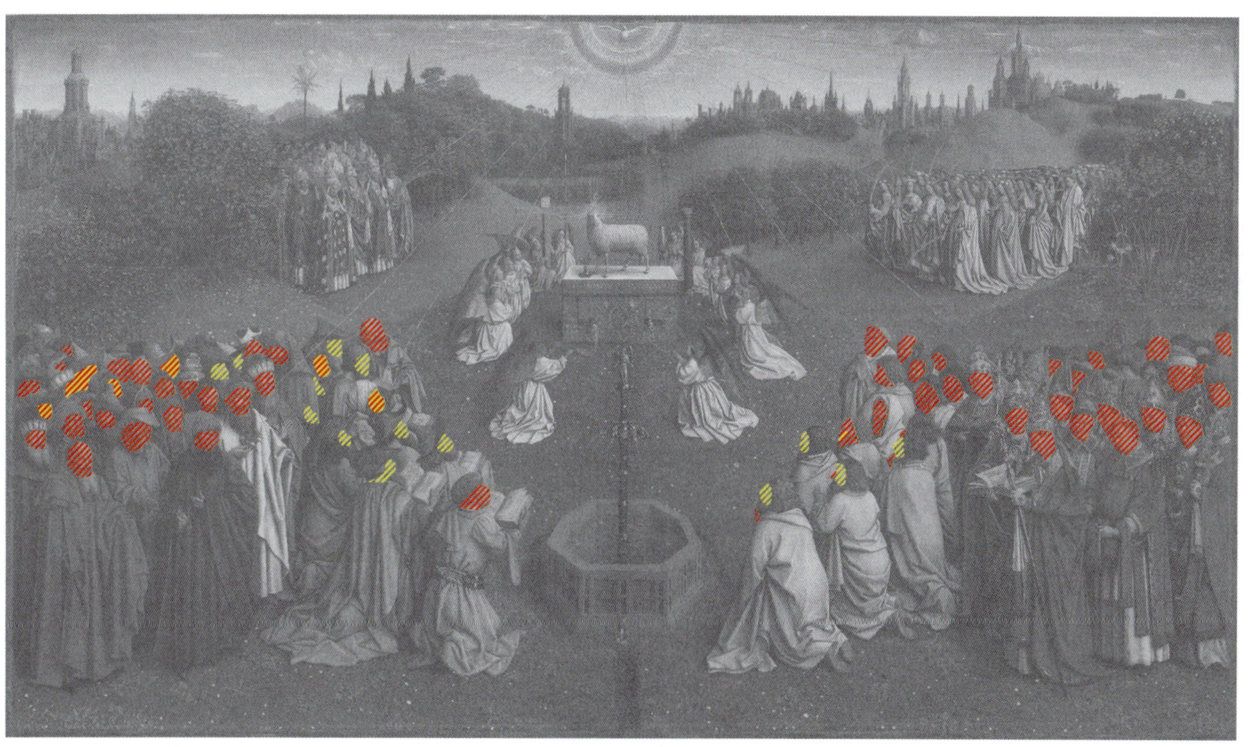

4.7

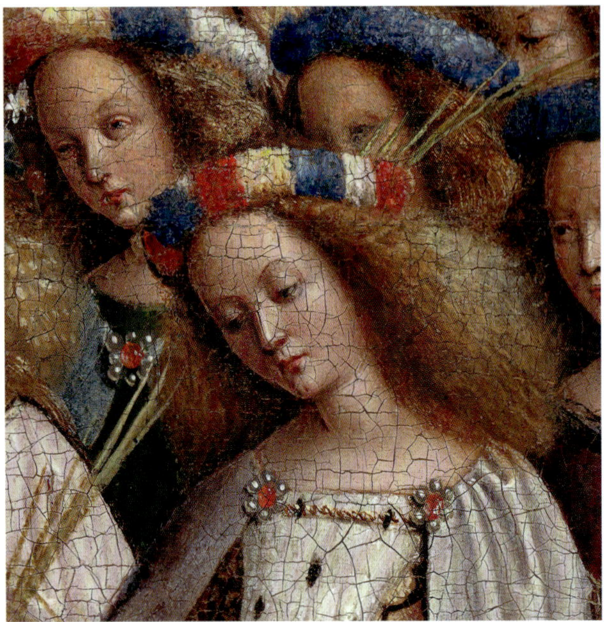
4.8a

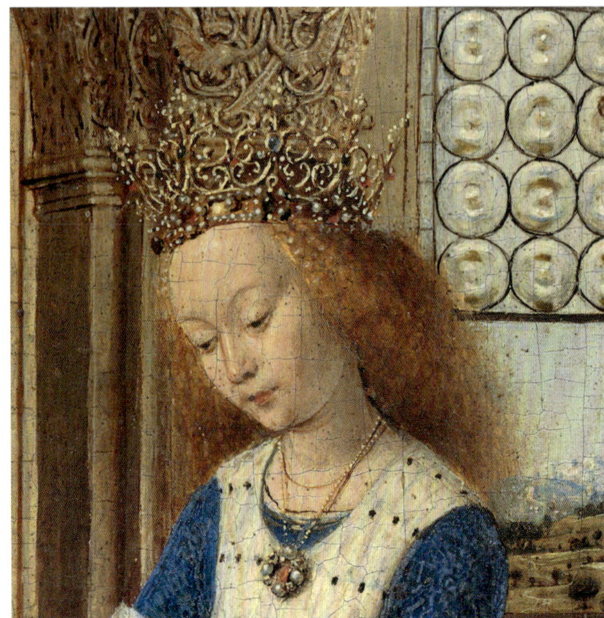
4.8b

Fig. 4.8a–b. *Adoration of the Lamb*, heads of virgin martyrs attributed to Jan van Eyck (a); Jan van Eyck, *Dresden Triptych*, detail of the head of St Catherine, 1437, Dresden, Staatliche Kunstsammlungen Dresden, inv. 799 (b).

meadow was laid down around these figures could mean that Hubert had already painted a first version, perhaps even to a very advanced stage, as suggested by a cross-section from the blue gown of one of the virgin martyrs, which comprises five layers.[31]

Our hypothesis that a second stage attributable to Jan van Eyck covers a first stage previously executed by Hubert and already well advanced in its painting, makes it highly likely that the preparatory layers too were done by Hubert.[32] Some authors have suggested that the preparatory drawing might, in theory, be his.[33] Others, studying the infrared images, have noted divergences in the underdrawing of the *Ghent Altarpiece* without concluding that it might have been done by a painter other than Jan or otherwise raising the possibility that Jan's assistants had a hand in it.[34]

The style of Jan van Eyck's drawing, as revealed by infrared reflectography in signed and dated works other than the *Ghent Altarpiece*, shows a high degree of coherence. As several authors have pointed out,[35] the main folds of the draperies are delimited by more strongly marked strokes, and the volumes are shaped using a more or less dense framework of fine, straight lines, set down parallel to the contour of the forms they define. These longer or shorter lines intersecting in deep shadows may bend slightly, but are very rarely curved. The drawing of *St Barbara* provides a good example.

The characteristics of the underdrawing observed in the *Adoration of the Lamb* differ from this,[36] most notably in the nervous strokes, often curved and crossing the broad lines that demarcate the folds, creating a more disordered impression than Jan's drawing. This type of drawing is clearly visible in the pale-coloured robes of the prophets, apostles and angels (figs. 4.9 and 4.10).[37] These short lines, can also be

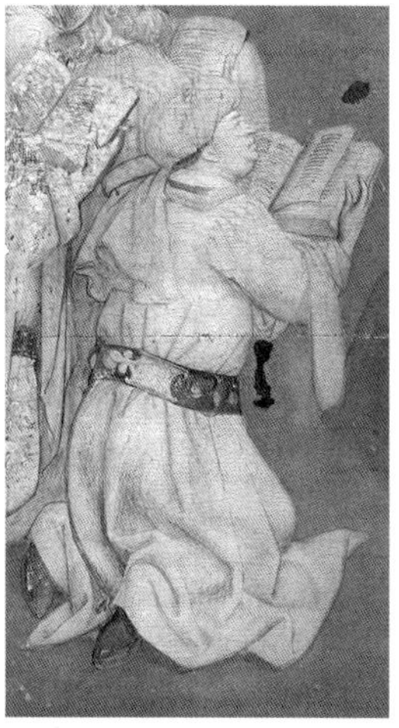
4.9a

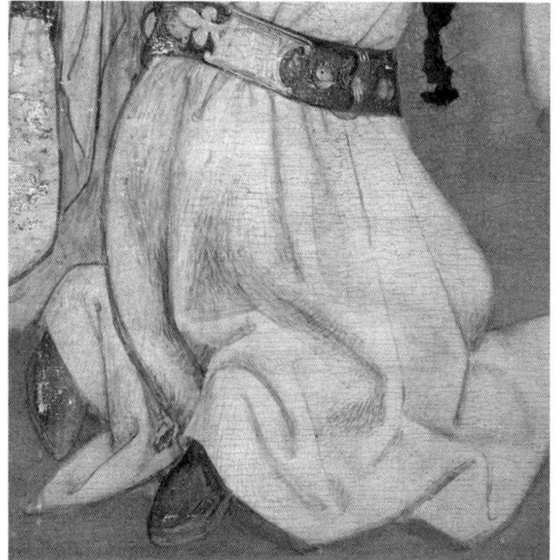
4.9b

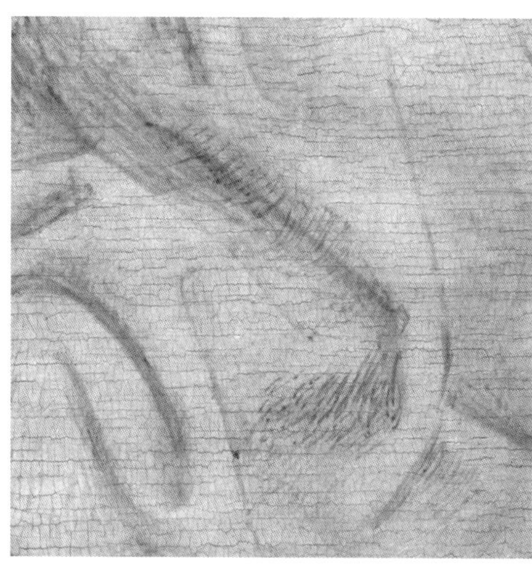
4.9c

Fig. 4.9a–c. *Adoration of the Lamb*, prophet in the foreground: IRR details.

seen in the infrared macrophotograph of the *Pilgrims* crossing the principal line of a fold in St Christopher's cloak (fig. 4.11). Such nervous strokes cutting across the folds might thus be idiosyncratic to Hubert's preparatory drawing.

In this context, comparative research could be carried out in the future on other works that have been associated with Jan or Hubert van Eyck. It is interesting, for instance, to compare this underdrawing with that of the diptych with *St John the Baptist* and the *Virgin and Child* in the Louvre.[38] The drapery folds of the Baptist's robe were drawn with similar strokes, especially in the numerous and complex folds beneath his hand. The diptych is generally attributed to a follower of Jan van Eyck and dated to around 1440.[39] However, given the similarities observed in the underdrawing, it is worth asking whether it might actually have been done by Hubert and at an earlier date.

Non-Eyckian interventions

Several interventions we consider to be non-Eyckian were detected in the technical analysis. They consist of touches that stick out, surface details added with a paint that is often opaque and quite granular. Some of the interventions are more substantial, as in the sky of the central panel and most of the mountains, certain grassy zones on the crags and a few large figures.

Numerous touches around the border between the meadow that Jan painted (the second stage) and the large figures (several from the first stage, painted by Hubert) stand out because of their weakness. This is the case with some hairs on top of a head, which are basically just repetitive straight strokes, and a highlight applied to a skull, which takes no account of the light reflected on the skin (figs. 2.64 and 2.65). Where, as we have seen, the distribution and even the form of Jan's touch contribute to the realistic rendering of what he was seeking to represent, these repetitive touches rigidify the representation rather than bring it to life.

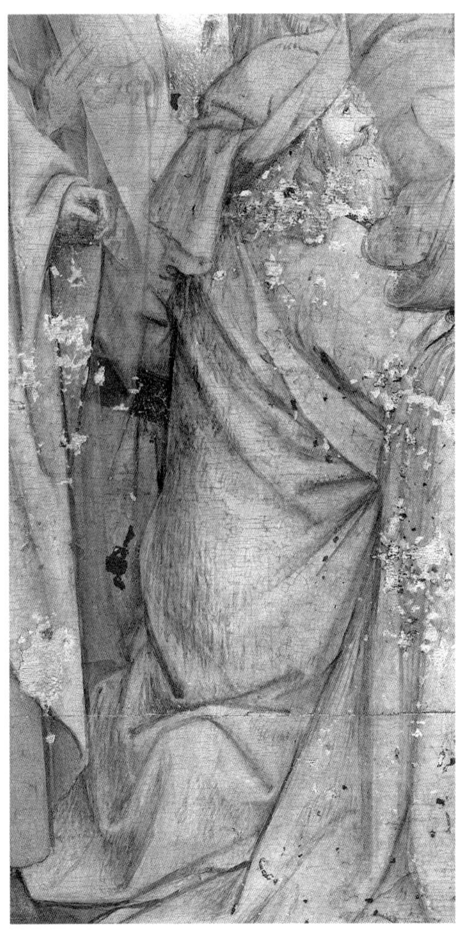

4.10a

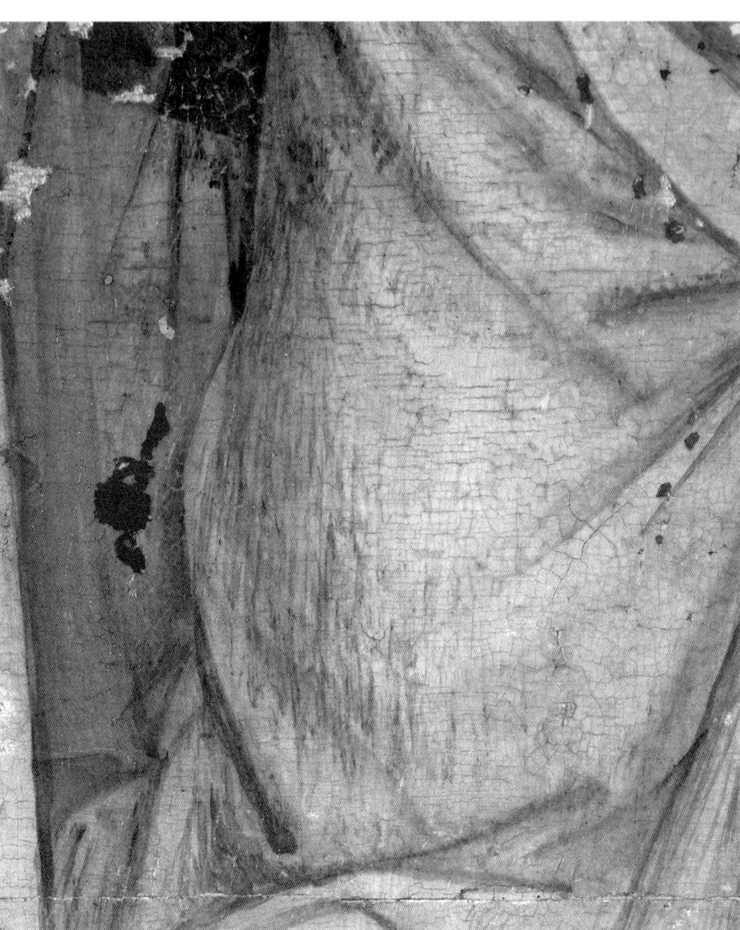

4.10b

Fig. 4.10a–b. *Adoration of the Lamb*, prophet: IRR details.

Examples include many of the trees in the shutters and the central panel, where these additions were executed in a highly repetitive manner (figs. 2.55–2.58).[40] The painter in question applied them with a routine gesture antithetical to Jan's art.[41]

The sky and mountains of the central panel, all based on ultramarine, were painted at the same time, and this after the buidings were finished. The openings of some of the turrets are filled with the ultramarine-based layer (fig. 2.46b), while others are not (fig 2.36b). We also find certain places along the horizon where the ultramarine covers fine painted details, such as the ornamentation and highlights of some of the turrets or the crest of a roof (figs. 2.36, 2.37 and 2.46). Tiny details like this and highlights were generally the last things to be added in early Netherlandish painting.[42] The *City View* in the altarpiece exterior reveals that all the architectural details standing out against the sky were painted after the application of the final blue layer.[43] The sky in *St Barbara* was nearly finished, even before the painting of the tower had begun.[44] The ultramarine layer, finally, makes the sky in the central panel milkier than the deep, subtly gradated skies of the shutters. All these features cast doubt on the Eyckian authorship of this ultramarine-based final layer.

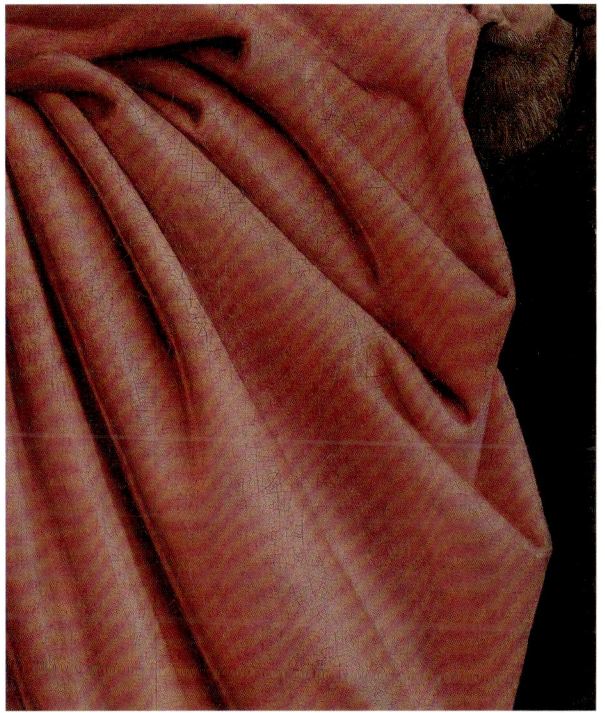

4.11a

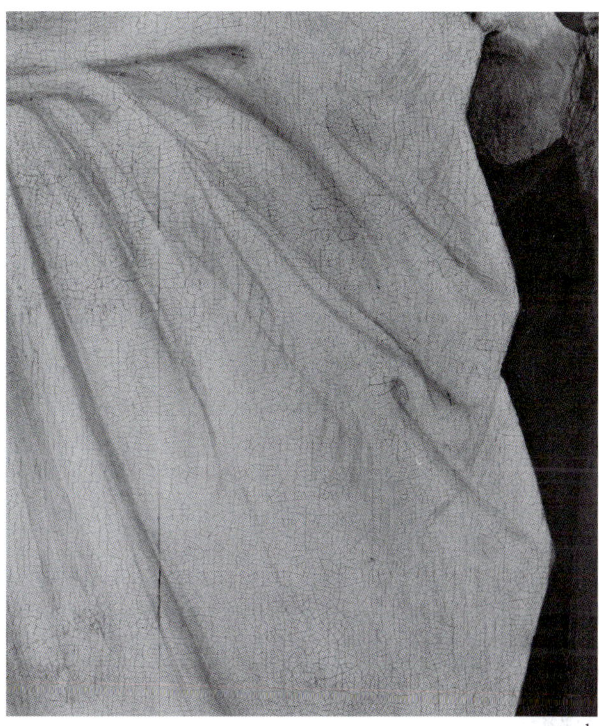

4.11b

Fig. 4.11a–b.
Pilgrims,
St Christopher's red cloak: VIS and IR details.

A horizon line and snow-topped mountains that may be compared stylistically to the mountains in the *Ghent Altarpiece* (fig. 4.12) are found in the *Virgin of Chancellor Rolin*. Those in the *Ghent Altarpiece* are flat, each painted with a single blue tone, whereas the mountains in the *Rolin Madonna* have a much more rugged relief within, with a wide variety of touches and nuances. The fortresses standing in the mountains in the *Knights of Christ* and in the *Rolin Madonna* (fig. 4.13) are both painted in similar tones but to very different effect. Brilliantly distributed brushstrokes evoke the impression in the latter of a citadel surrounded by a defensive wall that sparkles in the morning sun.[45] Each pink touch gives effective shape to a tower, a wall or even the face of the rocky outcrop on which the building stands. The mountains in the *Knights*, by contrast, are more like flat stage scenery, the fortified town is a two-dimensional silhouette and it is impossible to say precisely what the pink touches are meant to represent. Could it be that Jan van Eyck paid less attention to details as small as this fortress in a very large work like the *Ghent Altarpiece*, which was intended to be viewed from a greater distance? This argument can be dismissed on the grounds that the altarpiece is full of small details – not least in the architecture on the very horizon to which these mountains belong. Various elements seem to indicate, therefore, that the ultramarine-based mountains and sky were added after the landscape and buildings were finished. Stylistic comparison suggests that this addition cannot be attributed to Jan.

We have seen in chapter 2 that a relatively major change was made at some point in the groups in the foreground, where the kneeling and standing figures meet

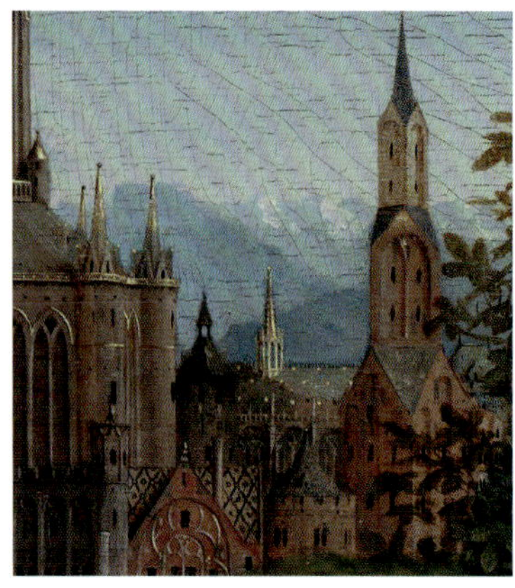
4.12a

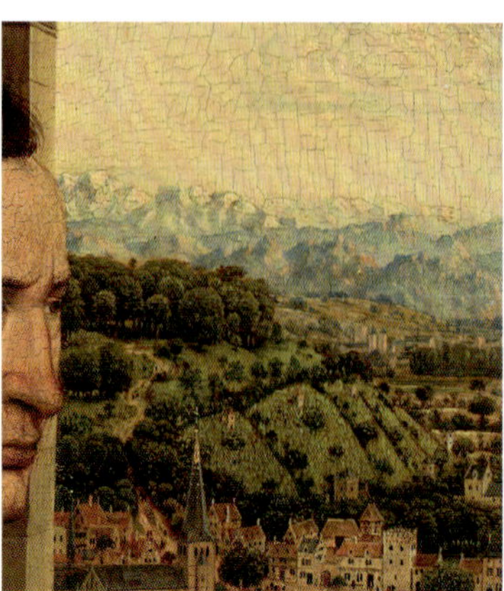
4.12b

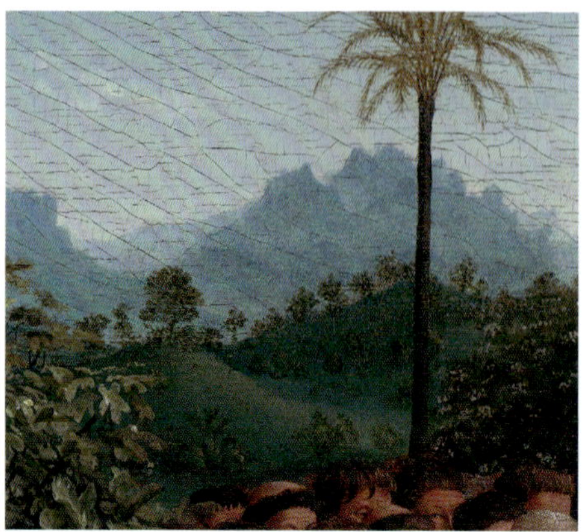
4.12c

Fig. 4.12a–c. Comparison of mountains: *Adoration of the Lamb* (a and c); Jan van Eyck, *Virgin of Chancellor Rolin*, Paris, Musée du Louvre, inv. 1271 (b).

on either side of the fountain (CVE-4). The left shoulder and the bottom of the chaperon worn by the philosopher in the pink robe, as well as the green cloak of the philosopher standing in front of him, have been enlarged to partially conceal three heads of already painted kneeling figures, one of whom was dressed in a gown with a belt. The face of this man, wearing a blue cap, can be attributed to Hubert (fig. 4.5d). On the other hand, the heads of two standing philosophers, and the head of the man in the background wearing a fur-lined hat,[46] can be attributed to Jan, but not the enlargements of the two philosophers. The contrast between shadows and highlights in the folds of skin and protruding veins of the hand added on top of the green drapery are too sharp and some of them are poorly placed, as are the highlights on the joints (fig. 4.14c). In other words, this painter tried to depict a hand in the same way as Jan, but lacked the talent. Weaker elements can also be made out in the chaperon of the philosopher dressed in pink (fig. 4.15b). The edge of his headgear is painted with dark, not very precise lines and the superimposition of the layers of fabric does not quite come off, unlike what we see in the large red figure on the left of the panel (fig. 4.15a). The painter also imitated the technique of scoring motifs in the fresh paint in the enlarged shoulder of the philosopher in

Fig. 4.13a–b. Comparison of fortresses in the mountains: *Knights of Christ* (a); Jan van Eyck, *Virgin of Chancellor Rolin*, Paris, Musée du Louvre, inv. 1271 (b).

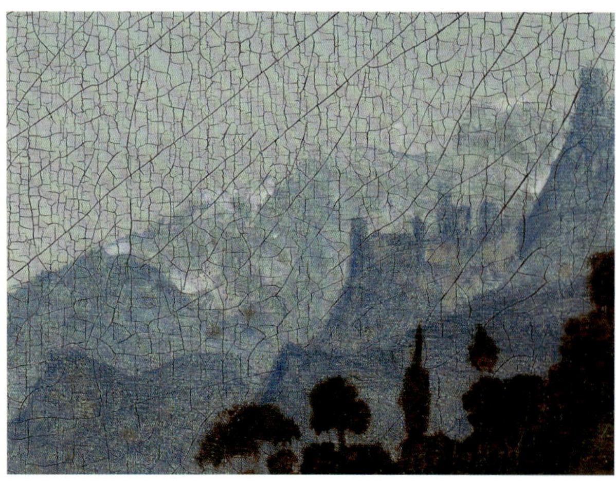
4.13a

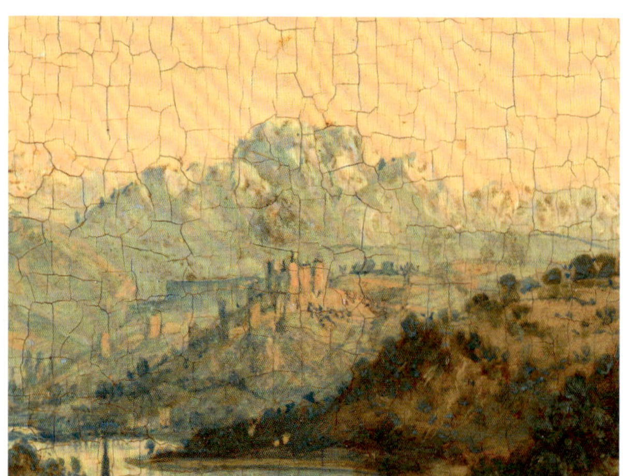
4.13b

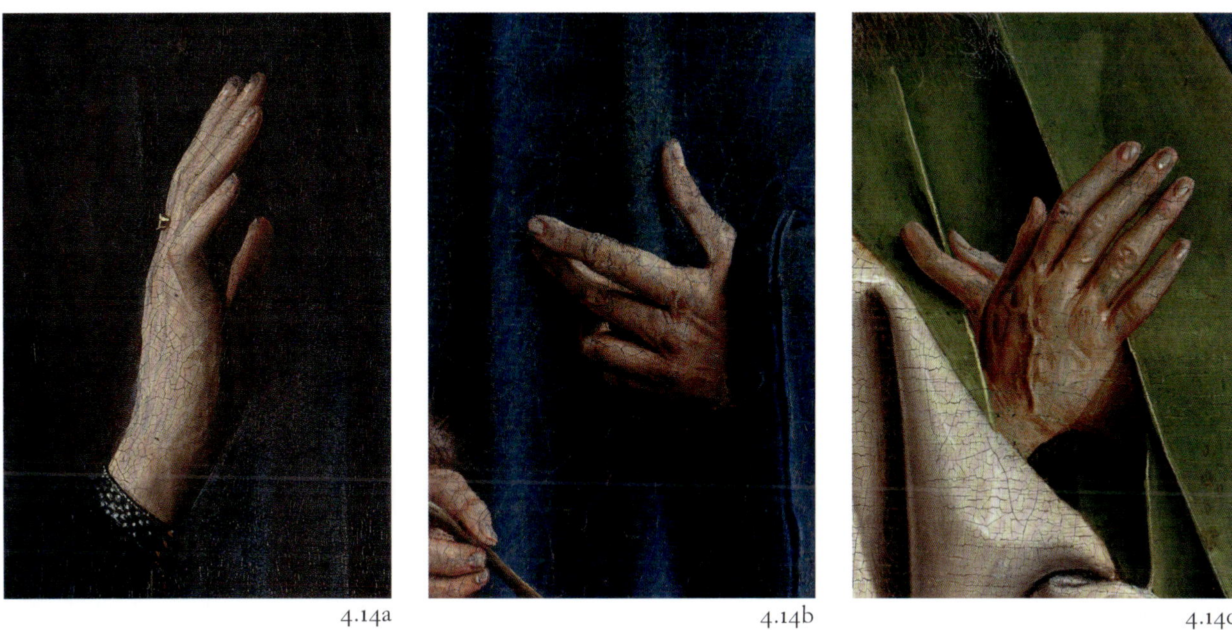

4.14a 4.14b 4.14c

Fig. 4.14a–c. Comparison of hands: Jan van Eyck, *Arnolfini Portrait*, 1434, London, The National Gallery, inv. NG186 (a); *Adoration of the Lamb*, hand of a philosopher attributed to Jan van Eyck (b); hand of a philosopher, non-Eyckian (c).

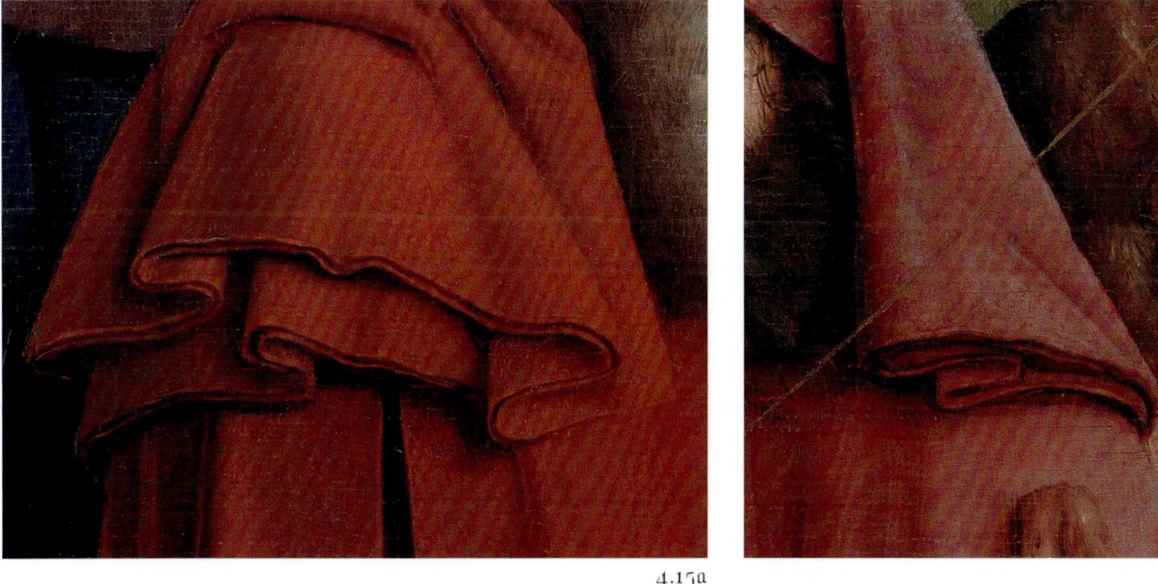

4.15a 4.15b

Fig. 4.15a–b. *Adoration of the Lamb*, red chaperon of a philosopher attributed to Jan van Eyck (a); pink chaperon of a philosopher, non-Eyckian (b).

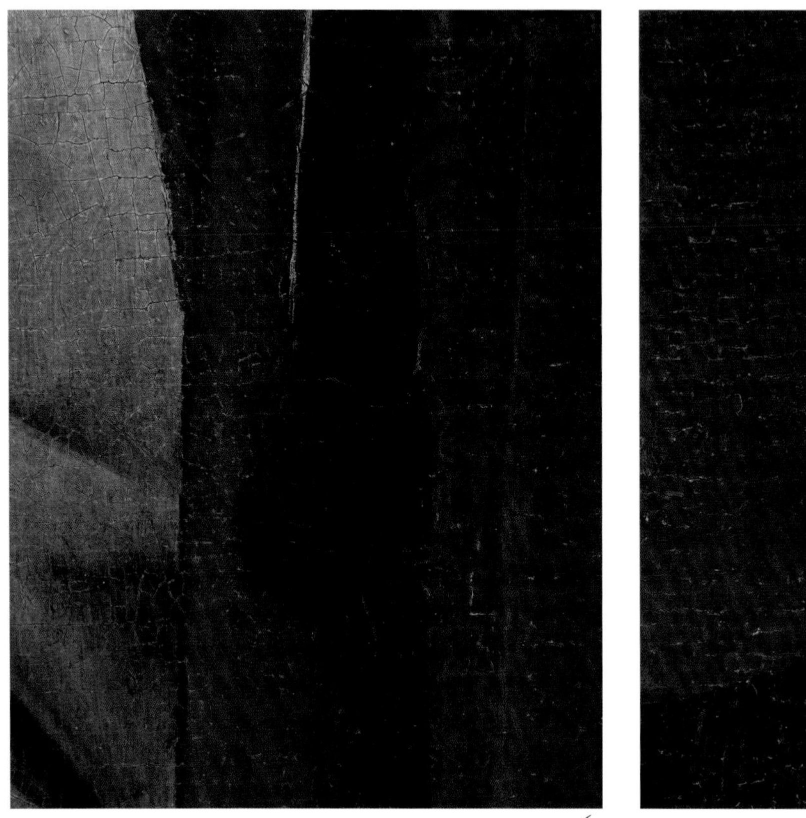

4.16a

4.16b

Fig. 4.16a–b. *Adoration of the Lamb*, green fringes at the bottom of the churchmen's cloaks, non-Eyckian (a), attributed to Jan van Eyck (b).

the pink chaperon, but the resulting grid is flat and in no way follows the volume of the shoulder (CVE-4). A similar change is found in the group to the right of the fountain, where the red robe of the third bishop has been enlarged to position it in front of rather than behind the kneeling apostle (CVE-14). While the bishop can be attributed to Jan, this enlargement does not seem painted by him. The green fringes at the bottom of the cloak (fig. 4.16a) are represented by a number of nondescript lines, unlike a similar detail lower down, in which the thickness and texture of the fringed border are tangible (fig. 4.16b).

Areas in which figures have been altered are also found in the wings, most notably in the *Knights of Christ*. The knight with the grey beard wore a brocade robe, over which a plain one was later painted (fig. 2.66). This alteration can probably be linked to the addition of a muzzle, meant to complete the head of a white horse in the *Just Judges* (fig. 4.17a–b). Comparison with the muzzles painted on the right in the *Knights of Christ* clearly shows that this addition cannot have been Jan's work.[47]

In order to paint the purple robe over the brocade, the painter first narrowed the edge of the beautiful green sleeve of the knight in armour. The MA-XRF maps show that the vermilion base layer of this reworking (MA-XRF Hg-L), overlaps the already painted green sleeve (MA-XRF Cu-K) (fig. 4.18). Then, after the purple robe had been glazed, the edge of the narrowed sleeve was reworked with more repetitive and much less precise strokes than those placed elsewhere by Jan to indicate the

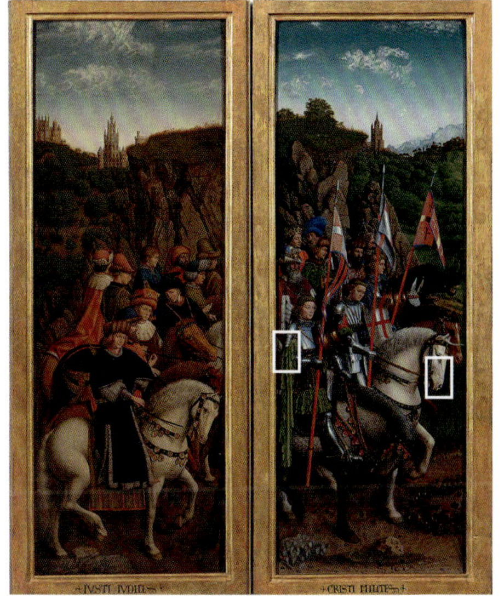

4.17a

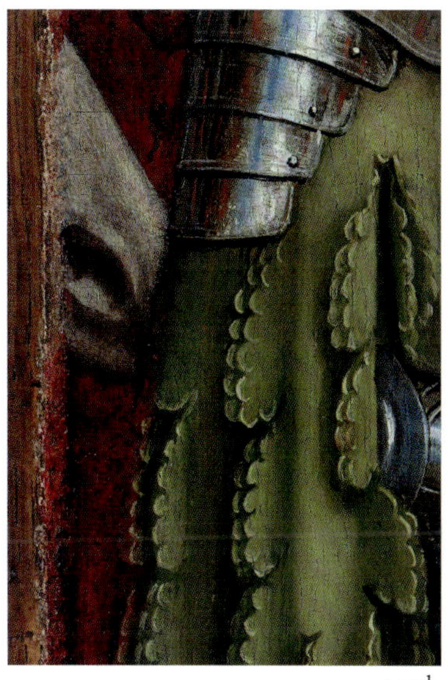

4.17b

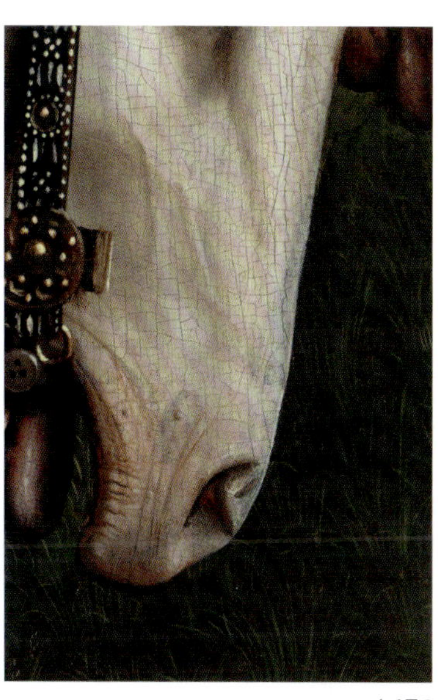

4.17c

Fig. 4.17a–c. Head of horse, continuity between the *Knights of Christ* and the *Just Judges* (a); muzzle, non-Eyckian horse (b); muzzle, Jan van Eyck (c).

dagging. Adjustments have also been made to the female figures in the *Hermits* (CVE-23). The blue cloak was painted over an earlier version with a decorative border around the neckline (visible in the infrared macrophotograph), and the neck was widened with a light pink layer that also continues into the woman's face. The latter's pupils have not been correctly placed and cannot be Jan's work.

The dove we see now can hardly be attributed to Jan either.[48] Comparison with the one in the *Annunciation* scene on the altarpiece exterior or with the parakeet in the *Virgin of Canon Van der Paele* (fig. 4.19) shows that the heads of the two other birds were painted with particular attention to the smallest details, be it the fixed, round eyes, the tiny feathers around the beak or the nostrils at its base. Eyes and beak in the *Adoration of the Lamb* are rendered by three clumsy spots of the same red. The fact that the dove is smaller than the other two birds is not enough to explain this lack of precision, as is demonstrated by the tiny head of the peacock painted in the background of the *Virgin of Chancellor Rolin*,[49] where the smallest details have been rendered meticulously. Although there is no evidence that there is another dove below the present one,[50] the uppermost white layer has been slightly damaged on the left side of the existing dove, at the base of the tail, revealing a light-grey layer beneath with a few sharp black lines (fig. 4.20). This zone resembles the black stripes in the corresponding location in the dove of the *Annunciation* and might be a trace of the original bird.

Non-Eyckian interventions seem to have been made for a variety of reasons. Some of the retouches were apparently intended to 'improve' Jan's work,[51] such as those along the boundary between the first-stage figures painted by Hubert and the second-stage meadow done by Jan. Others seem to have been placed in order to fill empty spaces – such as the leaves added to many of the trees – or to create a certain continuity between the different panels, as in the case of the horse's muzzle and a

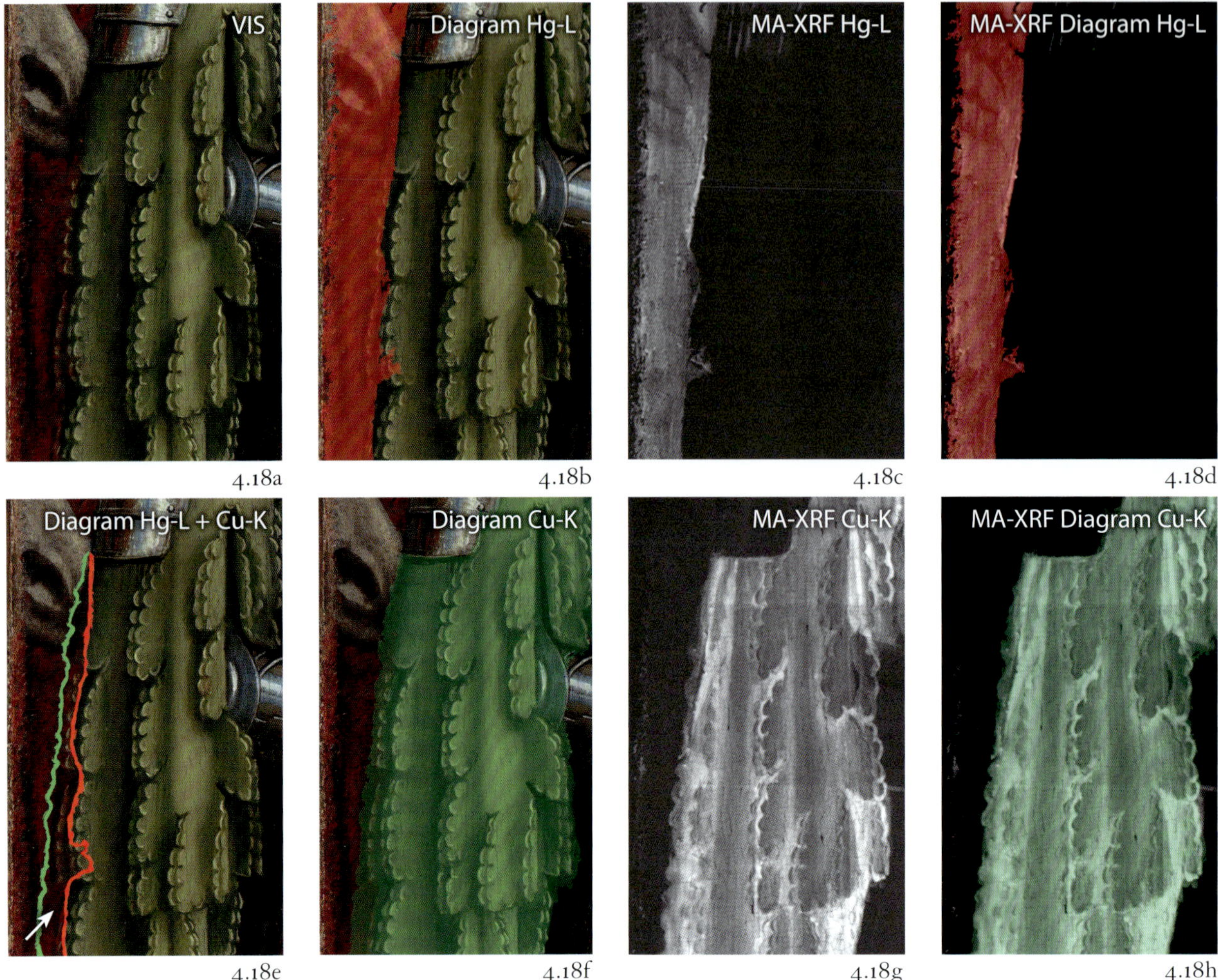

Fig 4.18a–h. *Knights of Christ*. In order to paint the purple robe over the brocade, the non-Eyckian painter narrowed the edge of the green sleeve. The MA-XRF maps show that the vermilion base layer of this reworking (Hg-L and red in the diagrams) overlaps the already painted green sleeve (Cu-K and green lines in the diagrams). After the purple robe had been completed (white arrow), the edge of the green sleeve was reworked (VIS and diagram).

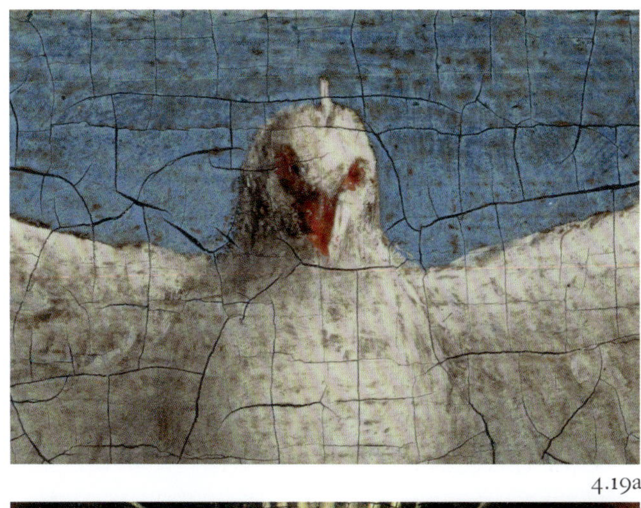

4.19a

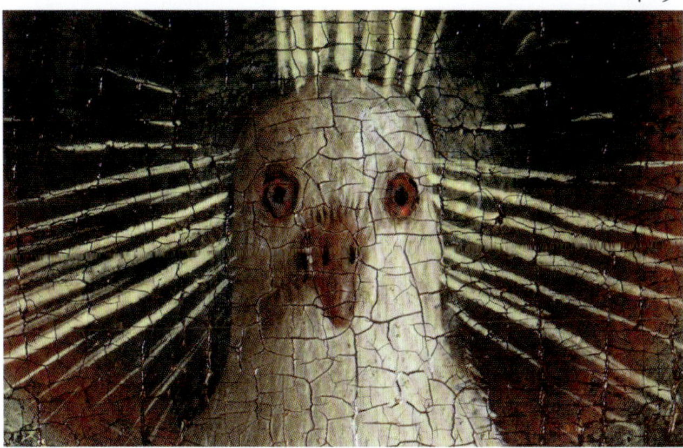

4.19b

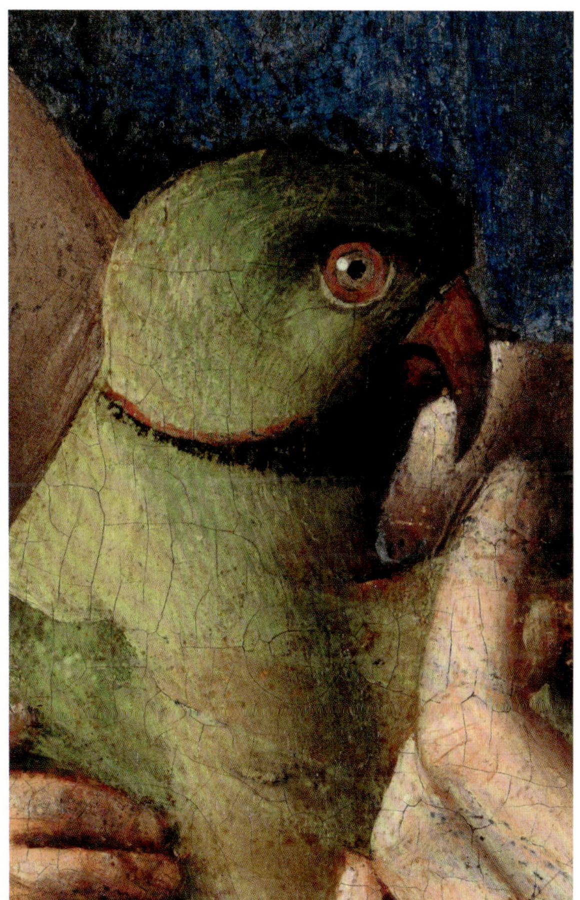

4.19c

Fig. 4.19a–c. Comparison of birds' heads: *Adoration of the Lamb*, detail of the dove (a); *Virgin Annunciate* from the altarpiece exterior, detail of the dove (b); *Virgin of Canon Van der Paele*, 1436, Bruges, Groeningemuseum, inv. 0000.GRO0161.I, detail of the parakeet (c).

patch of grass on the crags on the left of the *Knights of Christ*, or the mountains to the right of the same panel.[52] Some changes were also made to the organization of space, as in the perspective adjustment of the altar or the more marked separation between the kneeling and standing figures in the foreground of the central panel. An iconological or iconographical motive might also be sought in the addition of gilded rays in the sky and around the head of the lamb.[53] In one instance we encountered reworking in an area where a lacuna is embedded in the underlying paint layers (fig. 2.63),[54] and further research may eventually allow damage to be detected elsewhere too, as in the sky in the central panel. It is, indeed, still not known why the ultramarine layer was applied to the sky in the *Adoration of the Lamb*.

It is not possible to determine at this time whether these non-Eyckian interventions were the work of one person or several. We consider it unlikely that this reworking was carried out by an assistant of Jan, given the implausibility of the master allowing a subordinate to 'improve' his own work. It should be borne in mind that these non-Eyckian retouches were covered by the repaints removed during the 2016–19 conservation campaign, which dated from the mid-sixteenth century (before 1557 at any rate).[55]

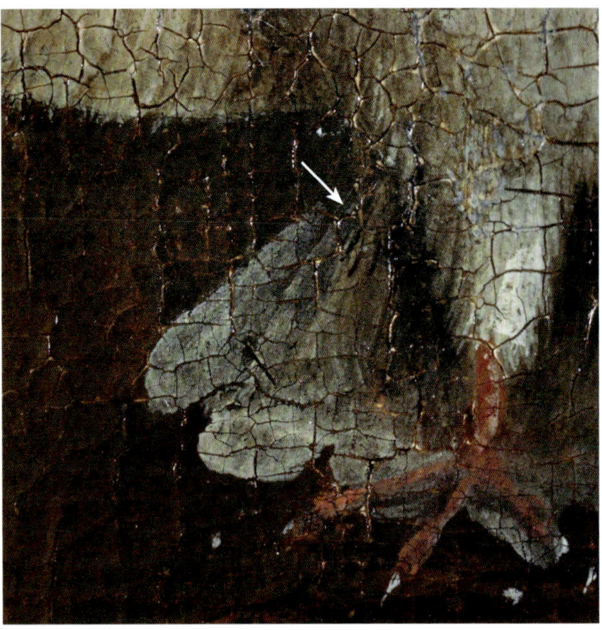

4.20a

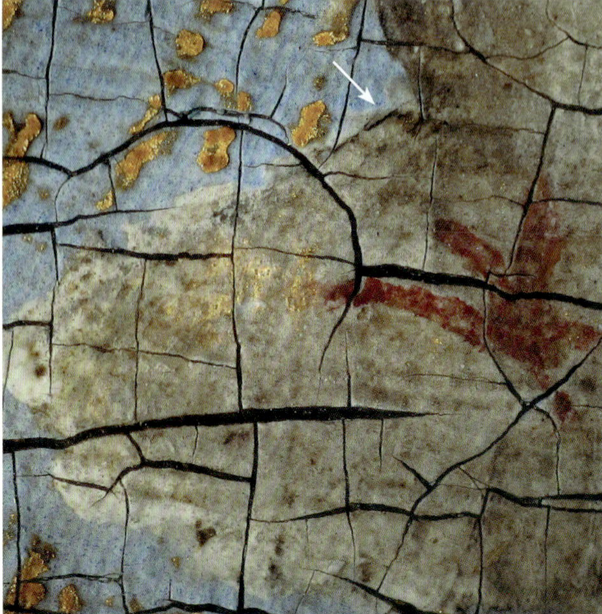

4.20b

Fig. 4.20a–b. *Adoration of the Lamb*, clear black lines in the dove (b) similar to those found in the dove of the *Annunciation* on the altarpiece exterior (a).

Conclusion

This stylistic study, in combination with the technical analysis, supports our hypothesis that the lower register of the altarpiece interior as it appears today was the result of three successive stages: the first by Hubert, the second by Jan, and the third post-dating the Van Eyck's work. While we have paid particular attention to these non-Eyckian interventions, they are nevertheless quite limited: most of the painted surface now visible in the lower register is the work of Jan van Eyck. Jan did not retain the design of the spring, which he replaced with a majestic fountain. He did, however, keep about fourteen faces around this central area, which can be attributed to his brother Hubert.

Notes

1 See Introduction.

2 Dhanens 1980; Campbell 1998a, p. 174; http://closertovaneyck.kikirpa.be/.

3 Including the *Virgin of Chancellor Rolin*, Paris, Musée du Louvre, inv. 1271; and the *Annunciation*, Washington, National Gallery of Art, inv. 1937.1.39.

4 Campbell 2017; Martens 2020.

5 Jan van Eyck, *The Virgin at the Fountain*, 1439, Antwerp, Royal Museum of Fine Arts, inv. 411.

6 To compare the details, see http://closertovaneyck.kikirpa.be/.

7 Jan van Eyck, *Arnolfini Portrait*, 1434, London, The National Gallery, inv. NG186.

8 Jan van Eyck, *The Virgin of Canon Van der Paele*, 1436, Bruges, Groeningemuseum, inv. 0000.GRO0161.I.

9 See fig. 2.22.

10 Campbell 2017.

11 The nose of this apostle and the top of his forehead were later retouched, as we will see in due course.

12 See http://closertovaneyck.kikirpa.be/.

13 See chapter 2, sections 'Meadow and fountain' and 'The large figures in the central panel'.

14 Especially the grass beneath the Madonna in the *Virgin at the Fountain*. See also 'Sequence of pictorial execution' and note 24.

15 The apostles' robes were reworked locally.

16 Cross-section 10/81.

17 Jan and Hubert had a sister, Margaretha (died before 1426), and a brother, Lambert. Both were painters. None of their work is known to us today. Unlike Hubert, they are not mentioned in the quatrain. Paviot 2020, pp. 60, 79.

18 Other authors have detected Hubert's hand in the groups in the foreground of the central panel, but without citing specific areas and offering only general arguments: Dvorák 1904; Panofsky 1953, vol. 1, pp. 205–32; for a summary, see Kemperdick 2014, pp. 19–22; Martens 2019, pp. 126–28.

19 Cross-section 09/20.

20 See chapter 2, sections 'Meadow and fountain' and 'Soils in the wings'.

21 Martens 2019, pp. 127–28; Borchert 2019, pp. 148–50.

22 It is interesting to note that Hubert also took account of the incidence of light from the right in the altarpiece's original location.

23 The reserves are visible in the XR and in the MA-XRF map.

24 Years of experience (visual observation, including stereomicroscopy and X-radiography) have taught us that this method is also found in other fifteenth-century Flemish masters, although as far as we know it has not been described in detail in the literature. Cennino Cennini advised painters 'to work on clothes and buildings before faces' (Broecke 2015, p. 187). A similar sequence of pictorial execution is found in certain unfinished miniatures, such as folios 41v and 55 in Guido delle Colonne, *History of the Destruction of Troy*, painted around 1500 by François Colombe (Paris, Bibliothèque nationale de France, NAF 24920).

25 Jan van Eyck, *St Barbara*, 1437, Antwerp, Royal Museum of Fine Arts, inv. 410. Van Hout 2012, pp. 34–37. When he died, Dirk Bouts left two works that displayed both finished and unfinished areas; Stroo et al. 1999, pp. 56–104, see pp. 76–78; Steyaert 2005.

26 Hubert worked in Ghent and died, according to his epitaph, on 18 September 1426. Jan was employed by John of Bavaria until the latter's death in The Hague on 5 January 1425, at which point he immediately moved to Bruges. He entered Philip the Good's service on 19 March 1425, but was allowed to accept other commissions. Sometime before 2 August 1425, the duke ordered him to move to Lille, where he remained for three years. Paviot 2020, pp. 61–66.

27 See http://closertovaneyck.kikirpa.be/.

28 Depoorter 2020b, p. 52.

29 Depoorter 2020a, p. 215.

30 Jan van Eyck, *Triptych of the Virgin and Child*, 1437, Staatliche Kunstsammlungen Dresden, inv. 799.

31 See chapter 3, section 'Ultramarine' and fig. 3.10.

32 These characteristics were not dealt with in our technical study of the

paintings of the altarpiece exterior (Postec, Steyaert 2020, pp. 200–216). We hope that the final study, which will follow the treatment of the upper register of the altarpiece interior, will provide an opportunity to take stock of this issue.

33 Panofsky 1953, p. 223.

34 Van Asperen de Boer 1979, pp. 205–13; Périer-D'Ieteren 2017, pp. 120–35.

35 Van Asperen de Boer, Faries 1990, pp. 38, 43, 46; Van Asperen de Boer 1995, p. 81; Faries 1999, pp. 223–25; Gifford, Metzger, Delaney 2013, p. 133; Billinge 2000, pp. 94–95; Périer-D'Ieteren 2017, pp. 122, 123, 127.

36 See chapter 2. These features were not as visible in the images (the *Virgin of Chancellor Rolin*) analysed by Van Asperen de Boer 1979, pp. 208–10. In the new IRRs (see http://closertovaneyck.kikirpa.be/), these small, transverse lines cannot be found in the *Virgin of Chancellor Rolin*.

37 The drawing is less visible in the IRRs of the clothes of the other figures, possibly due to a higher concentration of pigments that absorb infrared or the larger number of paint layers.

38 See http://closertovaneyck.kikirpa.be/. *St John the Baptist and the Virgin and Child*, Paris, Musée du Louvre, inv. RF 1938–22.

39 Comblen-Sonkes, Lorentz 1995, pp. 5 and 7. Hand, Metzger, Spronk 2006–07, pp. 78–79.

40 See chapter 2, section 'Trees'.

41 Campbell 2017; Postec, Steyaert 2020, p. 234.

42 See note 24.

43 It might appear in the *Virgin at the Fountain* that the blue upper layer of the sky was laid down after the figures were painted, as the brushstrokes follow the contours of the figures (the wings of the angels, for instance). However, the sky was painted first, around the contours of the figures indicated in the underdrawing. We also find that the painted sky runs around the forms of the drawing in Jan van Eyck's *St Barbara*. See further: Van Asperen de Boer 1979, p. 195, note 71.

44 The brush that applied the blue layer left clearly visible striations. Similar, albeit slightly less defined, brushstrokes can be made out in the sky of the *City View* of the *Ghent Altarpiece* exterior and in the *Virgin at the Fountain*. The white, slightly impastoed touches that define the clouds and the way the moon is represented in *St Barbara* are comparable with similar details in the *Knights of Christ*. In *St Barbara*, the birds were drawn before the blue layer was applied over the drawing and then the birds were painted (http://closertovaneyck.kikirpa.be/: compare the macrophotograph with the infrared macrophotograph to the left of the tower).

45 Comblen-Sonkes, Lorentz 1995, II, p. 58.

46 The milky pupils of this philosopher appear to suggest some kind of visual impairment.

47 The head of the horse on the right has been painted with subtle nuances of colour and every anatomical detail has been precisely observed – the veins, the fold of the nostril, the wrinkles in the lips, and even the hair on the muzzle. These are all details and nuances that are entirely absent in the horse on the left.

48 Panofsky 1953, pp. 218–19; Coremans 1953, p. 108; Van Asperen de Boer 1979, pp. 195–96 and 200–201.

49 See http://closertovaneyck.kikirpa.be/.

50 The dove is highly likely to have been present in the *Ghent Altarpiece* before 1458, when the polyptych was staged as a tableau vivant. Dubois, Sanyova, Vanwijnsberghe 2017, p. 73.

51 Regarding the restoration of works in the fifteenth and sixteenth centuries, see Campbell 1998b, p. 21.

52 See chapter 2, sections 'Trees', 'The large figures in the wings' and 'Rocks in the wings'.

53 See also chapter 1, note 23.

54 See chapter 2, sections 'The sky and the horizon' and ' The large figures in the central panel' and note 124.

55 Dubois 2018a; Depuydt et al. 2020, pp. 124–35; see also chapter 1.

Conclusion

The recent conservation campaign carried out on the paintings of the lower register of the altarpiece interior and the removal of several layers of degraded varnish and the sixteenth-century overpaints revealed the incredible richness of the Van Eycks' work, while also allowing it to be studied. The findings of that research add significantly to the knowledge previously gained regarding the *Ghent Altarpiece*. Nevertheless, a great deal remains to be explored. We very much hope that this data – which will no doubt be supplemented further by the forthcoming conservation of the upper register of the altarpiece interior – will offer pointers for future research.

The restoration campaign carried out in 1950–51 by Paul Coremans and Albert Philippot was itself accompanied by a technical and scientific study, which provided important information from interdisciplinary work. At that point, however, it was not possible to determine the extent of the overpaints, due to the presence of many layers of degraded varnish and to analysis techniques that were less advanced than those of today. Consequently, earlier research featured zones that were largely covered by sixteenth-century overpaints, the presence of which was not suspected at the time.

In the six decades that separate Coremans and Philippot's campaign from the one commenced in 2012 and not yet completed, our understanding of historic pictorial techniques – fifteenth-century Flemish painting in this instance – has advanced considerably. Scientific progress continues to expand our knowledge of the materials making up the pictorial layers, pigments and binders, but also of how they were manufactured and how they age. Not to mention the presence of additives, the very existence of which was not even suspected until recently. The interactions between all these materials, lastly, are likewise understood better today, allowing a more refined or more nuanced interpretation of the analysis results.

(facing page) *Hermits*, heads attributed to Jan van Eyck (see also fig. 4.6).

All the data collected in the course of the years required for the restoration of the paintings of the lower register of the altarpiece interior have been carefully examined both during and after treatment, enabling us to present a number of hypotheses. Some had been outlined before, but never expanded on in such detail – particularly as regards the share of the Van Eyck brothers in the work. Even though many questions remain, the degree to which the altarpiece was unfinished on Hubert's death in 1426 has begun to emerge. It is not always easy to distinguish the pictorial layers attributable to each stage of intervention. What is clear, however, is that several layers have been added to an already complete stratigraphy in a number of locations. In other words, a first stage consisting of several layers and completed with a surface glaze was then covered with another stratigraphy comprising multiple layers and ending once more with a glaze. Two distinct stages of development can be found in the meadow, for instance. Study of the scientific imagery – particularly MA-XRF scans and infrared macrophotographs – as well as examination under the stereomicroscope of painted layers discernible in losses beneath the currently visible composition, also allowed this first stage to be visualized elsewhere. Differences have been detected in, among other places, the horizon line – where other mountains and architecture had already been painted and possibly even completed – and the soil and rocks in the shutters. Determining the authorship of these interventions remains a challenge. Nevertheless, stylistic comparison suggests that the second stage can be attributed to Jan and the first stage, which remains visible in certain places on the surface, is different and might be Hubert's.

It seems quite possible, therefore, that the first layers of painting of the entire lower register of the altarpiece interior, which correspond with the first stage, had largely been completed by the time of Hubert's death, implying that all the work in the preparatory layers was finished in 1426, including the underdrawing. Jan van Eyck not only finished the paintings, he also made numerous adjustments. Some of these are formal in character: he repainted some of the buildings on the horizon and added others; he reworked many of the garments and altered the position of some of the large figures and certain horses, while adjusting the soil. He also reworked the landscape, which he transformed by painting a new meadow in the central panel with a varied and abundant flora. Other changes were more significant, notably in the central axis of the *Adoration of the Lamb* panel. In the first stage, there was a simple spring in the earth below the altar, which Jan covered in the second stage with a majestic fountain. It would seem that the dove we see now was not planned in the sky in the first stage – only rays of light that were not executed, possibly because that could only be done when the work was otherwise complete. Jan abandoned the rays and, although we have no proof, it might be to him that we owe the addition of the dove.

There are rays in the sky, however, that were covered by the now-removed sixteenth-century overpaint. They are far more numerous than the initially planned rays, increasing from around 28 to 129. We think that – like the current dove, the mediocrity of which cannot be attributed to Jan – the rays, too, were added by a painter other than the Van Eycks. This represents a third stage in the development of the paintings of the interior lower register as it appears today following conservation. The three stages observed here were detected because they are superimposed, but they also occur in juxtaposition. Laboratory analyses of samples do not allow the execution of the dove and the rays to be dated precisely, but they do show that they are contemporary and that they differ from the materials used elsewhere. The final blue layer of sky in the central panel, lastly, on which the gilded rays are laid, and the many touches scattered over the paintings of the lower register of the altarpiece interior seem to us to have been added during this third stage. These adjustments alter the perspective – especially in the altar of the *Adoration of the Lamb* – they ensure continuity between the different shutters and dispel a certain *horror vacui*. Certain changes were likewise made to the organization of space, as in the more marked separation between the four groups of figures in the foreground of the central panel. All the indications are that these additions also post-date the second stage, over which they have been placed. Laboratory analyses have so far been unable to demonstrate that they were done after the Van Eycks, but stylistic comparison suggests that they can hardly be attributed to Jan. They were superimposed in areas completed by him. It seems unlikely that they were done by assistants, since it is barely credible that they would have altered the master's finished work. It can be assumed that most of these non-Eyckian reworkings date from the second half of the fifteenth century or the beginning of the sixteenth at the latest. These additions have been retained during the recent conservation campaign.

The extra year of in-depth study enabled us to collate the team's observations and also to make fresh discoveries. This prospecting work deserves to be continued. The question of the lacunae observed in the lower strata of the paintings, for example, has not been completely resolved, and their extent has yet to be evaluated. Combining the findings of both the abundant scientific imagery and the meticulous observation of the paintings is, after all, a long-term process. We hope to have demonstrated, however, that it can result in significant discoveries.

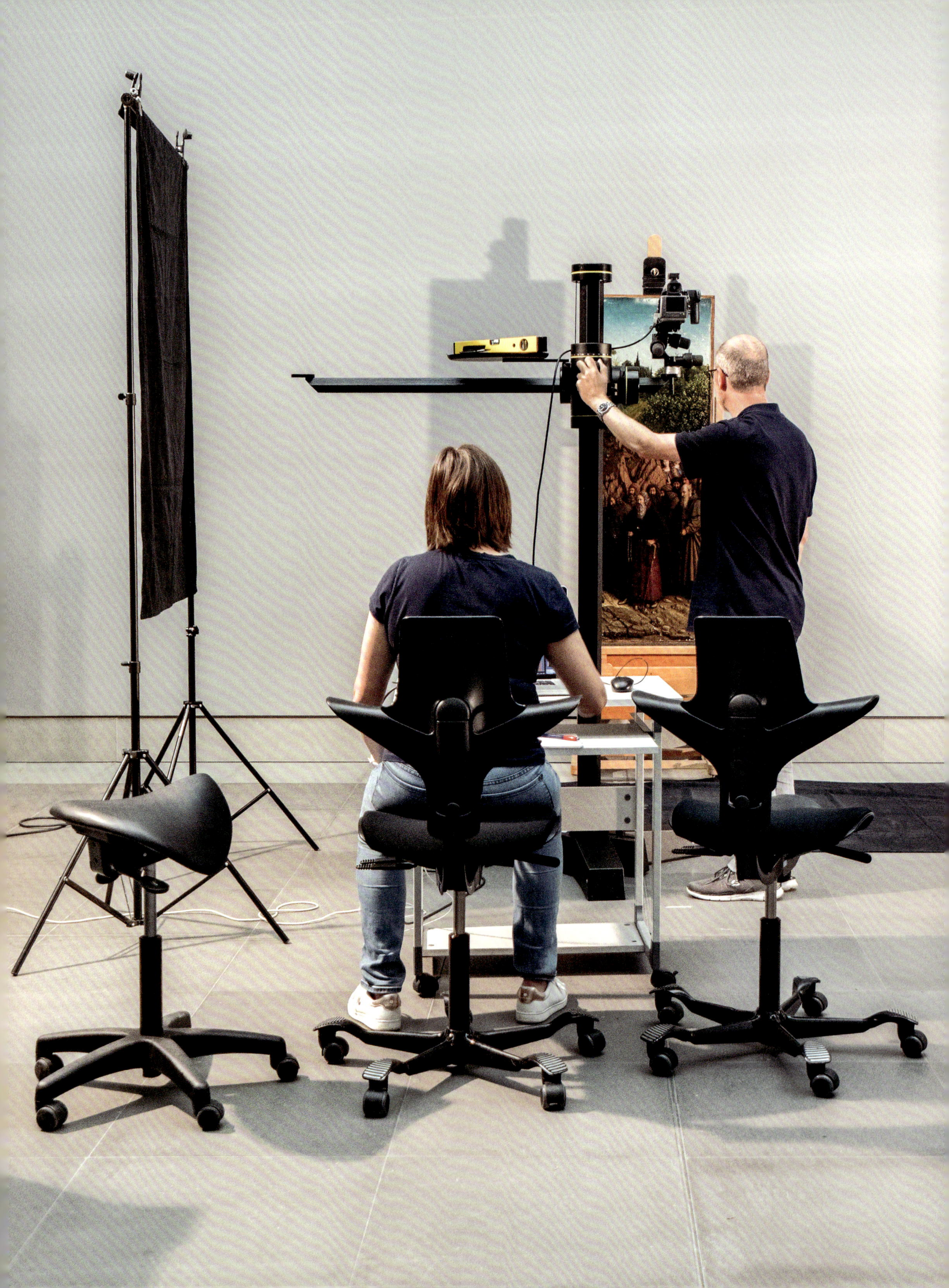

Photography before and after Treatment

All high-resolution images, before, during and after treatment, as well as scientific imagery, are available in open access on http://closertovaneyck.kikirpa.be. They have been made by the KIK-IRPA team, Sophie De Potter, Katrien Van Acker, Catherine Fondaire, Stéphane Bazzo and Hervé Pigeolet, under the direction of Christina Currie.

Fig. 1. *Just Judges*, before
Fig. 2. *Just Judges*, after

Fig. 3. *Knights of Christ*, before
Fig. 4. *Knights of Christ*, after

Fig. 5. *Adoration of the Lamb*, before
Fig. 6. *Adoration of the Lamb*, after

Fig. 7. *Hermits*, before
Fig. 8. *Hermits*, after

Fig. 9. *Pilgrims*, before
Fig. 10. *Pilgrims*, after

(facing page)
The photographers of KIK-IRPA make an ongoing visual record of the work as a whole and its details in normal, raking, ultraviolet and infrared light.

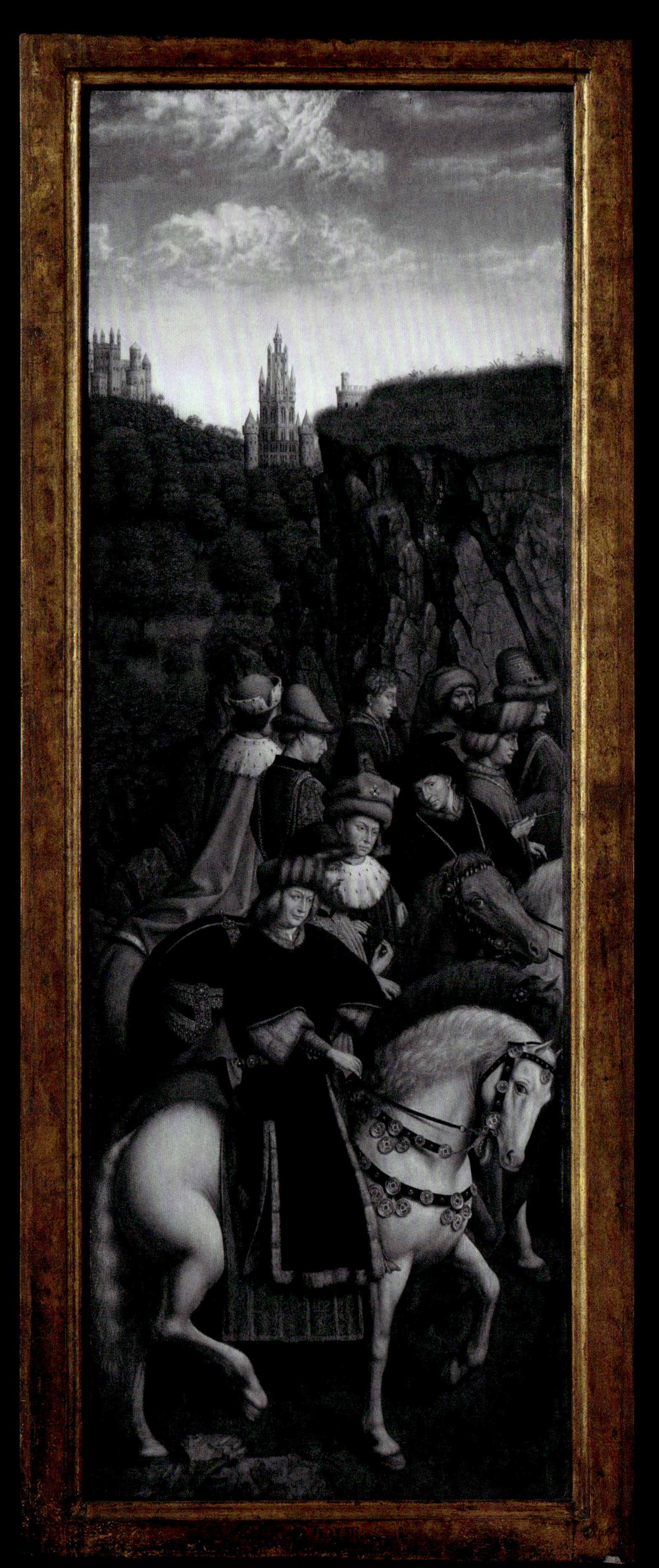

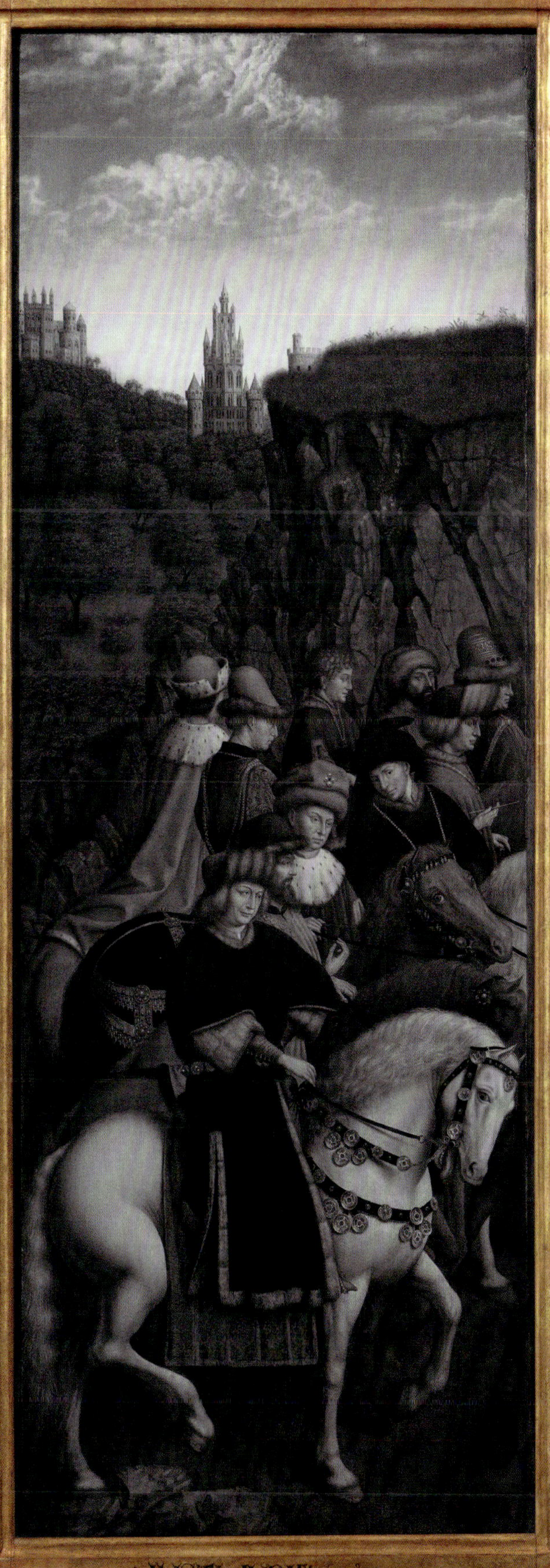
IVSTI IVDICES

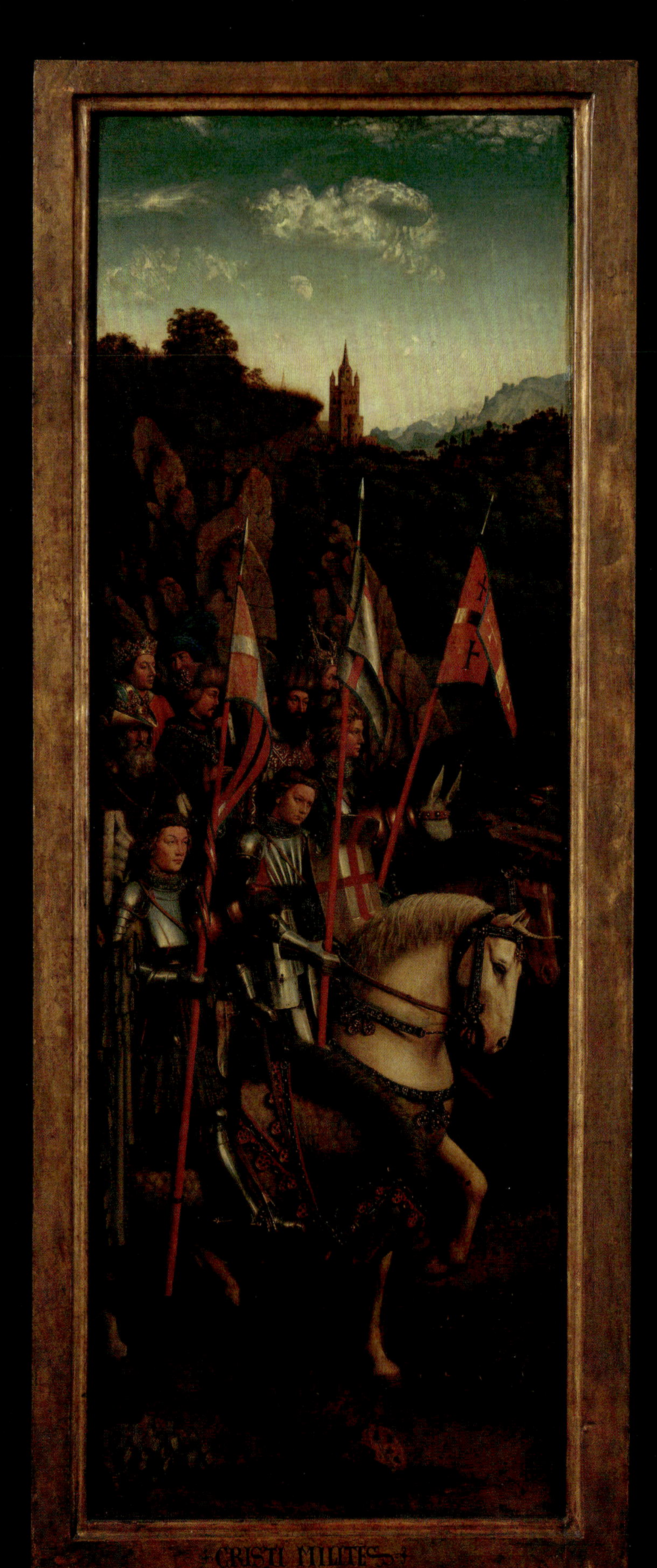
CRISTI MILITES

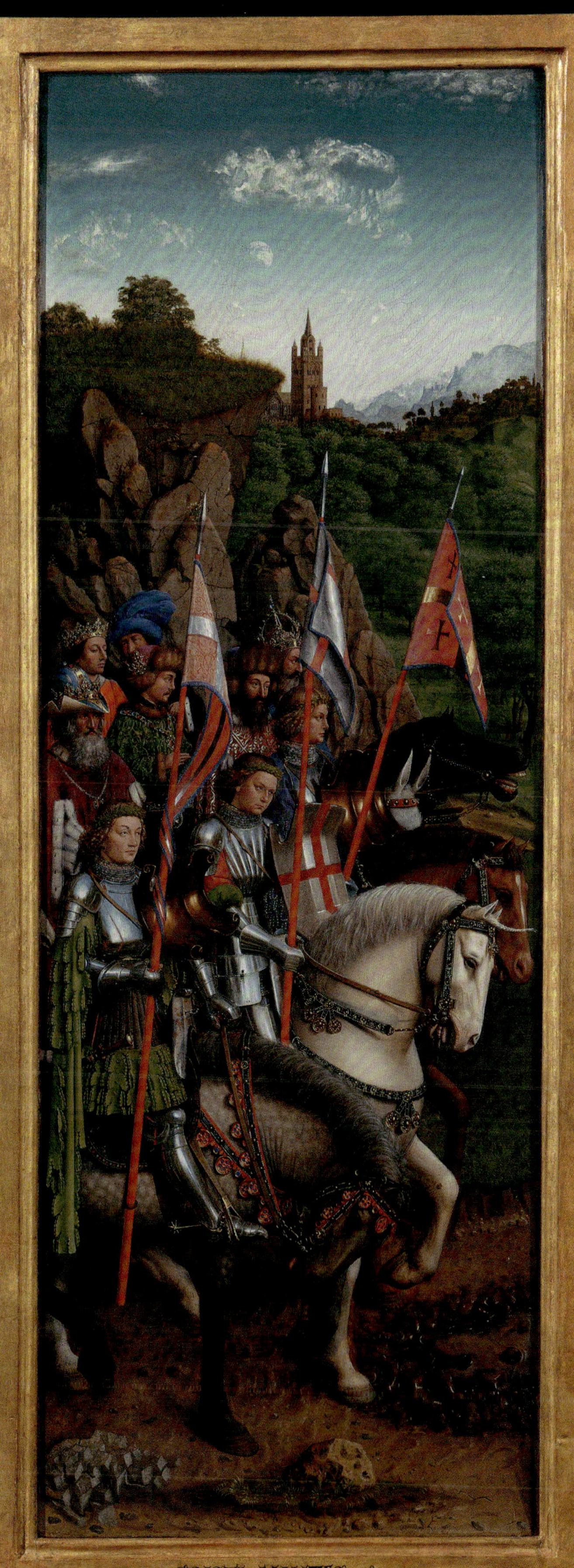
CRISTI MILITES

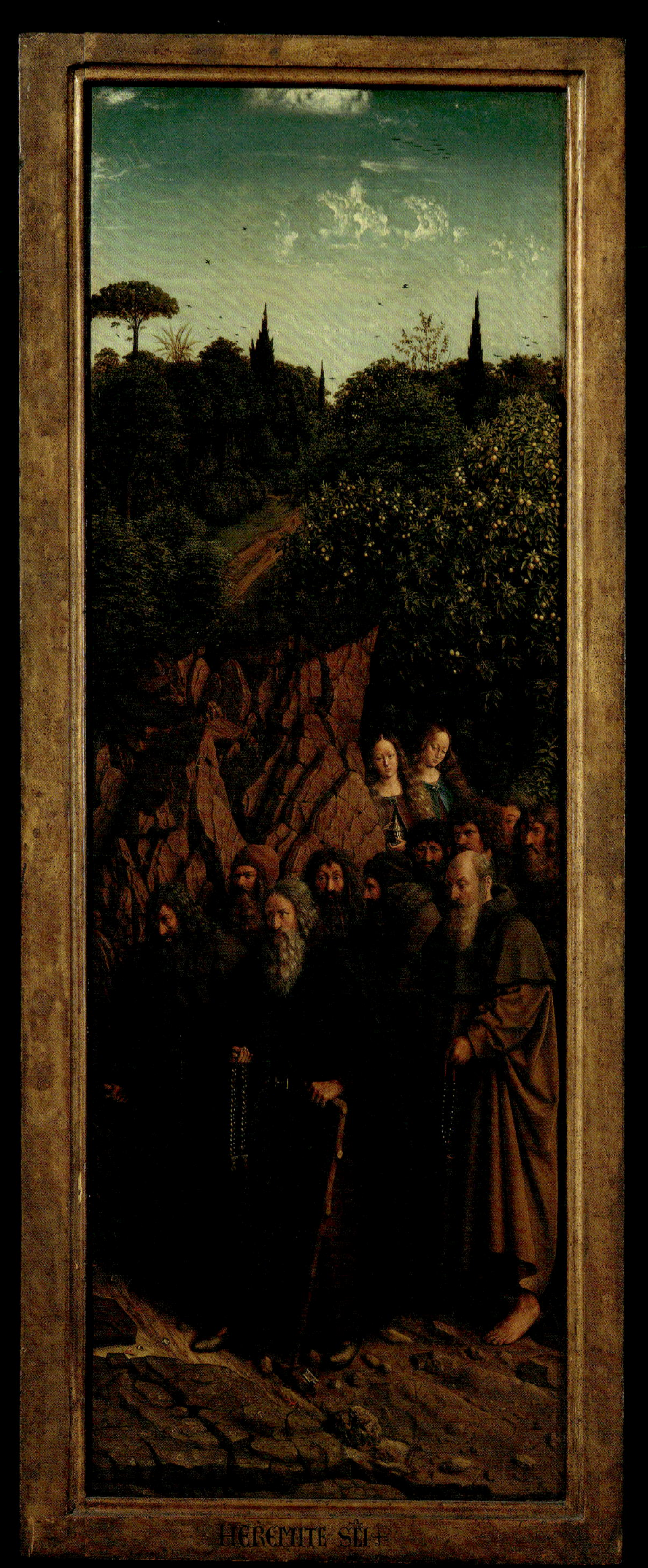
HEREMITE SCI +

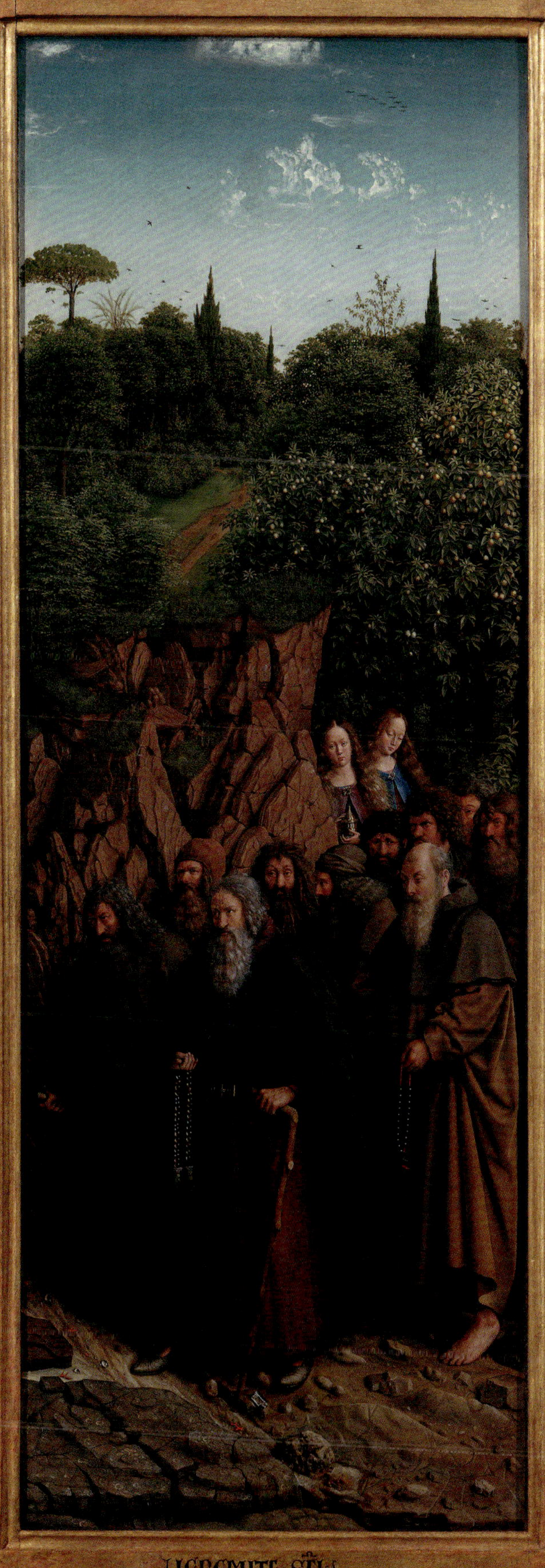
HEREMITE SCI

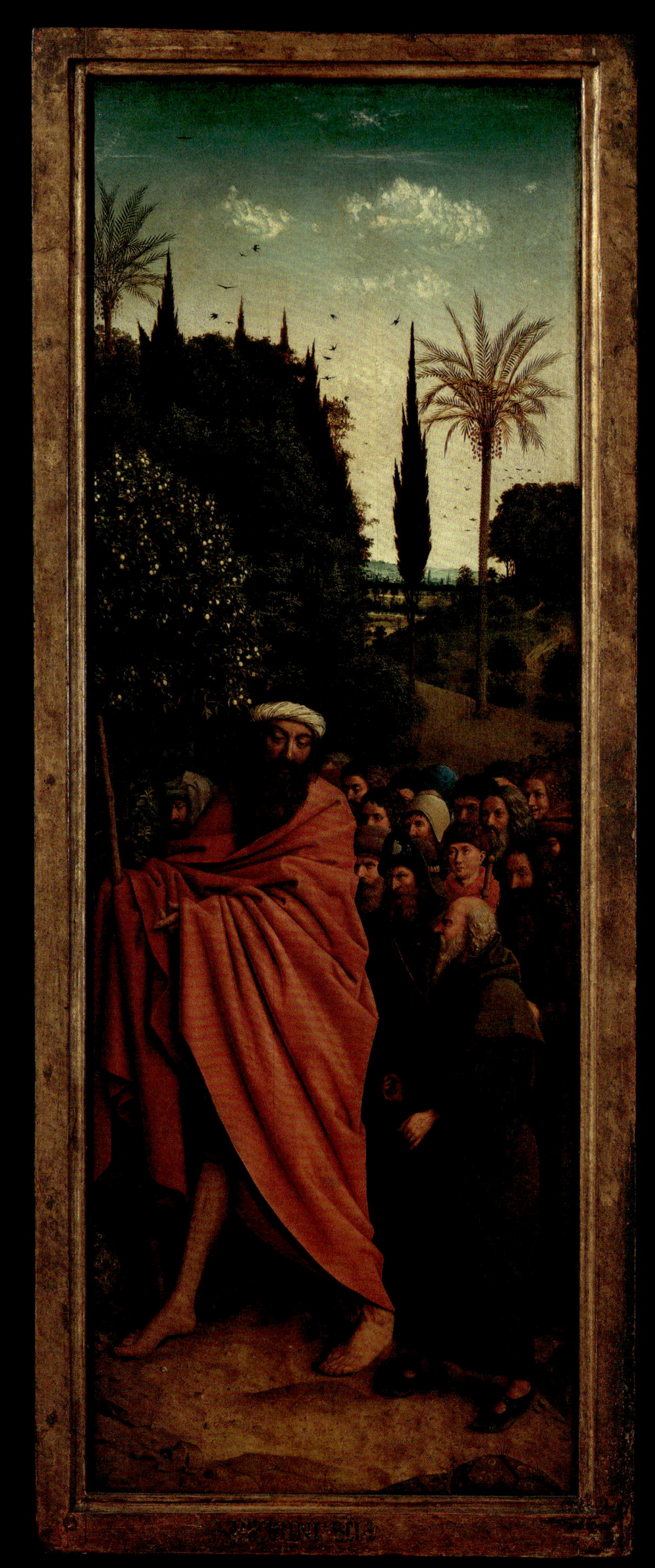

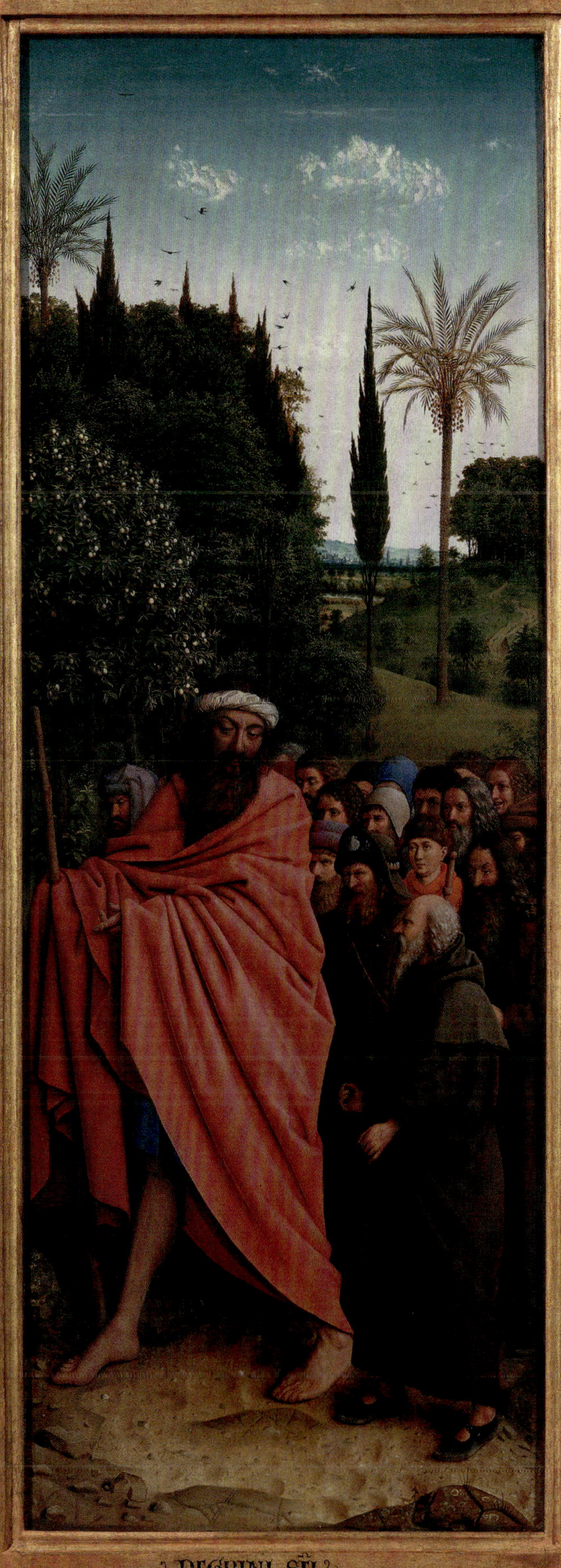
PEGRINI SCI

Bibliography

Alfeld et al. 2011
Matthias Alfeld, Koen Janssens, Joris Dik, Wout de Nolf and Geert Van der Snickt, 'Optimization of mobile scanning macro-XRF systems for the in situ investigation of historical paintings', in *Journal of Analytical Atomic Spectrometry*, 26, 2011, pp. 899–909.

Anaf et al. 2015
Willemien Anaf, Olivier Schalm, Koen Janssens and Karolien De Wael, 'Understanding the (in)stability of semiconductor pigments by a thermodynamic approach', in *Dyes and Pigments*, 113, 2015, pp. 409–15.

Augustyniak et al. 2017
Anne-Sophie Augustyniak, Bart Devolder, Livia Depuydt-Elbaum, Hélène Dubois, Jean-Albert Glatigny, Jochen Ketels, Nathalie Laquière, Claire Mehagnoul, Laure Mortiaux, Marie Postec, Françoise Rosier, Cyriel Stroo and Griet Steyaert, *Behandeling van het Lam Godsveelluik. Verslag van fase 1: het gesloten altaarstuk (2012–2016)*, KIK-IRPA, Brussels, 2017 http://closertovaneyck.kikirpa.be/ghentaltarpiece/#home/sub=documents.

Baumer et al. 2019
Ursula Baumer, Charlotte Höpker, Patrick Dietemann and Katharina von Miller, 'On the Use of Bistre in Transparent Wood Varnishes: Analysis, Application and Reconstruction', in *Studies in Conservation*, 64, Suppl. 1, 2019, pp. 115–25.

Beenken 1933
Hermann Beenken, 'The Ghent van Eyck Re-Examined', in *The Burlington Magazine*, 63, 365, August 1933, pp. 64–72.

Beenken 1933–34
Hermann Beenken, 'Zur Entstehungsgeschichte des Genter Altars Hubert und Jan von Eyck', in *Wallraf-Richartz Jahrbuch*, 2–3, 1933–34, pp. 176–232.

Bielman 1993
Johan H. Bielman 'Driers', in Oil and Colour Chemists' Association (ed.), *Surface Coatings*, Dordrecht, 1993, pp. 592–610.

Billinge 2000
Rachel Billinge, 'Examining Jan van Eyck's underdrawings', in Susan Foister, Sue Jones and Delphine Cool (eds), *Investigating Jan Van Eyck*, Turnhout, 2000, pp. 83–96.

Billinge, Campbell 1995
Rachel Billinge and Lorne Campbell, 'The Infra-red Reflectograms of Jan van Eyck's Portrait of Giovanni(?) Arnolfini and His Wife Giovanna Cenami(?)', in *National Gallery Technical Bulletin*, 16, 1995, pp. 47–60.

Billinge et al. 1997a
Rachel Billinge, Lorne Campbell, Jill Dunkerton, Susan Foister, Jo Kirby, Jennie Pilc, Ashok Roy, Marika Spring and Raymond White, *Early Northern European Painting, National Gallery Technical Bulletin*, 18, 1997. http://www.nationalgallery.org.uk/technical-bulletin/van_der_weyden1997.

Billinge et al. 1997b
Rachel Billinge, Lorne Campbell, Jill Dunkerton, Susan Foister, Jo Kirby, Jennie Pilc, Ashok Roy, Marika Spring and Raymond White, 'Methods and materials of Northern European Painting in the National Gallery, 1400–1550', in *National Gallery Technical Bulletin*, 18, 1997, pp. 6–55.

Billinge, Verougstraete, Van Schoute 2000
Rachel Billinge, Hélène Verougstraete and Roger Van Schoute, 'The Saint Barbara', in Susan Foister, Sue Jones and Delphine Cool (eds), *Investigating Jan Van Eyck*, Turnhout, 2000, pp. 41–48.

Borchert 2019
Till-Holger Borchert, 'The Creators. Jan Van Eyck and his Workshop: Organisation, Collaborators, Legacy', in Praet, Martens 2019, pp. 138–81.

Borrodaile, Borrodaile 1966
Viola and Rosamund Borrodaile, *'The Strasburg Manuscript – a medieval painters' handbook. Translated from the Old German*, Munich/London, 1966.

Brinkman 1993
Pim Brinkman, *Het geheim van Van Eyck, Aantekeningen bij de uitvinding van het olieverven*, Zwolle, 1993.

Brinkman et al. 1984/85
Pim Willem Frederik Brinkman, Léopold Kockaert, Luc Maes, Liliane Masschelein-Kleiner, Francis Robaszynski and Evert Thielen, 'Het Lam Godsretabel van Van Eyck. Een heronderzoek naar de materialen en schildermethoden, 1. De plamuur, de isolatielaag, de tekening en de grondtonen', in *Bulletin de l'Institut royal du Patrimoine artistique / Bulletin van het Koninklijk Instituut voor het Kunstpatrimonium*, 20, 1984/85, pp. 137–66.

Brinkman et al. 1988/89
Pim Willem Frederik Brinkman, Léopold Kockaert, Luc Maes, Evert Thielen and Jan Wouters, 'Het Lam Godsretabel van Van Eyck. Een heronderzoek naar de materialen en schildermethoden. 2. De hoofdkleuren blauw, groen, geel en rood', in *Bulletin de l'Institut royal du Patrimoine artistique / Bulletin van het Koninklijk Instituut voor het Kunstpatrimonium*, 22, 1988/89, pp. 26–49.

Broecke 2015
Lara Broecke, *Cennino Cennini's Il Libro dell'Arte: A new English language translation and commentary and Italian transcription*, London, 2015.

Burroughs 1938
Alan Burroughs, *Art Criticism from a Laboratory*, Boston, 1938.

Buse et al. 2019
Juliana Buse, Vanessa Otero and Maria J. Melo, 'New Insights into Synthetic Copper Greens: The Search for

Specific Signatures by Raman and Infrared Spectroscopy for Their Characterization in Medieval Artworks', in *Heritage*, 2, 2019, pp. 1614–29.

Caen et al. 2006
Joost Caen, Olivier Schalm and Koen Janssens, '15th century stained glass windows in the former county of Flanders; a historical and chemical study related to recent conservation campaigns', in Koen Janssens et al. (eds), *Annales du 17e Congrès de l'Association Internationale pour l'Histoire du Verre*, Antwerp, 2006, pp. 459–66.

Campbell 1998a
Lorne Campbell, *The Fifteenth-Century Netherlandish Schools (National Gallery Catalogues)*, New Haven/London, 1998.

Campbell 1998b
Lorne Campbell, 'The conservation of Netherlandish Paintings in the Fifteenth and Sixteenth Centuries', in Christine Sitwell and Sarah Staniforth (eds), *Studies in the History of Painting Restoration*, 1998, pp. 15–26.

Campbell 2017
Lorne Campbell, 'The Speed of Illusion', in Currie et al. 2017, pp. 256–61.

Campbell, Foister, Roy 1997a
Lorne Campbell, Susan Foister and Ashok Roy (eds), 'Methods and materials of Northern European Painting in the National Gallery, 1400–1550', in *National Gallery Technical Bulletin*, 18, 1997, pp. 6–55.

Campbell, Foister, Roy 1997b
Lorne Campbell, Susan Foister and Ashok Roy (eds), 'The materials and technique of five paintings by Rogier van der Weyden and his Workshop', in *National Gallery Technical Bulletin*, 18, 1997, pp. 68–86.

Cennini (ed. Thomson) 1960
The Craftsman's Handbook. 'Il libro dell'Arte' by Cennino d'Andrea Cennini, D.V. Thompson (ed.), New York, 1960.

Claes et al. 2019
Marie-Christine Claes, Hélène Dubois and Jana Sanyova, 'Le quotidien d'un idéal: *L'Agneau mystique*, catalyseur de l'interdisciplinarité', in Deneffe, Vanwijnsberghe 2019, pp. 140–57.

Clarke 2011
Mark Clarke, *Medieval painters materials and techniques. The Montpellier Liber diversarum arcium*, London, 2011.

Comblen-Sonkes, Lorentz 1995
Micheline Comblen-Sonkes and Philippe Lorentz, *Le Musée du Louvre Paris (Corpus de la peinture des anciens Pays-Bas méridionaux et de la Principauté de Liège au quinzième siècle*, 17), Brussels, 1995.

Coremans 1953
Paul Coremans, *L'Agneau mystique au Laboratoire. Examen et traitement (Contributions à l'étude des Primitifs flamands*, 2), Antwerp, 1953.

Coremans, Thissen 1953
Paul Coremans and Jean Thissen, 'Matériaux originaux et technique picturale eyckienne', in Coremans 1953, pp. 69–76.

Coremans, Loose, Thissen 1953
Paul Coremans, Louis Loose and Jean Thissen, 'Quelques problèmes particuliers', in Coremans 1953, pp. 98–122.

Cotte et al. 2016
Marine Cotte, Emilie Checroun, Wout De Nolf, Yoko Taniguchi, Laurence De Viguerie, Manfred Burghammer, Philippe Walter, Camille Rivard, Murielle Salomé, Koen Janssens and Jean Susini, 'Lead soaps in paintings: Friends or foes?', in *Studies in Conservation*, 62 (1), 2016, pp. 2–23.

Currie 2009
Christina Currie, 'Genesis of a Pre-Eyckian Masterpiece: Melchior Broederlam's Painted Wings for the Crucifixion Altarpiece', in Stroo 2009, pp. 23–86.

Currie et al. 2017
Christina Currie, Bart Fransen, Valentine Henderiks, Cyriel Stroo and Dominique Vanwijnsberghe (eds), *Van Eyck Studies. Papers Presented at the Eighteenth Symposium for the Study of Underdrawing and Technology in Painting, Brussels, 19–21 September 2012 (Underdrawing and Technology in Painting. Symposium*, 18), Paris/Louvain/Bristol, CT, 2017.

De Mey et al. 2012
Marc De Mey, Maximiliaan P.J. Martens and Cyriel Stroo (eds), *Vision and Material. Interaction between Art and Science in Jan van Eyck's Time*, KVAB Press (Koninklijke Vlaamse Academie van België voor Wetenschappen en Kunsten), Brussels, 2012, pp. 235–53.

Deneffe, Vanwijnsberghe 2019
Dominique Deneffe and Dominique Vanwijnsberghe (eds), *'A Man of Vision'. Paul Coremans and the Preservation of Cultural Heritage Worldwide. Proceedings of the International Symposium Paul Coremans Held in Brussels, 15–17 June 2015 (Scientia Artis*, 15), Brussels, 2019, pp. 120–39.

Deneffe, Peters, Fremout 2009
Dominique Deneffe, Famke Peters and Wim Fremout, *Pre-Eyckian Panel Painting in the Low Countries*, 1. *Catalogue (Contributions to Fifteenth-Century Painting in the Southern Netherlands and the Principality of Liège*, 9), Brussels, 2009.

Depoorter 2020a
Matthias Depoorter, 'Jan Van Eyck's Discovery of Nature', in Martens et al. 2020b, pp. 205–35.

Depoorter 2020b
Matthias Depoorter, 'Birds on the Ghent altarpiece', in Van den Bremt, Van Crombrugge 2020, pp. 45–52.

Depuydt-Elbaum et al. 2020
Livia Depuydt-Elbaum, Françoise Rosier, Bart Devolder and Nathalie Laquière, *Conservation and Restoration Treatment, The Painted Surface*, in Fransen, Stroo 2020, pp. 111–66.

De Schryver, Marijnissen 1953
Antoine De Schryver and Roger Henri Marijnissen, *Histoire matérielle*, in Coremans 1953, pp. 21–68.

Dhanens 1980
Elisabeth Dhanens, *Hubert en Jan van Eyck*, Antwerp, 1980.

Dietz et al. 2016
Stephanie Dietz, Christoph Krekel, Andrea Obermeier and Heike Stege, 'Ground glass in Holbein the Elder's work', in Arie Wallert (ed.), *Painting techniques: history, materials and studio practice, 5th International Symposium, Rijksmuseum, Amsterdam, 1820 September 2013*, Rijksmuseum, Amsterdam, 2016, pp. 43–47.

Dubois 2017
Hélène Dubois, 'Michiel Coxcie's Copy as a Formal Reference of the Material Condition of the Ghent

Altarpiece in 1557', in Stephan Kemperdick, Johannes Rößler and Joris Corin Heyder (eds), *Der Genter Altar. The Ghent Altarpiece. Reproduktionen, Deutungen, Forschungskontroversen. Reproductions, Interpretations, Scholarly Debates*, Berlin/Petersberg, 2017, pp. 78–93.

Dubois 2018a
Hélène Dubois, 'The Art of Conservation XV. The Conservation History of the Ghent Altarpiece', in *The Burlington Magazine*, 160, 1386, September 2018, pp. 754–65.

Dubois 2018b
Hélène Dubois, 'The Adoration of the Lamb' http://balat.kikirpa.be/doc/pdf/Saisies_147.pdf, 'The Virgin, The Deity and John the Baptist enthroned' http://balat.kikirpa.be/doc/pdf/Saisies_059.pdf. in *Inventaris van de schilderijen en beeldhouwwerken die ten tijde van de Franse Revolutie in België werden in beslag genomen en naar Frankrijk overgebracht (1794–1795)*', KIK-IRPA, Brussels. http://balat.kikirpa.be/tools/saisies/indexnl.html.

Dubois 2020a
Hélène Dubois, 'Transformations in the Sixteenth and Seventeenth Centuries', in Fransen, Stroo 2020, pp. 11–46.

Dubois 2020b
Hélène Dubois, 'When, by Whom and Why? Decisive Material and Optical Alterations of the Ghent Altarpiece', in Martens et al. 2020, pp. 237–57.

Dubois, Deneffe 2019
Hélène Dubois and Dominique Deneffe, 'Construction of a Vision: Coremans' Approach to the Study of Flemish Primitives before the Restoration of the Adoration of the Mystic Lamb (The Ghent Altarpiece)', in Deneffe, Vanwijnsberghe 2019, pp. 120–39.

Dubois et al. 2009
Anne Dubois, Roel Slachmuylders, Géraldine Patigny and Famke Peters, *The Flemish Primitives* V. *Anonymous Masters* (*Catalogue of Early Netherlandish Painting in the Royal Museums of Fine Arts of Belgium*), Brussels, 2009.

Dubois, Sanyova, Vanwijnsberghe 2017
Hélène Dubois, Jana Sanyova and Dominique Vanwijnsberghe, '"Revenons à notre mouton". Paul Coremans, Erwin Panofsky, Martin Davies and the Mystic Lamb', in Currie et al. 2017, pp. 270–79 and pp. 66–75.

Dumolyn, Buylaert 2020
Jan Dumolyn and Frederik Buylaert, 'Van Eyck's World', in Martens et al. 2020b, pp. 85–121.

Dunkerton 2011
Jill Dunkerton, 'Leonardo in Verrochio's Workshop: Re-examining the Technical Evidence', in *National Gallery Technical Bulletin*, 32, 2011, pp. 4–31.

Dunkerton, Billinge 2005
Jill Dunkerton and Rachel Billinge, *Beyond the naked eye. Details from the National Gallery*, London, 2005.

Dunkerton, Morrison, Roy 2017
Jill Dunkerton, Rachel Morrison and Ashok Roy, 'Pigments, Media and Varnish Layers on the *Portrait of Margaret van Eyck*', in Currie et al. 2017, pp. 270–80.

Duverger 1945
Jozef Duverger, 'Het grafschrift van Hubrecht Van Eyck en het quatrain van het Gentsche Lam Gods-retabel' (*Verhandelingen van de Koninklijke Vlaamsche Academie voor Wetenschappen, Letteren en Schoone Kunsten van België. Klasse der Schoone Kunsten*, 7, 4), Antwerp, 1945, pp. 1–89.

Dvorák 1904
Max Dvorák, 'Das Rätsel der Kunst der Brüder Van Eyck', in *Jahrbuch der kunsthistorischen Sammlungen des allerhöchsten Kaiserhauses*, 24, 5, 1904, pp. 161–318.

Eastaugh et al. 2004
Nicholas Eastaugh, Valentine Walsh, Tracey Chaplin and Ruth Siddall, *The Pigment Compendium: A Dictionary of Historical Pigments*, Amsterdam, 2004.

Faries 1997
Molly Faries, 'Jan van Scorel's Clerical Patronage', in *Bolletino d'arte*, Suppl. vol. 100, 1997, pp. 107–16.

Faries 1999
Molly Faries, 'The Underdrawing in Jan van Eyck's Dresden Triptych', in Hélène Verougstraete and Roger Van Schoute (eds), *La peinture dans les Pays-Bas au 16e siècle. Pratiques d'atelier. Infrarouges et autres méthodes d'investigation. Symposium 11–13 septembre 1997 (Le dessin sous-jacent et la technologie dans la peinture, 12)*, Louvain-la-Neuve, 1999, pp. 221–29.

Faries 2011
Molly Faries, 'Jan van Scorel's Drawing and Painting Technique', in Liesbeth M. Helmus and Dorien Tamis (eds), *Utrecht Painting, 1363–1600. The Collection of the Centraal Museum, Utrecht*, 2011, pp. 22–42.

Fondaire, Vanwijnsberghe 2008
Catherine Fondaire and Dominique Vanwijnsberghe, 'Van der Veken et Van Eyck aux rayons X', in Dominique Vanwijnsberghe (ed.) in collaboration with Catherine Bourguignon and Jacques Debergh, *Autour de la Madeleine Renders. Un aspect de l'histoire des collections, de la restauration et de la contrefaçon en Belgique dans la première moitié du XXe siècle* (*Scientia Artis*, 4), Brussels, 2008, pp. 283–86.

Fraiture 2017
Pascale Fraiture, 'Results of Three Campaigns of Dendrochronological Analysis on the Ghent Altarpiece (1986–2013)', in Currie et al. 2017, pp. 76–95.

Fransen 2017
Bart Fransen, 'Van Eyck in Valencia', in Currie et al. 2017, pp. 469–78.

Fransen, Stroo 2020
Bart Fransen and Cyriel Stroo (eds), *The Ghent Altarpiece – Research and Conservation of the Exterior* (*Contributions to the Study of the Flemish Primitives*, 14), Brussels, 2020.

Froyen, Dubois 2020
Kathleen Froyen and Hélène Dubois (eds), *Conservation and restoration treatment of the Adoration of the Mystic Lamb polyptych (The Ghent Altarpiece); Phase 2: the lower register of the open altarpiece (2016–2019)*, Brussels, KIK-IRPA, April 2020. http://data.closertovaneyck.be/ec2/data/GhentAltarpiece_treatment_Phase2.pdf.

Gifford 1999
Melanie E. Gifford, 'Van Eyck's Washington Annunciation: Technical Evidence for Iconographic Development', in *The Art Bulletin*, 81, 1999, 1, pp. 108–16.

Gifford 2000
Melanie E. Gifford, 'Assessing the Evolution of Van Eyck's Iconography through Technical Study of the Washington

Annunciation, I.', in Delphine Cool et al., *Investigating Jan van Eyck*, Turnhout, 2000, pp. 59–66.

Gifford et al. 2017
Melanie E. Gifford, John K. Delaney, Suzanne Quillen Lomax, Rachel Morrison and Marika Spring, 'New Findings on the Painting Medium of the Washington Annunciation', in Currie et al. 2017, pp. 281–90.

Gifford, Metzger, Delaney 2013
Melanie E. Gifford, Catherine A. Metzger and John K. Delaney, 'Jan van Eyck's Washington Annunciation: painting materials and techniques', in Daphne Barbour and Melanie E. Gifford (eds), *Facture: conservation, science, art history, Renaissance Masterworks*, 1, 2013, pp. 128–53.

Glanville 1995
Helen Glanville, 'Varnish, Grounds, Viewing Distance, and Lighting: Some Notes on 17th-century Italian Painting Technique', in Arie Wallert, Erma Hermens and Marja Peek (eds), *Historical Painting Techniques, Materials, and Studio Practice. Preprints of a Symposium, University of Leiden, the Netherlands, 26–29 June 1995*, The Getty Conservation Institute, Los Angeles, 1995, pp. 12–19.

Glatigny et al. 2010
Jean-Albert Glatigny et al., 'Report of the research on the structural condition of the panels and the frames of the Ghent Altarpiece, 2010'. http://legacy.closertovaneyck.be/#home/sub=documents.

Gonzalez et al. 2017
Victor Gonzalez, Didier Gourier, Thomas Calligaro, Kathleen Toussaint, Gilles Wallez and Michel Menu, 'Revealing the Origin and History of Lead-White Pigments by their Photoluminescence Properties', in *Analytical Chemistry*, 89, 2017, pp. 2909–18.

Hand, Metzger, Spronk 2006–07
John Oliver Hand, Catherine A. Metzger and Ron Spronk, *Prayers and Portraits: Unfolding the Netherlandish Diptych*, Antwerp, 2006–07.

Hedley 1993
Gerry Hedley, 'Long Lost Relations and New Found Relativities. Issues in the Cleaning of Paintings', in Caroline Villers (ed.), *Measured Opinions, Collected Papers on the Conservation of Paintings*, London, 1993, pp. 172–78.

Janssens et al. 1998
Koen Janssens, Ine Deraedt, Olivier Schalm and Johan Veeckman, 'Composition of 15–17th Century Archaeological Glass Vessels Excavated in Antwerp, Belgium', in *Microchimica Acta*, 15, 1998, pp. 253–67.

Jones, Augustyniak, Dubois 2020
Susan Frances Jones, Anne-Sophie Augustyniak and Hélène Dubois, 'The Authenticity of the Quatrain and the other Frame Inscriptions', in Fransen, Stroo 2020, pp. 273–307.

Keller 1973
Renate Keller, 'Leinöl als Malmittel: Rekonstruktionsversuche nach Rezepten aus dem 13. bis 19. Jahrhundert', in *Maltechnik Restauro*, 79, 1973, pp. 74–105.

Kemperdick 2014
Stephan Kemperdick, 'The History of the Ghent Altarpiece', in Stephan Kemperdick and Johannes Rößler, *The Ghent Altarpiece by the Brothers Van Eyck. History and Appraisal*, Berlin, 2014, pp. 8–69.

Kemperdick, Lammertse 2012
Stephan Kemperdick and Friso Lammertse, *The Road to Van Eyck*, Rotterdam, 2012.

Ketels, Glatigny, Augustyniak 2020
Jochen Ketels, Jean-Albert Glatigny and Anne-Sophie Augustyniak, 'Frames and Support: Technique and Structural Treatment', in Fransen, Stroo 2020, pp. 47–76.

Keune, Boon 2005
Katrien Keune and Jaap J. Boon, 'Analytical imaging studies clarifying the process of the darkening of vermilion in paintings', in *Analytical chemistry*, 77, 15, 2005, pp. 4742–50.

Kirby 2008
Jo Kirby, 'Some Aspects of Medieval and Renaissance Lake Pigment Technology', in *Dyes in History and Archaeology*, 21, 2008, pp. 89–108.

Kirby 2012
Jo Kirby, 'Aspects of Oil-Painting in Northern Europe and Jan van Eyck', in De Mey et al. 2012, pp. 255–78.

Kirby et al. 2014
Jo Kirby, Maarten van Bommel, André Verhecken and Marika Spring, *Natural Colorants for Dyeing and Lake Pigments: Practical Recipes and Their Historical Sources*, London, 2014.

Kirby, Saudners, Spring 2006
Jo Kirby, David Saudners and Marika Spring, 'Proscribed Pigments in Northern European Renaissance Paintings and the Case of Paris Red', in *Studies in Conservation*, 51, Suppl. 2, 2006, pp. 236–43.

Kirby, Spring, Higgitt 2005
Jo Kirby, Marika Spring and Catherine Higgitt, 'The Technology of Red Lake Pigment Manufacture: Study of the Dyestuff Substrate', in *National Gallery Technical Bulletin*, 26, 2005, pp. 71–87.

Klaassen et al. 2021
Lizet Klaassen, Marie Postec, Geert Van der Snickt and Marika Spring, 'Materials and Painting Technique of Memling's Nájera Panels', in Lizet Klaassen and Dieter Lampens (eds), *Harmony in Bright Colors. Memling's God the Father with Singing and Music-Making Angels Restored*, Turnhout, 2021, pp. 86–123.

Kockaert 1995
Léopold Kockaert, 'Problems concerning the Brussels Lamentation by Petrus Christus', in Maryan W. Ainsworth (ed.), *Petrus Christus in Renaissance Bruges, an interdisciplinary approach*, 1995, pp. 189–92.

Kühnen, Hern 2016
Renate Kühnen and Christoph Hern, 'Protein fibres as intermediate layer on medieval shields, panel paintings and altarpieces', in *Zeitschrift für Kunsttechnologie und Konservierung*, 3, 2016, pp. 36–46.

Lutzenberger, Stege, Tilenschi 2010
Karin Lutzenberger, Heike Stege und Cornelia Tilenschi, 'A note on new findings of glass and silica in oil paintings from the 15th to the 17th century', in *Journal of Cultural Heritage*, 11, 2010, pp. 365–72.

Martens 2015
Maximiliaan P.J. Martens, 'Leave it or take it away: ethical considerations on the removal of overpaintings. The case of the Ghent Altarpiece', in *Conservation, Exposition, Restauration d'objets d'art* (CeROArt), June 2015, http://journals.openedition.org/ceroart/4765, accessed 24 January 2021.
Martens 2019
Maximiliaan P.J. Martens, 'De Makers, De rol van Hubert van Eyck in het Lam Gods', in Praet, Martens 2019, pp. 116–29.
Martens 2020
Maximiliaan P.J. Martens, 'Jan van Eyck's Optical Revolution', in Martens et al. 2020b, pp. 140–79.
Martens et al. 2020a
Maximiliaan P.J. Martens, Christina Ceulemans, Ron Spronk and Anne van Grevenstein-Kruse, *Introduction*, in Fransen, Stroo 2020, pp. 1–9.
Martens et al. 2020b
Maximiliaan P.J. Martens, Till-Holger Borchert, Jan Dumolyn, Johan De Smet and Frederica Van Dam (eds), *Van Eyck – An Optical revolution*, Ghent, 2020.
Mayer 1973
Ralph Mayer, *The artist's handbook of materials and techniques*, Edwin Smith (ed.), 1951; 3rd edn. London, 1973.
Meiss 1974
Millard Meiss, *French painting in the time of Jean de Berry: the Limbourgs and their contemporaries*, London/New York, 1974.
Melo et al. 2020
Helena P. Melo, António João Cruz, Sara Valadas, Ana Margarida Cardoso and António Candeias, 'The use of glass particles and its consequences in late 16th century oil painting: a Portuguese case based on the analytical results and the technical treatises', in *Journal of Cultural Heritage*, 43, 2020, pp. 261–70.
Merrifield (1849) 1967
Mary Philadelphia Merrifield, 'Original treatises dating from the XIIth to XVIIIth centuries on the Arts of Painting, in *Oil, Miniature, Mosaic, and on Glass; of Gilding, Dyeing, and the Preparation of Colours and Artificial Gems*, London, 1967.
Metzger, Steyaert 2009
Cathy Metzger and Griet Steyaert, 'Painting, A Distinct Profession', in Lorne Campbell and Jan van der Stock, *Rogier van der Weyden 1400/1464 – Master of Passions*, Zwolle/Louvain, 2009, pp. 162–79.
Mund et al. 2003
Hélène Mund, Cyriel Stroo, Nicole Goetghebeur and Hans Nieuwdorp, *The Mayer Van den Bergh Museum, Antwerp* (*Corpus of Fifteenth-Century Painting in the Southern Netherlands and the Principality of Liège*, 20), Brussels, 2003.
Nadolny 2001
Jileen Nadolny, 'The techniques and use of gilded relief decoration by northern European painters, c. 1200–1500', unpublished PhD thesis, The Courtauld Institute, Department of Conservation and Technology, University, London, 2001.
Nadolny 2008
Jileen Nadolny, 'European documentary sources before c. 1550 relating to painting grounds applied to wooden supports: translation and terminology', in Joy Townsend et al. (eds), *Preparation for Painting: the artist's choice and its consequence, ICOM–CC Paintings Specialty Group Interim Meeting Postprints, London, 31 May–1 June, 2007*, London, 2008, pp. 1–13.
Neven 2016
Sylvie Neven, 'The Strasburger Manuscripts. A Medieval Tradition of Artists' Recipes Collection (1400–1570)', London, 2016.
Panofsky 1953
Erwin Panofsky, *Early Netherlandish Painting. Its Origins and Character* (*The Charles Eliot Norton lectures, 1948–48*), Cambridge, 1953.
Paviot 2020
Jacques Paviot, 'The Van Eyck Family', in Martens et al. 2020b, pp. 58–83.
Pérez Preciado 2018
José Juan Pérez Preciado (ed.), *La Fuente de la Gracia: una tabla del entorno de Jan van Eyck*, Madrid, 2018.
Périer-D'Ieteren 2017
Catheline Périer-D'Ieteren, 'Le rôle du dessin sous-jacent et de l'ébauche préparatoire au lavis dans la genèse des peintures de l'Agneau Mystique', in Currie et al. 2017, pp. 121–35.
Philippot 1953
Albert Philippot and René Sneyers, 'Examen pictural avant traitement', in Coremans 1953, pp. 77–78.
Philippot, Sneyers 1953
Albert Philippot and René Sneyers, 'Etat matériel avant traitement', in Coremans 1953, pp. 79–88.
Plahter 1992
Unn Plahter, '*Likneskjusmiå*: fourteenth-century instructions for painting from Iceland', in *Zeitschrift für Kunsttechnologie und Konsentierung*, 6, 16, 1992, pp. 7–73.
Plahter 2003
Unn Plahter, 'The Norwegial frontals from Odda and Tresfjord: materials and technique', in Ann Massing (ed.), *The Thornham Parva Retable: Technique, Conservation and Context of an English Medieval Painting*, Turnhout, 2003, pp. 159–71.
Plahter 2014
Unn Plahter, 'Norwegian art technology in the twelfth and thirteenth centuries: materials and techniques in a European context', in *Zeitschrift für Kunsttechnologie und Konservierung*, 28, 2014, pp. 298–332.
Postec 2006
Marie Postec, 'Découverte d'un vernis ancien', in Godelieve Denhaene (ed.), *Lambert Lombard, peintre de la Renaissance, Liège 1505/06–1566: essais interdisciplinaires et catalogue de l'exposition* (*Sciencia Artis*, 3), Brussels, 2006, pp. 229–31.
Postec, Sanyova 2016
Marie Postec and Jana Sanyova, 'Were metalpoints used for the Van Eyck's Saint Barbara? A new hypothesis on the genesis based on its re-examination', in A. Wallaert (ed.), *Painting Techniques – History, Material and Studio Practice, Rijksmuseum Amsterdam, 18, 19 and 20 September 2013*, Amsterdam, 2016, pp. 22–29.
Postec, Steyaert 2020
Marie Postec and Griet Steyaert, 'The Van Eycks' Creative Process. The Paintings: from (Under)drawing to the final touch in Paint', in Fransen, Stroo 2020, pp. 194–247.

Praet, Martens 2019
Danny Praet and Maximiliaan P.J. Martens (eds), *The Ghent Altarpiece: Van Eyck. Art, History, Science and Religion*, Ghent, 2019.

Radepont et al. 2011
Marie Radepont, Wout de Nolf, Koen Janssens, Geert Van der Snickt, Yvan Coquinot, Lizet Klaassen and Marine Cotte, 'The use of microscopic X-ray diffraction for the study of HgS and its degradation products corderoite (-Hg3S2Cl2), kenhsuite (-Hg3S2Cl2) and calomel (Hg2Cl2) in historical paintings', in *Journal of Analytical Atomic Spectrometry*, 2011, 26, pp. 959 ff.

Roldan et al. 2014
María L. Roldan, Silvia A. Centeno, Adriana Rizzo and Yana van Dyke, 'Characterization of Bistre Pigments Samples by FTIR, SERS, Py-GC/MS and XRF', in *MRS Online Proceedings Library (OPL), Volume 1656: Symposium PP – Materials Issues in Art and Archaeology X*, 2014, pp. 139–48.

Sanyova et al. 2020
Jana Sanyova, Geert Van der Snickt, Hélène Dubois, Alexia Coudray, Koen Janssens and Peter Vandenabeele, 'Paint and Polychromy: Chemical Investigation of the Overpaints', in Fransen, Stroo 2020, pp. 77–110.

Sauerberg et al. 2009
Marie Louise Sauerberg, Ashok Roy, Marika Spring, Spike Bucklow and Mary Kempski, 'Materials and Techniques', in Paul Binski, Anne Massing and Marie Louise Sauerberg (eds), *The Westminster Retable: History, Techniques and Conservation*, London/Turnhout, 2009, pp. 233–51.

Scott, Taniguchi, Koseto 2001
David A. Scott, Yoko Taniguchi and Emi Koseto, 'The verisimilitude of verdigris: a review of the copper carboxylates', in *Studies in Conservation, Volume 46*, Suppl. 1, 2001, pp. 73–91.

Schmidt 2005
Peter Schmidt, *Het Lam Gods*, Louvain, 2005.

Serrat 2019
Judit Verdaguer Serrat, 'The Earliest Painted Panels of Europe, Technical Characteristics', in Justin Kroesen, Micha Leeflang and Marc Sureda I Jubany (eds), *North & South, Medieval art from Norway and Catalonia 1100–1350*, Zwolle, 2019, pp. 67–77.

Skaug 2006
Erling Skaug, '"The Third Element": Preliminary Notes on Parchment, Canvas and Fibres as Structural Components Related to the Grounds of Medieval and Renaissance Panel Paintings', in Jileen Nadolny (ed.), *Medieval Painting in Northern Europe: Techniques, Analysis, Art History*, London, 2006, pp. 182–201.

Smeyers 1996
Maurits Smeyers, 'Jan van Eyck, Archaeologist? Reflections on Eyckian Epigraphy', in Marc Lodewijckx (ed.), *Archaeological and historical Aspects of West-European Societies. Album Amicorum André Van Doorselaer (Acta Archaeologica Lovaniensia Monographiae*, 8), Louvain, 1996, pp. 403–14.

Spring 2012
Marika Spring, 'Colourless powdered glass as an additive in fifteenth- and sixteenth-century European paintings', in *National Gallery Technical Bulletin*, 33, 2012, pp. 4–26.

Spring 2017
Marika Spring, 'New Insights into the Materials of Fifteenth- and Sixteenth-Century Netherlandish Paintings in the National Gallery, London', in *Heritage Science*, 2017, pp. 1–20. https://heritagesciencejournal.springeropen.com/articles/10.1186/s40494–017–0152–3.

Spring et al. 2012
Marika Spring, Rachel Billinge, David Peggie and Rachel Morrison, 'The technique and materials of two paintings from fifteenth-century Cologne in the National Gallery, London', in *Die Sprache des Materials – Kölner Maltechnik des Spätmittelalters im Kontext. Zeitschrift für Kunsttechnologie und Konservierung*, 26, 1, 2012, pp. 88–99.

Spring, Grout 2002
Marika Spring and Rachel Grout, 'The Blackening of Vermilion: An Analytical Study of the Process in Paintings', in *National Gallery Technical Bulletin*, 23, 2002, pp. 50–61.

Spring, Morrison 2017
Marika Spring and Rachel Morrison, 'Van Eyck's technique and materials: historical perspectives and contemporary context', in Currie et al. 2017, pp. 194–218.

Stege et al. 2007
Heike Stege, Patrick Dietemann, Ursula Baumer, Irene Fiedler and Cornelia Tilenschi, 'Investigations into the Painting Materials of the Adoration of the Kings in Winterthur', in *Venite Adoremus – Geertgen tot Sint Jans and the Adoration of the Kings*, Winterthur, 2007, pp. 73–87.

Stege, Tilenschi, Sanyova 2012
Heike Stege, Cornelia Tilenschi and Jana Sanyova, 'Neues zu den Pigmenten der Altkölner Malerei', in *Die Sprache des Materials – Kölner Maltechnik des Spätmittelalters im Kontext. Zeitschrift für Kunsttechnologie und Konservierung*, 26, 1, 2012, pp. 71–79 (English translation pp. 281–85).

Stehr, Dubois 2014
Ute Stehr and Hélène Dubois, 'The Splitting and Restoration History of the Six Wings of the Ghent Altarpiece in Berlin', in Stephan Kemperdick and Johannes Rößler (eds), *The Ghent Altarpiece by the Brothers Van Eyck. History and Appraisal*, Berlin, 2014, pp. 122–37.

Steyaert 2005
Griet Steyaert, 'De triptiek met de Marteling van de heilige Hippolytus, begonnen door Dirk Bouts en afgewerkt door Hugo van der Goes en zijn leerling of medewerker, Aert van den Bossche', in Arnout Balis et al. (eds), *Florissant. Bijdragen tot de kunstgeschiedenis der Nederlanden (5de–17de eeuw, Liber Amicorum Carl van de Velde)*, Brussels, 1, 2005, pp. 51–63.

Steyaert 2012
Griet Steyaert, 'The Seven Sacraments. Some Technical Aspects observed during the Restoration', in Lorne Campbell, Jan Van der Stock, Catherine Reynolds and Lieve Watteeuw (eds), *Rogier van der Weyden in Context. Papers presented at the Seventeenth Symposium for the Study of Underdrawing and Technology in Painting Held in Leuven, 22–24 October 2009 (Underdrawing and Technology in Painting*, 17), Paris/Louvain/Walpole, 2012, pp. 119–35.

Stroo 2009
Cyriel Stroo (ed.), *Pre-Eyckian Panel Painting in the Low Countries. 2. Essays (Contributions to Fifteenth-Century Painting in the Southern Netherlands and the Principality of Liège*, 9), Brussels, 2009.

Stroo et al. 1999
Cyriel Stroo, Pascale Syfer-d'Olne, Anne Dubois and Roel Slachmuylders, *The Dirk Bouts, Petrus Christus, Hans Memling and Hugo van der Goes groups (The Flemish primitives: catalogue of early Netherlandish painting in the Royal Museums of Fine Arts of Belgium*, 2), 1999.

Stroo, Martens 2020
Cyriel Stroo and Maximiliaan P.J. Martens, 'Epilogue: Implications and Perspectives', in Fransen, Stroo 2020, pp. 353–55.

Van Asperen de Boer 1974
Johan Rudolf Justus Van Asperen de Boer, 'An Examination of Particle Size Distributions of Azurite and Natural Ultramarine in Some Early Netherlandish Paintings', in *Studies in Conservation*, 19, 4, 1974, pp. 233–43.

Van Asperen de Boer 1979
Johan Rudolf Justus Van Asperen de Boer, 'A Scientific Re-Examination of the Ghent Altarpiece', in *Oud Holland*, 93, 3, 1979, pp. 141–214.

Van Asperen de Boer 1992
Johan Rudolf Justus Van Asperen de Boer, 'Over de techniek van Jan van Eycks De heilige Barbara', in *Jaarboek van het Koninklijk Museum voor Schone Kunsten Antwerpen*, 1992, pp. 9–18.

Van Asperen de Boer 1995
Johan Rudolf Justus Van Asperen de Boer, 'Infrared reflectograms of two Paintings by Jan Van Eyck in Bruges', in Roger Van Schoute and Hélène Verougstraete-Marcq (eds), *Le dessin sous-jacent dans le processus de création. Colloque 5–7 septembre 1993 (Le dessin sous-jacent dans la peinture*, 10), Louvain-la-Neuve, 1995, pp. 81–84.

Van Asperen de Boer, Faries 1990
Johan Rudolf Justus Van Asperen de Boer and Molly Faries, 'La Vierge au chancelier Rolin de Van Eyck: examen au moyen de la réflectographie à l'infrarouge', in *La Revue du Louvre et des Musées de France*, 40, 1, 1990, pp. 37–49.

Van den Bremt, Van Crombrugge 2020
Paul Van den Bremt and Hilde Van Crombrugge, *Op zoek naar het paradijs. Flora op het Lam Gods – A la recherche du paradis: La flore sur l'Agneau mystique – In Search of Paradise: Flora on the Ghent Altarpiece*, Ghent, 2020.

Van der Snickt et al. 2017
Geert Van der Snickt, Hélène Dubois, Jana Sanyova, Stijn Legrand, Alexia Coudray, Cécile Claude, Marie Postec, Piet Van Espen and Koen Janssens, 'Large-Area Elemental Imaging Reveals Van Eyck's Original Paint Layers on the Ghent Altarpiece (1432), Rescoping Its Conservation Treatment', in *GDCh, Angewandte Chemie, International Edition 2017*, 56, 17, 2017, pp. 4797–801.

Van der Snickt et al. 2020
Geert Van der Snickt, Kathryn A. Dooley, Jana Sanyova, Hélène Dubois, John K. Delaney, Melanie E. Gifford, Stijn Legrand, Nathalie Laquiere and Koen Janssens, 'Dual mode standoff imaging spectroscopy documents the painting process of the Lamb of God in the *Ghent Altarpiece* by J. and H. Van Eyck', in *Science Advances*, 6, 31, 29 July 2020. https://advances.sciencemag.org/content/6/31/eabb3379.

Vandivere 2013
Abbie Vandivere, '*From the ground up*', PhD thesis, University of Amsterdam, 2013.

Vandivere, Clarke 2012
Abbie Vandivere and Mark Clarke, 'Changing Drapery, Recipes and Practice', in De Mey et al. 2012, pp. 235–53.

Van Eikema Hommes 2004
Margriet Van Eikema Hommes, *Changing Pictures: Discolouration in 15th–17th Century Oil Paintings*, London, 2004.

Van Grevenstein et al. 2011
Anne van Grevenstein (ed.), Hélène Dubois, Marie Postec, Anne-Sophie Augustyniak, Jana Sanyova, Ingrid Geelen, Steven Saverwyns and Griet Steyaert, with the collaboration of Jean-Albert Glatigny, Aline Genbrugge, Jessica Roeders, Renzo Meurs, Bart Vekemans, Henk Van Keulen and Gwendoline Fife, *Verslag van het onderzoek naar de materiële conditie en van de urgente conservatiebehandeling (april tot november 2010)*, Brussels/Ghent, 2011. http://data.closertovaneyck.be/legacy/data/Conservatie%20en%20materieel%20onderzoek%202010.pdf.

Van Grevenstein 2015
Anne van Grevenstein, 'The ongoing conservation of the Ghent Altarpiece 2012–2015', in *Conservation, Exposition, Restauration d'objets d'art* (CeROArt), June 2015. http://journals.openedition.org/ceroart/4625, accessed 24 January 2021.

Van Hout 2012
Nico Van Hout, *The Unfinished Painting*, Antwerp, 2012.

Van Loon, Noble, Burnstock 2012
Annelies van Loon, Petria Noble and Aviva Burnstock, 'Ageing and Deterioration of Traditional Oil and Tempera Paints', in Joyce Hill Stoner and Rebecca Rushfield (eds), *Conservation of Easel Paintings*, New York, 2012, pp. 214–241.

Verougstraete 1987
Hélène Verougstraete-Marcq, 'L'imprimatura et la manière striée. Quelques exemples dans la peinture flamande du 15e au 17e siècle', in Roger Van Schoute and Hélène Verougstraete-Marcq (eds), *Le dessin sous-jacent dans la peinture, colloque IV, 12–14 septembre 1985*, Louvain-la-Neuve, 1987.

Verougstraete 2015
Hélène Verougstraete, *Frames and supports in 15th- and 16th-Century Southern Netherlandish Painting (Contributions to the Study of Flemish Primitives*, 13), Brussels, 2015 [e-book http://balat.kikirpa.be/tools/frames/].

Verougstraete, Van Schoute 1995
Hélène Verougstraete and Roger Van Schoute, 'La Lamentation de Petrus Christus', in Maryan W. Ainsworth (ed.), *Petrus Christus in Renaissance Bruges, an interdisciplinary approach*, Turnhout, 1995, pp. 193–203.

Verougstraete, Van Schoute 2000
Hélène Verougstraete and Roger Van Schoute, 'Frames and Supports of Some Eyckian

Paintings', in Susan Foister, Sue Jones and Delphine Cool (eds), *Investigating Jan Van Eyck*, Turnhout, 2000, pp. 107–17.

Von Baum et al. 2014
Katja Von Baum, Patrick Dietemann, Ulrike Fischer, Peter Klein, Roland Krischel, Theresa Neuhoff, Caroline Von Saint-George, Iris Schaefer, Martin Schawe, Heike Stege and Jeanine Walcher, *Let the Material Talk: Technology of Late-medieval Cologne Panel Painting*, Cologne/Munich, 2014.

Project Participants

Participants of the 2016–2019 conservation/restoration treatment of the *Ghent Altarpiece* (phase 2). The affiliation given corresponds to the participant's function within the project.

The Project

Commissioning authority

Churchwardens of St Bavo's Cathedral, Ghent (KKSB)

Project planning

Bressers Architects bvba, Ghent (BA), with Christina Ceulemans (KIK/IRPA), Hilde De Clercq (KIK/IRPA), Ludo Collin (KKSB), Maximiliaan Martens (UGent) and Ron Spronk (QU, RUN)

Administrative support

Johan De Ridder (KKSB), Johan Vandenberghe (KKSB)

Advisory committee

Liesbeth De Belie (KMSKB/MRBAB), Christiaan Beyaert (KKSB), Maaike Blancke (BBA), Till-Holger Borchert (GM, VKC), Véronique Bücken (KMSKB/MRBAB), Gonda Callaert (AOE), Christina Ceulemans (KIK/IRPA), Annemie Charlier (POV), Hilde De Clercq (KIK/IRPA), Ludo Collin (KKSB), Dirk Cuvelier (G), Ingrid Depoorter (KE), Philippe Depotter (BA, CHAIR), Bart Devolder (KIK/IRPA), Hélène Dubois (KIK/IRPA, UGent), Hans Feys (ACE), Bart Fransen (KIK/IRPA), Kathleen Froyen (KIK/IRPA), Jean-Albert Glatigny (ASAJAG), Anne van Grevenstein (TR, UVA), Natalie Honraet (BA), Margriet Van Houtte (KKSB), Beatrice Janssens (KKSB), Andrea De Kegel (MOV), Jochen Ketels (KIK/IRPA), Christian Lardinoit (KKSB), Thomas Leysen (TR), Jacques Lust (BELSPO), Madeleine Manderyck (AOE), Maximiliaan Martens (UGent), Catheline Metdepenninghen (AOE), Pascale De Meyer (MSK), Halewijn Missiaen (AOE), Timothy Naessens (LAF), Anne-Cathérine Olbrechts (POV), Evelien Oomen (AOE), Philip Oosterlinck (KKSB), Martine Pieteraerens (POV), Jo Rombouts (POV), Peter Schmidt (KUL), Johan De Smet (MSK), Wesley De Smet (MSK), Ron Spronk (QU, RUN), Cyriel Stroo (KIK/IRPA), Peter Vandenabeele (UGent), Johan Vandenberghe (KKSB), Cathérine Verleysen (MSK), Hélène Verougstraete (formerly UCL), Ben De Vriendt (KKSB, TV), Jørgen Wadum (SMK), Catherine De Zegher (MSK)

Project management

Liesbeth De Belie (KMSKB/MRBAB), Maaike Blancke (BA), Véronique Bücken (KMSKB/MRBAB), Christina Ceulemans (KIK/IRPA), Hilde De Clercq (KIK/IRPA), Ludo Collin (KKSB), Ingrid Depoorter (ACE), Philippe Depotter (BA), Bart Devolder (KIK/IRPA), Hélène Dubois (KIK/IRPA, UGent), Hans Feys (ACE), Kathleen Froyen (KIK/IRPA), Lieven Gerard (MSK), Maximiliaan Martens (UGent), Pascale De Meyer (MSK), Jan Mortier (AOE), Martine Pieteraerens (POV), Jo Rombouts (POV), Johan De Smet (MSK), Wesley De Smet (MSK), Cyriel Stroo (KIK/IRPA), Johan Vandenberghe (KKSB), Cathérine Verleysen (MSK), Peter De Wilde (TV, KKSB), Catherine De Zegher (MSK)

Site monitoring committee

Griet Blanckaert (UA), Till-Holger Borchert (GM, VKC), Christina Ceulemans (KIK/IRPA), Hilde De Clercq (KIK/IRPA), Ludo Collin (KKSB), Ingrid Depoorter (ACE, coordination), Bart Devolder (KIK/IRPA), Hélène Dubois (KIK/IRPA, UGent), Hans Feys (ACE), Koen Janssens (UA), Evelien Oomen (AOE)

Working group art history

Till-Holger Borchert (GM, VKC), Bart Fransen (KIK/IRPA, coordination), Maximiliaan Martens (UGent), Ron Spronk (QU, RUN), Cyriel Stroo (KIK/IRPA)

Working group communication

Nele Bogaert (POV, coordination), Tim Bottelberghe (TOV), Catherine Bourguignon (KIK/IRPA), Bart Devolder (KIK/IRPA), Valerie Evers (RWO), Kathleen Froyen (KIK/IRPA), Simon Laevers (KIK/IRPA), Stephanie Lenoir (UGent), Bart Ooghe (MSK), Evelien Oomen (AOE), Martine Pieteraerens (POV), Johan De Ridder (KKSB), Jabez Sinnesael (PCC), Birgit Vandamme (RWO), Ann Vervaeke (UGent), Ben De Vriendt (KKSB, TTV), Céline De Waegenaere (TG), Leen Van Wezemael (CJSM), Erwin van de Wiele (TG)

Working group education

Bart Devolder (KIK/IRPA), Kathleen Froyen (KIK/IRPA), Lies Ledure (MSK), Anneke Lippens (POV), Els Otte (pov, coordination), Jabez Sinnesael (PCC), Amand Vilyn (KKSB)

Working group relocation

Till-Holger Borchert (MB, VKC), Ingrid Depoorter (ACE), Philippe Depotter (BA), Hans Feys (ACE), Anne van Grevenstein (TR, UVA), Jan Mortier (AOE), Anne-Cathérine Olbrechts (FARO), Mira van Olmen (AOE), Philip Oosterlinck (KKSB), Jan Van der Stock (TR, KUL), Lieve Watteeuw (TR, KUL)

Working group technical imaging and web application

Bruno Cornelis (IMEC-ETRO–VUB), Christina Currie (KIK/IRPA), Bart Devolder (KIK/IRPA), Ann Dooms (VUB),

Bart Fransen (KIK/IRPA), Kathleen Froyen (KIK/IRPA), Margriet Van Houtte (KKSB), Simon Laevers (KIK/IRPA), Maximiliaan Martens (UGent), Timothy Naessens (AF), Edwin De Roock (KIK/IRPA), Ron Spronk (QU, RUN, coordination), Frederik Temmermans (UD, IMEC-VUB)

Conservation-restoration treatment and scientific research

Contractor

Royal Institute for Cultural Heritage, Brussels (KIK/IRPA)

Conservation/restoration team

Anne-Sophie Augustyniak (KIK/IRPA), Isabel Bedós (KIK/IRPA), Cécile de Boulard (KIK/IRPA), Marta Darowska (KIK/IRPA), Bart Devolder (KIK/IRPA, onsite coordinator), Hélène Dubois (KIK/IRPA, UGent, head of team, coordinator of the international committee of conservation/restoration advisors), Kathleen Froyen (KIK/IRPA, onsite coordinator), Jean-Albert Glatigny (ASAJAG, treatment of supports), Nathalie Laquière (KIK/IRPA), Laure Mortiaux (KIK/IRPA), Marie Postec (KIK/IRPA), Françoise Rosier (KIK/IRPA), Griet Steyaert (KIK/IRPA)

Conservation/restoration advisors

Maryan Ainsworth (MMA), Till-Holger Borchert (GM, VKC), Véronique Bücken (KMSKB/MRBAB), Lorne Campbell (formerly NGL), Leslie Carlyle (UNL), Christina Ceulemans (KIK/IRPA), Livia Depuydt-Elbaum (KIK/IRPA), Bart Devolder (PUAM), Jill Dunkerton (NG), Susan Farnell (independent conservator/restorer), Michael Gallagher (MMA), Melanie Gifford (NGA), Nicole Goetghebeur (formerly KIK/IRPA), Anne van Grevenstein (TR, UVA), Régine Guislain-Witterman (independent conservator/restorer), Babette Hartwieg (SMB-GG), Lizet Klaassen (KMSKA), Maximiliaan Martens (UGent), Uta Neidhardt (SKD), Elke Oberthaler (KHM), Catheline Périer-D'Ieteren (formerly ULB), Marika Spring (NG), Ron Spronk (QU, RUN), Jørgen Wadum (SMK)

Scientific imaging & photography (KIK/IRPA)

Katrien Van Acker (photography), Stéphane Bazzo (photography), Christina Currie (head of imaging team), Jean-Luc Elias (photography), Catherine Fondaire (X-radiography), Pascale Fraiture (dendrochronology), Hervé Pigeolet (photography and X-radiography), Sophie De Potter (infrared reflectography and infrared photography)

Image processing web application

Bruno Cornelis (VUB–ETRO), Ann Dooms (VUB–ETRO, coordination), Frederik Temmermans (IMEC-ETRO-VUB, UD, coordination), Iris Vanhamel (UD)

Scientific chemical research

Marine Cotte (ESRF), Alexia Coudray (KIK/IRPA), John Delaney (NGA), Arnaud Delcorte (UCL), Steven De Meyer (UA), Kate Dooley (NGA), Cécile Glaude (KIK/IRPA), Catherine Higgitt (NGL), Koen Janssens (UA, coordination), Štěpánka Kučková (VŠCHT), Stijn Legrand (UA), Francisco Mederos-Henry (KIK/IRPA), Claude Poleunis (UCL), Jana Sanyova (KIK/IRPA, coordination), Geert Van der Snickt (UA), Marika Spring (NGL), Frederik Vanmeert (UA)

Additional scientific research

Aleksandra Pižurica and research group TELIN (UGent)

Subcontractors

ArcelorMittal, Ghent
ASAJAG, Etterbeek
Mobull Art Transport, Zaventem
Eeckman Art & Insurance, Brussels
Meyvaert Glass Engineering nv, Ghent

Support

Financial support

Flemish Government, Agentschap Onroerend Erfgoed (AOE)
Flemish Government, Agentschap Kunsten en Erfgoed (KE)
Fonds InBev-Baillet Latour, Louvain
Ghent University (UGent), Bijzonder Onderzoekfonds (GOA)
Gieskes-Strijbis Fonds, Amsterdam

Financial support web application

The Getty Foundation, Los Angeles
Gieskes-Strijbis Fonds, Amsterdam

Support in kind

Churchwardens of St Bavo's Cathedral, Ghent (KKSB)
City of Ghent (G)
Ghent University (UGent)
Museum of Fine Arts, Ghent (MSK)
Province of East Flanders (POV)
Provinciaal Cultuurcentrum Caermersklooster, Ghent (PCC)
Royal Institute for Cultural Heritage, Brussels (KIK/IRPA)
Royal Museums of Fine Arts of Belgium (KMSKB/MRBAB)
Vrije Universiteit Brussel (VUB)

Additional support in kind

Amsterdam University, Faculty of Humanities (UVA)
Antwerp University (UA)
Belgian Federal Science Policy Office (BELSPO)
Cultuur, Jeugd, Sport en Media Vlaanderen (CJSM)
Doerner Institut, Munich (DI)
Duke University, Durham, NC (DU)
Ebury Street Studios, London (ESS)
European Synchrotron Radiation Facility (ESRF)
FARO. Vlaams steunpunt voor cultureel erfgoed vzw (FARO)
Gemäldegalerie Alte Meister, Staatliche Kunstsammlungen Dresden (SKD)
Gemäldegalerie, Kunsthistorisches Museum, Vienna (KHM)
Groeningemuseum, Bruges (GM)
Katholieke Universiteit Leuven (KUL)
Metropolitan Museum of Art, New York (MMA)

Musea Brugge, Bruges (MB)
Museo Nacional del Prado, Madrid (MNP)
National Gallery of Art, Washington D.C. (NGA)
National Gallery, London (NG)
Queen's University, Kingston, Ontario (QU)
Radboud University, Nijmegen (RUN)
Royal Museum of Fine Arts Antwerp (KMSKA)
Staatliche Museen zu Berlin – Gemäldegalerie (SMB-GG)
Statens Museum for Kunst, Copenhagen (SMK)
Toerisme Gent (TG)
Toerisme Oost-Vlaanderen (TOV)
Toerisme Vlaanderen (TV)
Topstukkenraad, Flemish Government, Afdeling Cultureel Erfgoed (TR)
Universidade Nova de Lisboa (UNL)
Université Catholique de Louvain (UCL)
Université Libre de Bruxelles (ULB)
Vysoka Skola Chemicko-Technologicka Prague (VSCHT)

Additional partners

Art in Flanders (AF)
Bougie VZW (BOU)
City of Ghent, Werken aan Onderwijs, Cultuur en Kunst (WOCK)
Helicon Conservation Support BV (HCS)
IMEC, Louvain/Ghent
JAAP Enterprise for Art Scientific Research, Amsterdam (JE)
Klimaatnetwerk Vlaanderen-Nederland
Lukas-Art in Flanders VZW (LAF)
Monumentenwacht Vlaanderen (MV)
Nicolaus Copernicus University, Torun (NCU)
Universum Digitalis, Brussels (UD)
Visser & Van Rijckevorsel Filmprodukties, Amsterdam
Vlaamse Kunstcollectie (VKC)
VRT, Brussels

Photographic Acknowledgements

All illustrations of the Ghent Altarpiece are made by KIK-IRPA, Brussels. The copyright of these images belongs to: Sint-Baafskathedraal © Lukasweb.be – Art in Flanders vzw, photo KIK-IRPA. Stratigraphic cross-sections of the Ghent Altarpiece belong to KIK-IRPA's Polychrome Artefact Laboratory. Diagrams belong to the authors. Exceptions and other illustration credits are listed below. Every effort has been made to contact copyright-holders of illustrations. Any copyright-holder whom we have been unable to reach or to whom inaccurate acknowledgement has been made is invited to contact the publisher.

Antwerp University: fig. 1.8b, 2.14a, 2.31b, 2.35c, 2.39c, 2.39d, 2.39e, 2.41a, 2.42b, 2.47a, 2.52b, 2.53b, 2.53c, 2.59b, 2.63b, 2.66b, 2.66d, 2.68, 2.72b, 3.4d, 3.4e, 3.4f, 3.4g, 3.7b, 3.7c, 3.7d, 3.7e, 3.7f, 3.9b, 3.9c, 3.9d, 3.9e, 3.9f, 3.12b, 3.12c, 3.13b, 3.13c, 3.13d, 3.16c, 3.16d, 3.16e, 3.16f, 3.16g, 3.16h, 3.18b, 3.18c, 3.18d, 3.18e, 3.19a, 3.19b, 3.19c, 3.19d, 3.19f, 3.20b, 3.20c, 3.21b, 3.21c, 4.18c, 4.18g.

Antwerp, Royal Museum of Fine Arts: fig. 4.3b.

Musea Brugge – Groeningemuseum, Lukasweb.be – Art in Flanders vzw, photo KIK-IRPA: fig. 4.2c, 4.4b, 4.19c.

Brussels, KIK-IRPA, Polychrome Artefact Laboratory: fig. 3.1, 3.2a, 3.2b, 3.2c, 3.2d, 3.3a, 3.3b, 3.3c, 3.3d, 3.4 b, 3.4c, 3.5a, 3.5b, 3.5c, 3.5d, 3.6, 3.10 b, 3.10c, 3.11b, 3.11c, 3.11d, 3.12d, 3.12e, 3.12f, 3.14b, 3.15b, 3.15c, 3.15d, 3.16b, 3.17, 3.18f, 3.18g, 3.22a, 3.22b, 3.22c, 3.22d, 3.22e, 3.22f, 3.22g, 3.22h, 3.22i, 3.22j, 3.22k, 3.22l.

Dresden, Staatliche Kunstsammlungen: fig. 4.8b.

London, © The National Gallery, London: fig. 4.1b, 4.14a.

New York, Metropolitan Museum of Art: fig. 1.26.

Paris, Bibliothèque nationale de France: fig. 2.15.

Paris, Musée du Louvre: fig. 4.2a, 4.4c, 4.12b, 4.13b.

© RMN-Grand Palais (domaine de Chantilly) / Michel Urtado: fig. 2.16.

Abbreviations

ATR-FTIR	attenuated total reflection – Fourier transform infrared spectroscopy
AXES	Antwerp X-ray Analysis, Electrochemistry & Speciation, Research Group, University of Antwerp
CHARISMA	Cultural Heritage Advanced Research Infrastructures: Synergy for a Multidisciplinary Approach to Conservation/Restoration
CVE	Closer to Van Eyck website
EDX	energy dispersive X-radiography
ESRF	European Synchrotron Radiation Facility
GC-MS	gas chromatography–mass spectrometry
HLLA	high-lime and low-alkali
HPLC	high performance liquid chromatography
IR	infrared macrophotography/ macrophotograph
IRR	infrared reflectography/reflectogram
KIK-IRPA	Koninklijk Instituut voor het Kunstpatrimonium – Institut royal du Patrimoine artistique – Royal Institute for Cultural Heritage
LC-MS/MS	liquid chromatography–tandem mass spectrometry
MA-XRPD	macro X-ray powder diffraction
MACRO-XRF	macro X-ray fluorescence
METOX	Metal-Oxalates Project
MOLAB	Mobile LABoratory
MRS	micro-Raman spectroscopy
MS	mass spectrometry
MSK	Museum voor Schone Kunsten (Museum of Fine Arts), Ghent
PY-GCMS	pyrolysis-gas chromatography–mass spectrometry
SEM-EDX	scanning electronic microscopy-energy dispersive X-ray spectroscopy analysis
SR	synchrotron radiation
SR-XRPD	synchrotron radiation-based X-ray powder diffraction
SR-XANES	synchrotron radiation-based X-ray absorption near-edge structure
SR-XRF	synchrotron radiation-based X-ray fluorescence
SR-µ-XRPD	synchrotron radiation-based micro-X-ray powder diffraction
STAM	Stadsmuseum Gent – Ghent City Museum
TOF-SIMS	time of flight-secondary ion mass spectrometry
UGent	Universiteit Gent – University of Ghent
UV	Ultraviolet
VERONA	Van Eyck Research in OpeN Access
VIS	visible light
XR X	radiography